Sheldonian Theatre

River Cherwell

Wadham

Kings Arms

llege

BROAD ST

Exeter

Brasenose

New

Hertford

Radcliffe Camera

All Souls

St Edmunds Hall

Queens

Magdalen College

Addisons Walk

HIGH ST

The Bear

Oriel

University

Corpus Christi

Merton

London
Garsington

Botanic Gardens

Christ
Church

Head of the River

GATSBY'S OXFORD

ALSO BY CHRISTOPHER A. SNYDER:

The Making of Middle-earth: A New Look Inside the World of J.R.R. Tolkien (2013)

The Britons (2003)

The World of King Arthur (2000)

An Age of Tyrants: Britain and the Britons, A.D. 400-600 (1998)

GATSBY'S OXFORD

Scott, Zelda, and the Jazz Age
Invasion of Britain: 1904–1929

Christopher A. Snyder

PEGASUS BOOKS
NEW YORK LONDON

GATSBY'S OXFORD

Pegasus Books, Ltd.
148 W 37th Street, 13th Floor
New York, NY 10018

Copyright © 2019 Christopher A. Snyder

First Pegasus Books cloth edition April 2019

Interior design by Maria Fernandez

ISBN: 978–1–64313–009–5

10 9 8 7 6 5 4 3 2 1

Printed in the United States of America

Distributed by W. W. Norton & Company, Inc.

To God

Hope

Dream

Love

Contents

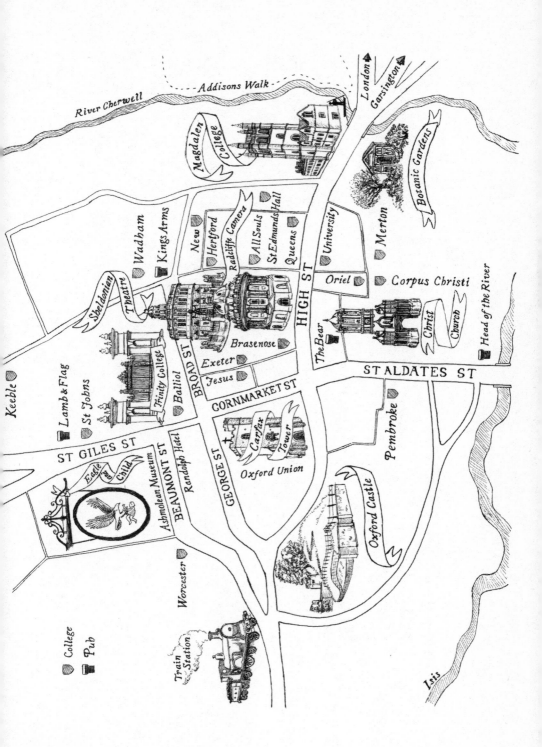

River Cherwell

Addisons Walk

London

Garsington

Magdalen College

Botanic Gardens

Wadham

Kings Arms

New

Hertford

Radcliffe Camera

All Souls

St Edmunds Hall

Queens

University

Merton

Sheldonian

Theatre

Oriel

Corpus Christi

HIGH ST

Keeble

Lamb & Flag

St Johns

Trinity College

Balliol

BROAD ST

Brasenose

Exeter

Jesus

The Bear

Christ Church

Head of the River

CORNMARKET ST

ST ALDATES ST

ST GILES ST

Eagle and Child

Ashmolean Museum

Randolph Hotel

BEAUMONT ST

GEORGE ST

Carfax Tower

Oxford Union

Pembroke

Oxford Castle

Worcester

Train Station

Isis

College

Pub

GLOSSARY OF OXFORD TERMS

Battels. Expenses incurred in a college by students and fellows, including accommodation, food, and beverages.

The Bird & Baby. Nickname used by the **Inklings** for the Eagle & Child pub on St. Giles' Street.

Blues. Colors awarded for making a varsity (university) sports team, the equivalent to the American letter.

The Bod. The Bodleian Library, the university's main library founded in 1602 by Sir Thomas Bodley. Now a copyright library holding more than 13 million volumes, in reality a vast network of general and specialized libraries and rare manuscript collections.

The Broad. Broad Street, on which the Bodleian Library, Exeter College, Trinity College, and Balliol College lay.

Chancellor. The lord chancellor is the honorary head of the university. The vice-chancellor is, in reality, the chief administrator of the university.

The Cher'. The Cherwell River, which flows past Magdalen College and the Botanic Gardens and into the **Isis** (Thames). A popular spot for punting.

Commoner. Undergraduate student who does not hold a scholarship.

Congregation. The sovereign governing body of the university, consisting of all college faculty and administrative staff, as well as university and library administrators.

Convocation. A body consisting of all members and retired members of **Congregation** and all former degree students of the university. Its sole function is to elect the Chancellor and the Professor of Poetry.

Dean. A title at Oxford usually pertaining to the head of undergraduates in a college (often Junior Dean), sometimes to the **Head of House**. The Dean of Christ Church is both Head of House and head of the cathedral.

Digs. Private rooms rented by students living outside of College.

Don. The generic term for a member of the faculty (professor, lecturer, or tutor) at Oxford.

Double-First. Achieving first class honors in two Oxford school examinations.

Encaenia. Literally "Renewal," Encaenia is Oxford's Commencement ceremony held annually on the Wednesday of ninth week during of Trinity Term. It includes a formal academic procession, the bestowing of honorary degrees, and the Vice-Chancellor's garden party.

Fellow. A voting member of the faculty of a college.

Fresher. First-year Oxford student, equivalent to the American freshman.

Gaudy. A formal event for old members of a college.

Greats. Nickname for *Literae Humaniores* ("More Humane Letters"), the old Classics undergraduate degree at Oxford, featuring Greek and Roman history, literature, and philosophy.

Head of House. The chief administrator of a college, variously termed dean, master, principal, warden, etc.

Head of the River. The term for finishing in first place in Oxford boat races. Also the name of a pub on St. Aldates.

The High. High Street, which runs from Magdalen Bridge to Carfax Tower.

The House. Traditional name for Christ Church.

The Inklings. A fluid and informal group of scholars and friends who gathered regularly around C. S. Lewis and J.R.R. Tolkien from around 1930 to 1960.

The Isis. The name for the River Thames in Oxford.

J.C.R. Junior Common Room, the name for both the social space and quasi student government of an Oxford college. The M.C.R., or Middle Common Room, is the lounge for the postgraduate students, and the S.C.R., or Senior Common Room, the room (more often rooms) for the faculty fellows and their guests.

Moderations or **Mods**. The name for Oxford's comprehensive examinations, usually taken at the end of the first and third years for either "Pass" or "Honours."

Old Members. Alumni, or former students of a college or hall.

The Other Place. The University of Cambridge.

Oxbridge. Referring to Oxford and Cambridge, or to those things the two ancient universities have in common.

Oxonian. Of or pertaining to Oxford, especially the University.

Porter. The member of the college staff responsible for monitoring the comings and goings of the students, appointments with faculty, and written communications.

Proctor. A University official responsible for upholding University statutes and monitoring the disciplinary behavior of undergraduates.

Punt. A small pleasure boat propelled by pushing off in shallow water with a long pole (which is known as "punting").

Quad. Short for "quadrangle," a central square enclosure in a college.

Rad Cam. The Radcliffe Camera, a neoclassical structure designed by James Gibbs c.1737 to house the Radcliffe Science Library. It now houses the undergraduate reading rooms of the Bodleian Library.

Schools. The Examination Schools, the facility where final examinations are administered and many university lectures are held. Also honor schools, the final examination leading to an honors degree.

Sent down. Forced to leave the university for academic or disciplinary reasons.

Summer Eights. End of the academic year boat races between eight-man (and now eight-woman) crews.

Teddy Hall. St. Edmund Hall, a college at Oxford dating back to the thirteenth century.

Term. Oxford has three eight-week academic terms: Michaelmas (beginning in October and ending before Christmas), Hilary (ending at Easter), and Trinity (or Summer Term, usually ending in mid-June).

Tom Quad and **Tom Tower.** The main quadrangle and the tower above the main gate at Christ Church. "Tom" is the nickname for the large bell in Tow Tower.

Torpids. The boat race for novice crews held during Hilary Term.

Tutor. A member of the college faculty responsible for weekly meetings with individual (or pairs) of undergraduate students, monitoring their reading, academic progress, and (until recently) their spiritual life.

PREFACE

One hundred and fifty-five strong we were when we fell upon the sleeping city—there was a full moon too. It isn't often that the profane enter unto the city of dreaming spires when they are really drenched in moonlight.[1]

A s the Great War came to an end, Major Jay Gatsby left the Argonne Forest for the City of Dreaming Spires, spending five months in Oxford in the spring of 1919 learning to appreciate, among other things, British tailors and grand libraries. Yet it was not F. Scott Fitzgerald who penned the lines above, but rather an American Rhodes scholar returning to Oxford in 1919 as part of a continuing education project for American army officers. This "American Invasion," as the January 1920 edition of the *American Oxonian* described it, included nearly two hundred soldier-students—from Alabama to Princeton to St. Paul—whose biographies shed some light on the experience of Americans in Oxford in the first decades of the twentieth century.

The present study is committed to the preposterous premise that Jay Gatsby was an historical figure who walked among them. I do not say "a real person," because that can be taken and debated several ways. No one can doubt that the impact of this character from F. Scott Fitzgerald's 1925 novel *The Great Gatsby* is very real to a great many people. The 2013 film directed by Baz Luhrmann and starring Leonardo Dicaprio is only the latest manifestation of our fascination with Gatsby, the Jazz Age, and that peculiar, unwavering optimism and romanticism that first captivated the book's narrator, Nick Carraway.

By "historical figure" I mean that Jay Gatsby will here serve as a lens through which to view this age, and in particular the town and university of Oxford from 1904 to 1929. Why was this particular American soldier in Oxford? What was the experience of Americans in Oxford like at the time, and why do many still come seeking the City of Dreaming Spires? Fitzgerald's early novels and short stories came to define the Jazz Age in America and, in the case of *Gatsby*, American modernism. But Britain experienced its own Jazz Age and many black American jazz artists sought refuge in Europe after the Great War. Fitzgerald is rightly seen in conversation with authors of the Old World and the New, caught between the medieval dreams of European poets and the materialist realities of Wilsonian America, just as jazz poured new American sounds through classical European instruments. The Great American Novel to many, *Gatsby* was written mostly in France, and Fitzgerald writes about his encounters on Oxford's High Street with characters from the pages of the Oxford Novel as he began his European sojourn in England. This dimension of Fitzgerald deserves lengthy exploration, as does the experiences of other Americans during this period in Oxford.

This book is truly interdisciplinary, with the lines between the study of literature and the study of history blurred, if not erased. My approach to literature and the creative culture of the Age of Gatsby might be considered New Historicist. The Dutch literary critic Hans Bertens, in discussing the similarities between New Historicism and cultural materialism, describes the relationship between any work of art and its historical context:

> Far from being untouched by the historical moment of its creation, the literary text is directly involved in history.

> Instead of transcending its own time and place . . . the
> literary text is a time- and place-bound verbal construc-
> tion. . . . Literature is not simply a product of history, it also
> actively *makes* history.[2]

While both New Historicists and cultural materialists (heavily
influenced by Marx and Foucault) might focus on the political nature
of the novel, the present study focuses on *narrative* as a common ground
for both history and literary criticism, a space that may be political and
time-bound, but may also be transcendent according to an individual's
own interaction with the narrative. New Historicism often engages in a
back-and-forth discussion of the literary work and its context, bringing
us face-to-face with issues of gender, race, and the construction of social
identities. These areas will be touched upon as we look at Fitzgerald's
Irish-American Catholic upbringing, discuss the first women and students of color to study at Oxford, and examine diversity—or the lack
thereof—in the early years of the Rhodes scholarships.

Fitzgerald was inspired in his early novels by that particular type
of bildungsroman known as the Oxford Novel, and in the 1920s the
first of these novels written from the perspective of female students
from Oxford and Cambridge began to appear. Zelda Fitzgerald herself
would produce a bildungsroman, and the flamboyant and androgynous
"flapper"—which for a while she embodied—provided an important
link between the Jazz Age in New York and that in London. After
the war, women were invading male spaces at Oxford as well as in
industry, in politics, and in the jazz clubs. In *The Great Gatsby*, the
characters Daisy and Jordan test the limits of feminine agency in the
Jazz Age, while their romantic counterparts, Gatsby and Nick, explore
ideas of masculinity and male friendship. Ultimately these friendships
and amorous pairings are crushed by Tom's cruelty and insistence on
maintaining the status quo.

I am also taking liberty herein to allow a literary character to step
outside the text to interact with actual historical figures, introducing
them to the reader as Major Gatsby or his better-documented army
comrades might have encountered them. This gives some idea of the

approach I am taking to the novel and its Oxford context. It is a bit Carrollian—and entirely Oxonian—to imagine Jay Gatsby in such a role, as if Bill the Lizard and the Carpenter stepped through the looking glass to meet Benjamin Disraeli and John Ruskin at a tea in Dean Liddell's garden at Christ Church. Pass the treacle, if you don't mind. In *Zuleika Dobson*, one of Fitzgerald's favorite Oxford Novels, Clio herself muses

> how fine a thing history might be if the historian had the novelist's privileges. Suppose he could be present at every scene which he was going to describe, a presence invisible and inevitable, and equipped with power to see into the breasts of all the persons whose actions he set himself to watch . . .[3]

A (qualified) New Historicist reading of the novel will thus lead to a cultural history of Oxford, a history emphasizing the experience of Americans in Oxford as well as the literary and intellectual output of famous Oxonians of the period—Oscar Wilde, T. S. Eliot, J.R.R. Tolkien, C. S. Lewis, Evelyn Waugh—who had a major impact on America. Above all, this book will aim to paint a picture of the Oxford through which Gatsby and other dreamers walked in 1919. Crossing "Trinity Quad" is to cross a threshold, to leave behind the baggage of modernity and enter a timeless realm of books and ideas. Some writers, like Tolkien and Lewis, embraced this world, while others, like Eliot and Waugh, turned away from it. Jay Gatsby wandered into this enchanted realm already carrying his grail—his love for Daisy—and the news of her marriage to Tom Buchanan seems to have prevented Gatsby from falling under Oxford's spell. The university, for him, became, as it still does for some, merely a cloak of legitimacy for his created persona, providing a crucial rung in the social ladder he tried so desperately to climb.

Or did it? Did Gatsby return to America with more than just a photograph of Trinity Quad and "the Merton College Library" for his new home on Long Island? Who were his companions in Oxford? What were New Yorkers of the 1920s supposed to make of Gatsby as "an Oxford man"? Why was this phrase both the first label Fitzgerald employed for Gatsby and the last veil removed, by Tom, to reveal that Jay Gatsby was really Jimmy Gatz, Mr. Nobody from Nowhere? Gatsby confesses to Tom that he cannot really call himself an Oxford man because he spent only five months there. What would those five months at Oxford in early 1919 have been like for an American, particularly for one as ill-prepared for the venerable university as Gatsby was? Alain Locke, the first African American Rhodes scholar, observed after his first term that "Oxford to most Americans" is the same as that of tourists, "the Oxford of the summer vacation . . . little more than a heap of legends and a pile of stones."[4]

There are many meanings to the term "an Oxford man," and some of these will be explored in the present study. Tom insists that Gatsby cannot be an Oxford man because he wears *pink suits*. But is that true? Has the staid and conservative Tom rightly seen through Gatsby's disguise—colorful but gauche shirts and suits that mark Gatsby as a wannabe who will never be accepted into America's aristocracy? Or is it that Gatsby has true knowledge of Oxford (he at least spent some time there as a student, unlike Tom), performing a particular Oxonian aestheticism through his dress and speech? Oxford had been home to Oscar Wilde and other English aesthetes who flaunted their wealth and witticisms, read poetry, and carried flowers and teddy bears, oft to confront the "Hearties" (athletes like Tom) with an androgynous dandyism. Locke—a gay black man who rode horses and fenced at Oxford—presented a similar challenge to many of his fellow American Rhodes scholars, who, as Tom with Gatsby, refused to accept him into their society. Horace Kallen, the Jewish American scholar who befriended Locke at Oxford, could partly appreciate Locke's status as an outsider, having himself confronted the anti-Semitism that controlled access and acceptance into the WASPish Ivy League. How sensitive was Fitzgerald to these prejudices? Did he perpetuate the racist, anti-Semitic, and homophobic attitudes of his day in his writings, or, as some have suggested, was the pink-suited Gatsby really a black man trying to pass as white, a German Jew trying to erase his origins, or an American dandy of fluid sexuality?

The Great Gatsby is also a novel that can also be read like a map. We begin in the American heartland, and journey with both Nick and Gatsby to Europe, to the battlefields of France in the world's first modern and total war. But these Americans are also being taken to the Old Word, and Gatsby, at least, steps back in time to medieval Oxford, a city of dreams and books and men with ancient titles. Finally, we return to America, and specifically to New York and the Jazz Age, where the glitter and glamour is of a new fay and fell lay. In other words—*pace* Professor Tolkien—we go from Middle America to Middle-earth, and back again.

In the geography of the novel, then, Oxford is the unexpected destination of the hero. Like the medieval world of Faërie, the wanderer can enter in and experience many strange adventures there, but upon leaving it he finds that time has sped past him, and his world has changed dramatically and often tragically. Gatsby returns from Oxford with the Faërie glamour still clinging to him, and takes up residence in a castle that he fills with newly gotten (ill-gotten?) treasures. But he also brings with him some mementoes from his journey—a medal, a photograph, books—and these become crucial in his plan to regain his lost love. Gatsby is a symbol of the scores of Americans who have made such journeys to the Old World—and to Oxford in particular—bringing back trinkets of an alien culture, remnants of a medieval past clinging to modernity, only to find that history has continued its unstoppable progress in America.

Why should history be so elevated in criticism of *The Great Gatsby*? According to Fitzgerald-scholar Matthew Bruccoli, a "characteristic quality of Fitzgerald's fiction is his ability to endow place and time with a sense of authenticity."[5] This makes sense for a novel hailed as a classic of American realism. Hence we are drawn into the Jazz Age by this bard, who sings to life a strip of land stretching from the pulsating city to the villages and estates of Long Island. In the middle lies the purgatory of ash heaps, where ethical choices made in error lead to tragedy and destruction. Is it fair that Gatsby dies while Tom and Daisy live on in comfort? Even our narrator, Nick, is left scarred by the events that have created a wasteland stretching from West Egg to the bridge. Gone are the fay castle and its king, to live on only in song.

In the early 1920s, Fitzgerald and his muse, Zelda, left America for the Old World, and there on its shores he wrote the *The Great Gatsby*. Passing through Oxford in 1921 he remarked on its great beauty and ancientry. "There one day I shall live," he wrote to friends. He never did, but his most unforgettable and indefatigable hero sojourned there in the winter of 1919. In a letter to Princeton friend and poet John Peale Bishop, dated August 9, 1925, Fitzgerald writes from Paris:

> Thank you for your most pleasant, full, discerning and helpful letter about *The Great Gatsby*. . . . Also you are right about Gatsby being blurred and patchy. I never at any one time saw him clear myself—for he started as one man I knew and then changed into myself—the amalgam was never complete in my mind.

Was Jay Gatsby really, for Fitzgerald, *one man I knew*? Is there a "shadow Gatsby" who sailed to France, fought on the Western Front, and then spent a good part of the year 1919 in Oxford?

We must get a sense of what Oxford was like in this period, a sense of its particular history and character, to understand a key part of Fitzgerald's greatest work. As it turns out, he and Gatsby were not the only Americans in Oxford during that time. They had been coming for more than a century, and thus Victorian Oxford was making its impress on the visiting students, while the Victorian Oxonian dreamer and imperialist Cecil Rhodes made it possible, starting in 1904, for an even larger contingent of Yanks to spend time in Oxford. When Gatsby arrives in the winter of 1919, the university and the city were coming back to life following the decimation of its students and dons during the Great War. And some of the greatest thinkers and writers of modernity—W.B. Yeats and T. S. Eliot, Virginia Woolf and Aldous Huxley, not to mention Lewis and Tolkien—were passing through Oxfordshire then, or else studying or teaching at the university. Like their Victorian predecessors, these Edwardian artists and intellectuals were carrying on a conversation with Oxford's medieval past.

This is a study of that time and place—of Gatsby's Oxford—where great songs were sung in great halls, where myths were being made (and unmade) by learned men and women, and where an American could fashion his or her dream beneath stone arches and spires built in an Age of Faith. It is precisely when Gatsby describes truthfully his time in Oxford that Nick has "one of those complete renewals of faith in him." We, like everyone in that room in the Plaza Hotel, are looking at Gatsby at this moment. Let us freeze this moment in the narrative—before the almost unbearable tragedy that ensues—and follow Gatsby back to Oxford, back to a time when both faith and progress were being challenged, but also renewed. Among the city's spires and gargoyles, let us both dream and remember.

1
Jay Gatsby: An Oxford Man

*T*he *Great Gatsby* is, for many, The Great American Novel. Not only does it appear on nearly every book critic's list of candidates, it has also sold more than twenty-five million copies worldwide and defined an entire era of American history. And yet, for a twentieth-century American novel, *Gatsby* brings with it so much of the Old World: Platonism, classical inspiration (*The Satyricon*), Romanticism (of the Keatsian variety), Gothic (or at least Neo-Gothic) elements, medieval imagery and symbolism, Arthurian and quest motifs. In the last lines of the novel, Nick wonders how Manhattan would have looked to the first Dutch explorers, the "fresh, green breast of the new world" (140).[1] Oxford functions in a similar way in the novel, bringing the American war hero to "the English Athens" to remake him into the cultured, old-moneyed figure that Gatsby believes will win him a life with Daisy. Oxford is both the key to his new identity and the lie by which Tom hopes to bring him down. It is worth exploring at length the role of Oxford in *Gatsby* and the appearance of the ancient university town, little commented on, in Fitzgerald's other writings. That is the aim of this chapter, presenting the evidence of Fitzgerald's own words along with the musings of Fitzgerald scholars to begin answering the question: Was Jay Gatsby an Oxford man?

Oxford in *The Great Gatsby*

There is a dramatic buildup to the introduction of Jay Gatsby in the novel. Fitzgerald first presents his narrator, Nick Carraway, and it is important to remember that everything we know about Gatsby comes through the filter of Nick. Nick tells us first about himself: that he is the most honest person he knows, that he "is inclined to reserve all judgments" as "a matter of infinite hope," but also that his "tolerance . . . has a limit" (5). In college, Nick was rather literary, he confesses, and was unjustly accused of being a politician because he "was privy to the secret griefs of wild, unknown men." He did not seek out the confidences of such men. They found him, as did so many of the characters he would meet and socialize with in New York in the summer of 1922.[2]

Despite his claim of disinterest in these "privileged glimpses into the human heart," one figure alone stands out from the rest and haunts Nick: Jay Gatsby. Though "he represented everything for which [Nick] had unaffected scorn . . . there was something gorgeous about" Gatsby, "some heightened sensitivity to the promises of life" (6). Gatsby had "an extraordinary gift for hope, a romantic readiness such as I have never found in any other person."

Gatsby's dreaming romanticism contrasts with Nick's practicality. Nick has come East after the war to sell bonds, renting a modest cottage in West Egg, on Long Island Sound. His cottage is dwarfed by that of his neighbor, an imitation of a French-Gothic town hall with an ivy-covered tower on one side (8). Our introduction to Gatsby is again delayed; Nick first visits the only people he knows on Long Island, the Buchanans of old-money East Egg. Tom Buchanan (from Chicago) was a friend of Nick's at Yale, while Daisy Fay Buchanan (from Louisville) is Nick's second cousin. Staying with the Buchanans that summer is

Jordan Baker, a recently famous golfer. Nick gets swept up in the affairs of these three people—rich, careless, and often dishonest. They are his initiation to life in New York, and ours.

Apart from a glimpse of Gatsby's silhouette—trembling arm reaching out to a distant green light across the bay—Nick's first meeting with his neighbor is delayed, once more, by the Buchanans. Tom whisks Nick off to the city, stopping in the "valley of ashes" to collect his mistress, Myrtle Wilson, right from under the nose of her husband and under the watchful eyes of Dr. T. J. Eckleburg, brooding high on a billboard (21). Against his wishes, Nick is swept away into a house-party, and domestic melodrama, of sorts, in middlebrow Washington Heights. Apart from Nick getting drunk (for only the second time in his life, he tells us), the episode serves mainly as a contrast to the next party, just as the volatile Myrtle and Tom serve as a contrast to Gatsby and Daisy.

Nick receives a formal invitation soon after to a party at his neighbor's mansion, one of the few guests who do. ("People were not invited—they went there" [34].) At first, lost in a sea of unfamiliar people, Nick was surprised by the number of young Englishmen at the party, "all well dressed . . . and all talking in low, earnest voices to solid and prosperous Americans" (35). Then he sees Jordan Baker, and the pair are drawn into conversation regarding their mysterious host, one person suggesting that Gatsby had killed a man, another that he was a German spy, and yet another who insisted that he fought in the American army in the war (36–37).[3] Nick and Jordan leave the gossips to go find their host, and end up walking into "a high Gothic library, paneled with carved English oak, and probably transported from some ruin overseas" (37). When they return to their table they are joined by new faces, and, after more glasses of champagne and a lull in the entertainment, a stranger approached Nick:

> "Your face is familiar," he said, politely. "Weren't you in the Third Division during the war?"
>   "Why, yes. I was on the ninth machine-gun battalion."
>   "I was in the Seventh Infantry until June nineteen-eighteen. I knew I'd seen you somewhere before." (39)

The man invites Nick to go for a ride in his hydroplane in the morning, and Nick is surprised to learn that this "elegant young roughneck, a year or two over thirty, whose elaborate formality of speech just missed being absurd," is none other than Gatsby himself.

> "I thought you knew, old sport. I'm afraid I'm not a very good host."
>
> He smiled understandingly—much more than understandingly. It was one of those rare smiles with a quality of eternal reassurance in it, that you may come across four or five times in life. It . . . concentrated on *you* with an irresistible prejudice in your favor. It understood you just as far as you wanted to be understood. . . . (39)

After Gatsby leaves them, Nick asks Jordan who his mysterious neighbor is.

> "He's just a man named Gatsby" [replied Jordan].
>
> "Where is he from, I mean? And what does he do?"
>
> "Now *you're* started on the subject," she answered with a wan smile. "Well, he told me once he was an Oxford man."[4]
>
> A dim background started to take shape behind him, but at her next remark it faded away.
>
> "However, I don't believe it."
>
> "Why not?"
>
> "I don't know," she insisted. "I just don't think he went there." (40–41)

Then, one morning in late July, Gatsby shows up in his shining roadster, and invites Nick to lunch with him in the city. Gatsby blurts out a confession before they leave the island:

> "We'll, I'm going to tell you something about my life," he interrupted. "I don't want you to get a wrong idea of me from all these stories you hear. . . . I was brought up in

America but educated at Oxford, because all my ancestors have been educated there for many years. It is a family tradition."

He looked at me sideways—and I knew why Jordan Baker had believed he was lying. He hurried the phrase "educated at Oxford," or swallowed it, or choked on it, as though it had bothered him before. (52)

After showing Nick a medal he received for heroism in the war, Gatsby returns to the subject of Oxford:

"Here's another thing I always carry. A souvenir of Oxford days. It was taken in Trinity Quad—the man on my left is now the Earl of Doncaster."

It was a photograph of half a dozen young men in blazers loafing in an archway through which were visible a host of spires. There was Gatsby, looking a little, not much, younger—with a cricket bat in his hand.

Then it was all true. (53)

Speeding through Astoria, the pair are approached by a policeman on a motorcycle just before the Queensboro Bridge. When Gatsby waves something at the frantic officer, Nick asks him if that was the picture of Oxford (54). Knowing the police commissioner, it turns out, is more important than having gone to Oxford when caught speeding in New York. When they reach their destination, a cellar restaurant on 42nd Street, Nick is introduced to Gatsby's business associate, Meyer Wolfsheim. "He's an Oggsford man," states Wolfsheim as Gatsby leaves the room. "He went to Oggsford College in England. You know Oggsford College?" he then asks Nick. "It's one of the most famous colleges in the world" (57).[5]

Oxford and England appear again in the romantic high point of the novel, the reunion of Gatsby and Daisy. When Gatsby is showing off his mansion to Nick and Daisy, he takes them to his library, which apparently he has named after Oxford's Merton College library (71).[6]

Gatsby also displays his lavish wardrobe, including piles of shirts of many colors and designs that he has a man purchase for him in England (72–73).

As Daisy and Gatsby become lovers again, Tom becomes suspicious of Gatsby and his wealth. Driving Nick and Jordan to the Plaza Hotel,[7] he confesses that he has launched an investigation into Gatsby:

> "And you found he was an Oxford man," said Jordan helpfully.
>
> "An Oxford man!" Tom was incredulous. "Like hell he is! He wears a pink suit."
>
> "Nevertheless he's an Oxford man."
>
> "Oxford, New Mexico," snorted Tom contemptuously, "or something like that." (95)

Tensions build as the temperature climbs in the Plaza Hotel, and in the novel's emotional climax, Tom confronts Gatsby with his suspicions. Nick narrates the conversation between the two rivals for Daisy's love:

> "By the way, Mr. Gatsby, I understand you're an Oxford man."
>
> "Not exactly."
>
> "Oh, yes, I understand you went to Oxford.
>
> "Yes—I went there."
>
> A pause. Then Tom's voice, incredulous and insulting: "You must have gone there about the time Biloxi went to New Haven."
>
> . . . This tremendous detail was about to be cleared up at last.
>
> "I told you I went there."
>
> "I heard you, but I'd like to know when."
>
> "It was in nineteen-nineteen. I only stayed five months. That's why I can't really call myself an Oxford man. . . . It

6

was an opportunity they gave to some of the officers after the Armistice," he continued. "We could go to any of the universities in England or France."

I wanted to get up and slap him on the back. I had one of those renewals of complete faith in him . . . (100–101)[8]

Nick's renewal of faith in Gatsby is seriously challenged when he returns home with Tom and Jordan only to find that Myrtle Wilson has been hit and killed by Gatsby's car. Confronting Gatsby, who is hiding outside the Buchanan house, Nick realizes that it was a distraught Daisy who was driving the car. Late into the night, Gatsby confesses the truth to Nick about his humble background, about how he became Jay Gatsby, and about his relationship with Daisy in Louisville before the war (117–18). He had been so successful in the war that he was promoted to captain before he reached the front, followed by another promotion to major following heroic command of the machine guns in his division during the Argonne campaign. After the Armistice, he tried to return home, but due to some complications he was sent to Oxford instead. Then Tom Buchanan entered Daisy's life, and swiftly, they became engaged, Daisy's letter reaching Gatsby while he was still at Oxford. By the time he returned to Louisville, Daisy was on her honeymoon.

After Gatsby's death, Nick pays a visit to Meyer Wolfsheim to invite him to Gatsby's funeral, and begins putting together more pieces about the past of Jimmy Gatz. "When he told me he was at Oggsford," confesses Wolfsheim, "I knew I could use him good" (133).

Part of what makes it such a pathetic ending for Gatsby is the vast number of people who "use[d] him good." While the actions of Daisy and Tom are perhaps the most criminal, the hordes of party guests, Wolfsheim, and even Nick used Gatsby and his wealth. Only Nick and Owl Eyes (the inebriated man Nick and Jordan meet in Gatsby's Merton College Library) had the decency to show up for Gatsby's funeral. Then again, Gatsby himself used people and things in his single-minded quest for Daisy. He certainly used Oxford: The question is, how? What did he take from his five months there? And why does Fitzgerald place Oxford in so many key moments in his novel?

Oxford in Other Fitzgerald Fiction

The first appearance of Oxford in Fitzgerald's fiction may have been in the short story, "Sentiment—and the Use of Rouge," written while he was at Princeton, in 1917.[9] It is the story of an English officer, Captain Clayton Harrington Syneforth, who headed off to the front "with the first hundred thousand," was severely wounded, but survived, and returned to England muddled. After he and Sergeant O'Flaherty crawl, bleeding profusely, into a shell crater for protection, the Irishman delivers a dying social sermon to his captain:

> ". . . Father O'Brien, he says: 'Go on in [boys] and bate the Luther out o' them'—great stuff! But can you see the Reverent Updike—Updike just out of Oxford, yellin' 'mix it up, chappies,' or 'soak 'em blokes'?—No, Captain, the best leader you ever get is a six-foot rowin' man that thinks God's got a seat in the House of Commons. All sportin' men have to have a bunch o' cheerin' when they die. Give an Englishman four inches in the sportin' page this side of the whistle an' he'll die happy—but not O'Flaherty."[10]

Oxford makes a handful of appearances in Fitzgerald's first novel, *This Side of Paradise* (1920), whose working title was *The Romantic Egoist* and which is described by its author as "a quest novel."[11] In it, the fifteen-year-old Amory Blaine pleads with his absentee mother, Beatrice, to be sent away from Minnesota to a preparatory school. She consents to St. Regis, in Connecticut: "I'd have preferred for you to have gone to Eton, and then to Christ Church, Oxford, but it seems impracticable now" (28).[12] Beatrice then connects Amory to Monsignor Darcy, who turns out to be a mentor and kindred-soul:

"Well, if you're like me, you loathe all science and mathematics—"

Amory nodded vehemently.

"Hate 'em all. Like English and history."

"Of course. You'll hate school for a while, too. . . ."

"I want to go to Princeton," said Amory. " . . . I think of Princeton as being lazy and good-looking and aristocratic. . . ." They slipped briskly into an intimacy from which they never recovered.

"I was for Bonnie Prince Charlie," announced Amory.

"Of course you were—and for Hannibal—"

"Yes, and for the Southern Confederacy." [Amory] was rather skeptical about being an Irish patriot—he suspected that being Irish was being somewhat common—but Monsignor assured him that Ireland was a romantic lost cause and Irish people quite charming, and that it should, by all means, be one of his principal biases. (31)

Oxford, then, is connected in the narrative with Princeton, Catholicism, "English and history," "lazy and good looking and aristocratic" Irish patriotism, and romantic lost causes: in other words, with formative influences and characteristics of Fitzgerald's own youth.[13] In *Gatsby*, many of these elements will reemerge, but rather than fixed to one alter ego like Amory, they are dispersed among the characters of Nick, Tom, and Gatsby. This divergence from the obvious autobiographic to an "infusion" of the personal is one reason why Fitzgerald's third novel achieves much more than the first two.

In *This Side of Paradise*, Fitzgerald describes Amory's first encounters with Princeton with imagery recalling Matthew Arnold's famous description of "the dreaming spires" of Oxford: "topping all, climbing with clear blue aspiration, the great dreaming spires of Holder and Cleveland towers" (47). There is a chapter in *This Side of Paradise* titled "Spires and Gargoyles," which Fitzgerald admitted "was possibly suggested by 'Dreaming Spires,'" the lengthy Oxford section in Compton Mackenzie's novel *Sinister Street* (1914).[14]

Princeton's "Gothic halls and cloisters were infinitely more myste-rious as they loomed suddenly out of the darkness," awaking in Amory "a deep and reverent devotion to the gray walls and Gothic peaks and all they symbolized as warehouses of dead ages" (57). But for Amory the Gothic spire "with its upward trend" was not dead, but rather a chaste symbol of imagination and dreaming ambition. "Yet he knew that where now the spirit of spires and towers made him dreamily acquiescent, it would then overawe him" when he actually began his work as a writer (58). Princeton began "to live up to its Gothic beauty" during Amory's third year, when he immersed himself in what he christened "quest books" (115).

Amory falls in love after his first year at Princeton with a girl named Isabelle Borgé, who, like Fitzgerald, has ties to both Minnesota and Baltimore. While spending time with Isabelle at her family's summer home on Long Island, Amory reaches "the high point of [his] vanity, the crest of his young egotism":

> Amory rushed upstairs to change into a dinner coat. As he put in his studs he realized that he was enjoying life as he would probably never enjoy it again. Everything was hal-lowed by the haze of his own youth. He had arrived, abreast of the best in his generation at Princeton. He was in love and his love was returned. . . . There was little in his life now that he would have changed. . . . Oxford might have been a bigger field. (88)

Amory soon falls from the crest of his vanity when Isabelle rejects him, and he fails his mathematics qualifying exam at Princeton. Crushed and aimless, he turns once more to Monsignor Darcy for advice:

> "Why do I make lists?" Amory asked him one night. "Lists of all sorts of things?"
> "Because you are a mediævalist," Monsignor answered. "We both are. It's the passion for classifying and finding a type." (97)[15]

Amory joins the Army as America enters the war in 1918, as a second lieutenant in the 171st Infantry, and is stationed in Camp Mills, Long Island, where Fitzgerald himself awaited embarkation. Unlike Fitzgerald, Amory does make it to Europe before the Armistice is signed, but we hear nothing of his war adventures. He writes from Brest to his friend Tom in March 1919, musing about entering politics upon his return to New York and asking, "Why is it that the pick of young Englishmen from Oxford and Cambridge go into politics and in the U.S.A. we leave it to the muckers?" (152). But it is a career in advertising, rather than politics, that Amory begins in New York, making him a poor match for debutante Rosalind Connage. Though they fall deeply in love, Rosalind ultimately rejects Amory, and he marks that this love affair "ended at exactly twenty minutes after eight on Thursday, June 10, 1919" (185). This is almost precisely the date that Jay Gatsby, in Oxford, receives the news that Daisy Fay has married Tom Buchanan.

In 1920, shortly after the publication of *This Side of Paradise*, Fitzgerald wrote a short story titled "The I.O.U." instructing his agent, Harold Ober, to submit it to *Harper's Bazaar*. Neither *Harper's* nor *The Saturday Evening Post* showed interested in publishing it, however, and it has only recently escaped the archives and appeared in print.[16] In the story, an unnamed publisher narrates how he acquired the manuscript of a "psychic research man" named Dr. Harden, "no intellectual upstart. He was a distinguished psychologist, PhD Vienna, LL.D. Oxford and late visiting professor at the University of Ohio."[17] This pedigree is very similar to that of Dick Diver in Fitzgerald's *Tender is the Night*. Dr. Harden's book, *The Aristocracy of the Spirit World*, tells the story of Harden's communion with his nephew, Cosgrove, who had been killed in the Great War. The short story parodies both psychic claims and the publishing world—Harden and the publisher are both running cons—with a bit of a shot taken at academic credentials.

In Fitzgerald's second novel, *The Beautiful and Damned* (1922), Amory Blaine has graduated and become Anthony Patch, an aspiring medieval historian wandering aimlessly the streets of Manhattan, talking of a character called "the Chevalier" and the need for a new chivalric code.[18] Though finding love and marriage, Anthony spirals in degradation, failing as a soldier, reaching heroic levels only in his pretension and his drinking. Oxford is not explicitly referenced in the novel.

In *Tender is the Night* (1934), Oxford makes only two appearances. A man on the beach in the Riviera approaches the young actress Rosemary with some advice about sharks. "He was of indeterminate nationality," writes Fitzgerald, "but spoke with a slow Oxford drawl." Rosemary's tormented lover, psychiatrist Dick Diver, is described as a Rhodes scholar at Oxford, in 1914, but though the Western Front and American casualties in the Great War are important components of this novel of American adventurers in Europe, Oxford does not seem to figure in any significant way.

The most explicit literary connection to Oxford came toward the end of Fitzgerald's career, while he was writing screenplays in Hollywood. In 1937, under contract with MGM, Fitzgerald was asked to doctor the screenplay for a movie called *A Yank at Oxford*. On the top of his copy of the typescript—dated July 12, 1937, and now at Princeton's Firestone Library—is this description:

> The story is about an extremely fresh American who is razzed at Oxford, and in an embittered moment, lets his enemy suffer for a blow he struck. He grows* to love Oxford and the enemy's sister and seizes an opportunity for attonement [sic]. Accidently, all is set right. . . . Why does he grow to like Oxford?"[19]

With such limited evidence in Fitzgerald's fiction, is there justification for making so much over the role of Oxford in *Gatsby*? Bonnie McNeil draws our attention to a comment Nick makes during the Plaza Hotel scene.[20] In the midst of Tom's interrogation of Gatsby over his being "an Oxford man" hangs Nick's commentary, "This tremendous detail was about to be cleared up at last." *This tremendous detail* of Gatsby's connection to Oxford is, writes McNeil, "the keystone in the arch that supports the grandiose but fragile structure Gatsby has created." Once it is removed, Gatsby begins to unravel and Daisy begins to have doubts about their future together.

Even the seemingly random references to Oxford in *This Side of Paradise* may have been more purposeful for Fitzgerald. In a letter from April 1925 to his Princeton friend John Peale Bishop, Scott praises a poem by Bishop, writing, "It was wonderful that when you wrote that [poem] you had never seen Italy—or, by God, now that I think about it, never lived in the 15th century. But then I wrote *T.S. of P.* without having been to Oxford." Oxford, it would appear from this comment, was also a tremendous detail in his first novel. It must have functioned symbolically, since Amory never goes to Oxford in the novel. In 1921 Fitzgerald *did* visit Oxford, and in August 1925 he writes again to Bishop stating that he and Zelda "go Nice for the Spring, with Oxford next Summer."[21] It would seem, then, that in the period in which Fitzgerald was writing *Gatsby*, Oxford had, for him, become more than just a generic symbol. He was making personal connections to Oxford as well as sensing the great poetic power Oxford still had for writers, some of whom were his early literary heroes, and we will discuss these in chapter three.

Fitzgerald Criticism, Medievalism, and the Problem of Narrative in *Gatsby*

A substantial body of literary criticism has grown around F. Scott Fitzgerald and, especially, *The Great Gatsby*. But this did not begin until nearly a decade after the author's death, when a general reevaluation of the Jazz Age occurred in America. The availability now of Scott and Zelda's letters, Scott's *Ledger*, and other Fitzgerald and Perkins family records has resulted in a rich corpus of scholarly articles as well as several good—and readable—biographies. Rather than competing with these works, for this study, I want to draw particular attention to the heretofore-overlooked importance of Oxford in the novel, and, more broadly, to the influence of both Romanticism and medievalism on Fitzgerald.

Apart from McNeil's essay, the role of Oxford in *The Great Gatsby* has attracted very little attention from Fitzgerald scholars. Lionel

Trilling, one of the first, attributed a "heroic quality" to Fitzgerald's writing in 1945 and pointed to the romantic tragedy of *Gatsby*.[22] The first full-length biography of Fitzgerald did not appear until 1949, the year after Zelda's death. Arthur Mizener's *The Far Side of Paradise* is aided by an abundance of material about Fitzgerald made available to the author by Mrs. Frances "Scottie" Lanahan, Scott and Zelda's daughter.[23] It is a fast-paced sweep through Fitzgerald's career and life with Zelda, but *Gatsby* itself merits a scant ten pages. For his biography, *Scott Fitzgerald* (1962), Andrew Turnbull had the advantage of a friendship with Fitzgerald that lasted from 1932 to 1941. Turnbull's beautiful prose is complemented by his early editorial work on Fitzgerald's letters.[24] Henry Dan Piper's *F. Scott Fitzgerald: A Critical Portrait* (1965) eschews traditional biography and focuses instead on Fitzgerald "as a writer and artist."[25] His lengthy treatment of *Gatsby* (three chapters) includes some discussion of Fitzgerald's medievalism.[26] Matthew Bruccoli, widely recognized as the most important Fitzgerald scholar of his day, has very little to say about the Fitzgeralds' 1921 trip to Oxford in his otherwise comprehensive biography, *Some Sort of Epic Grandeur* (1981).[27] The most recent Fitzgerald biographer, David S. Brown, is a historian who emphasizes the historical dimension of Fitzgerald's writing in *Paradise Lost: A Life of F. Scott Fitzgerald* (2017).[28] For Brown, Fitzgerald was a "cultural historian" as much as a writer of fiction, who "was able to write as powerfully as he did about historical change in America because he identified with it in such a personal way."

There are many articles and collections of essays dealing with the historical context of *The Great Gatsby* and other Fitzgerald works. Of the latter, *The Cambridge Companion to F. Scott Fitzgerald* (2001), *A Historical Guide to F. Scott Fitzgerald* (2004), and *F. Scott Fitzgerald in Context* (2013) are the most noteworthy.[29] Yet, like the Fitzgerald biographies, these tend to focus almost exclusively on America. This is true of one of the most original book-length studies of *Gatsby* in recent years, Sarah Churchwell's *Careless People: Murder, Mayhem, and the Invention of* The Great Gatsby (2013).[30] Churchwell, drawing our attention to a 1922 murder mystery in New Jersey with Gatsby-esque details, offers lengthy discussion of Tommy Hitchcock, Max Gerlach, and other Long Island associates of the Fitzgeralds.

In *The Great Gatsby: Limits of Wonder* (1990), Richard Lehan suggests that Jay Gatsby merely "exploits his brief contact with Oxford" along with his war record and his "natural physical elegance."[31] Lehan also draws our attention to the connections between *Gatsby* and T. S. Eliot's *The Wasteland*, observing that, "the two works function thematically in the same way. *The Great Gatsby* is a kind of prose-poem, held together by image and symbol in the same way that *The Wasteland* shores up broken images against their ruin."[32] In chapter five, we will explore Eliot's time in Oxford, his own medievalism, and his thoughts about Fitzgerald's writings. Nick's credibility as a narrator is scrutinized by Lehan, both because Nick engages in a relationship with known liar Jordan and because he smugly boasts at the outset of the novel of his tolerance and later that he is one of the few honest people he has ever known. Ultimately, however, argues Lehan, "we never lose an affinity with him because his deceit seems more unintentional than calculated."[33] Nevertheless, the narrative voice in *Gatsby* remains problematic, and we will examine Nick's role along with several key themes in the novel in chapter eleven.

This book will also devote a lot of attention to the medieval and Romantic dimensions of *The Great Gatsby*. Fitzgerald had a lifelong passion for medieval history, chivalric literature, and the poetry of the Romantics. He was as an amateur, however, not an academic, and so he reimagines the Middle Ages in ways similar to those of the Romantics, the Pre-Raphaelite painters, Alfred Tennyson, and other nineteenth-century figures. This reimagining of the Middle Ages is what scholars call "medievalism," and it continued intermittently through the twentieth century—T. S. Eliot, C. S. Lewis, and J.R.R. Tolkien all reimagined the Middle Ages in their writing (Lewis and Tolkien were also professional medievalists, for they taught and produced scholarship on the Middle Ages). Fitzgerald's medievalism will be the subject of chapter seven of this book. Michael Alexander in a new study defines medievalism as "the offspring of two impulses: the recovery by antiquarians and historians of materials for the study of the Middle Ages; and the imaginative adoption of medieval ideals and forms."[34] Movies and television series in this century—*Harry Potter*, *Game of Thrones*, the Narnia and Middle-earth films—carry on the work of the Victorian novels and paintings in keeping us fascinated with our medieval past.

Most scholars have treated Fitzgerald's novels as exemplars of American and modernist realism. The first-person narrative of Nick Carraway in *The Great Gatsby* is largely what makes the novel such a seminal work of modernist realism. James Nagel defines two important aspects of realism—"a limited, humanistic method of narration and a central theme of personal growth and ethical maturity"—and asserts the importance of both to the artistry and meaning of *Gatsby*.[35] "In the tradition of the best of Realistic fiction, *The Great Gatsby* has narrative integrity, consistency and unity," writes Nagel, but all of it is "limited, unreliable, and profoundly human recollection, speculation, and summation by Nick."[36] These limitations resulted in Gatsby being fragmented and unclear, at least in the first versions of the novel. Maxwell Perkins, Fitzgerald's editor at Scribner's, wrote a long report to the author, in November 1924, after reading the first complete manuscript of *Gatsby*, suggesting that Fitzgerald "might find ways to let the truth about some of [Gatsby's] claims like 'Oxford' and his army career come out bit by bit in the course of actual narrative."[37] Fitzgerald took Perkins's advice in this matter, and rewrote the character of Gatsby so that he becomes more real and relatable, if only gradually and not completely until after his demise. Jay Gatsby, for all his greatness, is still *Nick's version* of Gatsby, a compilation of first-person confessions, third-party rumors, and Nick's own assessment of Gatsby's character and his actions.

In a sense, Tom is right about Gatsby when he calls him "Mr. Nobody from Nowhere." He does not have aristocratic roots or even a nouveau riche family, he does not carry his real name, and we only know that name and his geographic origins after his death when we meet his mortal father, a poor farmer from Minnesota. The only real exception to Gatsby's proletarian upbringing is the five months he spends in Oxford, which were arguably insufficient in enabling him to familiarize himself completely with the social nuances of the upper classes and establish him as an "Oxford man," as evidenced in the doubtfulness of Nick, Jordan, and Tom when they are first confronted with Gatsby's claim. Nick and Jordan, for instance, suspect he is lying, while Tom responds with the incredulous explosion of "Like hell he is!"[38]

"Do *you* think of *Gatsby* as an Oxford novel?" asks Olivia Sung in Oxford's independent student newspaper, *Cherwell*. "Despite its being located in New York, Oxford in the novel is a pervasive spectre: a place never visited except, at first, in rumor, and then eventually in memory."[39] Rumors, deception, glimpsed memories, an enigmatic narrator—these things all problematize the text, and yet add to its power.

Even if Jay Gatsby could not really call himself "an Oxford man," he was, nevertheless, an American in Oxford. For nearly two centuries America had sent her sons (and a few daughters) to Oxford, though never in such large numbers as the American Army experiment in 1919, the subject of chapter six. The chronological focus of this book is the twenty-five year period between the arrival of the first American Rhodes scholars in Oxford in 1904 (examined in chapter three) and the beginning of the end of Prohibition in America and the climax of the Bright Young People in England in 1929 (the focus of chapter ten), marking the end of the Jazz Age on both sides of the Atlantic. But to understand both the allure of Oxford to Americans and the Oxonian traditions that influenced Fitzgerald, especially Oxonian aestheticism, we must begin well before 1904. It is to Victorian Oxford that we turn in the next chapter, to a century of piety, polo, painting, and Romantic poetry that would have resonated in the first decades of the twentieth century and hence made some impression on Major Jay Gatsby in 1919.

2

"Our Young Barbarians All at Play":
Oxford from Percy Shelley
to Oscar Wilde

For three years [Oxford] men are in possession of what the
world does not enjoy—leisure; and they are supposed to be
using that leisure for the purposes of perfection.
—Andrew Lang, *Oxford: Brief Historical
and Descriptive Notes* (1902)

Oxford is not just a medieval university; for many it is *the* medieval university. [1] While not the oldest—Bologna (1088) and
Paris (ca. 1150) predate it among European institutions—it is
the oldest university in the English-speaking world, officially chartered
in 1214 as a *universitas magistrorum et scholarum*, "community of masters
and scholars," which could grant degrees. In truth, masters had been
teaching students in Oxford for a hundred years at least before this date,
renting rooms in private halls to teach the *artes liberales*, the liberal arts
or "Arts" course for which Oxford was most famed (Bologna specialized

in law and Paris excelled in theology). Oxford's first residential colleges (Merton, Balliol, University) appeared only in the thirteenth century and were created on the model of walled monastic houses with rooms for students and masters, a chapel, a library, and a dining hall. The Franciscan scholar Robert Grosseteste was one of the university's first chancellors, and medieval Oxford was the home of such noted philosophers and theologians as Roger Bacon, John Duns Scotus, William of Ockham, and John Wycliffe. The Arts course, consisting of the *trivium* and the *quadrivium*, taught solely in Latin, came to define Oxford for centuries, though professional graduate training in theology, law, and, eventually, medicine were added.

There were many changes to Oxford's undergraduate syllabus, pedagogy, administration, and student culture over the years before the great reforms of the Victorian Age. Most instruction was done through lecturing and students had to progress in steps toward a Bachelor's "degree" (*gradus*), which prepared them to be clerks at secular and ecclesiastical courts. To become a Master, a public disputation of a thesis was required. Although the Doctorate of Divinity (D.D.) and the Doctorate of Civil Law (D.CL.) were awarded in the Middle Ages, Oxford did not grant research doctorates (D.Phil.) until 1917. While the new learning of Humanism appeared at Oxford in the sixteenth century, Henry VIII's Dissolution of the Monasteries saw the destruction of Oxford's abbeys and convents, and Mary Tudor's bloody orders led to the deaths of the Oxford Martyrs. Oxford's status as a Royalist camp during the English Civil War was a major factor in the intellectual lethargy and conservatism that came to characterize Oxford in the early modern period. Thomas Hobbes and John Locke are two notable exceptions among Oxonian philosophers of this period, as are Robert Hooke in physics and Christopher Wren in astronomy and architecture.

Since Archbishop Laud's Constitution for the University (1636) established Oxford as the center for Anglican orthodoxy, intellectual dissent was infrequent and Oxford was becoming a finishing school for affluent gentlemen. Both Edward Gibbon and Adam Smith decried their student days at Oxford, and the university came under attack by critics writing for the *Edinburgh Review* in the early nineteenth century.

Although nominally a university, Oxford was, in Cardinal Newman's student days, "really a colony of practically autonomous colleges, situated in a picturesque Gothic little town, and quite dissociated from the great world of industrialism, political struggle, and European intellectual ferment."[2] Romanticism, the Tractarians, Lewis Carroll, and the aestheticism of Ruskin, Arnold, and Pater would change all that, returning the ancient university to a prominent role in English arts and letters, culminating in that brilliant but tragic Oxonian aesthete, Oscar Wilde. These Oxford poets, painters, and novelists would exert a powerful influence on many Americans, including F. Scott Fitzgerald, and it is their lyrical remembrances of Oxford—dreams as much as history—that would produce the Oxford Novel and the image that we still hold in our minds when we think of the City of Dreaming Spires.

Victorian Oxford

> To call a man a characteristically Oxford man is, in my opinion, to pay him the highest compliment that can be paid to a human being.
> —William Gladstone, "Oxford Union Speech" (1890)

William Gladstone was educated at Eton and Christ Church, served as president of the Union, and earned a double-first in Classics and mathematics in 1831. The same year that Gladstone made this remark at the Union (and two years before his fourth term as prime minister), Max Beerbohm came up to Oxford, "that little city of learning or laughter."[3] The *or* of his description was as important to Victorian Oxonians as it would be for those in the Jazz Age. Academic preparation *or* laughs and leisure—or could one have both? "How sad was my coming to the university!" Beerbohm continues:

> Where were those sweet conditions I had pictured in my boyhood? Those antique contrasts? . . . I wandered out into the streets . . . through which Apollo had once passed. [Now]

among the hideous trams and the brand new bricks—here, glared at by electric lights ... here, in a riot of vulgarity, were remnants of beauty, as I discerned. There were only remnants.

Industry had finally cast a dark shadow over Victorian Oxford, what John Ruskin described as a "plague-cloud ... made of dead men's souls."[4] Beerbohm's boyhood image of Oxford was a romantic image constructed by Percy Shelley and John Keats, John Henry Newman and Matthew Arnold. Was it now really a "riot of vulgarity"?

Inspired partly by the Romantic poets, Victorian Oxford was having an almost constant conversation with its medieval past. Indeed, throughout Europe and (though a bit later) in America, artists and writers were haunted by the Middle Ages, turning to it for inspiration and an escape from the materialism and industry of their own time. To be sure, it was not the Middle Ages of history, but rather medievalism that had ensnared them. From Victoria and Albert's Westminster to Woodrow Wilson's Princeton, a century of medievalism took hold in England and America and did not give way until the modernist concerns of the 1920s. Building construction in the Gothic Revival style continued throughout the Victorian era in Oxford. Even the new museum that would house science faculty and labs—the University Museum (1860), now the Museum of Natural History—was built (in part on Ruskin's advice) in Gothic to remind the University of its medieval roots, its chemical laboratory echoing the Abbot's Kitchen at Glastonbury Abbey.[5] It was here that mathematics tutor Charles Dodgson would see the last surviving specimen of the dodo bird, the character in the *Alice* books that most represents their author.

The early Victorian period also gave birth to the Oxford Novel and the Oxford Man. In *The Adventures of Mr. Verdant Green* (1853), Cuthbert Bede (born Edward Bradley) gives us the phrase with emphasis on the protagonist's maturity: "To divert his thoughts, and to impress upon himself and others the fact that he was an Oxford man, our freshman set out for a stroll."[6] Setting out for an afternoon stroll was indeed the most typical form of exercise at Oxford until the 1850s, and the virtues of country walks are extolled by Oxonians Percy Shelley,

Matthew Arnold, C. S. Lewis, and J.R.R. Tolkien; other social out-doors activities included hunting and golf. But by the middle of the nineteenth century, Oxford dons began asserting the belief that sport, especially intercollegiate athletic competition, was character building for undergraduates.[7] While in 1860 organized sports were mostly limited to cricket and rowing, by 1900 football, rugby, tennis, polo, and boxing were added to the list.

Rowing was the most popular intercollegiate sport at Oxford in the Victorian era, with two annual meets from 1852 on: Torpids, for novice crews and held during Hilary Term, and Summer Eights, the more serious competition held during "Commems" (Commemoration Week) in Trinity Term. From the 1860s every college had a boat club, and many supported the maintenance of a barge on the Isis, used by the rowers for changing and by their supporters for partying. Rowing crews could be quite democratic in composition, but victors—especially the crew that went "head of the river" during Summer Eights—were often treated as royalty, and a handful of colleges—Brasenose, University, New College, Magdalen, Trinity—dominated the races before World War II. These crews were also well represented among the winners at the annual Henley Regatta. As we will see, American rowers did quite well in the Oxford Eights in the first two decades of the twentieth century.

Like sports, clubs were founded at both the college and university level, and grew dramatically in number from 1850 to 1920. There were the dining clubs—Merton's Myrmidon Society (1865), Brasenose's Octagon (1866), Trinity's Claret Club (1870), the uber-aristocratic Bullingdon Club (begun in the late 1700s as a cricket club)—the debating societies—Magdalen's Waynflete Society, New College's XX Club, the Oxford Union (1823, but with a permanent hall in 1857)—the newspapers and literary magazines—the *Isis* (1892) and the *Cherwell* (1920) were the most prominent—and numerous musical, dramatic, and scientific societies.[8] The Oxford University Boat Club, formed in 1839, battled Cambridge in the annual Boat Race from 1856 and had its own private club, Vincent's on the High (1863), while Oxford began challenging Cambridge in polo from 1877. Members of these university sporting clubs earned "blues," or what Americans would call letters from "varsity" sports. Most of the societies and sporting clubs flowed from the interests of young men who came from the most prominent of the residential English public schools: Charterhouse, Eton, Harrow, Rugby, Shrewsbury, Westminster, and Winchester.

The undergraduate examination system began at Oxford in 1807, with students electing to sit for oral examinations for an "honours" degree. These examinations became written in 1830, and when Parliament passed the Examination Statute in 1850, Oxford candidates for the Bachelor's degree were required to sit for exams in two "schools": the first in Classics (including ancient politics, economics, and history in addition to Greek and Latin literature) and the other in mathematics, natural science, or history and jurisprudence. Residential fellows would serve as "tutors" to guide undergraduates and prepare them for these exams, supplemented by university lectures given by the most prominent scholars. The latter, often Professors who held Chairs, were increasingly married men, as clerical restrictions against fellows were lifted in most colleges by 1877.

"In the nineteenth century the old men saw visions," wrote a young Evelyn Waugh, "and the young men dreamed dreams."[9] Waugh likely had in mind "young men" like the poet Percy Shelley (sent down in his second term), the mathematics tutor Charles Dodgson (Lewis Carroll), and the flamboyant playwright and novelist Oscar Wilde; the elder visionaries were surely John Henry Newman, Matthew Arnold, and John Ruskin, all of whom made their reputations more as faculty at Oxford than as students. As a young boy and as a college student, Fitzgerald read and was deeply influenced by these Oxonians, and he mentions all of them in his fiction and letters leading up to the publication of *The Great Gatsby*. These Oxford writers developed a distinctly Oxonian aesthetic, one perceived and occasionally imitated by the young American novelist.

Poetic Truths: Shelley, Keats, and Arnold

"Romantic" is one of the most frequently used adjectives by Fitzgerald in *The Great Gatsby*.[10] Nick uses it often in his narration, Daisy and

Jordan use it, and even Tom must admit that the nightingale singing on his lawn is "very romantic." The Age of Romanticism had an enormous impact on the young Fitzgerald, who dreamed of being a great poet like Shelley and Keats, and, failing that, managed to develop an aesthetic style through his novels under the influence of these two Romantic poets and the literary critic Matthew Arnold. These three writers left their varying testimonials to Oxford spanning nearly the entirety of the nineteenth century, a time in which the university would experience great reforms and find itself in the center of theological and scientific debates. It would also continue to be a medieval university reimagining the Middle Ages. Inspired by its Gothic architecture, Arnold would famously dub Oxford "the City of Dreaming Spires," an image that would make its way into the dreaming mind of Fitzgerald.

The poet often considered the greatest of the Romantics would have the most troubled relationship with the university. Educated at Eton, Percy Bysshe Shelley was already author of two books when he went up to University College, Oxford, on October 10, 1810.[11] He would publish a second Gothic novel and another collection of poems during his first term. The Scottish antiquarian Charles Kirkpatrick Sharpe, still hanging about Oxford after receiving his MA in 1807, knew Shelley and wrote after reading *Posthumous Fragments of Margaret Nicholson*: "the author is a great genius, and if he be not clapped up in Bedlam or hanged, will certainly prove one of the sweetest swans in the tuneful margin of Cherwell."[12] Shelley's mind was then set on studying the physical sciences, especially chemistry, with an Enlightenment faith in their exalted ability to disclose truth and an adolescent bent toward mischief.[13] "He sees a male-dominated Oxford as an imperious and royalty-mongering theocracy," writes the anarchist poet Heathcote Williams, "and he determines to turn its cloistered, overprivileged world upside down with the recklessness of a gleeful prankster."[14]

At Oxford, Shelley took little sleep (he claimed three hours or less), entertained guests and conducted experiments in his rooms, and wrote (pseudonymously) provocative letters to famous clergymen. He read Greek studiously and Hume with fascination, appreciated Oxonian scholasticism (if not Aristotle), and read and recited poetry continuously. To James Roe, a student at Trinity College, he wrote simply: "Dear Roe, At ½ past 4 or 5. O'Clock there will be wine & Poetry in my room—Will you honor me with your Co. Your devoted, Percy Shelley."[15]

According to Oxford historian L.W.B. Brockliss, Shelley was "an unconventional student who dressed in slovenly fashion and played practical jokes."[16] His rooms at University College were on the first floor of the quad, overlooking the Fellows Garden, and were a chaos of books, expensive clothes, and scientific equipment.[17] Beyond even the eccentricity of his own grandfather, Shelley and his friends wondered if he was approaching the border of insanity. Small acts of rebellion included growing his hair long, skipping dining in Hall, leaving lectures early, and sprinting from chapel. The young Shelley enjoyed conversation and long country walks, strolling out on occasion to Shotover Hill and, on the pond formed by the old Headington Quarry (where now stands the Kilns, home of C. S. Lewis), he would sail little paper boats and write poetry. Most of Shelley's conversations, country walks, and pistol practice were taken with his University College mate, Thomas Jefferson Hogg. The two became virtually inseparable, and Hogg would call the frenetic Shelley "a whole university of himself."[18] The two would conspire in radical political and religious discussion, some of which was collected and edited by Shelley over Christmas holiday and printed anonymously as *The Necessity of Atheism* in February 1811. The tract was advertised in the ultra-liberal *Oxford University and City Herald,* and Shelley sent copies to all of the bishops and the heads of the colleges. On March 25, Shelley and Hogg came before the master and fellows of University College to answer questions about *The Necessity of Atheism,* the few copies of which had widely circulated at the university where some, including Sharpe, had guessed its authors. Given a chance to end the matter by denying their authorship, both students refused and were immediately expelled for "contumacious conduct."

After going down from Oxford, "the votary of Romance" would travel to Dublin in 1812 and write pamphlets in support of Catholic Emancipation, a cause that both Fitzgerald and Amory Blaine would have supported.[19] The following year, while reading Ariosto's *Orlando*

Furioso (1532), Shelley finished his first poem of substance: *Queen Mab* (printed for private circulation in 1813), nine cantos in the form of a fairy tale but tackling industrialism and political revolution. Mary Shelley would write after her husband's death that Shelley loved medieval romance and chivalry, though he "had not fostered these tastes at their genuine sources . . . but in perusal of such German works as were current in those days."[20] In 1816, Shelley adopted the pseudonym "Elfin Knight" when he submitted the poem "Hymn to Intellectual Beauty" to the *Examiner*, while in the dedication to *Laon and Cynthia* (1817) he compares himself to "some victor Knight of Faëry." In *A Defense of Poetry* (1821), Shelley makes grand historical and social claims for the medieval and Celtic inheritance:

> It was not until the eleventh century that the effects of the poetry of the Christian and Chivalric systems began to manifest themselves. . . . The incorporation of the Celtic nations with the exhausted population of the South, impressed upon it the figure of the poetry existing in their mythology and institutions. The result was . . . the abolition of personal and domestic slavery, and the emancipation of women. . . . [W]e owe this great benefit to the worship of which Chivalry was the law, and poets the prophets.[21]

Shelley's last collection of poems, *The Triumph of Life* (1824), much admired by both T. S. Eliot and C. S. Lewis, was strongly influenced by the poetry of Dante and Petrarch.[22] While living on the Riviera in 1924 and working on *Gatsby*, Fitzgerald read biographies of Lord Byron and Shelley.[23] Fitzgerald admitted to Maxwell Perkins, in 1924: "Shelley was a God to me once."[24] Lewis wrote of Shelley: "His writings are too generous for our cynics; his life too loose for our 'humanist' censors. Almost every recent movement of thought in one way or another serves to discredit him."[25]

John Keats, Fitzgerald's favorite poet, took a very different path to Oxford. He left school at age fourteen to study for a medical career at

Guy's Hospital, but he also began writing poetry seriously by 1816 and was introduced to London's literati, including Shelley, whom he met for the first time that December. By early 1817 he had given up his medical career to pursue poetry professionally, and was dining regularly with Leigh Hunt and the Shelleys by February.

In early 1817 Keats also met Benjamin Bailey, who had matriculated at Oxford the year before to study for holy orders. On September 3, Keats traveled to Oxford to stay with Bailey at Magdalen Hall (later subsumed by Magdalen College), where Thomas Hobbes had lived as an undergraduate.[26] Keats was enchanted by Oxford's Botanic Gardens, and he and Bailey boated frequently on the Isis and the Cher, taking breaks to read and discuss John Milton and William Wordsworth. Keats wrote in a letter to his sister Fanny, dated September 10, 1817, of his first visit to Oxford, where he was then engaged in writing the third book of *Endymion*:

> When I saw you last I told you of my intention of going to Oxford. . . . I am living in Magdalen Hall with a young Man with whom I have not long been acquainted, but whom I like very much. . . . This Oxford I have no doubt is the finest City in the world—it is full of old Gothic buildings—Spires—towers—Quadrangles—Cloisters Groves &(c.) and is surrounded with more Clear streams than I ever saw together.[27]

Keats would read to Bailey in the evenings his day's work on *Endymion*. He also composed a short poem that he included in a letter from Oxford to John Hamilton Reynolds. The first stanza reads:

> The Gothic looks solemn,
> The plain Doric column
> Supports an old Bishop and Crosier;
> The mouldering arch,
> Shaded o'er by a larch
> Stands next door to Wilson the Hosier.[28]

In *The Beautiful and Damned*, Fitzgerald makes reference twice to Keats's poem, "La Belle Dame sans Merci" (1820), once in English (215) and once in French (274).

Kirk Carnutt observes that, for Fitzgerald, language "was a means to rhapsody, and like the titular nightingale of the Keats poem he adored so much, he wanted his words to sing."[29] At Princeton, though uninspired by his poetry tutors, Fitzgerald talked endlessly with his classmate and friend John Peale Bishop about Wordsworth, Shelley, Byron, and Keats, and years later he would give his daughter Scottie advice about studying poetry in college, describing in particular his experience reading Keats's poems as "something that lives like a fire in you" and brings tears with every reading.[30]

Fitzgerald's original title for *The Beautiful and Damned* was *The Beautiful Lady without Mercy*.[31] Robert Sklar has written about how deeply influential Keats was on Fitzgerald's second novel, especially in its depiction of Gloria Gilbert.[32] Writing from the perspective of Anthony Patch, Fitzgerald describes Gloria as "beautiful—but without mercy. He must own that strength that could send him away" (116). The title of his novel *Tender is the Night* is a borrowing from Keats's "Ode to a Nightingale"—"Already with thee! tender is the night"—and the novel itself is, observes Sklar, "the story of a faery land like Keats's faery land, a land Fitzgerald learned at last to render with exaggerated sensuousness. . . ."[33]

Critics have long acknowledged Fitzgerald's debts to the Romantic poets, especially Keats and Shelley. By 1916, confessed Fitzgerald in the autobiographical essay, "Who's Who—and Why" (1920),

> I had decided that poetry was the only thing worth while, so with my head ringing with the meters of Swinburne and the matters of Rupert Brooke I spent the spring doing sonnets, ballads and rondels into the small hours. I had read somewhere that every great poet had written great poetry before he was twenty-one. I had only a year and, besides, war was impending. I must publish a book of startling verse before I was engulfed.[34]

"Keats and the Romantics taught Fitzgerald that truth was beauty," writes Sklar, "and [that] beauty was eternal."[35] Through the interpretive lens of Joseph Conrad, Fitzgerald came to grasp the Keatsian belief that the "loss of youth and beauty, even the loss of life, could be overcome by an art which was intense enough to preserve the quality of romance and power, even though their substance must disappear."[36]

Less often recognized is the influence of the Oxonian poet and critic Matthew Arnold on Fitzgerald's aestheticism. Arnold was the eldest son of Rev. Dr. Thomas Arnold, the famous headmaster at Rugby and reformer of the public school system.[37] Thomas had deep Oxford ties, having gone up to study Classics at Corpus Christi after schooling at Winchester, receiving a fellowship at Oriel in 1815, and becoming Regius Professor of Modern History in 1841. Matthew followed his father's footsteps to Winchester and Oxford but rebelled against him in just about every other way. Already a promising poet (Wordsworth was a family friend) before going up to Oxford in the autumn of 1841, Arnold was a dandy and a dilettante as an undergraduate at Balliol, acquiring then his "Olympian manners," in the words of his philology tutor Friedrich Max-Müller. According to his younger brother Tom, Arnold "read a little with the reading men, hunted a little with the fast men, and dressed a little with the dressy men."[38] "He earned a reputation [at Oxford] not as a scholar," writes biographer Clinton Machann, "but as a dandified dresser, a flippant wit, and an avid fisherman."[39] Unlike his father, who led the Broad Church opposition to the Oxford Movement, Arnold was drawn to the charismatic scholar who preached every Sunday from the pulpit of the University Church of St. Mary, John Henry Newman:

> [Then] in the very prime of his life . . . who could resist the charm of that spiritual apparition, gliding in the dim afternoon light through the aisles of St. Mary's, . . . breaking the silence with words and thoughts which were a religious music—subtle, sweet, mournful?[40]

Though never himself a Tractarian, Arnold would throughout his life express great admiration for Newman, particularly the latter's views on liberal education.[41] Arnold won the Newdigate Prize for his poem, "Cromwell," in 1843 and would have recited it in the Sheldonian Theatre had not, on that day, a great uproar occurred at Commemoration over the presence of an unpopular Christ Church proctor (who had attempted to ban dining clubs) and the granting of an honorary degree to Dr. Edward Everett, then the U.S. Ambassador to Great Britain, because the Harvard scholar and future secretary of state had once been a Unitarian minister.[42]

At the end of his third year, Arnold sat his Oxford exams and was rewarded, to the surprise of one of his friends, a second. Still, the Oxford faculty who knew Arnold and his famous father, who passed away shortly after taking up his Oxford professorship, expressed their disappointment. The Greek scholar and Dean of Christ Church, Henry Liddell (father of the Alice of *Wonderland*) lamented that "so able a man should have excluded himself from the highest honours."[43] Undaunted, he won an Oriel fellowship 1845, but spent much more of his time in Paris before leaving Oxford for a career in London in April 1847.

As Arnold grew into an accomplished poet and serious literary critic, however, he never truly left Oxford behind. The austere beauty of medieval Oxford would haunt his writing and lead to a distinctly Oxonian aesthetic theory. In the preface to the first of his *Essays in Criticism* (1865), Arnold would deliver perhaps the most poetic paean to Oxford:

> Beautiful city! so venerable, so lovely, so unravaged by the fierce intellectual life of our century, so serene! "There are our young barbarians all at play!" And yet, steeped in sentiment as she lies, spreading her gardens to the moonlight, and whispering from her towers the last enchantments of the Middle Ages, who will deny that Oxford, by her ineffable charm, keeps ever calling us nearer to the true goal of all of us, to the ideal, to perfection,—to beauty, in a word, which

is only truth seen from another side? . . . Adorable dreamer,
whose heart has been so romantic! . . . home of lost causes,
and forsaken beliefs.

Arnold takes up the concept of *Sehnsucht* from Novalis and Wordsworth, describing it as a "wistful, soft, tearful longing." This Romantic
cornerstone would later shape C. S. Lewis's more theological version,
which he called "joy."[44] Despite his labeling Arnold, "rather a pro-
pagandist for criticism than an critic," T. S. Eliot also owed much to
Arnold's writings in his own cultural criticism.[45] Arnold's agnostic
defense of the Classics and of humanism, delivered in the mid-Victorian
era's crisis of science versus religion, anticipates much of the Christian
humanism of G. K. Chesterton and Lewis. In *Culture and Anarchy*
(1869), Arnold wrote:

> Oxford, the Oxford of the past, has many faults; and she
> has heavily paid for them in defeat, in isolation, in want of
> hold upon the modern world. Yet we in Oxford, brought
> up amidst the beauty and sweetness of that beautiful place,
> have not failed to seize one truth:—the truth that beauty
> and sweetness are essential characters of a complete human
> perfection. When I insist on this, I am all in the faith and
> tradition of Oxford.

In the 1860s, Arnold would also develop his theory about the
Celtic-Germanic dichotomy of the English character, a theory that
would hugely influence Fitzgerald's thinking at Princeton and in
writing his first novel.[46] As Machann points out, Arnold was attracted
to the "melancholy and unprogressiveness" of the Celtic peoples (as he
describes in one letter) and associated these qualities with Oxford, home
of "lost causes, and forsaken beliefs . . . and impossible loyalties."[47]
These sentiments are echoed almost verbatim by Amory and Father Fay
in *This Side of Paradise*. Fitzgerald owned a copy of *The Poetical Works of
Matthew Arnold* (1893), now at Princeton, and he annotated the book.[48]
Gatsby's claim that all his ancestors had been educated at Oxford for

centuries "captures a poetic truth," writes Bonnie McMullen, "for where else could this passionate American dreamer look for antecedents but to Arnold's 'home of lost causes . . . and impossible loyalties.'"[49]

In 1883, the year he would make his first tour of America, Arnold complained that "practical people talk with a smile of Plato and his absolute ideas," while the Platonic vision of education that Arnold advocated was being eclipsed by the practical.[50] Things had not improved when Eliot began his short-lived career as an educator in 1916, writing that the young "should be taught to respect the values of truth, beauty and goodness for their own sake . . . They should learn *why* knowledge is valuable, apart from purely practical success."[51] Liberal education was indeed under assault in the increasingly technological Victorian age, but it would find one of its strongest defenders in Oxford's John Henry Newman.

John Henry Newman and the Oxford Movement

Beware of the Anglo-Catholics—they're all sodomites with unpleasant accents. In fact, steer clear of all religious groups; they do nothing but harm.

—Evelyn Waugh, *Brideshead Revisited* (1945)

The advice that stolid cousin Jasper gives to Charles Ryder, just up at Oxford in 1922, is almost immediately ignored as Charles becomes friends with the Catholic Sebastian Flyte and Anthony Blanche. While Waugh had his own personal reasons for exploring Catholicism in the novel, it also brought many readers back to the religious controversies at Oxford in the middle of the nineteenth century. Within the so-called Oxford Movement some of the university's greatest thinkers debated Anglican reform, leading some to Anglo-Catholic High Church and others to conversion to Roman Catholicism. At the center was the charismatic John Henry Newman, whose ideas about higher education, derived from his experiences at Oxford, were to have an impact well beyond England.

Newman went up to Trinity College, Oxford, in 1817, at the age of sixteen. He "had at first come to the University, as to some sacred shrine," he later recalled, and "from time to time hopes had come over him that some day or other he should have gained a title to residence on one of its old foundations."[52] That would come, but in his first year he excelled in mathematics and struggled with his Greek and Latin, spending almost no time with sport but rather attending plays and concerts and practicing violin.[53] In 1819, Newman founded a debating society at Oxford, and he practiced writing by emulating the styles of Homer, Shakespeare, and Edward Gibbon.[54] Nevertheless, he managed only a lower second in Classics and failed his mathematics exam. Undaunted, he stayed in Trinity to study and took the fellowship examination for Oriel College, one of Oxford's most academically eminent, in 1822. The Oriel examiners were impressed with Newman's writing and offered him the fellowship.

Newman was ordained as a priest in the Church of England in 1824, taking over as Curate of St. Clement's and Vice-Principal of St. Alban's Hall. He resigned both positions in 1826 when he was made Tutor of Oriel and two years later became vicar of the University Church of St. Mary's. As an Oriel scholar he wrote on Aristotle, Cicero, and the early Church Fathers, while the sermons he delivered at St. Mary's over the next fifteen years made him a local legend. Together with John Keble, Richard Hurrell Froude, William Palmer, and Edward Bouverie Pusey, Newman's mostly Oriel coterie formed a spiritual counterpart to the Romantic Movement, rejecting eighteenth-century ideas (Anglican and evangelical Methodism) in favor of a return to early Christian history in their "imaginative devotion," transcendental doctrines, and mysterious sacramental symbols.[55] Labeled "Tractarians" after the ninety *Tracts for the Times* (1833–41) that they jointly published, these leaders of the Oxford Movement questioned whether any real and significant theological differences divided Anglicanism and Catholicism and called for a return of medieval liturgical elements. Bitter intra-Oxford dispute came to a head with Newman's 1843 sermon preached before the university entitled "The Holy Eucharist a comfort to the penitent." After the sermon Newman was banned from preaching for two years.

By 1845, Newman had entered into the Roman Catholic Communion. He moved to Rome for further study and was ordained into the priesthood a year later.

Newman developed a particular Oxonian aestheticism around a longing for the divine, and was especially moved by the chiming of the bells in Oxford's churches and towers. "Bells pealing," he would write, "The pleasure of hearing them . . . [evokes] a kind of longing after something dear to us and well known to us. . . . Such is my feeling . . . as I hear them."[56] Newman wrote poetry, hymns, and novels, as well as sermons, exegesis, and hagiography. Praising the philosophical idealism of Wordsworth and Coleridge in 1839, Newman declared, "Poetry then is our mysticism," and adopted a form of Christian Platonism.[57] Newman's aesthetics, in addition to his theological radicalism, aimed at restoring long past institutions and doctrines that he believed still had value for the modern world. The neo-chivalric "Young England" political movement of the 1830s and 1840s was partially inspired by Newman and the Tractarians, led by Etonian and Oxbridge young Tories who attempted to bring back medieval *noblesse oblige* as a way to unite aristocrats and laborers against the exploitive members of the bourgeoisie.[58]

Oxbridge Torries were coming increasingly under attack in the British press and academic journals for not modernizing the ancient universities and for perpetuating their exclusivity. As one critic in *The Times* put it,

> The Conservatives think they can govern England because
> they have the support of . . . Oxford. That university is the
> seat of isolated barbarism amongst an ocean of wholesome
> knowledge and of useful action. It is a generation behind
> the rest of the kingdom.[59]

Lord John Russell, then prime minister, suggested that Royal Commissioners be established to reform Oxford and Cambridge, prompting the memorable response from Oxford's lord chancellor, the Duke of Wellington: "Two centuries ago—in 1636—the University revised the whole body of its statutes, and . . . the nature and faculties of the human mind were exactly [then] what they are still."[60]

Despite the lack of cooperation from many of the colleges, a Royal Commission was sent to both Oxford and Cambridge in 1850 and attempted to secularize and liberalize the institutions in the era defined increasingly by the German model research university. Gladstone and Jowett set to work on a response, which became the Oxford University Act of 1854, resulting in a newly middle-class university with modernized administration and curricula, moving away from an entirely social orientation—creating the well-mannered gentleman—toward the process of learning as an educational end.[61] Keble College was founded in 1870 by surviving Tractarians to address the issue of economic access and inclusivity at the new Oxford, while new religious diversity can be seen in the founding of the permanent private halls: Wycliffe Hall in 1877 (evangelical Christians), St. Benet's Hall in 1890 (Benedictines), Campion Hall in 1896 (Jesuits), and Regents Park College relocated from London in 1927 (Baptists). The Commission also led to the founding of the first women's colleges.[62] Newman and other Tractarians pushed for more tutorials as well, and Benjamin Jowett, Master of Baliol and later vice-chancellor of the university, emphasized attendance and regular review of students' performance in the tutorials. Hilaire Beloc, poet and Oxford Union president who had gone up to Balliol in 1891 to read history, noticed the change:

> "Can this be Oxford? This the place?"
> (He cries). "Of which my father said
> The tutoring was a damn disgrace . . . ?"[63]

The challenge of the research university to Oxbridge was addressed by Newman in his magisterial *The Idea of a University* (1852), the first half of which is based on a series of discourses Newman delivered in Ireland in 1852, where he was tasked with creating the first Catholic university on the island. In *The Idea of a University*, Newman delivers a defense of liberal education and study of theology in the modern research university. Universities exist, asserts Newman, for the purpose of teaching Universal Knowledge, and the purpose of learning that Knowledge is the pursuit of Truth.[64] Universities are not, however, the best entities for philosophical enquiry and scientific research—the European Academies and the various Societies in Britain are much better for this purpose, according to Newman. Universities provide a preliminary function to this scholarly enquiry, a "first step in intellectual training," to impress on a student's mind "the idea of science, method, order, principle, and system."[65] This education is called "Liberal," writes Newman, because a "habit of mind is formed which lasts through life, of which . . . I have ventured to call a philosophical habit."[66] The liberal arts are "the especial characteristic or property of a University and of a gentleman," writes Newman. "It is well to be a gentleman, it is well to have a cultivated intellect, a delicate taste, a candid, equitable, dispassionate mind, a noble and courteous bearing in the conduct of life—these are the connatural qualities of a large knowledge; they are the objects of a University."[67]

Newman's name became associated with Catholic educational revival around the world. Fitzgerald attended the Newman School in New Jersey, founded in part on the principles of Newman's Oratory School in Birmingham, including a classical curriculum and lay teachers and administrators.[68] Fitzgerald made references to its namesake throughout his early writings. Cardinal Newman is listed among the "personages" in a letter Fitzgerald wrote to Sally Pope Taylor (daughter of Cousin Ceci) while stationed at Camp Sheridan in 1918.[69] This concept of "personage" is explored by Fitzgerald in his first two novels. In *This Side of Paradise*, the concept arises in conversation between Amory Blaine and Monsignor D'Arcy, a character based closely on Fitzgerald's early mentor, Father Cyril Sigourney Fay. Fay had attended Episcopal seminary in Philadelphia, taught at an Anglican seminary near Milwaukee, and was a member of the Companions of the Holy Savior, a community devoted to the ultra-High Church principles of the Oxford Movement.[70] When the General Convention of the Episcopal Church curbed the Catholicising tendencies of the Companions in 1908, Fay converted to Catholicism.

Father Fay, who would become headmaster at Newman School in 1913, invited several urbane and literary friends to join his "fireside group" and the young Fitzgerald was brought into this circle. Among these visitors was Father William Hemmick, an aesthete with whom Fitzgerald would carry on a correspondence during the war, and the English novelist Shane Leslie.[71] Fay, Hemmick, and Leslie all saw literary promise in Fitzgerald and tried to get him to see the Church as a vibrant source of inspiration for writers and intellectuals. They steered Fitzgerald to the novels of Compton Mackenzie, an Oxonian and also a Catholic convert. Fitzgerald closely identified with Michael Fane, the Catholic hero of Mackenzie's *Sinister Street*, through at least the writing of his first two novels.[72] Fay also schemed to get Fitzgerald to accompany him on a secret mission (under cover of the Red Cross) to Russia in the summer of 1917, and when that fell through he hoped Fitzgerald would accompany him to Rome. Fay made it to the Vatican and charmed Pope Benedict XV, who made him a monsignor, but failed to take Fitzgerald with him. Instead, they kept up correspondence while Fay traveled on lecture tours and Fitzgerald began training in the army.

In December 1877, the president of Trinity College Oxford wrote to Newman offering him the position of Honorary Fellow of the College. In his eager acceptance of the honor, Newman confessed that Trinity College had ever been in his thoughts and that he kept photos of its buildings at his bedside.[73] Newman was made cardinal by Pope Leo XIII in May 1879 and his beatification was officially proclaimed by Pope Benedict XVI in September 2010. "To me Newman is almost Oxford, the very *genius loci*. His spirit haunts the place," wrote the American scholar Paul Elmer More visiting Oxford in 1924.[74] In the words of one recent historian, "For whatever else he was, Newman was first and foremost an Oxford man."[75]

Ruskin and the Pre-Raphaelites

In the 1935 short story "I'd Die for You (The Legend of Lake Lure)"—which features a Great War veteran and has several *Gatsby* echoes—Fitzgerald makes reference at a crucial moment to *Sesame of the Lilies* (1865), a collection of lectures by the esteemed Victorian art critic John Ruskin.[76] In addition to art and literary criticism, the Oxonian Ruskin wrote poetry and fairy tales and called for social reform—all things Fitzgerald would have admired. But Ruskin was also a tortured man and remains a controversial figure, responsible for these words about Fitzgerald's home in *Time and Tide* (1867):

> . . . Americans, as a nation, set their trust in liberty and in equality, of which I detest the one, and deny the possibility of the other; and because, also, as a nation they are wholly undesirous of Rest, and incapable of it: irreverent of themselves, both in the present and in the future; discontented with what they are, yet having no ideal of anything which they desire to become.[77]

Ruskin entered Christ Church in 1837 as a gentleman commoner and published that same year his first book, *The Poetry of Architecture*. In 1839 he won the Newdigate for his poem, "Salsette and Elephanta." Love and depression lead to his double-fourth at Oxford in 1842, but the following year he published the landmark survey of art history, *Modern Painters* I (1843), and, following trips to France, Switzerland, and Italy to investigate medieval art, published *Modern Painters* II (1846). He married Euphemia "Effie" Gray in 1848, but the unconsummated marriage was annulled in 1854.

Ruskin became Oxford's first Slade Professor of Fine Art in 1870 and was elected to a second three-year term in 1873. He was a very active and popular lecturer at Oxford, where he would interrupt his art lectures with exhortations to his students to fall in love and pursue beauty rather than in pointless games, in "fruitless slashing of the river," in learning "to leap and to row, to hit a ball with a bat"; instead, they should join him in improving the Oxford countryside by creating a flower-bordered country road. "It was to be an ethical adventure like building a Gothic cathedral," writes Richard Ellmann. "[Ruskin's] art criticism always harked back to the medieval period, with its faith and its Gothic, while he argued that the Renaissance, the more it bloomed, the more it decayed."[78]

Ruskin's art criticism, especially his praise for J.M.W. Turner and medieval art, provided part of the inspiration for the Pre-Raphaelite movement. The Pre-Raphaelite Brotherhood (P.R.B.) was officially founded in 1848 by three young students at the Royal Academy of Art in London—Dante Gabriel Rossetti, William Holman Hunt, and John Everett Millais—who issued a manifesto decrying the stale classicism of English Victorian painting, calling for a return stylistically to late medieval and early Renaissance painters like Giotto, Cimabue, and Fra Angelico, and a religious devotion to depicting nature with maximum realism.[79] They saw the Middle Ages as an ideal for the synthesis of art and life in the applied arts and hence drew frequently upon medieval, and especially Arthurian, themes and subjects.

Several founding members of the P.R.B. had Oxford connections. Dante Gabriel Rossetti (1828–82) organized a group of artists in 1857 to paint the Arthurian murals in the Debating Chamber (now the Library) of the Oxford Union. None of the artists working on the Union murals understood the difficulty in working on fresco painting, and the Arthurian scenes taken from Thomas Malory and Alfred Lord Tennyson began to deteriorate almost immediately. Though technically less gifted as a painter than other members of the P.R.B., Rossetti wrote poetry and translated the *Vita Nuova* of his namesake.[80]

Sir John Everett Millais (1829–96), perhaps the most gifted of all the Pre-Raphaelites and who became the most commercially successful, studied the medieval stained glass windows of Merton College Chapel, Oxford, for one of his greatest paintings, *Mariana* (1851). Millais would also paint the famous portrait of John Henry Newman (1851) that hangs in the National Portrait Gallery in London. When he described the halted suicide of a young woman in "I'd Die for You," Fitzgerald seems to have had in mind not only Ruskin but also Millais's famous painting *Ophelia* (1851/2), which captures the serene face of Shakespeare's medieval heroine floating just above the water before her drowning. Although Ruskin had been one of his chief early supporters, Millais fell in love with Ruskin's wife Effie and married her soon after their annulment. William Holman Hunt (1827–1910) had a work ethic, commitment to social change, and religious devotion that were legendary. His eventual fame came mainly from his religious painting, including *The Light of the World* (1851–53), now in the chapel at Keble College, Oxford.

The second phase of Pre-Raphaelitism came when Rossetti met two former Oxford students, Edward Burne-Jones and William Morris, and drafted them to help with the Oxford Union project. Sir Edward Coley Burne-Jones (1833–98) had gone up to Exeter College in 1852, reading Tennyson and Ruskin and Malory at Oxford; William Morris (1834–96) joined Burne-Jones at Exeter in 1853, and "Ned and Topsy" (as they were known by friends and family) shared their passion for art, poetry, and the Middle Ages. A visit to France with Morris solidified Jones's devotion to Gothic architecture and medieval art. While at Oxford the two founded *The Oxford and Cambridge Magazine*, and in 1861 they became (with Rossetti) founding members of the firm Morris, Marshall, Faulkner & Co. Burne-Jones would design stained-glass windows for churches throughout Britain, including work in Oxford for the Chapel at St. Edmund's Hall and the Cathedral at Christ Church (depicting St. Frideswide), and tiles painted with scenes from fairy tales.

Morris, who was reading Classics at Oxford, had been writing poetry but decided he wanted to be a painter; after the Oxford Union project he turned to architecture and design. The only extant Morris easel painting is *La Belle Iseult* (1858), the model for Sir Tristan's lover being a dark-haired, working-class beauty from Oxford named Jane Burden.[81] They would marry in April 1859 at St. Michael at the North Gate church in Oxford, and for a wedding gift, Burne-Jones gave them a wardrobe with scenes from Geoffrey Chaucer's *Canterbury Tales* painted on it (now in the Ashmolean Museum). The couple would spend the next six years living at the Red House, a neo-Gothic house designed by Morris and the Oxford-born architect Philip Webb. Morris translated Icelandic sagas and wrote medieval romances in modern prose form, inspiring both Tolkien and Lewis. Active in Liberal politics, Morris became increasingly attracted to Marxism and anarchism, founding the Socialist League in 1884. Like Ruskin, he held a passionate belief in making fine art and crafts affordable for the common man, and in the last years of his life he founded Kelmscott Press to produce beautifully made books in the style of medieval illuminated manuscripts.

The most popular literary subject for Pre-Raphaelite painters and book illustrators was the Lady of Shallot, the tragic Arthurian heroine who, locked away in a tower, is cursed to die from unrequited love when she looks out her window to see Sir Lancelot riding by. Her story comes from Malory's *Morte D'Arthur*—the new illustrated editions of which provided work for Aubrey Beardsley and Arthur Rackham, among others—but two poems by Tennyson revived her fame in the nineteenth century: Rossetti, Millais, Holman Hunt, Elizabeth Siddal, Arthur Hughes, and J. W. Waterhouse (three different times!) are just some of the Victorian artists who drew or painted her. In his early short story, "The Spire and the Gargoyle" (1917), Fitzgerald describes the college preceptor ("the gargoyle") as having two "Mirrors of Shalott."[82] Another medieval woman who captivated the Pre-Raphaelites was *la belle dame sans merci*, the fay enchantress of Keats's poem who lures knights to their death. Arthur Hughes, John William Waterhouse, Henry Meynell Rheam, and Walter T. Crane were among the artists "in her thrall," as was Fitzgerald, explicitly in his second novel, but also when creating Daisy Buchanan in his third.

John Ruskin was an active and generous patron to Millais, Rossetti, Elizabeth Siddal, Burne-Jones, and many others in the Pre-Raphaelite orbit. He strove to make art affordable in England, and to make Oxford a more beautiful place. Ruskin Hall, later Ruskin College, was founded in 1898 by two Americans, progressive historian Charles Beard and philanthropist Watkins Vrooman, its aim to provide a residential experience and liberal education for working-class men (especially miners).[83] Named in honor of Ruskin as social reformer, the British trade unions both provided income and chose the students. Yet despite his sometimes progressive social views, Ruskin was an ardent Victorian imperialist, calling in 1870 for Britain to establish colonies "as fast and as far as she is able, formed of her most energetic and worthiest men."[84]

Charles Dodgson would photograph Ruskin (ca. 1875), an image that conveys both Ruskin's gravitas and his sadness. The Rev. Charles Lutwidge Dodgson, better known to the world as Lewis Carroll, went up to Christ Church in 1851 and performed so well on his mathematics examination that he was offered a studentship, meaning a place at the House for the rest of his life as long as he took holy orders and did not marry. In addition to befriending the children of Dean Liddell and making Alice Liddell famous in his two books, *Alice's Adventures in Wonderland* (1862) and *Through the Looking-Glass* (1872), Dodgson became an accomplished amateur photographer. He met Ruskin in 1857 and soon thereafter became friends with Rossetti, Millais, Holman Hunt, and the pioneering English photographer Julia Margaret Cameron. In addition to Ruskin, Dodgson would photograph Tennyson, the actress Ellen Terry, and, most famously, Alice Liddell. [85]

Ruskin and the Pre-Raphaelites shared in a medievalism that informed their aesthetics and became a significant part of their legacy, especially for writers, from the late Victorian period to the present day. As Dennis Welland points out, W. B. Yeats "found a strong stimulus in their aestheticism, their love of a legendary past, and their technique," while a young D.H. Lawrence was particularly inspired by Rossetti's medievalesque poetry. [86] I have argued that Tolkien's admiration for Pre-Raphaelite painting has been quite overlooked, despite his well-known debt to the romances of William Morris. [87] Quieter still is talk of the Pre-Raphaelites' influence on the two bards of the Jazz Age—F. Scott Fitzgerald and Evelyn Waugh—who, on several occasions, independently dipped into an Oxonian aestheticism that owes partial debt to Rossetti, Millais, Morris, and their frequent champion, Ruskin.

Oscar Wilde and the Oxford Aesthetes

" . . . the infamous St. Oscar of Oxford, poet and martyr . . ."

Thus did Oscar Wilde refer to himself in the year of his infamous trial and imprisonment. [88] "The self-canonization was not devoid of substance," writes John Dougill, "for it was Oxford, the home of aestheticism, that had made him, and it was Oxford that broke him too."[89] His path from distinguished student of Classics at Magdalen, beginning in 1874, to imprisonment in Reading Gaol for a homosexual affair with an Oxford undergraduate in 1897, was one of fame *and* infamy. Under the influence of Oxford faculty Walter Pater and John Ruskin, Wilde became the central figure of the Oxford Aesthetes, whose mannerisms and lifestyle would continue to define Oxonian undergraduate culture through much of the twentieth century. The French journalist Jean Fayard would write of Oxford in the 1920s, "Whether one loved or hated him, Oscar Wilde was [still] king."[90]

After two and a half years at studying Classics at Trinity College, Dublin, Wilde sat the scholarship exam for Magdalen College and, winning the scholarship, he went up to Oxford in 1874 to study Greats. Soon gone were his Dublin accent and day clothes, replaced by tweed jackets matched with checkered trousers, bright blue neckties, tall collars, and curly-brimmed bowlers, "the first phase of his sartorial revolution" in the words of his biographer, Richard Ellmann.[91] His new airs of sophistication amused friends and annoyed college and university officials, while also piling up unpaid debts. The young Wilde listed Byron, Keats, Rossetti, and Morris among his masters, and later called Matthew Arnold, "one whose gracious memory we all revere."[92]

But at Oxford it was Pater and Ruskin who would exert the greatest influence on Wilde. Pater, the Oxford classicist and Brasenose tutor, had been a disciple of Ruskin's but had begun to diverge from Ruskin in his theory about art and beauty. Pater celebrated "the difference between the Greeks and the Victorians, lauding the former's pagan spirit and lust for beauty in all its forms," writes L.W.B. Brockliss, and the young Wilde "adopted his yearning for a new exuberant aesthetic."[93] Wilde called Pater's *Studies in the History of the Renaissance* "my golden book" and embraced Pater's definition of life as cultivating experiences and his call for passionate devotion to religion, politics, and especially to art. Wilde first developed a relationship with Ruskin after attending the latter's powerful lectures on Florentine art. Writing to him years later, Wilde confessed, "The dearest memories of my Oxford days are my walks and talks with you, and from you I learned nothing but what was good."[94]

Wilde's Oxford notebooks show a Victorian classicist in training with an expansive intellect not just interested in poetry and aestheticism but also evolutionary thought, historical criticism, and philosophical debates between idealism and materialism.[95] His letters from this time, however, show a flair for whimsical illustration and an increasing interest in Catholicism.[96] His Magdalen friend David Hunter Blair had converted on a trip to Rome in 1875 and Wilde became interested in the Oxford convert cardinals, Newman and Manning. Wilde himself made a trip to Italy that year and was reading Newman in Ireland, but even after a private meeting with Pope Pius IX he did not convert. At Oxford he attended both the newly-built Catholic church, St. Aloysius, as well as Freemason meetings. His sexual affairs at Oxford seem to have been with women, while he followed Pater down the path of a pagan-aesthetic adoration of the boy.[97] Contradictions continued to exist within him, for while he enjoyed boxing at Oxford, his style of dress became increasingly flamboyant and he was caricatured by his fellow students as the leader of the Oxford Aesthetes (Fig. 1). As his tall, flamboyant mother had performed in her eccentric attire at Saturday salons, so would Wilde at Magdalen host tobacco and cocktail soirées in his Magdalen rooms and long after leaving Oxford with a first in Greats in 1878.

Failing to win a fellowship in Classics and archaeology, Wilde embarked on a career as a professional critic in London in 1879. His first play and first book of poems both failures, Wilde found success in a most unusual way: caricatured by the artist George Du Maurier in *Punch* as the New Aesthete, he became famous for being famous. Aesthetic tastes were becoming mass-produced for an eager public. Both English and American audiences delighted at *Punch*'s images of aesthetes as effeminate flowers, further popularized by the Gilbert and Sullivan comic opera *Patience, or Bunthorne's Bride* (1881).[98] When approached with an offer by an American theatre agent to come to the United States to give lectures in conjunction with the touring *Patience*, Wilde eagerly agreed.

Wilde became an important vehicle in delivering the image of the Oxford Aesthete to America. In January 1882, he crossed the pond to begin his lecture tour, draped in a full-length sealskin coat much of the time, appearing before the press wearing a felt hat and flowing cape, then on stage in black velvet, knee-breeches, silk stockings, and patent leather pumps as he described the new aestheticism to audiences from New York to San Francisco. Boldly, Wilde would call his aestheticism "The English Renaissance." Michèle Mendelssohn's new book, *Making Oscar Wilde* (2018), details the ups and downs of Wilde's American tour, on which he was both mocked and acclaimed by critics. Posters advertising the tour depicted a brown-skinned Wilde (with the caption, "What's de matter wid de Nigga? Why Oscar you's gone wild!"), reviewers questioned his manhood, and *The Washington Post* and *Harper's Weekly* lampooned the Oxonian aesthete by depicting him in cartoons as a flower-loving monkey and as "Mr. Wild of Borneo," drawing on Victorian phrenology and social Darwinist views of the Irish Apeman.[99] Yet despite these racist and homophobic attacks, Wilde had trails of female admirers in America, women who now bought his early erotic poems.

In America, Wilde described aestheticism "as an intellectual and artistic family that had roots in Oxford thinking," writes Mendelssohn, name-dropping as his "spiritual kin" A. C. Swinburne, Burne-Jones, William Morris, Ruskin, and Pater.[100] Wilde's aesthetic vision owes much to the idealism and social thought of Ruskin. It carries on the Romantic litterateur tradition of Byron, Baudelaire, and Beau Brummel, and in turn spawned the fin de siècle version both epitomized and caricatured by Max Beerbohm, Wilde's friend and one of Fitzgerald's early literary heroes. "One should either be a work of art," quipped Wilde, "or wear a work of art." Wilde's aestheticism went far deeper than its sartorial veneer and friendship with artists, bringing together classical and medieval ideas about beauty under the influence of Ruskin and Pater. He would write reviews and critical essays on Keats, Whistler, Sidney, Pater, Rossetti, Morris, and Yeats, among others.[101] In a similar way, Fitzgerald developed his aesthetic sensibilities, adding the Romantic poets and Wilde himself to the mix, though he wrote only a few book reviews and no serious extensive theoretical essays. Rather, it is through Fitzgerald's short stories and novels that we see his aestheticism. "Fitzgerald was breathing romantic air when he wrote" *The Great Gatsby*, waxes Richard Lehan, "and works like Walter Pater's *Marius the Epicurean* . . . seem long stamped upon his imagination."[102] In *Gatsby*, Nick speaks of "aesthetic contemplation" and the "capacity for wonder" (140).

Fitzgerald's earliest aesthetic impulses can be seen in the way he idolized and imitated his father, Edward, as a very young boy. Edward carried a cane and wore a cutaway and gray gloves on Sundays, and young Scott would likewise carry a cane when he and his father would go to have their shoes shined.[103] "The Aesthetic dandyism introduced to America in the 1880s by Oscar Wilde," writes Fitzgerald scholar Catherine Mintler, "characterizes the sartorial preoccupations of both Edward Fitzgerald and his son, and provides the sartorial model that [Scott] Fitzgerald uses in constructing his dandy protagonists Amory Blaine, Anthony Patch, and Jay Gatsby. . . . Fitzgerald extends this adoption of aesthetic dandyism to undergraduates in elite American universities modeled after the British university system."[104] The young Amory's "taste for fancy dress" shocked and disturbed his mother Beatrice—"But, my dear boy, what odd clothes! . . . Is your underwear purple, too?"—while Anthony "became an exquisite dandy" after entering university, amassing a wardrobe full of silk pajamas and flamboyant neckties. Further examples of the American dandy can be found in early Fitzgerald short stories like "The Jelly-Bean" (1920), "The Camel's Back" (1920), and "May Day" (1920).

While Fitzgerald himself drew heavily on the romanticism of Keats, Pater, and Wilde, argues Lehan, Gatsby, the "product of a romantic vision . . . lacked the aesthetic values of a Pater or a Wilde, because he lacked the education that would differentiate genuine from ersatz beauty."[105] Would his short stay in Oxford have given Jay Gatsby the appreciation for fine tailoring and Gothic architecture without the philosophy and poetic sensibility of an Oscar Wilde or a John Betjeman? Or even of an F. Scott Fitzgerald, an Amory Blaine, or an Anthony Patch?

Fitzgerald quotes Wilde in one of the two epigraphs in *This Side of Paradise*: "Experience is the name so many people give to their mistakes."[106] In an interview conducted by Carleton R. Davis shortly after publication of his first novel, Fitzgerald admits to envying "the wit of Oscar Wilde" and aspiring to be able to emulate it.[107] In another interview, in 1927, Fitzgerald lists Wilde's *The Picture of Dorian Gray* as the most influential book he read at the age of eighteen.[108]

Wilde's diverse literary production included writing fairy stories. Pater wrote to him complimenting his book, *The Happy Prince and Other Tales* (1888), which was followed in 1891 by *A House of Pomegranates*.[109] Yet his career and his life turned infamously from fairy tale to tragedy. In 1895, as a result of a public feud with the Marquess of Queensbury, father of Wilde's new lover, Oxford student Lord Alfred "Bosie" Douglas, Wilde was convicted of sodomy and indecency and spent the next two years doing hard labor in prison. Max Beerbohm attended all three of Wilde's trials, and was present to hear Wilde's "The Love that Dare not Speak its Name" speech. "Such British aesthetes as Ruskin and Pater had gotten away with criticizing English industrialism," writes James Stewart, "but Wilde's sweeping criticisms of the essential bankruptcy of English bourgeois life had cost him his freedom."[110] Wilde died in 1900, just three years after being released from Reading Gaol, from an ear infection, perhaps related to syphilis contracted while a student at Oxford.

In 1885, Wilde returned to Oxford to watch an Oxford Dramatic Club production of Shakespeare's *Henry IV, Part II*. In his review of the play, Wilde delivers a loving ode to Oxford while encapsulating his own aesthetic theory and aspirations for the role of art in modern society:

> Oxford still remains the most beautiful thing in England, and nowhere else are life and art so exquisitely blended, so perfectly made one. . . .
> To her the clamour of the schools and the dullness of the lecture-room are a weariness and a vexation of the spirit; she seeks not to define virtue, and cares little for the categories; she smiles on the swift athlete . . . and rejoices in the young

Barbarians at their games; she watches the rowers from the reedy bank and gives myrtle to her lovers, and laurel to her poets, and rue to those who talk wisely in the street; she makes the earth lovely to all who dream with Keats; she opens high heaven to all who soar with Shelley . . . turning her head from pedant, proctor and Philistine. . . .

As I sat in the Town Hall of Oxford the other night, the majesty of the mighty lines of the play seemed to me to gain new music from the clear voices that uttered them, and the ideal grandeur of the heroism to be made more real to the spectators by the chivalrous bearing, the noble gesture and the fine passion of its exponents. . . .

I hope that the Oxford Dramatic Society will produce every summer for us some noble play like *Henry IV.* For, in plays of this kind . . . when we have the modern spirit given to us in antique form, the very remoteness of that form can be made a method of increased realism. . . .[111]

For Wilde at Oxford, as for Fitzgerald at Princeton, it is the young barbarians at play who will usher in modernity on the shoulders of ancient giants. Without these giants—and their nineteenth-century successors Shelley, Keats, Rossetti, Morris, Newman, Carroll, Ruskin, Arnold, and Wilde—there could be no Tolkien or Lewis, no Fitzgerald or Waugh.

3

"Old Sport":
The First American Rhodes Scholars

I'd like to have been a young Englishman during the first
decade of the present century. . . . Oxford and Cambridge
were turning out interesting men, and the inhibitions of the
Victorian era were passing away.

—F. Scott Fitzgerald, interview in
The Smart Set (April, 1924)

When F. Scott Fitzgerald made this comment, he was
not so much speaking about men he had met during
his 1921 visits to Oxford and Cambridge. He had been
reading *about* Oxford his whole life, and was especially fond of a genre
of writing, then quite popular, known as the Oxford Novel. Reading
Oxford writers like Matthew Arnold, Oscar Wilde, Max Beerbohm, Compton Mackenzie, and, most recently, Aldous Huxley, gave
Fitzgerald the sense that Oxford was a city of dreamers and poets, and

that the dreamers and poets of the years leading up to the Great War were ready to live freely in pursuit of aesthetic, intellectual, and often Bacchic pleasures. Would this have been the expectation of Americans who came to study at Oxford in the Edwardian period? Would this have been the actual experience of the first American Rhodes scholars?

"Glamor of Rumsies and Hitchcoks": The First Americans in Oxford

I.	Glamor of Rumsies + Hitchcoks
II.	Ash Heaps. Memory of 125th Grt Neck
III.	Goddards. Dwanns Swopes
IV.	A. Vegetable days in NY
	B. Memory of Ginevras Wedding
V.	The Meeting all an invention. Mary
VI.	Bob Kerr's story. The 2nd Party
VII.	The Day in New York
VIII.	The Murder (inv.)
IX.	Funeral an invention

Scribbled in the back of his copy of André Malraux's *Man's Hope* (1938), Fitzgerald years later recalled some of the sources for characters and plot lines for *The Great Gatsby* in a strange and enigmatic list.[1] But it is believed by most Fitzgerald scholars that the first item in this list refers to two famous American polo players, Pad Rumsey and Tommy Hitchcock. Scott and Zelda met Hitchcock at a party at the Long Island estate of Rumsey's wife, Mary Harriman Rumsey, in April 1923. In the shadow of the Rumsey faux Norman castle, Fitzgerald learned about the adventures of Hitchcock in the Great War and playing polo at Oxford. The glamor, or "enchantment," of the tale (as *glamour* meant in an earlier age[2]), proved irresistible to him. Not only would Hitchcock provide a model for characters in two of his novels, Hitchcock and his father, Thomas Sr., also provided an important link between Fitzgerald and generations of Americans who have been lured to the ancient university town.

Americans had been coming to Oxford since the Colonial era, but in small numbers before 1900 compared to other Anglophone nations like Australia, Canada, and South Africa.[3] Charles C. Pinckney and his brother Robert, from South Carolina, both studied at Christ Church (1764 and 1768 respectively). Robert went on to become governor of South Carolina, while Charles failed twice as the Federalist candidate for the presidency in 1804 and 1808.[4] During his visit to America, Edward, Prince of Wales (later King Edward VII) invited the Mohawk chief Oronhyatekha to study medicine at Oxford; he did so at St. Edmund's Hall in 1862.

Other Americans came simply as tourists, as lecturers, or as visiting dignitaries. Henry James stayed at the Randolph Hotel in 1869 and 1872, was a guest of the Warden of Merton College in 1884, and stayed to work on his writings at 15 Beaumont Street in 1894.[5] Colonel Thomas Wentworth Higginson visited Oxford twice, in 1872 and 1878, on the latter trip hearing Oscar Wilde recite his Newdigate Prize-winning poem, "Ravenna," during Commemoration.[6] An Abolitionist and social crusader, Colonel Higginson had commanded the Union's first black regiment during the Civil War, and in England he became acquainted with Charles Darwin, Thomas Carlyle, Robert Browning, Matthew Arnold, and the Pre-Raphaelites. Ruskin College was founded in 1899 by two Americans, Charles Austin Beard (aged twenty-four) and Walter Watkins Vrooman (aged twenty-nine), who conceived of a college designed principally for working men to study the social sciences.[7]

One of the most powerful allurements for Americans was sport. Sir Douglas Haig, the future Field Marshall and Earl Haig and a student at Brasenose College, was one of many Oxonians of the Victorian period drawn to the sporting life: "Hunting in the Bicester country; polo in Port Meadow; claret at the Octagon; port at the Phoenix; lunching with the Vampires; dining with the Bullingdon; pulling strings at Vincent's on the other side of the High—Haig floated smoothly into the smarter sporting set."[8] Polo was a lifelong passion for Haig. The Oxford University Polo Club was founded in 1874 (just three years after polo's introduction in England) by Walter Hume Long (1854–1929) of Christ Church, later Viscount Long of Wraxall and First Lord of the Admiralty.[9] Winston Churchill used to come over to Port Meadow from Blenheim to practice with and coach the Oxford team. The first varsity match against Cambridge was played at the Bullingdon Cricket Ground in Cowley on November 27, 1877. In 1882 Oxford defeated Cambridge in a legendary match, and helping the Oxford team was Haig and his close friend, an American Oxonian named Thomas Hitchcock.

Thomas Hitchcock Sr. (1860–1941) was born in New York City but moved to England to prepare for Oxford. He attended Brasenose College from 1880 to 1884, where he embraced sports and clubs and became friends with Haig. Hitchcock won a blue and was made a member of the Phoenix Common Room (Oxford's oldest dining club). He was also a member of the Vampires, a club founded in 1865 as, in the words of Brasenose historian J. Mordant Crook, "a cricket club that did not take cricket too seriously. Sunday lunch was a major consideration."[10] Hitchcock stayed in Oxford after graduation to hunt, play polo, and ride steeplechase. At one point in his life he was a member of five of the world's top private clubs: the Knickerbocker in New York, the Somerset in Boston, the Metropolitan in Washington, the St. James's in London, and the Travellers in Paris. Back home he became captain of the U.S. polo team that lost to England in the first international match in 1886 in Newport, Rhode Island. Hitchcock and his wife, Louise Mary Eustis, both played polo, and they wintered at their three-thousand-acre estate in Aiken, South Carolina, then a winter playground for such wealthy families as the Vanderbilts and the Whitneys. For the rest of his life, Hitchcock trained thoroughbreds (imported from England) for track racing and steeplechase (a sport he founded in the United States) and enjoyed fox hunting.

The next American Oxonian to dominate the sport of polo was Devereux Milburn (1881–1942). Born in Buffalo, New York, Milburn went up to Oxford in 1903 as a member of Lincoln College. He gained a rowing blue, was on the varsity swim team, and led Oxford to victory over Cambridge in successive matches. His son, Devereux Milburn Jr., graduated from Oxford in 1938 and was also a polo player of some renown, a back like his father and a six-goal handicap.

But the most famous of all American polo players was Tommy Hitchcock, "Ten-Goal Tommy," son of Thomas Hitchcock Sr. (Fig. 2). At the age of seventeen he tried to enlist with the U.S. Air Force. After being rejected as being too young, he sought the help of family friend Theodore Roosevelt who got Tommy into the Lafayette Escadrille, "the cavalry in the air."[11] As a fighter pilot in the Great War, Tommy was wounded and his plane shot down by the Germans. Taken as a prisoner to German camps, he escaped dramatically four months later by jumping out of a train window and walking to Switzerland!

Awarded the Croix de Guerre, Tommy enrolled in Harvard after the war and spent the 1920–21 academic year at Oxford (also at Brasenose). He played on the U.S. polo team with Pad Rumsey and Devereux Milburn that defeated the English and won the Westchester Cup.

Charles Cary "Pad" Rumsey had married the daughter of robber baron E. H. Harriman, owner of both the Union Pacific and Southern Pacific railroads.[12] Pad Rumsey was a sculptor who was often commissioned by polo players to model their horses in bronze, and was himself a member of every U.S. polo team to compete in international matches from 1913 on. Tommy Hitchcock was both a client and a teammate. On September 21, 1922, Pad Ramsay died in a car accident after being thrown from the back of an open roadster. Like the arrival of jazz music in this period, the automobile appeared as a wild, flashy, raucous, and cacophonous replacement of the horse.[13] Manufactured and democratic, the car replaced the polo pony and the cavalry of the aristocratic Old World. That such a replacement was problematic to Fitzgerald can be seen in the many references to reckless driving and automobile accidents in *Gatsby*. Often this is fatal—Pad Rumsey and Myrtle Wilson being two very different victims. But mechanized travel is like mechanized warfare—it does not discriminate in its killing. Tom, Daisy, and Jordan are all "careless people" as drivers. Nick, witnessing the fast-moving whir of drinking, parties, and driving, is also our witness to these fatalities. The most grotesque deaths in the novel—those of Myrtle and George Wilson—happen to the two characters who live with and make their living from automobiles.

Tommy Hitchcock would go on from Oxford and Harvard to work as an investment banker for Lehman Brothers. When America entered World War II, Tommy again tried to join the air force but was thought this time to be too old to fly. Instead he was appointed military attaché for air in the American Embassy in London, and later made a chief of a tactical research section in the Ninth Air Force fighter command. [14] In April 1944, while testing a P-51 Mustang, Tommy's plane crashed in Salisbury Plain and he was killed. His death was reported on the front page of the *New York Times*, and he has been called the Babe Ruth of polo.

Scott and Zelda Fitzgerald socialized with Mrs. Rumsey and Tommy Hitchcock frequently during their Long Island spring of 1923. Fitzgerald became fascinated by Tommy's combination of war hero and star athlete. He wrote to his cousin Ceci in August 1927 that he was "just leaving for Long Island to visit Tommy Hitchcock and watch the polo (Zelda prays nightly that the Prince of Wales will come down from Canada)." [15] But he also admired Hitchcock for his academic trajectory. Tommy enrolled as a freshman at Harvard after the war, wrote Fitzgerald, "because he had the humility to ask himself 'Do I know anything?' That combination is what forever will put him in my pantheon of heroes." [16] Strange it is, then, that Tommy Hitchcock would provide partial inspiration for Tom Buchanan, the polo player whose East Egg mansion may have been modeled on the Hitchcock estate at Old Westbury. More than anything, as Horst Kruse has pointed out, it may have been the contrast of the equestrian culture of old-moneyed East Egg with the shiny automobiles of Gatsby's nouveaux riches that Fitzgerald wanted to emphasize. [17] Tommy was among a small group of friends who purchased Zelda's paintings after her show at Cary Ross's New York art gallery in 1934. [18] In a 1940 letter to Edmund Wilson, Scott lists "Tommy Hitchcock and the two Murphys" as the only truly rich friends he associated with closely.

While Oscar Wilde, who did a little boxing and boating at Oxford, never fell victim to it, a great war raged between the "Aesthetes" and the "Hearties" (sportsmen) at Oxford between about 1900 and 1932. [19] Aesthete leaders like T. W. Earp of Exeter, Harold Acton of Christ

Church, and John Betjeman of Magdalen occasionally provoked and satirized the Hearties, who in turn often responded with destruction of the former's property. The first American Rhodes scholars were thus often caught up in these warring camps at Oxford, for while they ostensibly were coming to Oxford to further their education, they were also chosen for their athletic ability in accordance with the controversial terms of Cecil Rhodes's will.

The First Decade of American Rhodes Scholars

It has been said of the midwesterner T. S. Eliot, as he traveled from Boston to Paris to London and Oxford in 1914, that "being American, he invented himself as he went along."[20] Not only could the same be said of Jay Gatsby, but also of many American Rhodes scholars who came to Oxford beginning in 1904. It was only the second year of the Rhodes scholarships, but it may have been the most controversial, for many people on both sides of the Atlantic were curious—if not very nervous—about how a large number of American students would fair at the ancient university.

Their story begins with that of Cecil John Rhodes (1853–1902), the successful industrialist, generous philanthropist, and ruthless imperialist who has been at the center of controversy for more than a hundred years. The son of a British clergyman, Rhodes left for southern Africa when he was only seventeen and quickly developed an interest in agriculture and mining. After buying up several smaller diamond mines, he returned to Britain to study at Oxford in October 1873. He applied to University College but was rejected, so he turned to Oriel. It is perhaps merely legend that the Provost of Oriel was said to have complained, "all colleges send me their failures."[21] Rhodes joined few clubs, played no sports, did not live in college, never attended the Union, and returned to Africa after his first term.[22] He did manage to join Vincent's and the Bullingdon and belonged to the Freemason lodge (while Oscar Wilde was there, neither mentioning the other), and read just enough Classics to have acquired a lifelong appreciation of Aristotle and Marcus Aurelius. He also managed to alternate between Oxford and his business affairs in Africa over the next eight years, emerging in 1881 with his "pass" degree.

While still a student at Oxford, Rhodes dreamed of binding the British and German empires together, with America, "in one grandiose Anglo-Saxon alliance that would dominate the world for the general good."[23] The model for such an alliance, remarkably, was the Oxbridge student club or society: "Why should we not form a secret society with but one object, the furtherance of the British Empire and the bringing of the whole civilised world under British rule?"[24] The idea germinated over the next twenty year in the mind, and many wills, of Rhodes. At first he thought of establishing an Oxbridge collegiate and residential university at Cape Town, then became attracted to the idea of establishing scholarships to send South African students to Britain; the University of Edinburgh was first proposed, but rejected because it did not have the residential college system.[25] In his eighth and final will (dated July 1, 1899), Rhodes proposed the establishment of fifty-two scholarships throughout the English-speaking world, twenty to the British colonies (Rhodesia, South Africa, Natal, four specific schools in the Cape of Good Hope, Canada, Newfoundland, Australia, New Zealand, Jamaica, and Bermuda) and thirty-two to the United States. In a 1901 codicil to the will, five scholarships were granted to Germany, the selection process left in the hands of the Kaiser.

The terms of Rhodes's will also addressed the amounts of money, the means of disbursement, and the selections process. Before the scholarship is even mentioned, in term 12 of the will, Rhodes bequeaths £100,000 "free of all duty whatsoever to my Old College Oriel College" for the erection of new College buildings and the repair of the old, to support the work of the residential Fellows, and to maintain "the dignity and comfort of the High Table."[26] In term 16, after explaining that he prefers Oxford over Edinburgh because of the supervision provided by the residential college system, he then entreats the University of Oxford to "make its medical school at least as good as that of the University of Edinburgh," and instructs his trustees as soon as possible after his death to establish "Scholarships . . . for male students . . . of the yearly value of £300 . . . tenable at any College of the University of Oxford for three consecutive academical years." Term 23 addresses selection, stating that the elected scholars "shall not be merely bookworms," but that each must demonstrate "(i) his literary and scholastic attainments (ii) his fondness of and success in manly outdoor sports such as cricket football and the like (iii) his qualities of manhood truth courage devotion to duty sympathy for and protection of the weak kindliness unselfishness and fellowship and (iv) his exhibition during school days of moral force of character and of instincts to lead and . . . to esteem the performance of public duties as his highest aim." Helpfully, Rhodes then provides ratios for these last qualifications, item one ranking first. Term 24 states, "No student shall be qualified or disqualified for election to a scholarship on account of his race or religious opinions." Though Rhodes was himself a successful professional and entrepreneur, the ideal qualities of a Rhodes scholar he states are those of liberal education rather than technical training.

Terms of a will are one thing: administration of such a far-ranging scholarship program quite another. First, he created the Rhodes Trust, which included his lawyer, his banker, his business partner, and several distinguished statesmen. His Oxonian partners in this enterprise included Viscount Alfred Milner, founding father of the Union of South Africa, and Lord George Curzon, Viceroy of India and late chancellor of Oxford—both Balliol men. Curzon had been president of the Oxford Union and was a very engaged chancellor. The actual administration of the program would be in the hands of Dr. George Parkin, as Organizing Secretary, and Francis Wylie, as the Oxford Secretary. Sir George Robert Parkin (1846–1922), an ardent imperialist who had come up with Rhodes to do postgraduate study and had been secretary of the Union, was then headmaster of a prestigious college (prep school) in Canada. Sir Francis James Wylie (1865–1952), who had been a student at Balliol (receiving a first in Greats in 1888), was a Fellow of Brasenose where he lectured in philosophy and worked on the poetry of Matthew Arnold. Wylie would become the first Warden of Rhodes House in 1903 and he and his wife surrogate parents for a generation of Rhodes scholars.

As soon as the Rhodes scheme was announced, there was international reaction. American newspapers fretted over their native sons mixing with "*lords* wearing gold tassels on their caps and gorgeously gowned *gentlemen commoners*," hence undermining democratic ideals.[27] Harvard President Charles Eliot remarked that the American scholars would benefit more if they studied at a German institution, while the president of Stanford suggested that they do just that during their Oxford vacations. Britons feared the superior athletic ability of "frontier" Americans who would embarrass Oxford's amateurs, the Oxford Union debated whether to oppose the scholarships, and Oxford's *Varsity* magazine ran cartoons depicting invading Americans setting up lunch counters, lynching dons, and turning part of the Bodleian into a skyscraper![28] G. K. Chesterton was not at all impressed with Rhodes or his scheme, writing that Rhodes had no principles but only "a hasty but elaborate machinery for spreading the principles that he hadn't got. What he called his ideals were the dregs of a Darwinism which had already grown not only stagnant, but poisonous. . . . [H]e invoked slaughter, violated justice, and ruined republics to spread them."[29]

Dr. Parkin traveled across the United States in 1903 to canvass opinion about the Rhodes scholarship program from leaders in government, industry, and academe. Two American skeptics he met in his travels were Andrew Carnegie and Henry James. The former told Parkin that the best young American men would not go to Oxford "because what Oxford has to give is not what they are after . . . dollars."[30] James, lunching with Parkin in Philadelphia, "entered a vehement protest against the desecration of Oxford by an irruption of young barbarians from Kalamazoo and Wallamaroo, from Auckland, Arizona, and Africa. . . ."[31] Parkin also encountered many questions about eligibility for Americans, including age (commonly nineteen to twenty-four), marital status (scholars could not marry and retain their scholarship), gender (women were not eligible), and race. On this last issue, Parkin was at first clear in his intentions: "The terms of the will, as well as my own inclination, make me anxious to give every possible opportunity that the white man has to the black."[32]

The first scholars began arriving from Germany and the colonies in 1903, but not from America, for the sheer number and breadth required time for Parkin to set up selection committees consisting of statesmen and academic leaders. "1903 was [just] an overture," recalled Wylie. "The real performance began in 1904, when seventy-two Rhodes Scholars came into residence, twenty-four from the British Commonwealth, forty-three from the United States and five from Germany."[33] Each state was then allowed two Rhodes scholars, one each of two consecutive years, with the third year there being no election (thus equating to thirty-two per year). Student applicants needed to declare from which state they were applying, their home state or the state where they attended school (if different), then take a qualifying examination in Latin, Greek, and mathematics. In five of the American states in 1904 no candidate survived the qualifying exam (only half of all applicants passed it that year).[34] After the exam, some of the students were nominated by their institutions for a formal interview with the state selection committee, which then notified the winners. These students gave Mr. Wylie their list of preferred Oxford colleges, and Wylie would sort out affiliations and accommodations.

Most of the first cohort of American Rhodes scholars came over together on the ship *Ivernia*, vowing (according to a story which reached Wylie) "that they should be careful to preserve, against the influences of this alien society, their distinctive American character."[35] In some ways they were a diverse group, coming from middle and working-class families; there were Jews, Catholics, Protestants, and Mormons; and they were forty-three men from forty-three different institutions. Harry Hinds (North Dakota and Queen's, 1904) was from Fitzgerald's hometown of St. Paul, Minnesota. He "acquired brief notoriety," writes Michael O'Brien, "by chasing one of the college aesthetes around Queen's firing his revolver at the victim's feet to keep him on the move."[36] William Crittendon (California and Trinity, 1904) also brought his revolver with him, firing it outside his bedroom window to call for his scout.[37] Other scholars settled for wearing their Stetsons.

The Texas Selection Committee met at Austin, in 1903, and described their selection, Stanley Ashby (Texas and Merton, 1904), as follows:

> Mr. Ashby is six feet one-half inch high, weighs 150 pounds, has perfect health and has capacity for doing laborious work for long periods. . . . He is broad-minded, modest, courageous, sympathetic, and kind. . . . He is healthy and strong, . . . fond of rowing, wrestling, and other outdoors sports. . . . He [has received] fifty A's, six B's, and one C. [38]

Ashby became a professor of English at the University of Maine. Indeed, an extraordinary number of the first American Rhodes scholars went on to distinguished academic careers. John James Tiggert (Tennessee and Pembroke, 1904) would become President of Kentucky Wesleyan and the University of Florida (and U.S. Commissioner of Education), Richard Frederick Scholz (Wisconsin and Worcester, 1904) became President of Reed College, Paul Nixon (Connecticut and Balliol, 1904) became Dean of Bowdoin College, Willard Learoyd Sperry (Michigan and Queen's, 1904) became Dean of the Divinity School at Harvard, Robert Preston Brooks (Georgia and Brasenose, 1904) was a dean at the University of Georgia, Julius Arthur Brown (New Hampshire and New College, 1904) was a dean at the American University of Beirut, Neil Carothers (Arkansas and Pembroke, 1904) was a dean at Lehigh University, Lawrence Henry Gipson (Idaho and Lincoln, 1904) a professor of History at Lehigh and a Pulitzer Prize winner, Robert Llewellyn Henry Jr. (Illinois and Worcester, 1904) a former judge and dean of law at the University of North Dakota, Harvey Bruce Densmore (Oregon and Unversity, 1904) was a professor of Greek at the University of Washington, Francis Howard Fobes (Massachusetts and Baliol, 1904) a professor of Greek at Amherst, and Harold Guy Merriam (Wyoming and Lincoln, 1904) a professor of English at Montana State University. Charles F. T. Brooke (West Virginia and St. John's, 1904) had received both his AB and MA from West Virginia University by the age of nineteen and was in graduate school at the University of Chicago before arriving in Oxford that fall. He would go on to be a Marlowe and Shakespeare scholar and distinguished professor of English at Yale. All this academic success in America, despite only six of the forty-three American scholars in the 1904 cohort receiving firsts and only one an advanced degree at Oxford.[39]

While most of the early Rhodes scholars had some sports in their background, and many continued athletic activity at Oxford, no scholar had quite the same level of athletic attainment as Charles A. Keith (Arkansas and Exeter, 1907). Keith taught in rural elementary schools before enrolling at the University of Arkansas in the fall of 1905, and after only two years there he had won a Rhodes scholarship.[40] He entered Oxford in the Michaelmas Term of 1907, chose the honours school in Modern History, and spent two years at Exeter before asking for a leave of absence to study History and Political Science at the University of Texas at Austin. He was paid to coach the Texas baseball team in the spring of 1909, returning to Oxford in 1910 to complete his studies. While a Rhodes scholar, on his summer vacation in 1908, Keith was awarded a major league baseball contract by the St. Louis Browns. Years later he penned an autobiography in which he described his unusual academic course, attending the coronation parade for King George V, helping Exeter's rugby team to the Oxford championship, and attaining honors in Modern History in 1911.

The Americans wasted no time in starting a club, recalled Wylie, renting rooms in Cornmarket with "comfortable chairs" and tea served daily, "too tempting a refuge," complained the secretary.[41] "[I]f one's rooms were cheerless, or one's tutor unsympathetic—why, there was always that armchair awaiting one in the Corn, with one's College pennant on the wall above, and very likely another homesick American in a chair nearby." The American Club (1904–26) moved its headquarters to various rooms rented downtown. The Club would invite famous visiting Americans (Mark Twain, Teddy Roosevelt, William Jennings Bryan) to give talks, and sponsored a traditional Thanksgiving banquet at the Randolph Hotel.[42]

"The first American Rhodes Scholars have left Oxford; their successors have arrived. Long live the Rhodes Scholars!" trumpeted an article in the first issue of the American Rhodes scholar alumni magazine. "As far as Oxford is concerned, the Rhodes Scholarship scheme has passed the experimental stage."[43] This was not, however, the prevailing *British* opinion of the "experiment," at least the American part, for much of its first decade. The Oxford Union came out against the establishment of the Rhodes scholars, one speaker proclaiming, "all the world will send us its worst specimens."[44] On October 11, 1910, there appeared in the London *Daily Mail* an anonymous column titled "The Americans at Oxford: An Unfulfilled Bequest":

> As regards the American [Rhodes scholar], . . . he takes from Oxford everything she has to give, and withholds from her anything that may be in his power to give in return. . . . The American Rhodes scholar becomes an undergraduate of Oxford only in so far as the wearing of a cap and gown and the obtaining of athletic honours permit. For the rest, he keeps to himself and seeks to know nothing of his English surroundings and fellow undergraduates. . . . The only point in which he carries out the spirit of the bequest is in the field of athletics. Here he shows himself to be thoroughly well at home, though sometimes in a manner which raises grave doubts in English minds as to his comprehension of the word sportsmanship.[45]

The American spends his Rhodes stipend traveling on the Continent, the author also complains, rather than on entertaining his fellow students in college. At least the American "Blue" is of use to Oxford, he adds, in her friendly rivalry against "the sister university." The column spawned indignant denials by several American scholars, some of which were published in the *New York Times*. "They are a new and distinctive element within the University, but an element which fuses with the older elements without being lost in them," wrote Sidney Ball, a Senior Tutor at St. John's, in their defense:

> This is especially true of the American Scholars, just because they are more 'grown-up' and are of a more mature character

than the ordinary undergraduate. . . . [W]hile they certainly do not rank athletic honors low, they do not rank them too highly. There are things which an American Rhodes Scholar would not sacrifice for his 'blue'. . . . Still it must be admitted that the general level of both attainment and ability has been somewhat disappointing. . . . In the first place they come to the University when they are some ways too old to benefit to the full from Oxford training and Oxford life; they come with their minds already rather 'set.'[46]

The first generation of American Rhodes scholars included several men who were pioneers of educational reform in America. None more so than Frank Aydelotte (Indiana and Brasenose, 1905), an English professor who went on to become president of Swarthmore College and director of the Institute for Advanced Study in Princeton.[47] Rhodes historian David Alexander describes Aydelotte as "superbly able, thorough and industrious, . . . well liked and fiercely loyal to his friends, faithful to the causes in which he believed, and tough."[48] A football star at Indiana University, Aydelotte graduated in 1900, taught English, and worked as a reporter before going to graduate school at Harvard, where he received his AM degree in English in 1903. He was a Rhodes scholar from 1905–7, where he pursued the BLitt (research) degree.

Aydelotte studied at Brasenose College, long a magnet for American students, particularly athletes. " . . . very Brasenose they became," writes a Brasenose historian of these Americans. "Most read law or PPE [Philosophy, Politics, and Economics], a few read science or engineering. Directly or indirectly, nearly all of them read sport."[49] Aydelotte rowed with the Brasenose eight in 1907, ran track, played rugby, and was invited to join the exclusive Ingoldsby literary club.[50] He submitted a thesis in Elizabethan studies for his BLitt degree at Oxford, and married in June of that year, with the trustees allowing him to return with his family in 1912 to complete the third year of his scholarship in residence. Founding editor of the *American Oxonian*, Aydelotte served as American Secretary for the Rhodes Trust from

1918 to 1953. He began his academic career as an English professor at his alma mater, Indiana University, before taking a post at MIT in 1915. As a professor at MIT and as President of Swarthmore, Aydelotte was recognized as a pioneering educational reformer and was instrumental in the creation of the Guggenheim fellowships. In 1937, Oxford University awarded him the honorary degree of Doctor of Civil Law and he became an Honorary Fellow of Brasenose College, the first American to hold such an honor at Oxford. In 1953 at Buckingham Palace, Queen Elizabeth made Frank Aydelotte Knight Commander of the Order of the British Empire (KBE) for his work as American Secretary to the Rhodes Trust.

In "The Oxford Stamp" (1917) and other essays he wrote after returning from Oxford, Aydelotte proved a keen and well-qualified observer of the differences between American and Oxonian educational cultures. "Much in the work and atmosphere of an English university is strikingly different from the adaptations of German university methods which have prevailed in our higher education for half a century."[51] The life of the Oxford undergraduate was "luxurious without being soft," governed by "a discipline which is thorough without losing its humanity."[52] Having implemented some Oxford ideas both at Indiana and at MIT, Aydelotte was looking for a place to implement an Oxford-style honors program for American undergraduates.[53] Shortly after becoming president of Swarthmore in 1921, Aydelotte founded the nationally-recognized Honors Program in which qualified upperclassmen studied subjects in small groups—without grades—for two years until evaluated by outside scholars in a series of written and oral examinations. Inspired by the Oxford tutorial and examination system, Aydelotte's pedagogy would provide a model for honors programs and colleges that began appearing in other American universities in the 1930s and now number in the hundreds.

Aydelotte wrote the report *Honors Courses in American Colleges and Universities* in 1924, and it proved so impactful (the number of honors programs in American had doubled) that he had to update it only one year later.[54] "Aydelotte also heavily advocated for the appointment of Rhodes scholars as college and university presidents in order to further spread the influence of Oxford," writes Anne Rinn. "It is generally believed that dozens of Rhodes Scholars owe their high-ranking positions to Aydelotte's endless lobbying."[55]

Stringfellow Barr, who introduced the Great Books curriculum at St. John's College (Maryland) when he became president there in 1937, was selected as Virginia's Rhodes scholar in 1917. He studied at Balliol College along with Scott Buchanon, a fellow Rhodes scholar from Massachusetts, who served under Barr as Dean at St. John's. A very different kind of pioneer was Edwin Hubble (Illinois and Queen's, 1910), who came to Oxford to study English and law, and returned home sporting plus fours and a cape and speaking with a British accent.[56] He became a renowned astronomer for whom the Hubble Telescope was named.

Like most Americans in the period, Fitzgerald would have been following press coverage of the Rhodes scholarship program and the early Rhodes scholars. Three members of the class of 1914 and two alumni were awarded Rhodes scholarships the year Fitzgerald entered Princeton. He makes the protagonist of his fourth novel, Dick Diver, a Rhodes scholar, as is the hero of the MGM comedy whose script he doctored, *A Yank at Oxford*. Lehan draws our attention to the influence of Oswald Spengler on Fitzgerald at the time he was writing *The Great Gatsby*, particularly Spengler's theory of the medieval or "Faustian" phase of western civilization. "Faustian man finds himself longing for the unattainable," writes Lehan, "and his modern heirs try to conquer space or create vast empires in the tradition of Cecil Rhodes, for whom 'expansion is everything.'"[57] Though he reached different conclusions than those of Cecil Rhodes, Fitzgerald, in many of his stories and novels, is interested in the themes of westward expansion, colonialism, and the Oxbridge "making of a gentleman." On this last topic, he learned most not from newspapers and histories, but rather from the Oxford Novel.

Zuleika Dobson and *Sinister Street*: The Oxford Novel

After returning from his second visit to Oxford in 1921, Fitzgerald wrote about his feelings standing on High Street amid "the ghosts of ghosts," characters from *Sinister Street*, *Zuleika Dobson*, and *Jude the Obscure*.[58] These first two are the quintessential Oxford Novels, depicting the lifestyle of Oxford undergraduates of the Edwardian Era and influencing generations of writers and readers. Little read today, they were enormously popular in the years leading up to the Great War.

Sir Henry Maximilian Beerbohm was born in London in 1872. Max (as he was always known) went up to Oxford and Merton College in 1890, becoming an acquaintance of Oscar Wilde and meeting artist Aubrey Beardsley. He revered Wilde, whom he referred to as "the Divinity," and left Oxford to become a writer and caricaturist. In 1910 Beerbohm married the American-born British actress Florence Kahn, and they settled in Rapallo, Italy, where he was to reside for the remainder of his life. Beerbohm describes the early Rhodes scholars in his first and only novel, *Zuleika Dobson: An Oxford Love Story* (1911), an Oxford satirical romance centering on the relationship between the titular character and her ardent admirer, the Duke of Dorset, an undergraduate at "Judas College." The Duke, writes Beerbohm, went out of his way to cultivate Rhodes scholars, though "more as a favour to Lord Milner than of his own caprice." He "found these Scholars, good fellows though they were, rather oppressive. They had not—how could they have?—the undergraduate's virtue of taking Oxford as a matter of course. The Germans loved it too little, the Colonials too much."[59] But it is to the American scholars that the narrator devotes nearly two pages of description:

> The Americans were, to the sensitive observer, the most troublesome—as being the most troubled—of the lot. The Duke . . . held, too, in his enlightened way, that Americans have a perfect right to exist. But he did often find himself wishing Mr. Rhodes had not enabled them to exercise that right in Oxford. They were so awfully afraid of having their strenuous native characters undermined by their delight in the place. They held that the future was theirs, a glorious asset, far more glorious than the past. . . . And Americans, individually, are of all people

the most anxious to please. . . . Altogether, the American Rhodes Scholars . . . are a noble, rather than a comfortable, element in the social life of the University.

The Duke's dinner guest at the Junta (a fictional Oxonian club) was the American Rhodes scholar Abimelech V. Oover of Trinity College. "Mr. Oover's moral tone, and his sense of chivalry," states the narrator, "were of the American kind: far higher than ours, even, and far better expressed."[60] Objecting to the behavior of the eighteenth-century founder of the Junta, Mr. Oover declares, "[he] was an unmitigated scoundrel. I say he was not a white man." Oover later suspects the wavering Duke of not being a white man, and vows that, although he intends to take his own life for love of Zuleika, he will still be attending his lectures first: "While life lasts, I'm bound to respect Rhodes's intentions."[61]

Zuleika Dobson "is as much a story about the love *of* Oxford as about love *in* Oxford," writes John Dougill. "The city stands at the very heart of the story."[62] Moreover, it is an Oxford exuding "the last enchantments of the Middle Age" for Beerbohm.[63] In *The Beautiful and Damned*, Fitzgerald includes "Zuleika the Conjurer," along with Helen and Cleopatra, in a list of literary heroines gracing the shelf of Anthony Patch's Manhattan apartment. Beerbohm's novel won great popularity among Oxonians in the early years of the century, and still stands as a darkly entertaining yet affectionate satire. It owes something to the Oxford satires of the Victorian Age, notably Edward Bradley's *The Adventures of Mr. Verdant Green* (1853) and Thomas Hughes's *Tom Brown at Oxford* (1861), and perhaps James Baker's *The Inseparables: An Oxford Novel of To-Day* (1905). Fitzgerald listed *Zuleika Dobson* among a dozen "Books I Have Enjoyed Most" in a 1923 interview, along with *The Oxford Book of English Verse*.[64] In a review of Aldous Huxley's novel *Crome Yellow* (1921), Fitzgerald compares Huxley to Beerbohm via a scene in the novel that reminds him of *Zuleika*.[65]

The young Fitzgerald was also a great fan of the novels of Compton Mackenzie, whose *Sinister Street* (1913–14) was the bildungsroman that most influenced *This Side of Paradise*.[66] Mackenzie's novel "was still my 'perfect book,'" wrote Fitzgerald of his early years, and *Sinister*

Street influenced many Ivy League writers of his generation, including John Dos Passos.[67] Max Beerbohm heaped great praise upon *Sinister Street*: "There is no book on Oxford like it. . . . It gives you the actual Oxford *experience*. What Mackenzie has miraculously done is to make you feel what each *term* was like."[68] Henry James and Ford Maddox Ford thought it genius, and Edmund Wilson was also a devotee. Less admiring, Cyril Connolly called it a pastiche of Pater and Wilde.

Mackenzie had studied at Magdalen College and served in British intelligence in the eastern Mediterranean during the Great War. His Catholicism, Jacobitism, and ardent passion for things Gaelic may all have been appealing to a young Fitzgerald. "[I met] my old idol Compton Mackenzie" in Capri in 1925, he wrote to Princeton friend John Peale Bishop, and "I found him cordial, attractive, and pleasantly mundane. . . . The war wrecked him as it did [H. G.] Wells [sic] and many of that generation."[69] During that visit, wrote Zelda in 1934, "Compton Mackenzie told us why he lived in Capri: Englishmen must have an island."[70]

Before the war, *Sinister Street* was a controversial—though critically and commercially successful—work that came to define the Oxford Novel.[71] It set a trend that would continue unabated until World War II, at a pace of more than one imitation a year (and six in 1935 alone). The Oxford section, in the second volume of the eight-hundred-page novel, is titled "Dreaming Spires," and begins with protagonist Michael Fane's entry into Oxford by train: "Then suddenly, as Michael was gazing out the window, the pearly sky broke into spires and pinnacles and domes and towers. He caught his breath for one bewitched moment."[72] The first impression Oxford's architecture made on students and pilgrims became a commonplace of the Oxford Novel and many an Oxonian memoir. The aesthete Michael Fane, from London's St. James, navigates the streets, colleges, and rivers of Oxford as he takes his place at St. Mary's College (a thinly disguised Magdalen) amid a great hoard of Old Etonians and Harrovians. He soon chooses his circle of intimates, defined by their "disdain for factual knowledge and love for the abstract" and devotion to "the cult of Oxford."[73] This includes producing an undergraduate magazine, embracing athletics and student drama, skipping lectures, and penetrating "the innermost shrine at Oxford" by becoming confidant of Venner, St. Mary's J.C.R. steward.

Grasping the meaning of Oxford becomes the true goal of Michael Fane's undergraduate career. "I'm not surprised you like Oxford, Dear Michael," announced his mother as they punted on the Cherwell.

> "I like it—I liked it, I mean, very much more when it was altogether different from this sort of thing. The great point of Oxford—in fact, the whole point of Oxford—is that there are no girls."
>
> "How charmingly savage you are, dear boy," said his mother. "And now to pretend you don't care for girls."
>
> "But I don't," he asserted. "In Oxford I actually dislike them very much. They're out of place except in Banbury Road [where the women's colleges were clustered]. Dons should never have been allowed to marry. Really, mother, women in Oxford are wrong."[74]

Anna Bogen has argued that Mackenzie, inspired by Newman and Arnold, evokes in *Sinister Street*

> traditional arguments for the amateurism of liberal education, notably a refusal to specialize in favor of a broader understanding of life. Throughout the text, Michael and his friends continue to separate specialized academic work from learning. Instead, they identify liberal education with an intimate knowledge of Oxford, and concentrate their intellectual energies on college activities, including the production of an undergraduate magazine, aptly named *Oxford Looking-Glass*.[75]

Gatsby readers may recall Nick Carraway's description of his goal, early in the summer, of reading broadly to "become again that most limited of all specialists, the 'well-rounded man.'" (7). The cynicism and ambiguity here is typical of Nick—and of Fitzgerald, who was, after all, an amateur (not an academic) who returned again and again to books he read at Princeton, where he left without a degree or a specialization. Alain Locke, who left Oxford without a degree, similarly described in 1910 the "primary aim and obligation" of the Rhodes scholar as "to acquire at Oxford and abroad generally a liberal education."[76]

Though branding Mackenzie's novel a "middlebrow" text "presenting an argument [for liberal education] in the guise of a picture" of a sentimentalized Oxford, Bogen admits that "*Sinister Street* displays a complex narrative structure and a highly persuasive sophistication of tone, and its influence over the perception of Oxford education is still being felt today."[77] In America, that is due in part to Mackenzie's influence on the early writing of Fitzgerald. Both *This Side of Paradise* and "Spires and Gargoyles" have protagonists who approach the topography and social life of Princeton with the same mixture of reverence and nonchalance as Michael Fane and his friends give to Oxford. Fitzgerald's dwelling on the friends, clubs, and literary pursuits of Amory Blaine at Princeton is at once both autobiographical and an homage to his hero Mackenzie's descriptions of Oxford life.[78]

Oxford novels became quite the literary fashion following the success of *Sinister Street* (35,000 copies sold in the first year alone). In 1921, the year of Scott and Zelda's trip to England, two noteworthy Oxford novels appeared: Gerard Hopkins's *A City in the Foreground* and Beverly Nichols's *Patchwork*. In *Patchwork*, the character Ray Sheldon wonders: "Sometimes dreaming in the sun, sometimes dappled by rain, sometimes unnaturally white under a decrescent moon—today a fairyland of frost and spangled snow. What was it about this city that troubled so exquisitely one's senses?"[79] Such descriptions and sense of wonder became typical of the genre. We find, for example, in Hamish Miles and Raymond Mortimer, *The Oxford Circus* (1922): "starlit spires and Athenian groves of the dreambound colleges." While Old Oxonians could read and reminisce, critics debated whether these novels were, for the general reader, "a vicarious form of matriculation" or a voyeuristic "peepshow of the academic world."[80]

A much smaller group of books forms the sub-genre of Oxford Novels centered on an American's experience at Oxford. John Corbin, an 1892 graduate of Harvard College who become drama critic for the *New York Times*, wrote much of the non-fictional *An American at Oxford* (1902) while in residence at Balliol College at the turn of the century.[81] Corbin's treatise is partly in response to America's current infatuation with the German research university, partly in response to the recent announcement of the Rhodes scholarship in America. The book attempts to explain Oxford to the youth of America, whose imagination was piqued by the will of Cecil Rhodes. At Oxford "the college is supreme," declared Corbin, "a hybrid between a mediæval cloister and a nursery," and the only memory of the university for the student will likely be that of the matriculation ceremony: "the ceremony is important mainly as a survival from the historic past, and is memorable to him perhaps because it takes place beneath the beautiful mediæval roof of the Divinity School; perhaps because he receives from the vice-chancellor a copy of the university statutes, written in mediæval Latin."[82] Corbin offers very practical advice for the American student with a dose of humor, devoting equal time to academics and athletics. He also weighs in on the debate over the merits of Oxbridge versus the German university:

> A combination of the residential hall and the teaching university would reproduce the highest type of the university of the Middle Ages. . . . England has lost the educational virtues of the mediæval university, while Germany, in losing the residential halls, has lost its peculiar social virtues. When the American university combines the old social life with the new instruction, it will be the most perfect educational instruction in the history of civilization.[83]

A bold prediction for American higher education. In an article for Scribner's *The Lamp* written a year later, Corbin compares Oxford to Paris and proclaims: "The Oxford undergraduate is athletically primitive; his love-making is as without imaginative attenuation as it is ingenious and wholesome."[84] This is what American readers wanted to hear about the English.

Also appearing in 1902 was *The Adventures of Downy V. Green: Rhodes Scholar at Oxford*, a satire of both the Oxford Novel and the Rhodes scholar program penned by the English writer George Calderon.[85] With illustrations by the author, the novel tells the story of Verdant Green's American grandson, Downy, who competes for an American Rhodes scholarship. "I've been studyin' up Cecil J. Rhodes will purty keerfully," advises his American grandfather, Mr. Jonathan Downy, "an I see they reckin' up the qualifications this way—thirty per cent. for knowin' Lattun an' Greek, an' the other seventy for bein' tall" (18). Downy wins the scholarship and, instructed by the account of Verdant Green's stay at Oxford, is supplied for his journey with a Victorian Aesthete's wardrobe: "flowered dressing-gowns, coloured silk shirts, shaggy jackets, velvet waistcoats and pendulous cravats" (35). When situated in his college, Downy is pestered by questions from "the Britishers," including, "Do you carry a bowie-knife? "Don't you think baseball's awful rot?" and "Have you ever been a cowboy?" (58). The American Rhodes scholar was also the only fresher who seemed to notice the history of Oxford:

> "I'm walkin' the streets which John Ruskin has walked; I'm livin' on the vurray same ward as has once contained Arnold, Froude, and Newman."
>
> . . . They looked blankly at Downy with the least symptom of enthusiasm.
>
> "I would give a thousand dollars," said Downy, "to have been up here with Newman!"
>
> . . . "Which Newman do you mean?" he asked. (76–79).

The satire is light on Oxonian aestheticism and the sarcasm heavy on the so-called American accent (offensive, even), and Calderon lacks the light touch and grandeur of Beerbohm (not to mention his skill as an illustrator). Calderon had been schooled at Rugby and Trinity College, Oxford, before training as a barrister, teaching in Russia, and working as a librarian at the British Museum. He became an expert on and translator of Chekhov, then joined the British army at the age of forty-five, seeing action in Flanders and dying at Gallipoli on June 4, 1915.

Of an altogether more sober tone is James Saxon Childers's *Laurel and Straw* (1927), a portrait of Oxford life from the perspective of an American Rhodes scholar. Childers, from Birmingham, Alabama, interrupted his studies at Oberlin College to serve as a U.S. Navy pilot in World War I. He came to Oxford as a Rhodes scholar in 1923, reading history and literature. In *Laurel and Straw*, Childers records the typical culture-shock of an American scholar in Oxford. Dan Steele, the very pragmatic Rhodes scholar from Ohio, is impatient with Oxford's esoteric ways and has trouble finding anyone to teach him a course on finance and banking. His scout, Budkins, patiently explains to him:

> "You see, sir, many of the young gentlemen come up just for the life. They hunt and ride and play games and stay in residence for a time and go down without ever taking any examinations. . . . Yes, sir, the life's the thing. It's great just to have been in residence at Oxford. Just to be an Oxford man."[86]

Childers's novel seems sensitive to the kind of criticism and mis-understanding expressed in the article in the *Daily Mail* attacking the American Rhodes scholars. Childers's best-known work was *A Novel About a White Man and a Black Man in the Deep South* (1936). Then a professor at Birmingham-Southern College, Childers penned a bold narrative of institutionalized racism in southern society, arguing for racial integration.

Racism—in both individuals and institutions—is an important, though often overlooked, theme in *The Great Gatsby*. In the next chapter we will look at race, gender, and sexuality in Fitzgerald's novel, while also addressing the experiences of women, Jewish students, and students of color at Oxford in the years leading up to the Great War.

4

"Modish Negroes" and Mr. Wolfsheim:
Alain Locke, Horace Kallen,
and Cultural Pluralism

F. Scott Fitzgerald was introduced to Carl Van Vechten, one of the most prominent white patrons of the Harlem Renaissance, at a Manhattan party in 1922.[1] Van Vechten, an urbane gay man who patronized uptown black speakeasies and became a champion of Langston Hughes's poetry—and thus a rival with Alain Locke for Hughes's affection—had just written the novel *Nigger Heaven*, earning kudos from Locke (though he had misgivings about it), the black actor Paul Robeson, H.L. Mencken, Sinclair Lewis, as well as Fitzgerald.[2] Van Vechten was fond of partying with Scott, Zelda, Tallulah Bankhead, and other Jazz Age luminaries on both sides of the Atlantic, and he would photograph Scott in 1937. Neither he nor Fitzgerald, however, became social crusaders, and both could justly be accused of cultural appropriation in the Jazz Age. The mature Fitzgerald, however, did tackle the issue of anti-Semitism in Hollywood in his unfinished novel, *The Love of the Last Tycoon* (1941), with a complex portrait of Jewish film producer Monroe Stahr. Fitzgerald raises issues of sexuality, gender, race, and religion in his novels, often obliquely, in a period in which men and women in Oxford faced the serious consequences of being different.

Alain Le Roy Locke

> . . . a limousine passed us, driven by a white chauffeur, in which sat three modish Negroes, two bucks and a girl. I laughed aloud as the yolks of their eyeballs rolled toward us in haughty rivalry. (*The Great Gatsby*, 69)

Fitzgerald readers and scholars have long been disturbed by the author's use of racial and ethnic stereotypes. A reader named Earl Wilkins, from Missouri, wrote to Fitzgerald in 1934 complaining, "Must all the male Negroes in your books and stories be called 'bucks'?"[3] Critic Robert Forrey pronounced in 1967 that, "On the question of race, Fitzgerald does not belong to the liberal tradition of American letters."[4] Was Fitzgerald merely trying to capture the stereotypes and racist slang of his day, or are these offensive passages indicative of the author's own fears and insecurities? Fitzgerald was, for example, self-conscious of being poor (relative to his peers at Princeton) and from a working-class, Irish-Catholic family (in his words, "half black Irish"). The great tide of Irish-Catholic emigrants from the middle of the nineteenth century to the first decades of the twentieth resulted in most Irish being excluded from definitions of whiteness in both Britain and America.[5] Other immigrant groups, from eastern and southern Europe, suffered from similar exclusion, and thus there remains the question of Jimmy Gatz's ethnic identity. Joseph Vogel asserts the centrality of such issues to *The Great Gatsby*: "What happens when race, class, and other identity hierarchies are named and interrogated?"[6]

In *Gatsby*, Tom Buchanan lectures his affluent white audience—Daisy, Jordan, and Nick—about the global threat of the colored races, as he has recently learned from reading a book titled *The Rise of the Colored Empires* written by a man Goddard (12). "Tom's getting very profound," mocks his wife in response. This episode is likely an inside joke between Fitzgerald and Maxwell Perkins, for in 1920 Scribner and Sons had published the book *The Rising Tide of Color Against White World-Supremacy* by the eugenicist Lothrop Stoddard. Carlyle V. Thompson, a professor of African American literature at Medgar Evers College, has gone much farther, suggesting that Fitzgerald, deeply concerned with miscegenation in America, wrote Jay Gatsby as a black man "passing" as white.[7] His evidence: Gatsby is a bootlegger (thus a counterfeit); he wore his hair trimmed short; he owns 40 acres and a mansion, code for "40 acres and a mule"; he changes his name (from Gatz to Gatsby), just as many blacks did to pass in a white world; he tells Nick Carraway that his family is dead; and Gatsby is often associated with the color yellow, a common descriptor for pale-skinned blacks. Few Fitzgerald scholars have been convinced by Thompson's provocative theory.[8]

If any *historical* figure came close to being a black Gatsby, it is arguably America's first black Rhodes scholar, the pale-skinned and debonair Alain Le Roy Locke (1885–1954). Before becoming mid-wife to the Harlem Renaissance, Locke changed his given name, was circumspect about his actual home, became an overnight celebrity in America, lied about obtaining an Oxford degree, enjoyed a lifestyle of aesthetic and sensual pleasures (often on other peoples' money), trained army officers during the War, longed for acceptance by wealthy white elites, and was famous for his elaborate wardrobe. He was also one of the most eloquent and important writers about race in America.

The Rhodes scholar experiment in America was less than four years old when it faced the issue of racism and Jim Crow. In 1907 the Pennsylvania Selection Committee put forward as their candidate for the Rhodes scholarship Alain Locke. Born Arthur Roy Locke in Phila-delphia, son of Pliny Ishmael Locke, a lawyer, and Mary (Hawkins) Locke, a public school teacher, Alain Le Roy Locke (he had changed his name before college) was a product of the classical curriculum of

Philadelphia's public Central High School.[9] Locke had won admission to Harvard University, where he would go on to win the prestigious Bowdoin Prize for an essay on the influence of the Celtic romantic tradition on Tennyson's *Idylls of the King*. A disciple of George Santayana and Josiah Royce, Locke was about to graduate after three years with an AB in Philosophy (*magna cum laude*) from Harvard College and carried strong endorsements for the Rhodes scholarship from many of Harvard's top professors and from the Dean of the College.[10] He worked quite hard on the mandatory Oxford examinations and on strategy in applying for the Rhodes scholarship, ultimately deciding to apply from Pennsylvania even though his mother and he had been living in Camden, New Jersey.[11] "I shall try and try hard," he wrote to his mother before the Rhodes interview, "and the Pennsylvania Committee will see that one negro has the nerve and the backing to thrust himself on their serious consideration if but for a few hours."[12] Asked by the committee—which included the presidents of Swarthmore, Washington and Jefferson, and Muhlenberg Colleges—why he wanted the scholarship, Locke did not shy away from the racial insinuation: "Besides the further education . . . I want to see the race problem from the outside. . . . [I] want to see it in perspective."[13] He was a unanimous selection, even though his competitors came from the very colleges represented on the selection committee.[14]

Within the Rhodes organization, George Parkin was delighted by the choice of Locke, Francis Wylie at first expressed great reservation, and Lord Rosebury (a Rhodes Trustee) wrote Charles Boyd (the London secretary) that he does "*not* rejoice at the election of the negro scholar."[15] Locke's election made headlines in many American newspapers, with most reports about the first black Rhodes scholar to be elected quite positive—at least in the northern states. Locke confided to his mother that he was "not going to England as a Negro. I will leave the race question in New York and English people won't have any chance to enthuse over the Negro question. . . . None of it for me."[16]

While there were very few students of color matriculating at Oxford before well-to-do Indian students began arriving in the 1890s, Oxford's first black graduate dates to 1876, when Christian Frederick

Cole (1852–85) of Sierra Leone took his degree (a fourth in Greats).[17] Cole had been admitted to Oxford as a non-collegiate student in 1873, teaching music to pay his way, but he debated often in the Union and was accepted as a member of University College in 1877. He had become popular at Oxford, with shouts of "Three cheers for Christian Cole!" as he entered the Sheldonian for Commemoration in 1878. The man Oxford called "King Cole" was called to the Inner Temple in 1883 and became the first black African to practice law in an English court.

The will of Cecil Rhodes states that no one was to be "qualified or disqualified on account of his race or religious opinions" from obtaining a scholarship. While Rhodes may have meant "race" to be understood as "nationality," both Parkin and Wylie interpreted it to mean that discrimination was not to be conducted on the basis of skin color. In his 1903 visit to the United States, Parkin visited both W.E.B. Du Bois at Atlanta University and Booker T. Washington at Tuskegee Institute, the American educators advising Parkin of the difficulty that a black candidate would have appearing before a Southern selection committee.[18] The same means that were used in the South against blacks to prevent them from voting, they warned, would be used to prevent black candidates from receiving the scholarships.

It did not take long for Jim Crow to prove them right. The Harvard-educated lawyer Gustaf Westfeldt, a member of the board at Tulane University, wrote almost immediately after Locke's election to the British Embassy in Washington, asking that "the granting of Rhodes Scholarships to Negroes be discontinued because such awards would make the scholarships unpopular in the South."[19] The chancellor of the University of Georgia had excluded, on his own authority, Atlanta University from eligibility for the Rhodes scholarships, to the protests of Professor Du Bois and Atlanta University's Dean, the Rev. M. W. Adams.[20] Similarly the president of the University of North Carolina took it upon himself to declare that "a man of the colored race would be of little or no value" for "cementing links between the peoples of the English speaking race."[21] Fearing that the American Rhodes experiment was in danger of being extinguished by American racial prejudices, Parkin made it clear that "while the Trustees were perfectly ready to receive an American citizen of any class sent to them, it was no part of their business to solve the race problem . . . and that the negro people must rely for justice upon public opinion in their own country."[22]

It is worth quoting at length from Sir Francis Wylie's account of Locke's election:

> A more startling event in that year . . . was the election of a negro to an American Rhodes Scholarship. It was the Pennsylvania Section Committee who took this unexpected step. When the news reached Oxford the Rhodes Scholars who were from southern States were dumbfounded. As opinion was in the southern States in 1907, the election of a negro to membership of what Rhodes Scholars were being urged to regard as a 'Society,' almost a 'Brotherhood,' was bound to come as a shock, an offence even, to any Southerner. They met in protest . . . [one going] to London to interview the Trustees, who might, it was hoped, be willing to cancel the appointment. A vain hope. He . . . was reminded that there was plenty of 'colour' in the British Empire; and no British subject was going to be debarred from a Rhodes Scholarship on that ground. . . . Certainly in 1907 it was a bold experiment, something of a challenge even, to elect a negro to an American Rhodes Scholarship. A good many people at the time questioned its wisdom; and some, later, its success. What is incontestable is that, in the forty-two years that have passed . . . he has done notable work among his own people, both as a teacher and as a writer.[23]

These later recollections do not capture Wylie's near panic in 1907. He wrote to Boyd in March that "the Americans are all horrified" at the report of Locke's election, and that the Southerners would likely boycott the scholarships.[24] Some did protest, including scholars from Mississippi and South Carolina who requested to Wylie not to be placed in the same college as Locke. Lord Rosebury could not understand why the other American scholars should object to one black scholar: "They need have no contact with the 'untutored mind' or the black body of this American citizen, and I do not see how he touches them in any way."[25] Wylie launched an investigation into Locke's election, reviewing his preliminary Rhodes examination, but nothing came of it. Five Oxford colleges, however, refused to admit Locke before Hertford accepted him, he was denied membership in the American Club, and he was not invited to the annual Thanksgiving dinner for the American scholars in 1907.[26] In May 1908 some fifteen American scholars refused to attend a dinner given by the Rhodes trustees after Locke had accepted the invitation. For a luncheon hosted by the American Embassy at Dorchester House in London in March 1909, Wylie tried to convince Locke not to attend. He refused, and when at the luncheon all the American Rhodes scholars were seated at tables for two except for Locke, who was seated alone, the U.S. Ambassador, William Whitelaw Reid, entered, he "bowed to his guests, crossed the room and sat down with the black man."[27]

Such a subtle rebuke to the Southern scholars did not improve Locke's status in the Rhodes community. Solace was found, however, in a small circle of international students Locke would befriend at Oxford, men who shared with Locke outsider status to varying degrees.[28] The most significant of these friends was Pixley ka-Isaka Seme (1881–1951), a Zulu from South Africa, who wrote Locke encouragingly soon after his election and would introduce him to Oxford's Cosmopolitan Club (Fig. 3). Four years older than Locke, Seme had lived in America, studied at Columbia University, began reading law at Jesus College in 1906, and would go on to become the co-founder and president-general of the African National Congress.[29] At Oxford (though he could be found more often in London), Seme with Locke would launch the African Union Society, a diasporic student association committed to Pan Africanism. James Arthur Harley, an older Antiguan student and Locke's only black friend at Harvard, would join Locke in Oxford in 1908 as a research diploma student at Jesus.[30] Satya Mukerjea, a wealthy Bengali student who introduced Locke to several suffragettes at Oxford, was developing ideas about Indian nationalism along the lines of Seme's and Locke's thinking about Africa. Lionel de Fonseka, an Indian student from Ceylon who was at Merton College, would accompany Locke on his first Italian tour. Percy Philip, a Scottish student of modest background who graduated from Edinburgh and came to Oxford to work on the *Oxford English Dictionary*, was beloved by Locke as a "bohemian" and "democratic aristocrat" who took him on country walks.[31] Samuel Eliot (Missouri and Hertford, 1905) was one of the few American Rhodes scholars friendly with Locke. Locke's most intimate friend at Oxford, Carl Downes, was admitted to Merton College and would stay in Oxford for only a year, returning eventually to Harvard for his PhD in Philosophy.

Locke was not entirely alone in his fight. Harvard friend Horace Kallen (see below), along with one or two other "authentic" Americans in Oxford, refused to attend the American Club's Thanksgiving dinner in 1907 in protest over Locke's exclusion. A.V. Dicey, a liberal English constitutional law scholar at Oxford, instead hosted a reception for Locke the night before at Balliol College, while Louis Dyer, a Balliol alum and former Harvard professor, brought Locke into his own home on Banbury Road for Thanksgiving dinner with his family.[32] Nevertheless, the Rhodes administrators and college officials were not, at the time, very sympathetic to Locke's struggles. Wylie wrote in Locke's student file that his Harvard career was "not very successful" (that was certainly not the case) and that he was "superficial and wanting in solid character," while Wylie's American brother-in-law at Harvard commented that, "though clever he is decidedly objectionable. I do not know him personally but he is not at all pleasant to look at."[33] The Principal at Hertford, according to Wylie, found Locke's conduct to be satisfactory but his knowledge of Greek and Latin to be poor and his general academic work to be "not strenuous."

Locke did not disagree.[34] Ironically, he had used Harvard's new elective system to construct a true liberal arts education—mixing Greek, Latin, Philosophy, and English courses, even taking a course with T. S. Eliot's mentor, Irving Babbitt—akin to his Greats course at Oxford.[35] But he was poorly matched with his Oxford tutors (not uncommon for many Americans at Oxford) and having great difficulty learning Greek, and hence requested a change in degree to a BSc in

Philosophy. Locke would be required to write a thesis for this degree, which was considered a graduate research degree, and he wished to work under the Pragmatist philosopher Ferdinand Schiller, formerly of Cornell University and now at Corpus Christi.[36] Locke's supervisor at Hertford at first denied the request, but Locke persisted and was granted permission by the faculty to pursue a course of study titled "The Concept of Value in its Relation to Logic, Ethics, and Aesthetics" under the supervision of Schiller and Professor Cook Wilson (New College).[37] As he moved away from Greats and into a specialization in Philosophy, Locke also began to move away from the Absolute Idealism of his Harvard days and toward Pragmatic Pluralism; his records indicate that he attended (or planned to attend) lectures given by Schiller and William James, the Platonist J.A. Smith, the philosopher of aesthetics E. F. Carritt, and the anthropologist Edward B. Tylor.[38] Nevertheless, Locke remained miserable doing much of his academic work and considered resigning his scholarship.

Financial worries increasingly plagued Locke at Oxford. He spent a good deal on his first rooms in college, in Hertford's North Quad (which were so elegant in his mind that they required furnishings suitable for entertaining, including renting an English piano), while also paying for Italian wine and tailored clothes (required because of his small frame).[39] He ran up enormous debts after moving out of college his second year and into large and expensive digs on Beaumont Street, at which he would host meals for the Cosmopolitan Club (forty members could fit comfortably into his flat). In addition to the Cosmopolitan, Locke joined, was elected to, or invited to join, the Atlantic Union, Le Club Français, the Oxford Rationalist Society, the Harvard Club of London, the Oxford University Food Reform Society, the Oxford University Musical Union, and the Oxford Union Society (to name just a few). Increasingly, however, Locke kept only the company of a small group of intimates, most members of the Cosmopolitan Club, and his isolation from the Rhodes community, along with the departures of Kallen and Downes in the summer of 1908, took its toll on him.

Wylie and others speculated that the reason Locke was having such difficulties in Oxford was because he was not an athlete. A biracial scholar from Queensland (1908) and a black scholar from Jamaica (1910) were described as fitting in better because they were both good athletes.[40] While Locke was very small in stature and had health issues (heart and lung), this criticism could also have been code for Locke's homosexuality, "veiled but not hidden at Harvard," more out in the open in Oxford.[41] It was also not exactly true that he was no athlete, for he became a confident rider at Oxford and, as coxswain for the Hertford boat (he was also a cox at Harvard his senior year), won a silver cup for the Torpid Fours during his first term at Oxford. Locke's response to the hostility and ostracism was most often a hyper formality, and his elaborate dress and gastronomic excesses gave the impression of an Oxford Aesthete.[42]

At Harvard, Locke took great pains to play the part of the black dandy of 1904—a decade and a half before *Gatsby*'s "modish Negroes"— wearing often a gray coat, matching gray gloves, and a top hat.[43] While studying Greek philosophy and drama, medieval history, and German during his first year at Harvard, he ran with a crowd that appreciated Yeats's poetry, Harvard's museums, and Boston's fine art and music establishments. He was drawn to the myth of Prometheus, to the poetry of Keats and Shelley, and to the aestheticism of Wilde and Santayana.[44] "Spry and sophisticated," writes Mendelssohn, "Locke styled himself as Wilde's spiritual heir."[45]

Locke wrote to his mother from Oxford recommending opera, complaining about "the vulgarly unaesthetic Americans" who criticize it, and sent her a book on the Pre-Raphaelites (he seems to have particularly liked Holman Hunt).[46] On his first trip to London in 1907, with Seme, Locke began his lifelong fascination with Gothic architecture, commenting on "the beautiful old Gothic buildings" at Westminster and the Middle Temple.[47] He and Downes would spend the Christmas holiday of 1907 touring medieval towns and Gothic churches in Brittany and Normandy. Even Parkin commented after his first meeting with Locke that "he has the grace and politeness of manner of a Frenchman or Italian," and Stewart argues that Locke was already the "[Barrett] Wendell-like dandy, a man who had cultivated a persona that perfectly matched the Italianate manner then dominant at Oxford."[48]

Traveling on the Continent in search of beautiful buildings and paintings became salvific pilgrimages for Locke, and in Paris, Venice, and Rome he lounged at fashionable cafes rubbing elbows with the likes of Rudyard Kipling and Richard Strauss. But like many an Oxford Aesthete, Locke ran up large bills from entertaining and traveling first class and was unable to pay his creditors. He appeared in court several times and was asked by Hertford College to leave during his third year. In the summer of 1910 Locke headed for the Continent, inspired by French and Austrian philosophers, German modernity, and Berlin's openness to gay culture. In Berlin he managed to complete his thesis on "The Concept of Value" and submitted it before the deadline imposed by Hertford. An often-autobiographical exploration of the psychology of learning and assigning value, the four-hundred-page thesis marks Locke's beginning to see race and culture as fluid constructs. He attended lectures and took philosophy courses at the University of Berlin while waiting for Oxford's response to his thesis. In February 1911, the Oxford examination board rendered its decision: the thesis was not deserving of a degree, nor would Locke be allowed to revise it. He was sent down from Oxford on March 10.

The whole Oxford experience had turned out so much more differently than Locke had anticipated while at Harvard, where he dreamt of Magdalen College and of wearing the scarlet and gray robes (awarded Oxford doctoral recipients) and being coxswain for the Varsity boat.[49] By the end of his first year, however, Locke had stopped chasing English and Oxonian acceptance, instead becoming a transnational critic of imperialism along with his African and Asian friends, leading him to develop new ideas about cultural pluralism just as Seme and other Cosmpolitans were advancing their indigenous-focused political agendas. How much his race and sexual orientation played into the decisions at Oxford is a matter of debate; what was not was that Locke would never be granted a degree, graduate or undergraduate, from the University of Oxford. Returning to America in the fall of 1911, Locke decided to lie about this "tremendous detail," claiming publically that he had received a BLitt (Oxon). The first African American Rhodes scholar claimed his right to be considered an Oxford man.

Shortly after his first term at Oxford, Locke penned an essay titled "Oxford Contrasts," first appearing in the New York weekly *The Independent* in 1909. In the essay he struggled (and ultimately succeeded beautifully) to define the contrasts between Oxford's medieval ways and the modern educational philosophy pervading America and Germany:

> Education at Oxford, in brief, influences and influences for life everyone who becomes a part of its corporate life. This is its excellence. But the same system gives Oxford a sort of religious dominance over the province of knowledge that certainly makes the right to teach, and too often the right to be taught a matter of apostolic succession, and excommunicates all education that does not subordinate itself as directly preparatory to that system. This is its defect: both excellence and defect are medieval. These statements will seem unkind and adverse to those who think it a reproach to be called medieval—but by such Oxford never can be understood or appreciated. [50]

One day, "to the lasting and reasonable regret of many Oxonians," concludes Locke, "Oxford will probably choose to be modern." In the essay, Locke also makes observations about class and race that foreshadow his later philosophical writings:

> In a land of class distinctions, . . . I have found no race distinctions, and better still in cultured circles no race curiosity. . . . But racially, I prefer disfavor and . . . persecution even, to indifference. One cannot be neutral toward a class or social body without the gravest danger of losing one's own humanity. [51]

While Locke preferring the open and hostile racism of the Southern Rhodes scholars to the "indifference" of the English seems puzzling, Stewart argues that it gave Locke an opportunity to assert both his national and racial identity: "At Oxford, dealing with the Americans made him Black, but dealing with the English made him American."[52]

Locke would complete his doctoral thesis and earn the PhD from Harvard in 1918, and in 1921 he became Head of the Department of Philosophy at Howard University in Washington, D.C.

Locke and his mother Mary were vacationing in Germany in the summer of 1914 when the Great War broke out. From 1917 to 1919, race riots in America left dozens dead in Washington, Houston, and Chicago. Some 350,000 black soldiers would serve in segregated units in the A.E.F. (though often alongside French troops), and while General Pershing praised their service publicly, his private instructions to white officers were less congenial: "We must not eat with them, must not shake hands with them, seek to talk to them or to meet with them outside the requirements of military service. We must not commend too highly these troops, especially in front of white Americans."[53]

From 1918 to 1919, Locke served as an organizer of Student Army Corps Instruction, a personnel clerk, and an instructor in the SATC at Howard.[54] He would return to Europe after the War, on the *Aquitania* in 1922, a year after Scott and Zelda Fitzgerald took their maiden voyage to Europe on that same ship, and, like the Fitzgeralds, enjoyed its first class pleasures in food, drink, and classical music.[55] These European adventures included Parisian opera, a trip to see *Othello* performed at Stratford-upon-Avon, and then to Berlin, where Locke indulged in the seedy cabaret nightlife and experimental theatre of the Weimar years, indulging in the sensual as well as the intellectual. If Long Island's Gold Coast was a whir of flappers dancing with industrialists and movie directors in 1922 and 1923, Berlin throbbed with a darker mixture of communists, Jewish intellectuals and anti-Semites, Bauhaus painters and prostitutes. Berlin, too, was about to enter its own Jazz Age.

In 1924 Locke turned his attention increasingly to New York, staying in Harlem and frequenting Manhattan cabarets and gay nightclubs, living (as in Berlin) more freely as a homosexual than he could have in Washington.[56] That year the Irish-born critic Ernest Boyd described the American aesthete—a composite satire of many

Jazz Age writers—returning from Europe to find literary camaraderie in the Village:

> . . . the now complete Æsthete returned to New York and descended on Greenwich Village. His poems of disenchantment were in the press, his war novel was nearly finished, and it was not long before he appeared as Editor-in-Chief. . . . But it is essentially as an appraiser of the arts, as editor and critic, that the young Æsthete demands attention. [57]

Locke became an enthusiastic supporter of black writers like Countee Cullen and Langston Hughes while occasionally pursuing them romantically. Hughes ultimately failed to return Locke's invitation to be his lover, and Locke moved on, emotionally and physically, relocating from Paris to the Italian Riviera. These movements corresponded almost exactly with those of Scott and Zelda Fitzgerald in the second half of 1924, with Scott leaving the American expatriates in Paris to move to the Riviera as he concentrated on his next novel. [58] As Fitzgerald penned the words capturing the American Dream in the Great American Novel on the shores of the Mediterranean, Locke on the sands of San Remo collected his observations of race in America and the needed self-determination of African Americans in essays titled "Enter the New Negro" and "The Harlem Scene."

Nineteen twenty-five, the year that *The Great Gatsby* was published, also witnessed the birth of *The New Negro: An Interpretation*, an anthology of poetry, essays, plays, and art that gave cohesion to the concept of a Harlem Renaissance, a construct largely of Locke's own making. [59] In this landmark collection, Locke was able to capture the black voices of the previous generation, like Du Bois (though he had personally drifted far from Du Bois's ideas), while also championing the next generation of young African American writers and artists like Cullen, Hughes, and Zora Neale Hurston. [60] But as early as his Harvard undergraduate days, Locke had envisioned an expansion of Du Bois's arguments for black participation in the Western literary cannon by drawing comparisons with the Celtic Twilight in contemporary Ireland, where Yeats and other Irish writers were drawing inspiration from indigenous folk tales and ballads and turning out great literature.[61] Why couldn't black writers, also oppressed by an English-speaking majority, do the same with their African and African-American folk traditions?

Locke had witnessed the rise and near dominance of black culture in New York and the capitals of Western Europe in the early 1920s. Jazz and blues could be heard everywhere, with Bessie Smith, Louis Armstrong (who played on some of Smith's recordings), Fats Waller, Duke Ellington, Chick Webb, and their white imitators filling clubs and selling records. While Roland Hayes and the classically trained actor Paul Robeson paved the way for black artists in Europe, Sidney Bechet and Josephine Baker thrilled crowds in London, Paris, and Munich with hot jazz and risqué dancing. Much of this was done for segregated audiences, however, most infamously at Harlem's whites-only Cotton Club. "White interest in black art, entertainment, and culture in the Jazz Age," observes Joseph Vogel, "was often grounded in primitivism, voyeurism, and exploitation."[62] Much was written "*about* the Negro rather than of him," Locke would complain in *The New Negro*, "so that it is the Negro problem rather than the Negro that is known and mooted in the general mind."[63]

In the view of Locke's biographer, Jeffrey Stewart, "Locke was speaking as the 'Afro-American' Yeats when he suggested that the Negro artist who mattered embodied the Negro soul in his or her work."[64] Locke reached back to the criticism of Oxonian Matthew Arnold in his new interpretation of cosmopolitanism, where one could be both African American and cosmopolitan, an aesthete and a social reformer.[65] So committed was Locke to cultural studies (and, later in life, to adult education) that he did not publish a single article of philosophy until 1935's "Values and Imperatives," a revised version of his doctoral dissertation, when he was fifty years old.

In a biographical sketch that precedes his essay contribution to *American Philosophy Today and Tomorrow* (1935), Locke paints a self-portrait that places his Oxford years in the context of his developing socio-political awareness:

[I am] more of a pagan than a Puritan, more of a humanist that a pragmatist. . . . At Oxford, once more intrigued by the twilight of aestheticism but dimly aware of the new realism of the Austrian philosophy of value; socially Anglophile, but because of race loyalty, strenuously anti-imperialist; universalist in religion . . . cultural cosmopolitan, and accordingly more of a philosophical mid-wife to a generation of younger Negro poets, writers, artists than a professional philosopher.[66]

While achieving notoriety as both a literary critic and as a philosopher, Locke was an original thinker who drew from the American Pragmatists and presaged some of the ideas of Deconstruction and Derrida, especially cultural relativism. Locke grew into his role as a modernist and as patron and promoter of others. He had come a long way from the surface affectations of the Harvard dandy and Oxford Aesthete, a black Gatsby in search of his grail.

At first glance, it would appear that Alain Locke and F. Scott Fitzgerald had little in common. Paul S. Brown argues, however, that in having his alter-ego Amory in *This Side of Paradise* denounce American materialism and hypocrisy, and in his mocking of Tom Buchanan's racism in *Gatsby*, "Fitzgerald takes his place as part of an emergent and nontraditional intellectual class—including George Santayana and Alain Locke, Alice Paul and Margaret Mead, to name a few—that pushed for progressive ideas in a more open and pluralistic postwar nation."[67] Fitzgerald and Locke walked down the same streets and upon the same beaches of the Old World—at almost the exact same times—as they created their visions of a New America in the Jazz Age in 1924. Both writers indulged in aesthetic reveries of Oxonian and Gothic inspiration, if ultimately returning to America as motherland of very modern beauties.

Alain Locke died on June 9, 1954, in New York City. It would not be until 1963 that America elected its next black Rhodes scholar, and few black students applied in the more than fifty years since Locke left Oxford.[68] There were *two* famous men named Locke—both important philosophers and social critics—who attended the University of Oxford.

The first defined equality and individual rights in the Enlightenment, the second struggled to define and defend a culture denied full equality and individual rights in the twentieth century. Being a Rhodes scholar did not make that struggle any easier. I have found no greater description of the ideal Rhodes scholar, however, than the one penned by Alain Locke in 1909: "If he has served his time and purpose well, he will be, I take it, a man whose sympathies are wider than his prejudices, whose knowledge is larger than his beliefs, his work and his hopes greater than he himself."[69]

Horace Meyer Kallen

"Mr. Carraway, this is my friend Mr. Wolfsheim."
A small, flat-nosed Jew raised his large head and regarded me with . . . his tiny eyes in the half-darkness. (*The Great Gatsby*, 69)

Meyer Wolfsheim is one of the most clearly drawn characters in *The Great Gatsby*. The name Wolfsheim may have been inspired by *Wolfstein, or The Mysterious Bandit* (1822), a Gothic chapbook based on Percy Shelley's 1811 Gothic horror novel, *St. Irvyne; or, The Rosicrucian.*[70]

Nick, Tom, Jordan, and many of Gatsby's party guests display a great deal of curiosity about Jay Gatsby's origins. Nick is more willing to believe Gatsby is from the rural South or the Lower East Side of Manhattan than to accept that he went to Oxford. Obscure southern origins or those of the immigrant seem synonymous here. But it is Manhattan that is the island "where anything can happen," and it is significant that the scene of Nick and Gatsby passing southern Europeans and affluent blacks on the Queensboro Bridge is followed by Nick's meeting Meyer Wolfsheim in a speakeasy. Keith Gandal has written about the ethnicity of Jimmy Gatz and how it would have been perceived by the army, by Oxford, and especially by Tom Buchanan, who appears also in the club scene and begins to have doubts about Gatsby's background.[71] Indeed, many readers have wondered if

Gatsby's elaborate makeover and half-lies were meant to cover up the fact that he was a Jew. Was the Oxford mask the key for Wolfsheim's using Gatsby as a front for his illegitimate business ventures?

Oxford's history with Jewish students begins with the arrival of the first Jewish undergraduates in 1869.[72] No synagogue existed in Oxford until one was established (short-lived) in Paradise Square (ca. 1847), followed by St. Aldate's in 1871, the year of the passing of the University Tests Act.[73] The Oxford University Reform Act of 1854 and the Tests Act had removed admissions barriers for professing Jews, and F. D. Schloss of Corpus Christi became in 1869 the first of a succession of Jewish students to win Oxford scholarships. There were twenty-five Jewish undergraduates at Oxford by 1882, twenty-nine in the academic year 1908–9, and forty-three in 1912—not insignificant numbers given the size of Oxford then (less than three thousand students), but far fewer than at Cambridge.[74]

As a result of the growing number of European Jewish émigrés in the American northeast, Chicago, and other urban areas, and of their sons' success on college entrance exams, the practice of *numerus clausus* (quotas) was instituted at Harvard, Princeton, and other elite private universities to limit the number of Jewish students.[75] Columbia University, which had the largest number of Jewish students at 40%, was the first Ivy League institution to administer an explicit quota in 1921, dropping its Jewish population to 22%. While Radcliffe Heermance, Princeton's first Director of Admissions (from 1922 to 1950) claimed that Princeton never had a Jewish quota, President John Grier Hibben and his wife admitted to the practice to University of Chicago President Robert Hutchins.[76] Asked by President Hutchins how many black students were at Princeton (ca. 1930), President Hibben responded that "there weren't any. . . . They just don't seem to want to come."[77] Princeton's exclusive eating clubs perpetuated the anti-Semitism, and neither the progressive Woodrow Wilson nor his immediate presidential successors at Princeton changed this exclusion. Fitzgerald records socializing with several prominent Jewish-Americans while he and Zelda resided in Long Island. *The Great Gatsby* is in part about "the convoluted possibilities of Jews mixing with Gentiles," writes historian Judith

Goldstein, for Great Neck was one of the few Gold Coast communities that welcomed or even allowed Jews at the time, for most were mixed in with the theatrical and literary crowd that flocked to the suburb.[78]

Gatsby is also about cultural pluralism and cultural appropriation, two concepts unknown to Fitzgerald but very much part of the conversations that Alain Locke and T. S. Eliot were having (separately) with a man named Horace Kallen. "Locke utilized the intellectual scaffold of James and Dewey," writes Rutledge Dennis, "but he was to gain a firsthand account of pluralism from Horace Kallen, who coined the term *cultural pluralism*."[79] Locke met Kallen at Harvard University in the Fall of 1906 when he was an undergraduate student there and Kallen was a graduate teaching assistant for George Santayana. The German-born son of an émigré Orthodox rabbi in Boston, Horace Meyer Kallen (1882–1974) went to Harvard on scholarship and studied philosophy under Santayana and William James, graduating (*magna cum laude*), like Locke, in only three years.[80] Woodrow Wilson, then president of Princeton University, hired Kallen to teach English there in 1903, Kallen becoming the first Jew on the faculty at Princeton. After two years he returned to Harvard to begin his doctoral studies, and in 1907 he came to Oxford on a Sheldon Traveling Fellowship and stayed for two years, studying philosophy in preparation for his PhD examination and thesis under F.C.S. Schiller, Fellow and Senior Tutor at Corpus Christi.

While at Oxford, Kallen corresponded with Santayana, James, Bertrand Russell, Schiller, and Barrett Wendell.[81] Kallen was also one of the first to witness and comment upon Locke's ostracism at Oxford. He wrote to Wendell asking advice in late October of 1907:

> some people have been . . . mean-spirited enough to draw "the color line" for the benefit of Englishmen. The boy earned his scholarship in open competition. He has said nothing to me himself. Others have deprecated his being there. But he is here, one of America's scholars, and a Harvard man. He finds himself suddenly shut out of things,— unhappy, and lonely and doesn't know why.[82]

While Kallen is clear in his letter to Wendell that his kindness to Locke is a matter of individual, rather than racial, justice, Locke's treatment by most of the Rhodes scholars was enough to drive Kallen to anger and to action. He would become, by choice, a big brother to Locke, holding the Rhodes scholar in great esteem if not others of his race. He would introduce Locke to both Schiller and Russell, then at Cambridge. As for Locke, he would describe to his mother his Oxford ally as "a Ghetto Jew I met at Harvard who is making a social sensation" at Oxford. [83]

Kallen was back at Harvard to give a series of lectures in February and March 1909. After finishing his PhD in 1911 with a dissertation titled "Notes on the Nature of Truth," Kallen joined the philosophy faculty at the University of Wisconsin and stayed in Madison until 1918, when he became one of the founding members of The New School for Social Thought in New York City, serving as dean of its Graduate Faculty of Political and Social Science from 1944–46 and remaining there for the rest of his academic career.

William James wrote Kallen a glowing letter of recommendation for a teaching position in 1910. [84] Harvard College Dean L.B.R. Briggs described him in a 1909 letter to his colleague E.H. Wells as "a brilliant fellow of high aims and self-sacrificing character" who "was thoroughly good" in teaching English Composition at Princeton despite "the Princeton objection to Jews [and] . . . a tendency to discuss theological questions in a radical manner." [85] In his obituary, the *New York Times* reported that Kallen had been dismissed from the Princeton faculty in 1905 "for being an avowed unbeliever," was denied a regular faculty position at Harvard, and was forced to resign from the University of Wisconsin "for being an advocate of the rights of pacifists in the heat of World War I." [86]

A widely published philosopher, Kallen is credited with creating the concept of "cultural pluralism," inspired in part by his Harvard teachers, William James and Barrett Wendell, and just as importantly through conversations with Locke at Harvard and Oxford beginning in 1906. [87] The two disagreed over the importance of racial or ethnic difference, Kallen asserting that Locke had not gone far enough, the latter seeing race (at this early point in his career) as merely performative.[88] Kallen first published his theory in a 1915 essay for *The Nation* titled "Democracy Versus the Melting Pot," responding to critiques emanating from the social sciences that saw Italian, Slavic, and other European immigrants of the period as "a rootless proletariat" subverting America's major cities. "For Kallen," writes William Toll, "this xenophobic literature expressed a deep-seated fear of cultural diversity by a social elite losing its authority."[89]

Kallen also carried on a thirty-three year long correspondence (beginning in 1927) with T. S. Eliot, from whom Kallen solicited help in creating a British version of the International League for Academic Freedom in December 1933.[90] Eliot immediately wrote to the Oxford historian A. L. Rowse (a classmate of Evelyn Waugh's) asking him for ideas about forming academic groups to help Jewish refugees. Eliot would himself give personal assistance to Jewish refugees during the war.[91] While renewing their acquaintance in the late 1920s, Kallen and Eliot had known each other at Harvard from 1906, Eliot's freshman year (the same year Kallen met Locke), to 1911, when Kallen left for Wisconsin. The two may have met when Kallen was a graduate teaching assistant for Josiah Royce's open seminar. Kallen finally convinced Eliot to come to lecture at the New School in the spring of 1933, and Eliot stayed with Kallen during his residency there. Though dialectically opposed in much of their social thought, they remained committed humanists and close friends, Eliot contributing to a *festschrift* honoring Kallen at his retirement: "to a man whose mind and achievements I have always admired, and whose personality I hold in enduring affection."[92]

In a 1949 essay titled, "That Education has Become Big Business," Kallen praises America for being a pioneer in tax-supported, free public education "from kindergarten to the university and beyond," and observes that American institutions of higher learning have embraced either "the Gothic building or the colonial meeting house."[93] Both architectural styles represent America's inheritance from Great Britain, be it from Oxonians John Locke and Christopher Wren or the medieval liberal arts tradition of Oxford and Cambridge. Thomas Jefferson, who lived in the Wren Building while studying law at the College of William and Mary in Virginia, expressed a radical notion of equality, and Locke and Kallen strove to make good that promise.

The Man in the Pink Suit

"About Gatsby! . . . [I've] been making a small investigation of his past."

"And you found he was an Oxford man," said Jordan helpfully.

"An Oxford man!" [Tom] was incredulous. "Like hell he is! He wears a pink suit." (95)

Tom Buchanan's incredulity is brought on by the incongruity he sees between being "an Oxford man" and wearing a pink suit. Earlier we saw that Fitzgerald's own dandyism dates to his boyhood mimicking of his father and expressed itself in both his personal style of dress and in his depiction of protagonists like Amory Blaine, Anthony Patch, and Jay Gatsby.[94] As with his depiction of the radically dressed and coiffed "flappers" in his early short stories and novels, Fitzgerald's dandies raise questions about sartorial expressions of masculinity in the 1920s. In particular, does Fitzgerald give us a queer Gatsby?

For Tom Buchanan, Oxford must be a staid, conservative environment that would never tolerate a man wearing a pink suit—or a "caramel-colored suit" (52) or a "white flannel suit, silver shirt, and gold-colored tie" (66), for that matter. While there is certainly some truth in this, Tom knows nothing of the Oxonian Aesthetes (nor of the Bright Young People), nor does he realize that even Oxford has occasions for white flannel suits and brightly-colored blazers: garden parties, croquet matches, and boat races, for example. "In terms of dandiacal influence," writes Catherine Mintler, "we might remember here that when Gatsby was in Britain after the war, allegedly as an Oxford undergraduate, he would have encountered fellow undergraduates emulating various forms of dandiacal dress. What he may not have realized is that this posturing was typically generational—that most young Oxford men sporting dandiacal dress would dress more conventionally upon taking their degree."[95] In other words, an Oxford man of Tom's age would most often have dressed like Tom.

Should Gatsby, then, have grown out of such undergraduate displays of dandyism? Anthony Patch does not change his sartorial habits after graduating from Harvard to the leisured lifestyle of a twenty-something in Manhattan. A pink suit was not necessarily too garish for Fitzgerald himself, it seems, if we can trust the evidence of the pink shirt and pink tie Zelda made for the paper doll version of Scott produced for their daughter, Scottie, in the 1920s.[96] The persistence of dandyism throughout Fitzgerald's novels and short stories, argues Mintler, draws attention to acceptable, normative forms of masculinity in the Edwardian Era and the Jazz Age, and how these can be challenged sartorially.[97] What Fitzgerald is doing with his own style of dress (he carried a cane throughout the 1920s), as well as that of his male protagonists, furthermore, becomes a social challenge parallel to the risqué and androgynous style of Zelda and the so-called "flappers."[98]

While much contemporary *Gatsby* criticism deals with issues of gender and sexuality, a few critics have taken a more radical step in arguing that both Nick Carraway and Jay Gatsby engage in homoerotic if not homosexual relationships in the novel. Both men, these critics would argue, were gay or bisexual characters "passing" as straight men in 1922 New York, just as Fitzgerald cherished throughout his life homosocial bonds that may have risen to the level of homoerotic desire.[99]

The evidence for this theory in *The Great Gatsby* begins with Nick's description of his first New York party, at Tom and Myrtle's apartment in Washington Heights. Nick and Chester McKee leave the party, and as they "groaned down in the elevator," McKee is warned, "Keep your hands off the lever," by the elevator boy (32). They end up in McKee's apartment, the inebriated Nick later recalling: ". . . I was standing beside his bed and he was sitting up between the sheets, clad in his underwear, with a great portfolio [of photos] in his hands." Fitzgerald's use of the ellipsis between the elevator incident and McKee's bed has suggested to some an indication of a sexual encounter too risqué for detailing in print.

Critic Maggie Froehlich suggests that Gatsby was not above prostituting himself for social and monetary gain, particularly during the time he spends with the debauched Dan Cody "in a vague personal capacity" on his yacht.[100] As for Nick and Gatsby, there is no indication that they have a sexualized relationship, but Nick is increasingly drawn to the elegance and charm of Gatsby and chooses their friendship over his relationship with Jordan Baker. Similarly, Jordan appears to be drawn to the beauty and charm of Daisy from an early age, voyeuristically observing Daisy's flirtations with various young men, and ultimately chooses allegiance to Daisy over Nick.

While Fitzgerald may have been drawn to the aesthetic tastes of Oscar Wilde, he overtly rejected homosexuality and ridiculed gay men in his fiction.[101] *Tender is the Night* is particularly harsh in its depiction of the gay subculture of Paris, and in Fitzgerald's letters he derisively uses the term "fairy" to describe gay men. This may, in large part, be due to Zelda's hurtful accusations beginning in 1929 that her husband was a homosexual, and in particular was in love with Ernest Hemingway. Scott publicly and privately refuted this and he believed that the accusation derived from Zelda's own lesbian leanings.[102] In his *Ledger* under May 1929 he wrote "Zelda & Dolly Wilde," and in a 1930 letter to Zelda, then institutionalized, he referred to "the Dolly Wilde matter."[103] Dolly was the niece of Oscar Wilde and was a Parisian libertine who was openly gay and introduced Scott and Zelda to lesbian artists and intellectuals in Paris like Natalie Barney and Romaine Brooks. Zelda believed that women like Dolly shared her own aesthetic values, and Zelda indicated that she was herself in love with her dance teacher, Madame Egorova. Egorova had "symbols of beauty in her head that I understood," Zelda would later confess, "[she] had everything of beauty in her head, the brightness of a Greek temple."[104]

While the evidence is not strong that Fitzgerald intended to depict Gatsby as homosexual, the pink suit does stand out as one indicator of a "queer" Gatsby. Fitzgerald's own friendships in New York City, on Long Island, and in Paris included more than a few gay men, lesbians, and others performing queerness in a variety of ways. Dandies and aesthetes had been challenging norms of masculinity for more than a century before the publication of *The Great Gatsby*. To do so, however, was often to risk questions about one's sexuality. "Men who gravitated toward or sought to express masculinity differently were labeled feminine," writes Mintler, "because sartorial display was considered to be a feminine or effeminate behavior that deviated from essentialist masculine norms."[105] Fitzgerald seems to have been more or less comfortable balancing his dandyism with normative masculine tastes for football and war. Zelda saw the machismo of Hemingway, on the contrary, as overcompensation, calling him "a pansy with hair on his chest." Zelda's observation was echoed by Robert Menzies McAlmon, who described the gay subculture in 1920s Berlin (of which Alain Locke was a frequent participant) in his *Distinguished Air: Grim Fairy Tales*, published the same year as *Gatsby*. McAlmon, who grew up in South Dakota and Minnesota and later became a member of the Fitzgerald and Hemingway circle of American expatriates in Paris, was a gay man married to the lesbian writer Annie Winifred Ellerman, better known as Bryher. McAlmon angered Fitzgerald when he suggested that he and Hemingway had similarly married women to pass as heterosexual.[106]

To be queer in the 1920s did not necessarily mean deliberately shocking conservatives with your sexuality or style of dress: it could also be a statement of Romantic longing in the age of modernism. Fitzgerald struggled between these two worlds in his first two novels. Amory Blaine sets out on romantic quests in *This Side of Paradise* but finds himself, at the end of the novel, spouting a Marxist critique of American capitalism. Anthony Patch, "the romantic, always lets his 'superior intellect' slide into a vague aestheticism," writes Robert Sklar, "and his aestheticism descend into erotic yearning."[107] Finding love with the provocative Gloria does not, however, satisfy these yearnings. Nor do all the silk shirts tossed at his rediscovered lover bring Gatsby ultimate happiness. Gatsby "is a dandy of desire," writes Malcolm Bradbury, "a desire that has been redirected from its human or material object into a fantasy, one which seeks to retain a past moment in an endless instant of contemplation."[108]

There are many parallels between the turbulent marriages of Scott and Zelda and that of T. S. Eliot and his first wife, Vivienne, whom he met in Oxford in 1915. In the next chapter we will examine the Oxford episode in the life of a poet much admired by Fitzgerald, and visit a medieval manor house outside Oxford where an eccentric bisexual aristocrat presided over parties that drew artists, writers, and intellectuals from Oxford and London and America.

5

An American at Merton College:
T. S. Eliot, Garsington, and
the Women of Oxford

"I'm glad it's a girl. And I hope she'll be a fool—that's the
best thing a girl can be in this world, a beautiful little fool."
                    —Daisy Buchanan in *The Great Gatsby* (1925)

Neither Daisy nor Zelda (who inspired these lines) were fools,
nor were the women living in Oxford in the late Victorian
and Edwardian eras. Yet the vote was denied them—until
1920 in America and full suffrage for British women in 1928—as
was the ability to matriculate and take a degree from the University
of Oxford. The invisible women of Oxford worked, studied, and
occasionally socialized with their male counterparts from the 1870s,
and they often sat the same exams. Two Oxford women in particular,
Vivienne Haigh-Wood and Lady Ottoline Morrell, had an enormous

impact on the early literary career of the most famous American yet to study at Oxford—T. S. Eliot. Though, like Shelley, he spent but a little time studying at the ancient university, Oxford would continue throughout his life to shape the way Eliot thought and wrote. The man F. Scott Fitzgerald called "the greatest living poet" brought to life a new, modernist aesthetic that merged medieval, Christian, and Oxonian elements with the new philosophical and literary experimentation coming from Cambridge, Bloomsbury, and Paris.

Women, Eventually

What has the rosy-cheeked, laughing, chaperoned English girl to do with such a mystery of beauty as that of these mediæval walls and flowering gardens?
—John Corbin, "The Latin Quarter of England" (1903)

In 1866 women were given permission, for the first time, to attend some of the university's lectures.[1] Classes just for women were organized shortly thereafter, and the first residential halls for women at Oxford were founded in the 1870s. The Association for the Education of Women founded Lady Margaret Hall in 1878 for Anglican women, and its first students were admitted a year later. Somerville Hall (later College) was founded for nondenominational students in 1879, St. Hugh's College in 1886, St. Hilda's College in 1893, and St. Anne's College (founded in 1879 for the home-students) formally incorporated in 1952. However, while female students could attend lectures and take examinations at Oxford, they were not allowed to matriculate at the university, nor were they allowed to take degrees, only diplomas, from their colleges. While some dons (including Charles Dodgson) encouraged young women to study at Oxford and sit university examinations to make them better prepared to be teachers, the university authorities struggled over female matriculation and felt no urgency as long as women were limited in vocation and political participation.

Between 1904 and 1907 the "Steamboat Ladies," as they came to be called, traveled from Oxford and Cambridge to Ireland where they were awarded *ad eundem* (courtesy) University of Dublin degrees through Trinity College, which had opened its doors to women in 1904. More than seven hundred Oxbridge women, passing the same exams as their male counterparts, had to settle for this compromise. Among them was Eleanor Rathbone, the suffragette who read Classics at Somerville College and went on to become an Independent MP for the Combined English Universities in 1929, campaigning for human rights and against appeasement of Nazi Germany. Many female Oxford students were also like their male counterparts in that they came from families of means. Once such was Ottoline Morrell, a home-student at Somerville College in 1899. She found digs in Oxford, attended lectures on Roman history, and was tutored on political economy by Miss Deverell.[2] Margaret Haigh Thomas, later Viscountess, left Somerville during her first year "because of its ugliness and bad food."[3]

Just as the Great War had led to female suffrage and expanded employment opportunities for women, so too would it lead to change at Oxford. Women were first granted Oxford degrees in 1920, Cambridge women having to wait until after World War II. However, a quota limiting the numbers of women at Oxford was instituted from 1927 to 1957. In 1957 the women's colleges were finally given equal status. This parallels the course of many private institutions in the United States, for example, Harvard, where Radcliffe College was chartered to educate women in 1894 but Radcliffe women were not granted Harvard degrees until 1963. There would be no female Rhodes scholar until 1977, when twenty-four women arrived in Oxford as scholars.

While inside their own halls and colleges before 1920, Oxford's women formed their sports teams, competed intercollegiately, had their own J.C.R.s and social clubs, they could not be members of most university societies and were excluded from most university events where they might mix with male undergraduates, attending Union debates only as spectators in the gallery.[4] Some American women made their way to the women's colleges at Oxford in this period. An American named "K.R." wrote in 1920 about her St. Anne's tutor: "The first impression was typical of the universal contrast between the impersonal mass treatment of students in American college and the instant personal relationship in which each of us found herself, with her tutor."[5] K.R. also wrote: "Nowhere else, nowhere but in Oxford, do [books] seem to be so thoroughly natives of the place, so natural and inevitable and withal so entrancing."

Also native to the place was Dorothy Leigh Sayers, born at the Headmaster's House of Christ Church Cathedral School, Oxford. Her father, the Rev. Henry Sayers, was a chaplain of Christ Church and headmaster of the Choir School. Dorothy won a scholarship to Somerville College in 1912, where she studied modern languages and medieval literature, finishing with first-class honours in 1915 (Oxford awarded her an MA in 1920). Blackwell's published her first book of poetry in 1916 and she later worked there, in addition to teaching abroad, before moving to London to work in an advertising agency. Sayers became a prolific writer, most famous for her Lord Peter Wimsey detective novels featuring the aristocratic Balliol grad and his novelist partner Harriet Vane. Harriet was a graduate of the fictional Oxford women's college Shrewsbury, and returns there for the matriarchy and mayhem of *Gaudy Night* (1936). Sayers wrote several plays and was also a respected medievalist, translating the Old French *Song of Roland* and the *Tristan* of the twelfth-century poet Thomas of Britain, as well Dante's *Divine Comedy* (having taught herself Old Italian). She numbered among her friends T. S. Eliot, Charles Williams, and C. S. Lewis, and hence is often grouped together with the Inklings. Her essay, "The Lost Tools of Learning" (1948), calls for a new model of primary and secondary education based on the *trivium* and *quadrivium* of the medieval liberal arts.

Gaudy Night balances the nostalgia of the masculine Oxford Novel with criticism of Oxford and its traditional gender roles. The gender imbalance at Oxford changed temporarily during the Great War when so many male students and dons went off to fight. Somerville College became a military hospital, forcing its staff and students into Oriel College housing. The women of Oxford did their part for king and country during the war, both on the home front and on the Western Front.[6] One of the most remarkable personal stories is that of Vera

Brittain (1893–1970). From Buxton in Derbyshire, Brittain attended a course of Oxford University extension lectures given by the historian John Marriot in 1912 and 1913 who encouraged her to try for Oxford. In March 1914, she was awarded an exhibition to Somerville College to read English. However, at the end of her first year she left Oxford to do war service as a nursing assistant, first in Buxton and London and then in military hospitals in Malta (1916) and Étaples, France (1917), where she nursed wounded German prisoners. When she returned to Somerville in 1919, Brittain changed her course of study to Modern History, in part to understand the origins of the conflict that had claimed the lives of her fiancé, her brother, and two close friends. In 1933 she would publish her most acclaimed work the memoir *Testament of Youth*, largely based on a diary she kept during the war.

As a burgeoning feminist and working journalist in London, Brittain wrote about the difficulties women experienced at Oxford during and immediately after the war. Women were discouraged from joining the conflict and were urged to stay at Oxford, but with constant reminders of the "abnormality" of their new status and privileges at the university.[7] When the male undergraduates returned from the war, they often aggressively reclaimed their privileged places. In the 1919 "Oriel raid," for example, a group of Oriel men took pickaxes to the wall that divided the men's and women's quarters, forcing the principal and female staff of Somerville to guard the hole all through the night, "sustained by students who brought them coffee, cushions and *The Oxford Book of English Verse*"![8] Postwar university women were, observed Vera Brittain, "in a state of transition," and this included more openness about women's sexuality. Brittain's first novel, *The Dark Tide* (1923), was a thinly disguised portrait of life at Oxford's women's colleges, and so does her classmate and London housemate, Winifred Holtby, comment on Somerville life in her novel, *The Land of Green Ginger* (1927). Significantly, both Brittain and Holtby turned down offers of academic posts to try to make it as writers.[9]

With the numbers of women increasing at Oxford and Cambridge in the period between the wars, there appeared a feminine counterpart to the masculine bildungsroman that was the Oxford Novel. Eventually the "Girton Girl," from Cambridge's Girton College (founded for women in 1869), emerged as a literary commonplace, representing the educated modern woman and sexual liberalism. The simultaneous appearance of the socially liberated "flapper" and the popularity of Freudian sexual theories drew increasing attention to these novels in the 1920s and '30s.

The first to capitalize on the new phenomenon of women at Oxbridge was Annie Edwards's *The Girton Girl*, serialized in *Temple Bar* in 1881 and published in three volumes in 1885. Cambridge is merely a backdrop to this romance, however, and the Girton College plays no significant role, but as Sally Mitchell points out, the motifs and customs were quickly established and soon copied.[10] The farce written by "Tivoli" (Horace William Bleackley), *Une Culotte, or, A New Woman: An Impossible Story of Modern Oxford* (1894), brings the heroine to Oxford disguised as a man to enter the fictional St. Chad's, one of the men's colleges, and romance with one of its male students. In L. T. Meade, *The Girls of Merton College* (1911), "Merton" is plainly Girton, depicting a strong community of young women at Cambridge. Rosamond Lehmann's first novel, *Dusty Answer* (1927), was less conventional as a Cambridge romance, depicting same-sex relations at Girton in the brief affair between heroine Judith Earl and her fellow student Jennifer. Lehmann later became friends with Leonard and Virginia Woolf. Virginia Woolf's short story, "A Woman's College from Outside" (1926), set at Newnham College, Cambridge, explores the university woman's romantic longing for meaning and sexual fulfillment and her frustration with the chaperone system and exclusion from the male world, which again leads to homosexual relationships.

A similar but darker treatment of the subject of sexuality within the world of women's colleges is Gertrude Eileen Trevelyan's *Hot-House* (1933), which takes place at the fictional Queen Anne's Hall at Oxford. This psychological thriller tells the story of the bitter decline of a bright Oxford undergraduate, Mina Cook, whose psychological instability ultimately results in suicide due to the darkness and pettiness of the university itself. Trevelyn (b. 1903) came up to Lady Margaret Hall, Oxford in 1923 and read English, receiving a second in 1927, the same year she won the Newdigate Prize. After Oxford she, too, moved to

London to try to make it as a professional writer, her first novel the acclaimed *Appius and Virginia* (1932). She died from injuries suffered in a London air raid in 1941.

Anna Bogen has studied these works and discerned a growing disillusionment, especially among the female writers, who avoid the "rosy glow that permeates so much Oxford fiction," replacing it with cynicism and even anger.[11] "In *Une Culotte* and *The Girls of Merton College*," writes Bogen, "the Girton Girl learned to negotiate successful heterosexual relationships at university," while in *"Dusty Answer* and *Hot-House*, although normality is still located in the heterosexual, the focus shifts to relationships between women. . . . All four writers struggle to contain the contradictory sexual expectations foisted on college women within the formal structures of the *Bildungsroman*. . . "[12]

While Scott Fitzgerald was more drawn to the light touch and nostalgia of Beerbohm and Mackenzie, Zelda Fitzgerald was perhaps more sympathetic to the approach of Lehmann and Trevelyan. Zelda produced something of a female bildungsroman in her first and only published novel, *Save Me the Waltz* (1932), drawing heavily on her relationship with Scott. In the novel, Zelda's and Scott's alter egos are southern belle Alabama Beggs and philandering artist David Knight, the surname an ironic nod to Scott's heroic self-image. A bored Alabama laments from the Riviera, "Philosophers and expelled college boys, movie directors and prophets predicting the end said people were restless because the war was over." Zelda finished the novel while recovering from a breakdown in 1932 at Phipps Psychiatric Clinic of Johns Hopkins University Hospital in Baltimore. Scott rented a house nearby called, ironically, La Paix ("The Peace"), and while in Baltimore in February 1933, the expelled college boy got to meet one of his literary heroes, the philosopher poet T. S. Eliot.[13]

T. S. Eliot and Garsington

While *Sinister Street* and *Hot-House* may not have risen to the level of the High Modernist canon, one American in Oxford had quite a lot to do with defining high modernism in the immediate post-war years. Thomas Stearns Eliot was born in St. Louis in 1888, the youngest of six surviving children of Henry Ware Eliot and Charlotte "Lottie" Champe Stearns. The St. Louis Eliots descended from New England Unitarians, and young Tom would follow the footsteps of his paternal grandfather, Rev. William Greenleaf Eliot, and brother Henry to "Unitarian Harvard" in 1906. He had read much as boy, but his grades on the entrance exams were hardly distinguished. After his first semester, he was already on probation for poor grades, even receiving a D from Charles Homer Haskins in Medieval History (despite Eliot's early love of Malory and Arthurian literature).[14] Eventually he was inspired by Harvard faculty like William James, Gilbert Murray (who returned to Oxford in 1908), and Bertrand Russell (visiting from Cambridge). He began publishing his poetry while at Harvard and earned his BA in comparative literature in three years. Becoming attracted to French writers and thinkers, Tom left for Paris in October 1910 and studied philosophy for one year at the Sorbonne. In Paris he sampled experimental art, music, and literature (Picasso, Braque, Ravel, Debussy, Proust, Dostoevsky), but he also read (for the first time) *The Divine Comedy* and experienced the medievalism of Wagner.[15]

While back at Harvard in 1911 for his AM in English Literature, Eliot's coursework included Chaucer, Medieval and Renaissance Drama, the History of Allegory, and Florentine Painting.[16] In his second year in graduate school he shifted to Philosophy, Philology, and Sanskrit, pursuing a PhD in Indian philosophy. Eliot was admitted as a Commoner to Merton College, Oxford, for the 1914–15 academic year, with a testimonial from Harvard's Dean ignoring Eliot's early failures and praising him as "a gentleman in whose character I have the utmost confidence."[17] He was later awarded a Sheldon Travelling Fellowship, and left in July 1914 for Marburg, Germany, where he was to attend a philosophy summer school. But that August Germany declared war on Russia and France, the summer school was suspended, and Eliot escaped Germany with little money—but, luckily, with American papers—reaching London by August 20. There he struck up friendships with Bertrand Russell and Ezra Pound, impressing the latter with his poem, "The Love Song of J. Alfred Prufrock." Eliot arrived at Merton to find less than fifty students at the college, among them six Americans, including fellow graduate student Percy Blanshard. Half of the British students then at Merton would perish in the war. At Merton, Eliot fell under the influence of Oxford idealist philosophers F.H. Bradley and Harold Joachim (his college tutor), attended Oxford lectures by R. G. Collingwood on Aristotle and J. A. Smith on Logic, and corresponded with fellow Harvard student abroad Norbert Wiener (then at Cambridge) regarding Wiener's essay, "Relativism."[18]

Eliot occupied rooms off staircase 2:1 in the St. Alban's Quadrangle at Merton, with a view across the quad to Christ Church Meadow. His letters and reminiscences of Oxford are puzzlingly contradictory. In one, he describes Merton and Oxford as "exceedingly comfortable and delightful," if "very foreign," while acquiring "the highest respect for English methods of teaching."[19] In a letter of October 1914 he wrote, "Oxford is not intellectually stimulating—but that would be a good deal to ask of a university atmosphere," and he complained to friends that he was fed up with "professors and their wives."[20] With the regular sports suspended for the duration of the war, Eliot joined the Merton Debating Society and spoke out against a motion from the president "that this Society abhors the threatened Americanization of Oxford."[21] "Mr. Eliot opposed and preserved the appearance of gravity," recorded the secretary, "which was more than the house did." Eliot pointed out, in a letter describing the debate to Eleanor Hinkley, how much the British owed to American culture in the form of movies, cocktails, and the fox trot![22] He despised the weather and food of Oxford, loved the countryside, took up rowing on the Isis, and made friends with both British and American students at Oxford. Among the latter were Blanshard, Francis Wendell Butler-Thwing (New College), and Scofield Thayer (Magdalen).[23] Christmas long vacation was spent in London, in Bloomsbury, where he could spend time reading Aristotle at the British Library, and at the seaside town of Swanage in Dorset.

Eliot was, of course, also writing poetry, with ironic detachment borrowed from Pound.[24] In all, six poems form the Oxford group

(1914–15), the most famous of which is "Mr. Apollinax," which contrasts the centaur-like Bertrand Russell with desiccated Oxbridge dons and their wives.

The following term Eliot started attending meetings of the Coterie, a mostly-undergraduate poetry-reading group, where he met Balliol undergrad Aldous Huxley and read "Prufrock." In March, at a lunch party in Scofield Thayer's Magdalen College rooms, T. S. Eliot was introduced to Vivienne Haigh-Wood, an aspiring artist from Lancashire and one of the "river girls" who occasionally came to Oxford to spend time with undergraduate men on the Cher or the Isis.[25] They punted, danced, and shared their love of poetry together. On the rebound from Thayer, Vivienne captivated Eliot and the two were married, almost secretly, at Hampstead Register Office on June 26, 1915. Vivienne and Pound believed that this would keep Eliot in England and spur his promising career as a poet. Harold Joachim wrote a letter to the Harvard Philosophy Department that June stating that "Mr. T. S. Eliot has . . . worked most thoroughly and enthusiastically," making much progress in "the study of Plato and Aristotle. . . . I am quite sure that Mr. Eliot's time at Oxford has been most profitably spent, and I am sorry to lose him as a pupil."[26] But Eliot had resigned from his assistantship at Harvard, and he and Vivienne took up residence in Soho. While he was to finish his thesis and send it to the philosophy faculty at Harvard, Eliot gave up on the doctoral degree.

Teaching now in a High Wycombe grammar school, and living in Russell's London flat, the newly married Eliot was quite done with Oxford, or nearly so. Mr. and Mrs. Eliot were regular visitors to Garsington Manor (Fig. 4), the Jacobean country house six miles from Oxford owned by the solicitor Philip Edward Morrell (an Old Etonian, Balliol man, and Liberal MP) and his wife, Lady Ottoline Violet Anne Cavendish-Bentinck Morrell, half-sister of the Duke of Portland. The flamboyant and bisexual Ottoline (Fig. 5), six feet tall with full, Pre-Raphaelite hair, was both adored and mocked by the Bloomsburies. The Morrells owned a townhouse at 44 Bedford Square, in Bloomsbury, where Lady Ottoline held salons in two rooms on Thursday evenings: In one room was a crowd singing and dancing, eating and drinking; in the other, "the sedate talkers."[27] Weekends and summer months were spent at Garsington, where Ottoline's guests for garden teas, lunches, swimming, and conversation included Virginia and Leonard Woolf, Eddy and Vita Sackville-West, Bertrand Russell (one of Ottoline's many lovers), Frieda and D. H. Lawrence, Lytton Strachey, the economist John Maynard Keynes, the art critic Roger Fry, the painters Augustus John and Mark Gertler, Aldous Huxley, Siegfried Sassoon, E. M. Forster, Ian Fleming, Lord David Cecil, Hugo Dyson, Henry James, Sir Winston Churchill, Lady Cynthia and Herbert Asquith, Lord Nuffield, the Duke of York (later King George VI), and George and W. B. Yeats.[28] In her memoirs, Ottoline described the Garsington gatherings as "theatre, where week after week a travelling company would arrive and play their parts. . . . How much they felt and saw of the beauty of the setting I never know."[29] Lytton Strachey described Garsington, with its poets and peacocks, as "Circe's cave." Ottoline was caricatured by D. H. Lawrence in his novel *Women in Love* (1920) and her rumored affair with a young stonemason at Garsington outed in *Lady Chatterley's Lover* (1928), while the whole Garsington crowd was bitingly satirized in Huxley's novel, *Crome Yellow* (1921).[30]

Ottoline was deeply hurt by these "betrayals" of her hospitality, especially by a man she described as "a son of the house"; one of the bedrooms at Garsington came to be known as "Mr. Huxley's room."[31] Aldous Huxley (1894–1963) read English at Balliol and graduated with a first in 1916. In *Crome Yellow*, his first novel, the stately house of Crome with "its three projecting towers" sits on the hills "like a fortification" above the town of Camlet, the same spatial relation of Oxford to Garsington (2–13, 10); hence Oxford is a Camelot and Garsington a mysterious castle luring young knights into its dark adventures. The lady of the manor, Priscilla Wimbush, is described as masculine and melodramatic, "with a massive projecting nose and little, green eyes, the whole surmounted by a lofty and elaborate coiffure of a curiously improbable shade of orange." (6). Huxley aims to avoid both "the dreary tyranny of the realistic novel" and the contemporary English bildungsroman, the latter "describing in endless fastidious detail, cultured life of Chelsea and Bloomsbury and Hampstead."[32]

Hurt as she might be by such caricatures, Ottoline never changed her ways. "Conventionality is deadness," she wrote in her diary in 1915, and lived true to that motto. She once presented a handwritten manifesto to Siegfried Sassoon urging him to join her at Garsington Manor, "to live the noble life: to live freely, recklessly, with clear reason released from convention." "She was a remarkable woman," asserts the curator of her vast library, Crispin Jackson, "a thrower of parties certainly but a friend to anyone in need, who made her house a centre of opposition to the Great War."[33] The Morrell's also had close ties to the university, and Oxford undergraduates like Huxley, Robert Graves, Harold Acton, Maurice Bowra, and Anthony Powell were among the visitors who flocked to Garsington soirees from 1915 to 1927. Despite a bad first impression made by Eliot, he and his wife became regular visitors to Garsington and frequent correspondents with Lady Ottoline.[34] It was through Garsington that Eliot met Virginia Woolf and became associated with the Bloomsburies, although he was never an integral part of the group.[35]

Despite the parties and famous friends, the thoroughly unhappy marriage between Tom and Vivienne Eliot "brought the state of mind out of which came *The Waste Land*."[36] Desperate for money, Eliot took up lecturing at the University of London (on John Ruskin, William Morris, Matthew Arnold, and William Pater, no less), writing reviews, and even banking—none of which could satisfy Vivienne's ambitions for him. Even the publication of his first book of poems, *Prufrock and Other Observations* (1917), paid for by Pound and exalted at Garsington, resulted in neither critical nor commercial success. Vivienne had long struggled with mental and physical illness—"lives on a knife-edge" according to Russell (who manipulated, if not outright seduced, her)—and she sought fame for herself by trying to take up a career in ballet: a pattern eerily similar to that of Zelda in Paris.[37] Her health worsened, and she became more and more dependent on Russell, while Tom attempted to join the U.S. Naval Intelligence Service once America had declared its entry into the war. Red tape prevented this before the Armistice was announced, and Tom began his transition from American Midwesterner to "European," in the way of his idol Henry James, "a consciously created identity, nourished by a peculiarly

American sense of the past."[38] For her part, Vivienne entertained such visitors as Ottoline Morrell, Huxley, and the Pounds for teas and dinner at their London flat.[39]

Midwestern author F. Scott Fitzgerald owned a copy of the book that would deliver the Arthurian version of the Waste Land myth to T. S. Eliot: Jessie Weston's *From Ritual to Romance* (1920).[40] In the very first sentence of the notes that accompany his poem, Eliot wrote: "Not only the title, but the plan and a good deal of the incidental symbolism of the poem were suggested by Miss Jessie Weston's book."[41] Among the many medieval and Oxonian allusions in *The Waste Land* are the dedication to Pound from (and numerous allusions to) Dante's *Divine Comedy*, references to both the Parsifal and Tristan/Isolde romances, a name borrowed from Huxley's *Crome Yellow*, a reference to Walter Pater's description of *Mona Lisa*, a mention of the Norse martyr St. Magnus, and a quote from Augustine's *Confessions*. While these are not as numerous as the classical and Shakespearean allusions in the poem, both Dante and Arthurian myth are crucial to the structure of *The Waste Land*.

The death of Eliot's father in 1919, Vivienne's constant health problems, his own exhaustion and depression (for which he was to receive psychiatric treatment in Switzerland), and a less than satisfying meeting with James Joyce in Paris all lay behind the writing of *The Waste Land*, revised by Pound, released serially in the *Criterion*, and published in book form in New York in late 1922.[42] Edmund Wilson and Fitzgerald were blown away by its jazz rhythms, while aesthete Anthony Blanche in Evelyn Waugh's *Brideshead Revisited* recited it from the window of his Oxford college rooms. But *The Waste Land*'s medievalism is too important to overlook. It hits the reader from the very beginning—the title derives from a sentence in Malory, the dedication is a quote from Dante's *Purgatorio*, and its first line borrows from a trope employed by Chaucer at the beginning of *The Canterbury Tales*.[43] Its closing scene depicts the narrator as the Fisher King, getting his lands in order before his impending death. Eliot, in his notes to this poem about ruin and death, recommends Weston with her assertion, "but of this one thing we may be sure, the Grail is a living force, it will never die."[44]

Cambridge University asked Eliot to deliver a series of lectures at the beginning of 1926, and he prepared by spending time in the south of France reading Jacque Maritain, wondering whether modernity might need the unity of the medieval world as expressed by Dante and Thomas Aquinas.[45] While preparing to deliver a paper at Oxford, Eliot expressed his appreciation of the audience:

> I am looking forward eagerly to coming down to Oxford. One always has hopes of undergraduates, almost the only kind of audience that is interesting to talk to. It would be a pity if we lost that hope, wouldn't it. The most hopeless of them are more intelligent and interesting than the same sort of man 10 years later.[46]

As early as 1921, Eliot tried to secure an affiliation with Oxford, and wrote to Ottoline for help.[47] His new employer Geoffrey Faber proposed Eliot for a research fellowship at Oxford, but the Fellows of All Souls declined to award the fellowship, perhaps finding his poetry too modern and iconoclastic. But Eliot was moving more toward the medieval in his spiritual life—which he described as "Anglo-catholic"—and began receiving training and attending morning services in the Church of England. Some members of the Bloomsbury Group turned on Eliot as he turned toward Christ. Virginia Woolf wrote bitingly to her sister in February 1928:

> I have had a most shameful and distressing interview with dear Tom Eliot, who may be called dead to us all from this day forward. He had become an Anglo-Catholic believer in God and immortality, and goes to church. I was shocked. A corpse would seem to me more credible than he is. I mean, there's something obscene in a living person sitting by the fire and believing in God.[48]

T. S. Eliot was baptized—in secrecy—on June 29, 1927, by the chaplain of Worcester College, Oxford, William Force Stead (1884–1967), at Finstock Church in the Cotswolds. Eliot's two adult sponsors were also members of the Oxford community, and he was later confirmed in the private chapel of the Bishop of Oxford, Thomas Banks Strong.[49] Born in Washington, D.C. and a graduate of the University of Virginia, William Force Stead was appointed to the U.S. Consular Service in 1908 and served in Liverpool and Nottingham. He was ordained in the Church of England in 1915 and served as curate at Ross-on-Wye before matriculating at Queen's College, Oxford, in 1917, taking his BA in 1921 and his MA in 1925. After serving two years as chaplain of St. Mark's Anglican Church in Florence, Italy, Stead returned to Oxford in 1925 and was chaplain at Worcester until 1933. A published poet, Stead was part of the circle of intimates of C. S. Lewis in his pre-Inkling days, and introduced Lewis to W. B. Yeats.[50]

T. S. Eliot and C. S. Lewis, both students of philosophy at Oxford, were each on a path from skepticism to Christianity in the late 1920s. Both were admirers of Dante and writing important literary criticism, and both became close friends and patrons of the writer and editor Charles Williams. They were not, however, fond of each other. It would take more than thirty years before these two famous Christian authors would have a true rapprochement.[51] In the 1920s they stood in opposition in a culture war over how language and poetry should convey truths in the modern world.[52] Fitzgerald was himself conflicted over these issues. Though a great admirer of Eliot's, Fitzgerald was, like Lewis, a failed poet who found prose fiction to be a more suitable outlet for his vivid imagery and colorful characters. Short stories and novels would serve as his tapestries, and like his Romantic heroes he would turn often to the Middle Ages for inspiration. Fitzgerald sent Eliot a copy of the *The Great Gatsby* in late 1925 with the following inscription:

> For T. S. Elliot [*sic*]
> Greatest of Living Poets
> from his enthusiastic
> worshipper
> F. Scott Fitzgerald

Eliot wrote back—after having read the novel three time—telling him that *Gatsby* "has interested and excited me more than any new novel I have seen, either English or American, for a number of years," and that the novel represented "the first step that American fiction has taken since Henry James."[53]

Eliot's sober and serious nature was sometimes at odds with the Garsington crowd. Lord David Cecil recalls a moment shortly after his conversion in which Eliot was provoked into defending his faith before a small crowd gathered for tea.[54] Eliot "must have turned to Christianity from a cowardly desire for comfort" said the attacker, Samuel Koteliansky. Far from being a comfort, Eliot replied,

> it had forced him to face the full dangers of the human predicament, not just in this life but in eternity; and it had burdened his soul with a terrible and hitherto unrealized weight of moral responsibility. . . . What he said [had] such a grave sincerity of conviction that it was impossible not to believe him. Koteliansky was silenced; and I myself listening felt that I had been given a glimpse into the depths of Eliot's grand and tragic spirit. I saw that Lady Ottoline felt so too.

"Eliot made occasional medieval gestures before 1927," writes Michael Alexander. "But after his conversion . . . medieval poems, prayers, rites and institutions became stations on his way in life."[55] His most blatantly medievalist work is, perhaps, *Murder in the Cathedral*, first performed in 1935. Oxford would award Eliot an honorary DLitt in 1948 and Merton College would name its new theater after him in 2010.

On a February day in 1933, T. S. Eliot and F. Scott Fitzgerald took a long walk near the estate of the Turnbulls in Maryland. Eliot was giving lectures at Johns Hopkins University and the Turnbulls hosted a dinner for him, inviting their dear friend Fitzgerald. Fitzgerald read some of Eliot's poetry aloud in tribute, and Eliot thought the performance good. As they walked they talked about many things, including Fitzgerald's next novel, *Tender is the Night*. Fitzgerald produced a carboy of gin to give to Eliot, and Mrs. Turnbull showed off her copy of Dante's *Divine Comedy*. Fitzgerald wrote soon after to Edmund Wilson: "T. S. Eliot and I had an afternoon + evening together last week. I read him some of his poems and he seemed to think that they were pretty good. I liked him fine. Very broken and sad + shrunk inside." "Fitzgerald seemed to me a very sick man at the time I saw him in Baltimore," Eliot later wrote to a friend. "I liked him and enjoyed our conversation, though I cannot now remember what topics were discussed. I *can* remember the . . . gin."[56]

Oxford, 1914—Towards War

At light of dawn,
When the May buds in the hedgerows
   White the thorn,
There's a song in Magdalen tower;
Then, as thunder in the blue,
A sound comes breaking through,
And we know it is not thunder as it comes;
We know it is the sound of distant guns.[57]

The lines above were written by an American student in Oxford in 1914, a Harvard student come to Oxford to do postgraduate work but whose experience of the City of Dreaming Spires differed significantly from that of T. S. Eliot. His name was John Brett Langstaff, and he left seminary in New York to study for the BLitt at Magdalen College that summer. Like many Americans who studied at Oxford in the nineteenth century, Langstaff came to "the dream city of the English intellect" with the intention of getting ordained as an Anglican priest.[58] At Magdalen he would become friends with Edward, Prince of Wales, and his cousin, Prince George of Teck, who were living together in undergraduate rooms in the Cloister at Magdalen. Both royals would leave Oxford in 1916 to join the British Expeditionary Force, and Langstaff (despite being an ordained priest) would join them as a volunteer. After being invalided out of service, he returned to New York to become a full-time minister and part-time scholar.

Decades later, Langstaff would write a memoir of his Oxford years, drawing on his personal diary and correspondence, which includes anecdotes of his meetings and friendships with an impressive array of writers, politicians, intellectuals, and nobles including George Santayana, the physician Sir William and Lady Osler, Lady Astor, Viscount Harcourt, Scofield Thayer, Violet Asquith, G. K. Chesterton, Kenneth Grahame, John Masefield, Sir George Parkin, Lewis Gielgud (Sir John Gielgud's brother), Robert Bridges, and Philip and Ottoline Morrell. Langstaff went out to Garsington on a motorcycle during Easter Vacation 1916:

> Great stone gates, a long low house rather startlingly deco-
> rated, and further down the side of the hill a large pond
> which can be used for bathing. . . . Lady Ottoline Mor-
> rell . . . is a woman of natural charm but a woman upon
> whom personal eccentricities have laid a heavy veneer.
> A strangely alluring drawl, a well painted face, costume
> clothes of costly material—can you see her seated in a smart
> trap driving a high-stepping tandem through the streets of
> Oxford![59]

Shortly after this visit, while performing the lead in *Ariadne in Naxos* at Magdalen, Langstaff drew noticeably on Ottoline's accent and affectations, and to his dismay he spied Lady Ottoline herself in the front row! While chastised afterward by John Masefield, Lady Ottoline slyly asked him later at tea where he found his accent, and commented, "Now we see what lurks behind these calm exteriors."[60]

Langstaff also describes meetings of the Nineties Club, an Oxford society which "conceives of the world as having come again to the same condition as it founds itself in the 1890s, and following the lead of the obscure men who followed Oscar Wilde they are busy marking time and making every effort to live only a sensuous life with no purpose in the future."[61] These aesthetes (mostly from Balliol and Christ Church, though Magdalen's Thayer had joined them) wore "long white cloaks, great rings on their fingers, [and kept] rare flowers in their rooms."

Despite the breezy prose and constant name-dropping, Langstaff's memoir is rooted in an Oxford worried and waning in the wake of the Great War. "A Rhodes Scholar has come back from his Red Cross work in Belgium," writes Langstaff, "and told me it was worth three years of Oxford."[62] Many American Rhodes scholars were swept into the war, whether through relief work or combat, and it is to their stories that we turn next.

6

Major Gatsby in Trinity Quad:
Oxford and the Great War

Dear Papa: This flying is much too romantic to be real modern war with all its horrors. There is something so unreal and fairy like about it, which ought to be told and described by Poets. . . .

—Victor Chapman (June 1, 1916)

Victor Chapman (1890–1916), an American aviator, wrote these lines in a letter to his father days before his plane was shot down behind German lines. The horrors of the Great War, more so than the sublimity of first flight, would be described famously by the British war poets, many of whom—Vera Brittain, Robert Graves, Julian Grenfell, Henry Newbolt, Robert Nichols, Charles Hamilton Sorley, Edward Thomas, Arthur West—had links to Oxford. But the celebrated war poets provide, typically, an aristocratic or upper-middle class—and almost exclusively white male—literary perspective on the war. A century later we are only now seeing the attitudes of the common soldier, the nurse, the family members on the home front. Through documents, but also through material culture, historians now recognize that the Great War was both global and local, both modern and a continuation of attitudes from an earlier age.[1]

"[H]e has been wise enough to keep God out of the war," wrote F. Scott Fitzgerald of H. G. Welles, "[for] if any war was made on earth it is this one."[2] While Fitzgerald had no direct experience with combat during the war, his characters Nick Carraway and Jay Gatsby did. In fact, remembrance of France during the war is what first brought these two characters together. But before we meet Gatsby in Trinity Quad, we need to meet his American comrades, those forgotten men who left but scant record on the pages of U.S. Army documents and Oxford college registers. What brought America into the war, and what brought these particular American soldiers to Oxford in 1919?

Oxford During the War

Blood was in the earth, the sea, and the air;
Yet fair in Oxford the City stood.
—Charles Williams, *The Advent of Galahad*, "Dedication"[3]

The Great War was one in which a generation of young men entered with visions of heroic action, and returned—if they returned—often with shattered views on war and politics. There had been much talk in Oxford in the first years of the twentieth century about German aggression and the threat it posed to the British Empire. In 1907, Britain abandoned its "Splendid Isolation" by joining France and Russia to form the Triple Entente, a response to Germany forming the Triple Alliance with Italy and Austria-Hungary. On June 28, 1914, Austrian Archduke and heir Franz Ferdinand was assassinated by Serbian nationalists, and Austria declared war against Serbia a few weeks later. The Great War had begun. Britain and France entered the war in August, following the

German invasion of Belgium, but America officially stayed out of the war until April 1917. Although the United States had been supplying munitions and money to the Allies, President Woodrow Wilson did not persuade Congress to declare war on Germany until after German submarines attacked several American ships and Britain turned over the intercepted "Zimmerman Telegram," in which Germany offered assistance to Mexico in regaining territory lost to the United States during the Mexican-American War.

Several American Rhodes scholars were caught on the Continent when the war broke out, and their accounts of getting back to Oxford are given in *The American Oxonian*, the quarterly periodical of the Association of American Rhodes scholars first published in 1914. Henry Furst, an American studying at Exeter College, and A. J. Dawe recounted their harrowing adventure in 1914 coming to the Belgian city of Louvain and witnessing German soldiers setting fire to houses and shooting the fleeing occupants.[4] These and stories of what British Oxford students were encountering in the first months of the war aroused desire in not a few Americans to do their part in the fighting.

Many Americans studying in Europe did not wait for an official declaration of war by their government. Hundreds volunteered to fight under British and French commanders, including several Rhodes scholars. In 1914 there were nineteen American Rhodes scholars serving in Belgian Relief, eighteen with the American ambulance corps in France, six working with soldiers through the YMCA, and two working for the Red Cross.[5] One of the Rhodes scholars drawn to the situation in Belgium was Charles Francis Hawkins (New York and Balliol, 1914).[6] An honors graduate of Williams College, Hawkins entered Harvard to conduct postgraduate research in Chemistry, receiving his MA in 1914 and beginning his doctoral study when he received the Rhodes. Three months after arriving in Oxford he volunteered for relief work in Belgium, returning to Oxford after six months to become president of the American Club and obtaining his BSc in 1917, after which he became an Instructor in Chemistry at Williams. He resigned after a term to enter the Chemical Warfare Service in Washington, D.C. as a private, soon after commissioned believed fervently that the men who went to war had been initiated into mysteries that they and only they could understand," writes J. M. Winter. "Whenever they met, in Oxford and elsewhere, they renewed this bond through reminiscence, conversation, regimental reunions, battlefield tours and the like. Those who didn't go . . . were outside this circle."[67]

In the original, handwritten manuscript of the novel that would become *The Great Gatsby*, there is a very different version of "that tremendous detail" about Oxford that Gatsby discloses to Nick:

> "No, I studied there—for six months. Perhaps you remember that a lot of American army officers were given a chance to go there just after the war."
>
> For some reason I wanted to slap him on the back but now suddenly he was telling me a lot of things. He had juxtaposed various events, he said, to make people wonder; his family were poor but he had inherited money or almost inherited it and the reason he had invented a golden spoon for himself was because he didn't believe he was the son of his parents at all.[68]

In this, the original version of his confession, Gatsby says that he *studied* at Oxford, that he was there *for six months*, and that Nick—as an officer in France himself—would be expected to know about the A.E.F. student program at Oxford. In the *Trimalchio* version of this scene, Fitzgerald simply has Gatsby say that "I was only there a few months."[69] But in the final version of *The Great Gatsby*, in the Plaza Hotel scene, Gatsby says, "It was nineteen-nineteen. I only stayed five months" (129). The original version takes for granted that Nick (and perhaps many readers) would know about the A.E.F. education programs, and that they involved actual studies. Following Maxwell Perkins's advice about providing more details about Gatsby's past one piece at a time, Fitzgerald adds in the final version the year, 1919, and correctly states that the A.E.F. program at Oxford lasted five months (March through July), not six.

as second lieutenant. Intending to return to Harvard after the war to finish his PhD, Hawkins was the victim of a chemical explosion at the American University Experiment Station in June 1918 and died a few months later from blood poisoning and pneumonia. Balliol College would remember his service in its *War Memorial Book*.

More famous still was William Alexander "Billy" Fleet, from Virginia, elected in 1904 as Magdalen's first Rhodes scholar. When he heard about his friends dying during the Great War, he returned to Britain in 1916 (on sabbatical from teaching) and persuaded the British authorities to allow him to join the Grenadier Guards.[7] He was commissioned and killed in Flanders in 1918, and his name is commemorated in the Fleet Fellowships at Magdalen. "He had a frank and boyish, I feel inclined to say guileless face," recalled Francis Wylie. "But there was nothing soft about him. . . . It was impossible not to like him."[8] The first American president of the Oxford Union, W. J. Bland (1913), was also killed in 1918 on the Western Front.[9] In all, 240 Rhodes scholars from the Dominions and Colonies participated in the war, and sixty-one scholars serving in allied services (in addition to eight of the forty-nine scholars serving in the Germany army) were among the casualties.[10]

In the first Somme Offensive, which began on June 1, 1916, more than in 420,000 British soldiers were killed or wounded. Before April of 1917 America had fewer men than that in its entire armed services, and relied on both the National Guard and conscription to quickly build and train an army. By the end of the war, over four and a half million American men—including some 200,000 African American soldiers—and 11,000 American women served in the U.S. armed forces.

Back at Oxford, life went on, but hardly as usual. Frank Aydelotte, then editor of *The American Oxonian*, wrote in October 1914:

> Oxford is open as usual this term although with only about one thousand undergraduates. The Schools have been transformed into a great hospital with beds and other equipment from the colleges. . . . Over a thousand Oxford

men have been given commissions in the English armies and most of the Colonial Rhodes Scholars have entered the service. . . . The newly elected Rhodes Scholars have gone up as usual; about thirty members of the class sailed from New York on September 23.[11]

By 1917, things had become quite precarious for the Americans in Oxford, and as the United States moved closer to joining the war effort, the Rhodes Trust was faced with canceling or postposing elections:

> The last two or three classes have melted away from Oxford without electing secretaries or leaving any trace of their whereabouts: for the 1914 and 1916 men we have only such addresses as chance has thrown our way. Almost all the younger men and many of the older ones are in military service, and the state of that service at present is such as to make definite information very hard to obtain.[12]

Rhodes scholar Wyatt Rushton (Alabama and Trinity, 1916) records that there were only two or three dons left in his college and "the small American fraternity" had been reduced to about thirty.[13] "Nearly all the candidates eligible by age and physical qualifications for holding the scholarships are also liable to be called upon for military service," Parkin wrote in a letter to the chairmen of the Committees of Selection, September 5, 1917. "I have learned that many intending candidates have already volunteered as soldiers and given up the thought of competing."[14] The Oxford correspondent for *The Times* wrote, on October 8, 1917:

> The American students, both the Rhodes Scholars and others, who have given it such a happy and friendly "stiffening" during the last three years, have now themselves, to their great satisfaction, gone to join their English brothers. There is left only an exiguous remnant, a few neutrals, a few very young students, who come for a term or two.

The American Oxonian records the following dramatic decline in numbers of undergraduates at Oxford during the war years:

1914–2,969
1915–1,030
1916–516
1917–434
1918–348[15]

One hundred and fifty undergraduates had been in residence at Trinity College during Trinity term 1914, but just fifty showed up in October, and only thirty remained by the end of the term. During Hilary and Trinity terms 1915 there were only twenty-five undergraduates, and a group photograph taken in summer 1917 showed only fourteen, six of whom were American Rhodes scholars. Wyatt Rushton, the first Rhodes scholar from Alabama, went to Paris to join the American Red Cross and later the U.S. military intelligence. Rushton was one of four Trinity College Rhodes scholars to die in the war.[16] In a farewell letter in *The Oxford Magazine* (October 19, 1917), the retiring vice-chancellor of the university mentions giving a tour of Christ Church to "a large party from a draft of ninety American cadets who are come to study here."[17]

Balliol had forty undergraduates in Trinity term 1918, while in other colleges five or six was the norm. There was only one Rhodes scholar then in Oxford, recorded *The American Oxonian*, a wounded man from the front, while the university hoped that its adoption of a new postgraduate degree, the Doctor of Philosophy (DPhil), in 1917, would bring more Americans to Oxford after the war.[18] The Rhodes Trustees also rescinded the rule that American candidates had to pass a qualifying exam. "We must picture Oxford, during World War I," write Philip and Carol Zaleski, "not as the neomedieval paradise it would like to be, but as the military compound it was obliged to become."[19]

There were, nevertheless, a few advantages of a depleted Oxford. Rushton comments that the remaining Englishmen in College are less reserved and less obsessed with their English friends and schoolfellows than would have been the case in peacetime.[20] Henry Canby, a Yale professor who visited Oxford for several months in the Spring of 1918, observed: "I shall always think of Oxford in wartime as a dreamy town, quiet in one hour except for the bells, and in the next hour stirred everywhere by the noise of marching feet and military commands and the buzz of dozens of aeroplanes over the towers."[21] T. S. Eliot, then at Merton College, describes in several letters the conditions of wartime Oxford. "Oxford even at this time is peaceful, always elegiac," he wrote in November 1914. "It is Alexandrine verse, nuts and wine."[22]

Too old to enlist, the English poet John Masefield instead joined the Red Cross as an orderly and was posted to France early in 1915.[23] Soon after that the future Poet Laureate was recruited by the Department of Information, who sent him to America on a lecture tour in the winter of 1915–16 and requested that he write accounts of the battle of Gallipoli, and later, the Somme.[24] In *The Old Front Line* (1917), he writes: "All wars end; even this war will some day end. . . . In a few years' time, when this war is a romance in memory, the soldier looking for his battlefield will find his marks gone." Masefield's lyrical and elegiac prose proved successful propaganda for Wellington House, which was particularly interested in his perception of American sentiment in areas settled by German-speaking immigrants. In January 1918 he returned to America for a second lecture tour that lasted until August.[25] He spent much of his time lecturing on college campuses and speaking to American soldiers waiting to be sent to Europe, including a battalion of African American soldiers. The American artist Jerome Blum painted Masefield's portrait during this 1918 visit, and both Yale and Harvard conferred honorary Doctorates of Letters on him.

Major Rogers: An American Rhodes Scholar Goes to War

America sent its own war poets and novelists to France—Alan Seeger, Joyce Kilmer, John Allan Wyeth, E. E. Cummings—both as early volunteers and as conscripts in 1918. Among the large numbers of

American troops arriving in June of 1918 were several Rhodes scholars, including one young officer who would receive his majority fighting in the Argonne campaign that Nick and Gatsby discuss at their first meeting. William Wayne McMillan Rogers Jr. (Fig. 6) was born on January 25, 1884, in Oxford, Mississippi, the son of William McMillan Rogers (1850–1890), a judge educated at Washington and Lee College and the University of Virginia. As a student at Mississippi Agricultural and Mechanical College (as Mississippi State University was then called), "Bill" Rogers studied electrical engineering and rose to first lieutenant in the "Lee Guards." He was a notable athlete, a two-year varsity football player and quarterback. Later he would play baseball and basketball as well at Southwestern Presbyterian University in Tennessee (now Rhodes College), and, like his father, he rushed Sigma Alpha Epsilon fraternity.

While at Mississippi A&M, Rogers served as associate editor of *The Reveille*, the school yearbook, and as president of the Engineering Society; he was also a member of the German Club and the Dialectic Society. In the 1907 *Reveille* he is described as

> alright as long as you lead him. . . . His greatest trouble is keeping his face washed and his hair parted. "Bill" has won fame for himself on the gridiron, and is an athlete of no small renown. He is an original thinker and does not fail to express his individual opinion. He has always been a leader in the classroom and out.

Rogers graduated in 1907 with a bachelor of science degree from Mississippi A&M and served as commencement orator. While at Southwestern from 1907–9, he played quarterback for the football team and was an editor for their yearbook, *The Sou'wester*. He also joined many social organizations, including The Mississippi Club and The Down-and-Out Club, whose motto was "Better to have loved and lost than never to have loved at all." As officer for the latter his title was "Knight of the Shattered Heart," an epithet that would have fit both F. Scott Fitzgerald and Jay Gatsby well.

William Rogers was awarded the Rhodes scholarship in 1911, the fifth student from Mississippi to be so recognized. He began his studies at Oxford that fall and was placed at St. John's College. Rogers read Law while at Oxford and was a member of the college's Essay Society. Rogers received a first in Jurisprudence and an Oxford BA in June 1914. After returning to the states, Rogers moved to Birmingham, Alabama, and practiced law with the firm Tillman, Bradley & Morrow (now Bradley Arant Boult Cummings LLP, Birmingham's largest law firm), becoming a partner on February 1, 1921.[26] With offices in the grand Empire Building on First Avenue, the firm acted as general counsel for several rail, steel, and oil companies.

William Rogers joined the National Guard in Alabama in June 1916, and was promoted to First Lieutenant, Field Artillery, that October. His first assignment was to the Mexican Border Service, as the United States attempted to locate Mexican revolutionary Pancho Villa and prepare for a possible German-funded invasion from Mexico in response to the Zimmerman Telegram. In August of 1917 Rogers was commissioned Captain in the U.S. Army and served for nearly a year in Alabama as an R.O.T.C. Instructor before departing for Southampton, England, on May 30, 1918.[27] As part of the 321st Field Artillery Regiment of the 157th Field Artillery Brigade, 82nd Division, he would have arrived at Le Havre, France, sometime that June and prepared with French troops for the St. Mihiel Offensive (Fig. 7).

Under the command of General John J. Pershing, the American Expeditionary Force (A.E.F.) had begun arriving in France in early June, at first in small numbers; eventually the A.E.F. included more than two million soldiers. The arrival of the American "doughboys" (as American soldiers had been dubbed) was at a crucial time, for a new peace treaty with Bolshevik-controlled Russia meant that Germany could commit as many as 260 divisions to the Western Front against an Allied force of just 169 divisions.[28] While Wilson and Pershing at first maintained strict independence of the A.E.F. from British and French commanders, Pershing allowed amalgamation at the division level after a successful German offensive in spring 1918 threatened Paris and the Channel ports. Coordinated Allied efforts along the Aisne and Marne rivers in July and August had pushed the Germans back, while defeats in the Middle East and Italy forced Austria-Hungary out of the war and the Ottoman Empire to collapse.

Oxonian Douglas Haig recorded his impressions of Pershing and the American doughboys in his private papers. General Pershing "hankers after a *great self-contained American Army*' but seeing that he has neither Commanders of Divisions, of Corps, nor of Armies, nor Staffs for same, it is ridiculous to think such an Army could function unaided in less than two years' time," wrote Haig in May 1918.[29] Pershing, "who is bed with flu, imagines now, though he said nothing at the time, that I had disparaged the American Army," recorded Haig in October. "Nothing was further from my thoughts. . . . The Americans have been so criticised by the French that they are very touchy."[30]

Captain Rogers successfully commanded F Battery of the 321st Field Artillery through the second half of 1918. Though part of an all-American division, the 321st nevertheless adopted the French 75mm guns. Rogers and his men set out from Toul Sector during the great Somme Offensive of 1918, as part of Pershing's independent First Army, and assaulted the German salient of St. Mihiel on September 12. Half a million American soldiers, supported by French tanks and an Allied air force of 1,500 planes, successfully drove out the Germans from this key position in northeastern France that September. This victory made possible the Meuse-Argonne Offensive, the last major offensive on the Western Front (Fig. 7). Gatsby asks Nick if he served in the Great War in the First Division (the first American division to suffer casualties but also the first to experience victory, at the Battle of Cantigny).[31] Finding out that they were indeed division comrades, Gatsby explains that he was commissioned as first lieutenant in the Seventh Infantry until June 1918, was promoted to captain before he reached the front, and following battle in the Argonne Forest he was promoted to major and given command of the divisional machine-guns (39, 117).[32]

Throughout October, Captain Rogers and the rest of his division cleared the Germans out of the Argonne Forest in what General Pershing would hail as the greatest victory in American history: twenty-two

American and four French divisions, extending from southeast of Verdun to the Argonne Forest, had engaged and beaten forty-seven different German divisions, representing 25 percent of the enemy's entire divisional strength on the Western Front.[33] As a revolution in Germany forced the abdication of Kaiser Wilhelm II, representatives of the Allied and the Central Powers met to sign the Armistice ending the Great War on November 11. William Rogers received his promotion to major and he was about to be called on to lead the largest and most ambitious international education project ever involving American students.

The A.E.F. Soldier-Students Invade Oxford

In mid-1918 American cadets and soldiers came to Oxford and were billeted in some of the colleges, the War Office having negotiated a flat fee for their room and board. The colleges were, for the most part, glad to receive this income given the reduction in matriculated student fees, though high-spirited British and American soldiers were the cause of some property damage in the colleges.[34] These soldiers stayed only for a short period of time before deployment, but in early 1919 the Armistice created a very different kind of "American Invasion."

There were many young Americans in Europe to be dealt with as the Allied leaders gathered to discuss peace. While former Princeton president Woodrow Wilson was still drafting his "Fourteen Points" for peace after the war, the presidents of American universities and colleges met to discuss methods of supporting American college students fighting in Europe. One result of these meetings was the creation of the American University Union in Paris (with an additional outpost in London), giving stranded American university students a temporary home and entertainments. Much more ambitious was a plan drafted by the Union's chairman, Dr. Anson Phelps Stokes, Secretary of Yale University, submitted to General Headquarters in February 1918 and approved soon thereafter by General Pershing. Stokes's recommendation was for continuous training in the French language and in the arts of war while hostilities continued, but after a ceasefire American soldiers could enjoy formal higher education suited for "a modern democracy," to make them more aware of "the duties of citizenship" and better equipped to solve "our nation's great social and industrial problems."[35] Curriculum would be supervised by the Y.M.C.A.'s new Army Education Commission, headed by Columbia University English professor Dr. John Erskine. The Y.M.C.A. would finance the entire project with $4.5 million in appropriations.[36]

The work of the Commission led to General Orders No. 30, in February 1919, which would place nearly 10,000 A.E.F. soldiers in universities throughout France and the United Kingdom for the duration of the Armistice. About 8,000 men applied for positions at British universities, but only 2,000 were selected, both officers and enlisted men, on the basis of their military record and academic standing (see Appendix B).[37] A requirement was that they had to have graduated or matriculated for at least two years in a university. As a column in *The Stars and Stripes* described it, "a college B.A. back in the States wants to take a post-graduate course in English literature or history or some other classical subject. The ways will be greased for him to listen to the best lecturers at Oxford or Cambridge, and the credits he gains will be counted toward his P.G. degree back in God's country."[38]

These A.E.F. students would be placed on "detached service" until June 30 in order to draw pay and commutation to cover expenses, and all were ordered to report in England by March 5 at the last remaining American army camp in Britain, Knotty Ash in Liverpool, where they would be sorted and assigned to one of sixty institutions of higher learning in the United Kingdom. The group was officially known as the University Detachment of the A.E.F. in the United Kingdom and its Commanding Officer was Colonel Francis F. Longley, C.E. Engineers, a graduate of West Point and MIT. On his staff of eighteen officers (headquartered at 47–50 Russell Square) were Major E. P. Hubble and Major William M. Rogers, both Rhodes scholars. Rogers would serve as Supervisor of the U.S. Army Students in London and Oxford, as well as Liaison Officer with the British Army. The application of each soldier selected was approved and signed by George E. MacLean (on behalf of the Army Education Commission) and F. F. Longley.[39] While special four-week courses were designed for the students at Aberystwyth, Cambridge, the Inns of Court, and medical schools in London, the intention was for most A.E.F. students to take regular term courses with British students and to interact as much as possible with college and university customs.

Majors Rogers and Hubble, assisted by First Lieutenant Lawrence Crosby (a Rhodes scholar at Trinity pressed into service), chose which of the A.E.F. students would attend Oxford and Cambridge.[40] Arrangements were made with the individual colleges at Oxford via Sir Francis Wylie, first Warden of Rhodes House. About 150 American soldiers, among them eight Rhodes scholars, began arriving in Oxford at 3 A.M. on March 17. "A whole trainload of 'blooming Yanks,'" predicted R. F. Taylor, "whose invasion of Oxford will go down in her archives as one of the most historic of the many eventful happenings of this war time" (Fig. 8).[41]

In early 1919 Oxford had started to come back to life, as both dons and students began returning from the British army. C. S. Lewis, just recently convalesced and back up at Oxford to resume his study of *Literae Humaniores*, described the atmosphere at University College in January 1919:

> There is of course already a great difference between this Oxford and the ghost I knew before: true, we are only twenty eight in College, but we *do* dine in Hall again, the Junior Common Room is no longer swathed in dust sheets, and the old round of lectures, debates, games, and whatnot is getting under weigh. The reawakening is a little pathetic: at our first [J.C.R. meeting] we read the minutes of the last [meeting]—1914. I don't know any little thing that has made me realize the absolute suspension and waste of these years more thoroughly.[42]

At the end of Hilary term 1919, there were 160 undergraduates at Balliol College, 113 of whom had been in the army.[43] In Trinity term there were 233, of whom 188 had seen service. Before the war the number of undergraduates had rarely exceeded 190.

Because the university began its Easter vacation three days later, many of the arriving Americans took the opportunity to attend lectures in London or else to tour the British Isles before the beginning of the next term. Lieutenant Melvin Brorby (Brasenose) wrote to his college alumni magazine that he would be spending his vacation "on a bicycle trip through southern England and Ireland."[44] There was also a depletion of tutors at Oxford (many dons had either perished in the war or not yet been released from the British army). When Trinity term at Oxford began, the Americans were free to attend whatever lectures suited them. On average the Americans attended about eleven lectures per week, more than that of the average Oxford undergraduate.[45] History, economics, and political science were the most popular academic subjects, but the dons were so overworked (writes one student) that "the old preceptorial system is not able to work to its best advantage, seminar courses taking its place."[46] The students were assigned to colleges, though only some lived in college, and at New College, at least, each student was assigned a "moral tutor" to introduce them to college life, give them academic advising, but also to keep an eye on them.

Many commented on the American students being drawn to sports, with rowing, tennis, and baseball—introduced to Oxford by these American students—being the most popular. Two American officers (Captain Lovejoy and Lieutenant Walker) were in the winning boat at the Summer Eights that year and later rowed at Henley, one Rhodes scholar (Hopkins of Balliol) made the varsity tennis team, while the Oxford-American baseball team was undefeated and won the championship of the British Isles![47]

Among the most prominent members of the group, there was "the curious case of Benjamin Selden Bacon," from Lyme, Connecticut, a member of one of the great families of Yale. His father, Benjamin Wisner Bacon, was a professor in the Yale Divinity School. His great-grandfather, Rev. Leonard Bacon, was a New Haven pastor active in the anti-slavery movement who taught the imprisoned passengers of the *Amistad*. Benjamin S. Bacon, a member of the Freshman Glee Club and president of his class, rowed in the second eight for Balliol.

In the same boat that summer was Lieutenant Clark Hopkins of New Haven, who became Professor of Art and Archaeology at the University of Michigan and founder of its Great Books Program. He was a Senior Fulbright Fellow, and rejoined the army in World War II as a Lieutenant Colonel. The son of a Yale professor of Sanskrit, Professor Hopkins led the joint French-American excavations at Dura-Europos in Syria.

Captain Aaron Bradshaw of Brasenose was a career military man from West Point. He would become commanding general of anti-aircraft in North Africa during World War II, a brigadier general who served under both George S. Patton and Mark Clark. He was decorated by America, Britain, France, and Italy (earning the Distinguished Service Medal, the Silver Star, the Bronze Star, the Legion of Merit, and the O.B.E.), retiring as Major General. Also at Brasenose was Bradshaw's West Point classmate, Captain Frank Markoe. Severely wounded in the Meuse-Argonne campaign, he entered a Trappist monastery after his time in Oxford and later attended the Georgetown School of Foreign Service. Markoe served as an army colonel in World War II, with the Fifth Army in North Africa and Italy, earning the Legion of Merit, and after the war worked for the CIA. He was also a member of the White Bear Yacht Club near St. Paul, Minnesota, where Scott and Zelda Fitzgerald would live in the summer of 1921, Scott making there his first plans for the novel that would become *The Great Gatsby*.

Lieutenant Lawrence Crosby, a football player and Rhodes scholar from Maine, had earned a law degree at Columbia before joining the A.E.F. When he returned to Oxford he took on the teaching duties of a Trinity College law tutor who had not yet been released from service by the British army. In 1923 he co-authored *A Manual for Prospective Rhodes Scholars* with Frank Aydelotte, and practiced law in New York City. Lieutenant Thomas A. Morgan, who had attended Harvard and served as aide-de-camp to Brigadier General Evan Johnson, survived being gassed and hospitalized for four months to join the American

Students' Detachment at Oxford.[48] While Harvard and Yale, predictably, accounted for more than a quarter of all the A.E.F. students, the state of West Virginia had quite a presence at Oxford in Trinity 1919: three Rhodes scholars (Corporal Frederick M. Smith, Rexford B. Hersey, and Sergeant Julian L. Hagen) and Army Chaplain Curtis Chenoweth were among the eight West Virginians in residence.

Many Oxford colleges offered placement to the A.E.F. students but minimal, if any, housing in-college.[49] In-college housing at Oxford was scarce in part because some 3,000 undergraduates also returned to Oxford during the Armistice. As for Major Rogers, he was "often seen playing about town" with Major Hubble, reported *The American Oxonian*. The idea of providing a rigorous, Oxbridge education to American soldiers must have struck some on both sides of the pond as rather amusing. Corporal Brown of the 51st Pioneer Infantry saw fit to lampoon the plan in a poem for *The Stars and Stripes* titled "HELL, YES!":

> "Private Perkins, take the floor,
> Scan this philosophic law,
> Who was Kant and who was Locke?
> Why did Hick'ry Dick'ry Dock
> Run about and play when he
> Might have read philosophy
> And learned to talk in high-brow strain?
> I dare you, sir, to make it plain."
>
> Now ain't that a scrumptious way
> For a hulkin' man to play?
> Next they'll teach us how to dress.
> HELL, YES!—HELL, YES![50]

With "To the Oxford Men in the War," Rhodes scholar and poet Christopher Morley (Maryland and New College, 1910) added more sober lines to those of the many British poets who commemorated Oxford's great losses in the Great War:

O my brothers, my more than brothers—
Big, intolerant, gallant boys!
Going to war as into a boat-race,
Full of laughter and fond of noise![51]

According to one of the A.E.F. students in Oxford, the Americans did, in fact, take to British civilian clothing ("Oxford bags" being more comfortable than American military uniforms) and adopted British ways of speaking: "'rawthuh' and 'I don't know at all' are bandied about almost without taking thought," while a "certain lieutenant" from Worcester College "is responsible for the following yell: *Righto-cheerio! / How's your fathah? / Can we play baseball / Rawthah! Rawthah! / Oxford! Oxford! Oxford!*"[52] Gatsby's favorite phrase, "old sport," it seems, would have fit right in.

"Eights' week was a dazzling experience for those of us who had known only a war-time Oxford," writes one Rhodes scholar. "It was very wonderful and beautiful . . . to see the Isis ablaze with color and life, the barges swarming with real girls . . . the Cher so jammed with punts that you could cross from bank to bank as safely as on the old pontoons on the Vesle!"[53] While Magdalen went to the head of the river that year followed by New College, the Rhodes House boat finished third.

There were two Oxford clubs that served the particular needs of American students at the university: the New American Club (with spacious quarters in George Street) and the British-American Club (whose American officers were both Rhodes scholars). The former hosted talks by Mr. Wylie and Dr. Parkin along with "other well-known Oxonians," while Mrs. Wylie hosted several tea parties for the men.[54] The British-American Club, newly formed as a result of increased interest in postwar international relations (and speculation about the roles America and Great Britain would play in the League of Nations), sponsored guest lectures in 1919 and 1920 given by visiting dignitaries, including the American Ambassador to the Court of St. James, James W. Davis, named as the American President of the Club.

We possess written accounts of these five months penned by a few of the A.E.F. students, as well as a description from one of their Oxford dons. Private Reuben Taylor, a Rhodes scholar from Kentucky, writes in *The American Oxonian*:

> I don't know what tales are told in the official semi-monthly reports that go into headquarters, but I'm sure, if the truth were told, the greatest thing these Yanks are deriving from their term in Oxford is found on the Cher and Isis, on the tennis courts, [and] along the deep cut lanes which lead through lush meadows. . . . Bikes are few and far between, but the more hardy have small need of them. . . . Some have clung to our National Sport, with the result that Oxford now boasts a champion baseball team which has administered severe trouncings to Cambridge and Manchester. . . . The punt pole, however, and the cricket bat are still objects of suspicion and are considered among those things which are better left in the hands of others. [55]

A note made in the minutes for April 25, 1919, by the sub-bursar of New College said, "It was agreed [by the Warden and Tutors] to excuse the American Officers in residence this term from Roll Call" for chapel. [56] "It is really too much to expect anyone to do any serious work," concurs Private Taylor, "but we are not without honors" (Lieutenant Crosby annexing two more Oxford degrees, Captain Ray and Sergeant Foster completing their BAs, and Sergeant Bosworth his master's).

Lieutenant John Dyer, from Ohio State University and assigned to Mansfield College, wrote a short reflection for his American camp newsletter:

> Oxford University is prouder of its history and age than of any other item. Many of its buildings are old and weather-beaten, and would not be considered a credit to the average American campus. . . . Despite its buildings and its antiquity, or perhaps because of them, the school is progressive and keenly awake to the great problems of the day, such as history, both ancient and modern. [57]

Modern history and economics had, in fact, much more charm for many Oxford students than did Classics after the war. One particularly popular lecturer was Professor C. Grant Robertson of All Souls, who delivered a series of lectures on "The Problems of the Versailles Peace Conference." Nearly every British and American officer in Oxford attended these lecturers, it is said. Professor Robertson himself wrote a very positive description of the A.E.F. program in Oxford for *The American Oxonian*:

> The visit of the American Army Students was welcomed by everyone in Oxford. As one who has some share both in the teaching and in the administration of the University I know that the proposal was most warmly supported from the very first. . . . We would gladly have had them for [an entire] year, because Oxford could have done more for them. We all regarded the visit . . . as a means of bringing Oxford into a closer relation with the American universities—as a beginning of that interchange of students and of teachers which in Oxford we wish to see accomplished as one of the great indirect results of the war. [58]

Robertson admits that there were skeptics at Oxford who expected the Americans to be both idle and the cause of idleness in other students. But he found it to be otherwise:

> First, the American Army Student came apparently determined to get all he could, all the more because he had only one term to get it in. He wanted to touch our Oxford life and teaching at as many points as possible. . . . He 'sampled' a good many teachers and lecturers. . . . Secondly, I was much impressed by the high level of keenness. The Americans came for business. They did not come for play. [N.b. that Robertson comments on the exception of baseball.] I don't know that he read much—I doubt whether he had time for serious reading—but he worked and in most cases he worked hard. . . . Thirdly, they struck one as being very appreciative

of any help one was able to give. . . . I was much touched by the way the American Army Student quickly appreciated what I was trying to do and how I was trying to teach and his thanks were embarrassing in their sincerity and cordiality. . . . I have no criticism to offer.[59]

This was not true of all their tutors, however, though only a couple of colleges kept any record of their comments. "A talker more than a worker," wrote one Keble tutor.[60] "Not the best of our Americans." "'Is real tickled' with lectures," wrote another. "A good American: earnest, no sense of humour, childlike." A student from Wisconsin was described as "A good, strong, simple hearted man, reading geology with a view to Mining engineering."

Rev. Chenoweth, one of two army chaplains in the group, left a brief account in the *Mansfield College Magazine*:

I perceive that it may be interesting, and must certainly be amusing, to note how much or how little an American mind can sense the truth as it is about Oxford in the course of one Trinity term. . . . In fact it is not possible to be here a much shorter time than has been our privilege without having sensed something of the power of [Oxford's] tradition, the delight of its social life, and the uniqueness of its efforts on the behalf of knowledge. . . . And it is little short of marvelous that in one hour's run from the great Metropolis [of London] one may drop right into the midst of another world, a world in which life has somehow got rid of that plodding, near-sighted regard to the present, and has lengthened itself out into the span of many centuries, where the now and the future may draw without stint on the treasures accumulated throughout all the yesterdays.[61]

This romantic view of Oxford does not cloud Chenoweth from seeing differences in study habits between English and American students at Oxford:

Oxford at play and Oxford at work are so difficult to distinguish, that one must observe caution in their treatment. . . . In America a large section of the student personnel finds its pleasure in work, . . . plain, exacting, monotonous work. And many students aspire to nothing else than to be known as workers. . . . Here apparently that sort of thing 'isn't done.' If a man must work the necessity arises from some weakness within himself. . . . Lectures are tolerated, books are treated with condescension. In America the drudgery of work is the penalty which the student must pay for his ignorance. Here there is no penalty. The student is to pass from his intellectual boyhood to maturity by the easy stages of natural growth.

As the author of the "J.C.R. Notes" in the same issue of the *Magazine* states more succinctly, "the overseas friends from the United States . . . contributed a great deal to the life of the J.C.R., and their stay will not be forgotten."[62] As for the American view, Lieutenant Dyer wrote that, "Almost without exception the two thousand" American soldier-students in Britain "have come home warm admirers of a really great people whom we have failed to understand."[63]

Failure to understand Oxford is a state in which American visitors often find themselves, visiting students and Rhodes scholars not excepted. Nevertheless, this was, for most, the happiest time of the war, and that certainly seems reflected in the survivors who taught and studied at Oxford. Many commented on the unusually sunny and dry months of Trinity Term 1919, and thus a great optimism undoubtedly colors these days leading up to the Treaty of Versailles. The American soldiers—like Gatsby—wanted first and foremost to go home, but most also took full advantage of academic, athletic, and social activities offered by their college and the university. While an impressive group of men, it was not a very diverse one, apart from representatives from different states and regions. Ambition and achievement in higher education are the most common factors among the A.E.F. students. Law, medicine, the professoriate, and the military were the most popular professional fields, along with a variety of careers in business. Dreaming of making money while playing sports at Oxford, dreaming of returning to America a hero and a man who commands respect—these are things that Jay Gatsby and Meyer Wolfsheim play to their advantage in the novel. But there must have been other dreams for Gatsby as well, inspired by the spires and quads of Oxford colleges.

Many A.E.F. students were on hand to witness Encaenia that June, when General Pershing and Field Marshal Haig were among those awarded the honorary degrees of Doctor of Civil Law (Fig. 11), and about thirty-five of the students performed in the Oxford Victory Pageant. A column in the June 13, 1919, issue of *Stars and Stripes* mentions "the conferring of a degree by Oxford University on Casual Buck Private Frank Reid, of the A.E.F., a former Rhodes scholar who already had three university degrees."[64] Frank Alphonso Reid (Virginia and Oriel, 1908), a student at and later president of the Board of Trustees of Roanoke College, was a skilled debater who became an attorney.

Before he was mustered out of service in August, Major William Rogers was awarded an honorary Order of the British Empire (O.B.E.) by King George V for distinguished service to Great Britain during the war. He returned to Alabama and to his law practice, and in 1925 married Lydia Edith Eustis (1894–1991), a nurse who had worked for the American Red Cross at Camp Sheridan during the war.[65] Rogers served as president of the Birmingham Bar Association in 1933, the year that his son William Wayne McMillan Rogers III was born.[66] After retiring from the practice of law, William Sr. would serve as chairman of the board and president of Birmingham Electric Company until 1948. He died May 10, 1951.

Major Jay Gatsby

It is significant that the first bond between Nick Carraway and Jay Gatsby is their common experience in the Great War. Acknowledging that they were both members of the same division, they identify their respective regiments and compare stories about gray French villages. Harold Macmillan, later prime minister, "was one of the many who

As we have seen, many of the records of the A.E.F. students in Oxford indicate that they embraced sports, both indulging in Oxford's traditional physical displays—rowing, polo, cricket, tennis, rugby—as well as introducing American baseball. One of the pieces of evidence substantiating Gatsby's claims about Oxford is the photo of him in cricket attire standing in Trinity Quad next to "the Earl of Doncaster." Bruccoli points out that the Earl of Doncaster was one of the titles borne by Walter John Montagu-Douglas-Scott, eighth Duke of Buccleuch, but that he did not succeed to this title until 1935.[70] The duke had attended Christ Church before the war, and from 1919–22 he was Earl of Dalkeith. Either Fitzgerald was ignorant of these facts or Gatsby was mistaken about the title of the man, who may indeed have returned to Oxford for a game of cricket, not an uncommon reason for old members to return to Oxford.

The reader is introduced to Tom Buchanan early in the novel as he finishes a polo match and rushes to greet Nick. Much later, Gatsby introduces Tom to his party guests as "Tom Buchanan, the polo player." Gatsby's calling Tom "the polo player" is at once both accurate and a dismissal of the relevance of his rival, hence Tom's irritation. "He is from old money and privilege," Gatsby seems to imply, "and plays sports rather than leading men in battle or industry, squanders inherited wealth rather than creating business 'opportunities.'" If this is so, then Gatsby misses the point of Oxonian sports: They are not just boys' games, but means of building social networks and business ties, as well as physical rigor for future soldiers, or, as in the case of the A.E.F. students, those on temporary leave.

There is no record other than *Gatsby* indicating that Fitzgerald knew the details of the A.E.F. education program. Fitzgerald's friend John Dos Passos, however, does mention the program briefly in his second novel, *Three Soldiers* (1921), in which the character Lieutenant Bleezer says, to a comrade wanting to study at the University of Paris, "I am going to Oxford myself." Dos Passos had joined the Norton-Harjes Ambulance corps in June 1917 and witnessed the Battle of Verdun in August. Scott and Zelda first met Dos Passos at the Plaza in October of 1922 and he was with them while they house-hunted in Great Neck, Long Island, with Ring Lardner. They all joined the party circuit along the Gold Coast over the succeeding months, and Scott would meet Tommy Hitchcock that April amidst talk of polo, Oxford, and the war.

Fitzgerald could have learned about the A.E.F. program at Oxford from Dos Passos or Hitchcock (though neither participated in it) or from a chance meeting with one of the participants like William Rogers (they were both at Camp Sheridan) or Frank Markoe (perhaps at White Bear Lake when the Fitzgeralds lived there). The evidence is circumstantial, but seems more than coincidental. What we do know for certain is that Fitzgerald had evolved as a writer steeped in medieval and Romantic poetry, inspired by the genre of the Oxford Novel, and after the success of his first two bildungsromans had the opportunity finally to travel to Europe and meet some of his literary heroes. By the time he reached Oxford in 1921, the university had rebounded after the war and was producing a generation of influential writers and thinkers unmatched even in its own illustrious history. A large part of the success of these Oxonian authors—J.R.R. Tolkien, C. S. Lewis, Aldous Huxley, Evelyn Waugh, Robert Graves—was due to their literary conversations with the past. In the next chapter we will eavesdrop on these conversations, and explore in more detail the ways in which Fitzgerald reimagines the Middle Ages.

7

The Castle and the Grail: J.R.R. Tolkien, C. S. Lewis, and Modern Medievalism

... to us remains
One city that has nothing of the beast,
That was not built for gross, material gains,
Sharp, wolfish power or empire's glutted feast.
We are not wholly brute. To us remains
A clean, sweet city lulled by ancient streams,
A place of visions and of loosening chains,
A refuge of the elect, a tower of dreams.
    —C. S. Lewis, "Oxford," in *Spirits in Bondage* (1919)

These colleges. . . . The spell was laid upon them long ago,
"the Dream of the Middle Ages."
    —Paul Elmer More, *Pages from an Oxford Diary* (1937)

Shortly after the arrival of the Fitzgeralds in the south of France in May 1924, Scott wrote a letter to Thomas Boyd: "This is the loveliest piece of earth I have ever seen without excepting Oxford or Venice or Princeton or anywhere. . . . I'm going to read nothing but Homer + Homeric literature—and history 540–1200 AD until I finish my novel. . . ."[1] The novel was *The Great Gatsby*, considered a classic example of American high modernism and the defining work of the Jazz Age. And yet, if Fitzgerald can be trusted here (he writes in the same letter that he and Zelda were "but a little tight and very happily drunk"), it was not modernity and contemporary literature that was on his mind as he wrote the bulk of his greatest work. Rather, perched in his Mediterranean villa, it was to ancient literature and medieval history that he would turn for inspiration.

He was not alone. For at Oxford at this time were two writers just beginning their careers, both veterans of the Great War, both scholars of medieval literature and great friends who gathered about them like-minded retrogrades forming a group at Oxford known as the Inklings. Though they had never met Scott Fitzgerald, never visited America, and would never have embraced the Jazz Age lifestyle, J.R.R. Tolkien and C. S. Lewis shared with Fitzgerald a love of epic, of poetry, and of the colors of the European Middle Ages. If Edith Wharton had, according to Fitzgerald in the same letter, "fought the good fight with bronze age weapons when there were very few people in the line at all," Tolkien and Lewis were then sharpening their Iron Age swords for a fight against modernism—against, indeed, modernity itself—from the sweet city of ancient streams and towering dreams.

J.R.R. Tolkien

John Ronald Reuel Tolkien (known to his family as Ronald) was born in Bloemfontein, at the time part of the Orange Free State of South Africa, on January 3, 1892.[2] His parents, Arthur Reuel Tolkien and Mabel Suffield, moved from Birmingham to the Boer Republic for Arthur's job in the Bank of Africa. He died suddenly in 1896 leaving Mabel to bring up two young boys in a rural suburb of Birmingham with no home and few possessions. When Mabel died from diabetes in 1904, Ronald Tolkien and his brother Hilary were put in the care of

Father Francis Morgan, a priest at the Birmingham Oratory who had guided Mabel's conversion to Catholicism. Ronald had, by then, won a place at King Edward VI School in Birmingham city center where he studied Classics but also became attracted to the Old English and Gothic languages. He and his school friends would found a club—the Tea Club and Barrovian Society (or T.C.B.S.)—dedicated to their mutual appreciation of ancient and medieval literature, history, and art. Most of the T.C.B.S. also excelled on the rugby pitch. At a boarding house in Birmingham he would also fall in love with Edith Bratt, a fellow lodger and orphan four years his senior.

On his second attempt, Ronald Tolkien won a scholarship to study Greats at Exeter College, Oxford, arriving (by motorcar!) in October 1911. His placement at Exeter was fortuitous, for as a practicing Catholic he was at a fourteenth-century college with the greatest number of Catholic students at Oxford in the Edwardian era.[3] Exeter had been the college of Pre-Raphaelites William Morris and Edward Burne-Jones (a fellow King Edward's grad), thoroughly Anglo-Catholic in the years that the Oxford Movement's Joseph Loscombe Richards was its rector. The Burne-Jones designed, William Morris and Company crafted tapestry, *The Adoration of the Magi*, still hangs in the Exeter College chapel. Tolkien adored his ancient-new home, "tower crownèd in its dreamy robe of grey/ . . . Proudly wrapt in mystic mem'ry . . . ," as he described it in an early poem.[4]

Not unlike the aristocratic and *ennui*-filled undergraduates of the Oxford Novel, Tolkien threw himself into sports, dining and debating, and reading for private pleasure rather than for the required examinations. The Oxonian journalist John Garth has recently disclosed insightful details about Tolkien's life as a student both at King Edward's and at Exeter College, and Exeter and the Tolkien family have also made public some photos and drawings from these years.[5] As a freshman Tolkien founded the Apolausticks, a group of twelve Exonians devoted to fine food (including at least one nine-course dinner at the Randolph Hotel!), drinking, and literary discussions. Comprised mostly of the sons of professionals—with three Rhodes scholars among them—the group's first topic for discussion was Lewis

Carroll.[6] Tolkien also belonged to the Exeter Essay Club, the Dialectical Society, and the Stapledon Society, Exeter's version of the Oxford Union. Despite his association with these literary societies, Tolkien was described by Exeter's sub-rector during his first year as "very lazy" and warned that he might lose his scholarship if he continued to play pranks like stealing a bus for a joy ride or scaling the Swiss Cottage (for which he was arrested). In 1912 he boasted of a prank played on American Rhodes scholar Milton Hoffman (Michigan and Exeter, 1910), tripping the latter on the Thames towpath and nearly causing him to fall into the river![7] Tolkien admitted, years later, to his son Michael that he had fallen "back into folly and slackness and misspent a good deal of my first year at College," due, he says, to the forced separation (mandated by Father Francis) from his beloved Edith.[8]

Despite his merry-making, however, Tolkien distanced himself from the aristocratic Aesthetes and the avant-garde early in his undergraduate days at Oxford. As an active participant in the Stapledon Society, Tolkien frequently debated the likes of T(homas) W(ade) Earp, the son of an affluent Liberal MP, described by Roy Campbell as "the last, most charming, and wittiest of the 'decadents.'" Tolkien called him "a blushing débutant" and "the original twerp," and both mocked and praised him for his witticisms.[9] As Oxford Union President, T.W. Earp drew the wrath of Oxonian rugby-players like Tolkien for lampooning sports. After Oxford, Earp became an art critic and friend of the Eliots and Lady Ottoline Morrell, who photographed him. "How different the young men are to the Cambridge undergraduates," wrote Ottoline of Earp and his Balliol friend Aldous Huxley:

> They seem so soft and effeminate, elegant with gentle unaffected movements and voices. Tommy Earp is an amusing character, with a high voice and an odd amusing mind. He is very rich and generous. . . . In spite of their apparent flippancy and frivolity they are seriously anti-war.[10]

Eventually Earp and Tolkien seem to have been on more friendly terms: both were Exonians in the English School, and they shared an interest in publishing good undergraduate poetry. One wonders if Tolkien would have read Earp's Arthurian and Keatsean poem, "Broceliande," published in *Oxford Poetry* in 1916:

> In the midst of the forest silence,
> Where even the leaves are mute,
> Where never bird wanders,
> She plays upon a lute.
> . . . bright with jewels,
> She would sit crowned on high,
> But if she left the forest,
> Alas, the trees would die.[11]

The undergraduate poetry of Earp and Tolkien, like that of Fitzgerald, shows an effort to imitate the meter and rhyme schemes of Shelley and Keats. Only later would Tolkien attempt poetry inspired by the alliteration and half-lines of Old and Middle English verse. His Oxford poetry also sought to convey the enchantments of Faerie, in a manner closer to Keats and Yeats, as in these lines from "Goblin Feet" (1915), a poem Earp would have known:

> I must follow in their train
> Down the crooked fairy lane. . . .
> And the echo of their padding feet is dying!
> O! it's knocking at my heart—
> Let me go! O! let me start!
> For the little magic hours are all a-flying. . . .[12]

Distracted from his study of Classics by an active social life, his longing for Edith, and his newly discovered love of Welsh and Finnish, Tolkien received only a second on his Honours Moderations in 1913 and was advised to change his course to the (newly founded) English School. The change was momentous—he was allowed to keep his Classics scholarship, and now he would be able to apply the philology he had learned in Greats to the Old and Middle English texts that had become his passion and would establish his future academic reputation. In July 1915 Tolkien won first class honours in English and soon after finished his training as a signaling officer (A.A. Milne was also a signaler), with the rank of second lieutenant, in the Lancashire Fusiliers. He married Edith in March 1916 and two months later embarked for France. Before he left Albion's shores, however, he penned a farewell ode to Oxford, not knowing if he would ever again see the ancient city, titled "The Wanderer's Allegiance":

> Thy thousand pinnacles and fretted spires
> Are lit with echoes and the lambent fires
> Of many companies of bells that ring
> Rousing pale visions of majestic days
> The windy years have strewn down distant ways;
> And in thy halls still doth thy spirit sing
> Songs of old memory amid thy present tears,
> Or hope of days to come half-sad with many fears. . . .
> O aged city . . .
> Most peerless-magical thou dost possess
> My heart, and old days come to life again. . . .[13]

Much has been written about Tolkien and his friends in the T.C.B.S., of this his first fellowship tragically sundered by the Great War. As Tolkien joined the Somme offensive in the summer of 1916, news began arriving of the loss of his Birmingham friends, only one (Christopher Wiseman) surviving the war. Tolkien managed to avoid the bullets and shrapnel only to contract trench fever in November and was invalided to hospital in France before being shipped home. The fever would plague him for nearly two years, as he moved between hospital bed and light defensive duty in Yorkshire and Staffordshire until the end of the war. Much of this time was spent on transforming his childhood love of fairy stories into rich, mature tales of the tragic race of the Elves of Middle-earth. Decades before the appearance of *The Lord of the Rings* (1954–55), the invalided philologist was inventing Elvish languages and early poetic versions of what he called his "mythology for England."

As Tolkien returned to life at Oxford in late 1918 he did so without fulltime academic employment and with a wife and child to support. In January 1919, just days before the "American invasion" of A.E.F. soldier-students in Oxford, Tolkien began working on the staff of the *Oxford English Dictionary*. This opportunity came by way of his Old Norse tutor William Alexander Craigie, the Rawlinson and Bosworth Professor of Anglo-Saxon at Oxford. In the *OED* offices on Broad Street, next to the Bodleian Library, Tolkien worked with a team of philologists on the volume *W*. He loved the work, and in June he was asked by Kenneth Sisam, another former tutor, to create a glossary of Middle English for Sisam's forthcoming book, *Fourteenth-Century Verse and Prose*. It took him more than two years to finish, missing the publishing deadline, but appeared to great critical acclaim in 1922. Tolkien also took on tutoring in English for extra pay. Many of his pupils were from the women's colleges, and at least one was a Rhodes scholar: the Canadian E. V. Gordon, who would become a colleague of Tolkien's at Leeds and collaborator on an edition of *Sir Gawain and the Green Knight*. In March of 1920 Tolkien also shared publicly, for the first time, one of his Elvish tales, reading the tragic "The Fall of Gondolin" to the Exeter College Essay Club.[14]

Tolkien's first full-time teaching post was at Leeds, where he was a popular teacher and eventually received a professorship, but he would return to Oxford in 1925 to take up the Rawlinson and Bosworth Professorship of Anglo-Saxon when William Craigie left for Chicago to work (ironically) on the *Dictionary of American English*, and he became a fellow of Pembroke College. A year later (May 11, 1926) Professor Tolkien met, for the first time, a young colleague named C. S. Lewis at a meeting of the Oxford English faculty over tea at Merton College. Their shared passion for medieval literature and "Northernness"—the bleak atmosphere and heroic values that undergird Norse mythology[15]—would lead to Lewis' religious conversion and to the publication of Tolkien's Middle-earth oeuvre and Lewis's Narnia books, together some of the most popular literature ever produced in the English language.

Unlike Lewis, Tolkien did not make public declamations against modernism. However, he made his views on many modernist authors clear in personal correspondence. In correcting a reporter on why Lewis disliked the poetry of T. S. Eliot, for example, Tolkien wrote, "it is possible to dislike Eliot with some intensity even if one has no aspirations to poetic laurels oneself."[16] Tolkien also made clear his views on Americans.[17] After the great success of *The Lord of the Rings*, Tolkien was disturbed by his cult-following in America, "horrors" causing him "great distress," arising from "an entirely different mental climate and soil, polluted and impoverished to a degree only paralleled by the lunatic destruction of the physical lands which Americans inhabit."[18] As for American music, he preferred Chopin to American jazz: "Music will give place to jiving. . . . This delicately cultured amusement is said to be a 'fever' in the U.S.A. O God! O Montreal! O Minnesota! O Michigan!"[19]

"Tolkien takes on the claims of modernity by creating characters who call into question the industrial or technological gains that have also produced the escalating devastation of two world wars," writes Michael D. Thomas. "In the final analysis, he seems to suggest that modernity is not worth the price of its violence and destructiveness."[20] The arrival of cars and buses had created canyons of unnerving sound in the streets of Edwardian Oxford, lined as they were (and are) with high stone walls and higher masonry Gothic structures. Tolkien, who never properly learned to drive a car and preferred bicycling, drew a cartoon of an autobus terrorizing a fleeing gowned don!

These prejudices, however, mask some important similarities with Eliot, Fitzgerald, and many modernist writers; Tolkien was, for example, drawn to the powerful medieval image of the Waste Land.[21] "Tolkien grapples with a Waste Land of war and quest and duty and death that threatens disaster," writes E. L. Risden, in comparing *The Lord of the Rings* with Eliot's *The Waste Land*, "but survives on the basis of a spiritual connection both of characters to a sense of something greater and of the author to his green and numinous creation."[22]

We do not know Fitzgerald's knowledge of Tolkien's writings, but it is likely that *The Hobbit* (published in 1937, three years before Fitzgerald's death) would have lain outside his mature tastes.[23] In a 2003 reader's poll conducted by the BBC, British readers chose *The*

Lord of the Rings as their best-loved novel of all time, with *The Great Gatsby* finishing at number 43.[24] Fitzgerald's friend Edmund Wilson described *The Lord of the Rings* as "juvenile trash," a thoughtless dismissal echoed by many mainstream literary critics of that time. Many of these critics—indeed, many today—accuse Tolkien of writing escapist fantasy (though fantasy hardly existed as a genre before *The Hobbit*). "Tolkien's fantasy is not so much an escape from modernity as a rejection of modern dehumanization," counters Lee Oser. "As such, it relates truth to goodness to beauty, in an analogue of Christian myth."[25]

It is also a true response to the horrors Tolkien witnessed on the Western Front, for much of his Middle-earth mythology was born in the misery of the trenches and in military hospitals during Tolkien's long recovery from trench fever. Witnessing a second world war, and worrying about his sons' survival while fighting in it, solidified for Tolkien his belief that there were still men who could fall under the dark spells of demagogues and tyrants willing to sacrifice all for powerful weapons of destruction.

Tolkien, in conversation with Lewis and other Oxonians, also developed the theory of "subcreation," or creating secondary worlds through fiction. Both Tolkien and Lewis—like Fitzgerald—entered university with aspirations to be poets. Through his academic scholarship and his own writing of verse (lyrical, epic, alliterative), Tolkien came to see the poet as a subcreator working under the Creator and carrying on this divine art. He was especially interested in *mythopoeia*, or the creation of myth, as a way of communicating divine truths. Lewis, already under the spell of the Romantic poets by the time he met Tolkien, came to view myth-creation in similar terms. Jay Gatsby is described by Nick as "a son of God . . . and he must be about His Father's business" (98)—creating the persona of Jay Gatsby as hero, with grace and chivalric virtues to match his enormous wealth. "the true romantic, as . . . in the case of Gatsby," writes Lehan, "is the son of God, repeating the godlike activity of creation. Such activity is not without its dangers."[26]

Such dangers are pervasive in Tolkien's Middle-earth writings. Like Fitzgerald's protagonists, many of Tolkien's heroes in these tales—be they men, elves, or dwarves—meet tragic ends, lovers are torn apart, and the ceaseless machines of war create waste lands of ashes and gloom out of a green-breasted world.

C. S. Lewis and the Magdalen Metaphysicals

The period between the wars in Oxford saw a battle in the discipline of philosophy between the Oxford Realists (Cook Wilson, H. A. Prichard, and H.W.B. Joseph) and a group of four loosely affiliated Magdalen College dons—Clement Webb, J. A. Smith, R. G. Collingwood, and C. S. Lewis—sometimes called the Magdalen Metaphysicals.[27] These men shared what James Patrick describes as an idealism born from a renewal of classical metaphysics and attention to the relationship between theology and philosophy. While Cambridge would fall almost completely under the spell of realists like G. E. Moore and Bertrand Russell, Collingwood and Lewis in particular would, in their different realms, make Oxford synonymous with idealism for much of the world.

The youngest of the four Magdalen dons was Clive Staples Lewis, the second son of a Belfast barrister. "Jack" Lewis (as he was known to family and friends) hoped that by entering Oxford early he could join the Officers Training Corps (OTC) and quickly receive his commission.[28] War was then on his mind and mixing with medieval legend, as we can see in his unpublished poem "Decadence" (written around Christmas of 1916), which begins:

Oh Galahad! My Galahad!
The world is old and very sad,
The world is old and gray with pain
And all the ways thereof are bad.[29]

He came to sit the Oxford scholarship exam in December 1916 (his first time in Oxford); passed over by New College, he received a Classics scholarship from University College.[30] Lewis took the Oxford entrance examination in March 1917 but failed mathematics, particularly algebra. He was allowed to take up his residence in University College in April, however, and to join the OTC while continuing to take algebra lessons. In these first few glorious months at Oxford, Lewis would begin his day rising early to read William Morris and the *Chanson de Roland*, later in the day discuss the poetry of W. B. Yeats with his Irish classmate, Theobald Butler. In June, however, he joined the OTC and was transferred as a cadet to more Spartan housing in Keble College. There were only 315 students in all of Oxford when Lewis took up his studies in April 1917, and 120 of them were in the OTC. After finishing his training Lewis became a second lieutenant in the Somerset Light Infantry and arrived at the Western Front on his nineteenth birthday on November 29, 1917. He received serious shrapnel wounds at the Battle of Arras on April 15, 1918 and was sent to hospital in Étaples.[31] Like Tolkien, Lewis spent his time in the trenches and in army hospitals (nearly eight months) reading and writing poetry, but what they wrote would never gain the attention that the war poets like Owen and Sassoon would achieve. Lewis was demobilized on December 25, 1918, and retained the rank of lieutenant when he resigned his commission.

Returning to student life at Oxford after the war, during Hilary term 1919, Lewis began his studies in *Literae Humaniores*. At that time Lewis's chosen academic path was philosophy, particularly ancient philosophy, with tutorials from A. B. Poynton and lectures by Gilbert Murray. He chose to sit the Classical Moderations exam after his first year, however, which meant reading all of Homer, Virgil, Cicero, and Demosthenes in addition to four Greek plays before moving on to classical philosophy.[32] Lewis won a first in Honour Mods and then resumed his study in Greats under tutors G. H. Stevenson (for history) and E. F. Carritt (for philosophy). Yet Lewis still aspired to be a poet, being then an admirer of Keats and Shelley, Tennyson and Arnold. Lewis had read T.S. Eliot's *Prufrock and Other Observations* shortly after it was published in 1917, and the next year he submitted to the publisher William Heinemann his own collection of verse, some of it written as a student, other poems written while convalescing. In 1919 Heinemann published the collection, *Spirits in Bondage: A Cycle of Lyrics*, under the pseudonym Clive Hamilton (Hamilton was his mother's surname). Lewis confessed to his friend, Arthur Greeves, that the poems centered on the idea that nature was malevolent and that God—if he exists—was outside of and opposed to the cosmic order. "I'm afraid I shall never be an orthodox modern," he wrote with sarcasm to Arthur, because "I like lines that will scan and do not care for descriptions of sea-sickness."[33] What he did care for was a blending of classical, Celtic, and Arthurian motifs and allusions with contrasting images of the Irish hills and the battlefields of France. Despite the unabashed atheism of the poems, Lewis's father responded with cautious pride to his son's first book: "I do think that if Oxford does not spoil him . . . he may write something that men would not willingly let die."[34]

In 1919 Lewis was still a committed atheist and danced on the edge of aestheticism, spending much time reading poetry, seeing plays, and attending performances of classical music. That year he met Leo Kingsley Baker, who was reading History at Wadham College; also a wounded veteran of the Western Front, Baker was an aspiring actor who excited Lewis with stories about meeting Mrs. Asquith (the wife of the prime minister), Princess Bibesco, and Vaughn Williams.[35] Baker introduced Lewis that same year to a fellow Wadham student, Arthur Owen Barfield, who would become Lewis's "Second Friend" (second only to childhood friend Arthur Greeves) and a future member of the Inklings. The two would begin a long debate (waged in person and later in epistolary form) that Lewis called "The Great War."[36] The Anthroposophist Barfield, a second lieutenant in the Royal Engineers sent to Belgium at the end of the war, came to Oxford first in early 1919 in an army education program based at Keble College (a British near equivalent to the A.E.F. program that Trinity term).[37] Barfield had already won a scholarship to read Classics at Oxford, but once discharged he requested to read English language and literature instead at Wadham College, earning a first in 1921 followed by a BLitt in 1923 (his thesis would become the book *Poetic Diction*) before becoming a solicitor in his father's London law firm. Writing poetry and criticism as an amateur, Barfield occasionally impressed Tolkien with his philological insights and played a significant role in Lewis coming to accept a Theist position in the late 1920s. Though he held no academic position, he was nevertheless prolific and respected as a poet and literary theorist, and, unlike Tolkien and Lewis, Barfield spent time in America and became friends with, among others, the American novelist Saul Bellow. "Barfield towers above us all," Lewis asserted, "the wisest and best of my unofficial teachers."[38]

Lewis would please his official teachers at Oxford in 1920 and 1921 with papers on Greek and Roman history, logic, ethics, and Plato and Aristotle. He would sit the Final Honour School exam in Greats, as well as the oral *viva*, in June 1922, and receive another first. He had by this time adopted what he called his "New Look," a flirtation with philosophical realism via the Oxford Realists, a group that now included his tutor Carritt.[39] With no position then open to him in Classics or philosophy, however, he decided to study for a third exam, in the relatively new English School. Lewis would win another first, in English language and literature, in only one year rather than the usual three. That year was also spent with poetry, new friends, and faculty whom he barely tolerated.[40] Among the new friends was fellow English student and Irish Protestant Nevill Coghill, a future member of the Inklings. Coghill would become a colleague and friend of Tolkien, as well, and a beloved tutor of W. H. Auden, landing a fellowship at Exeter in 1924.

Full-time employment still evaded Lewis, however, and he grew worried. He spent his free time finishing his second book of verse, the long narrative poem *Dymer* (1926), a *Faust*-like epic about an anti-hero who kills his son in a dystopic version of the myth of Theseus. His first teaching was in philosophy, filling in for his old tutor E. F. Carritt at University College in the 1924–25 academic year while Carritt lectured in America (Carritt had published *The Theory of Beauty* in 1914 and was developing an aesthetic philosophy that beauty was intuitive and expressive). Lewis gave fourteen lectures on "The Moral Good—Its Place among the Values." When his much sought after fellowship at Magdalen finally opened up in April 1925, however, it was in English, with additional tutoring in philosophy, renewable after five years.

Lewis would hold the fellowship at Magdalen College, Oxford, for twenty-nine years, and his scholarship would be almost entirely in the field of literary criticism, with courtly romance, Spenser, and Milton his special subjects. The wider world beyond medieval and Renaissance scholars, however, would soon be tutored in Lewis's philosophy through his fiction and Christian apologetics.

Never a devotee of Moore or Russell, Lewis began to drift away from philosophical realism in the mid 1920s and toward Platonic idealism. "Collingwood and Lewis both called their philosophy romantic," writes Patrick, meaning a continuation of the project of the Romantic Movement to reinvigorate Christianity and culture with a heavy dose of medievalism.[41] The Magdalen Metaphysicals all shared an interest in Plato's *Republic*, Aristotle, medieval texts, poetry, history, and religious truth. But for Lewis in his early years, as an Oxford student and a young don, it was the Romantics that held his greatest allegiance. Modern poetry and *vers libre*, however, was then replacing the universal, shared experiences of the Romantics (especially with regard to nature) with the more subjective and mundane experiences of the individual poet, experiences too often expressed in dark cynicism that Lewis termed "Saturnalistic."[42] This is how Lewis saw most of the verse of the war poets, and how he was to view *The Waste Land*—yet Western civilization did *not* fall in 1916, and patriotism *was* the proper response to war, at least the war he shared with Owen, Brooke, and Sassoon.

After the war, Lewis took on T.S. Eliot and contemporary critics over both form and content in poetry, and his long debate with Eliot often touched on the worth of the Romantics.[43] In his essay, "Shelley, Dryden, and Mr. Eliot," Lewis argued—against Eliot—that Shelley was not only a superior poet to Dryden, but also a more classical one.[44] As for their own poetry, Eliot and many of the Modernist poets "had abandoned their posts" in Lewis's view, observes Andrew Cuneo. "They would neither teach *(docere)* nor delight *(delectare)*," to use Philip Sidney's definition of the role of poetry.[45]

For Lewis, the journey from Plato to Romanticism to truth in religion was a long and arduous one, a journey he would later describe in

Pilgrim's Regress (1933) and *Surprised by Joy* (1955). Lewis continued to struggle with developing a personal philosophy—through poetry and conversation and correspondence—throughout the 1920s. He began moving away from his "New Look" and adopted what he calls in *Surprised by Joy* his "treaty with reality"—not escapism, but a "fixing of a frontier" between himself and the more destructive of realities (war, for example). "During the early 1920s, Lewis saw philosophy not simply as a human attempt to understand reality, but as a means of modulating its impact," writes Alistair McGrath. "Like T. S. Eliot, Lewis appears to have realized that 'Humankind cannot bear very much reality.' Reality had to be filtered or tempered, in order for human beings to cope with it—especially when it seemed meaningless and pointless. Many who experienced the horror and trauma of the Great War experienced such thoughts."[46] Unlike Eliot and Fitzgerald, Lewis and Coghill and Tolkien *had* experienced combat in the war, and Lewis was beginning to find an idealism consonant with logic—"a cosmic *Logos*"—to be a more satisfactory way of dealing with the sacrifices of the war and the moral seriousness of his Oxford friends.[47]

In a 1941 sermon delivered in Oxford titled "The Weight of Glory," as well in both *Surprised by Joy* and *Mere Christianity* (1952), Lewis makes what McGrath calls his theological "argument from desire." For Lewis, *joy* is a deep human desire or longing for something we glimpse from childhood—a land full of wonders—but flees from us the more we reach out to grab it. While it may be our eyes or other physical senses that point us to this object of desire, we also recognize in this joy that there are realities beyond what we can see or touch. This argument has its roots, of course, in Plato's theory of forms, and was expressed in the theology of Augustine, Anselm, Bernard of Clairvaux, and Julian of Norwich.[48] But it was also an idea that appealed strongly to the Romantics, especially Wordsworth and the German Romantics who called it *Sehnsucht*. Matthew Arnold had also explored the idea in 1907 and, as McGrath points out, even atheistic Modernists like Virginia Woolf and Bertrand Russell had written about the phenomenon as early as 1916. Russell described it as "a terrible pain," and Lewis agreed that his *joy* did not often bring to one what we think of as joy. This longing, rather, "was legitimized and satisfied only by its object," writes Patrick, "directed by reasoning, and capable of issuing in happiness among those who developed in themselves the life of virtue."[49] In Tolkien's writings, from his early poems like "Goblin Feet" to *Lord of the Rings*, this feeling is most commonly associated with the elves, who had once experienced paradise but were exiled from it, and thus inspire a great yearning in the hobbits Bilbo, Frodo, and Sam to see or live with the elves.

This type of *joy*, I would argue, is what Nick is trying to convey to the reader at the end of *The Great Gatsby*. "I thought of Gatsby's wonder when he first picked out the green light at the end of Daisy's dock," Nick tells us. "He had come a long way to this blue lawn, and his dream must have seemed so close that he could hardly fail to grasp it" (141). While the dream eluded Nick and Gatsby in the summer of 1922, "tomorrow we will run faster, stretch out our arms farther." This, for many readers and critics of *Gatsby*, is the essence of the American Dream, running faster and reaching farther toward a better tomorrow. For Lewis and the Magdalen Metaphysicals, this desire is not American particularism but rather part of the universal human condition. "So long as Gatsby does not have Daisy," writes Lehan, "he can keep his godlike state of romantic yearning alive."[50] Nick seems to be telling us in his last words that it doesn't matter that Gatsby did not fulfill his longing—in fact, Daisy would not likely have led Gatsby to a life of virtue—but rather it is the longing itself that matters, for *it* makes us run faster and reach farther.

Oxford had long been the home of such runners and dreamers, but things began changing there around Lewis and Tolkien in the postwar years. For the irreverent John Betjeman, the future poet laureate who had been a pupil of Eliot's at Highgate Junior School, Oxford between the wars was almost synonymous with C. S. Lewis. In the poem "May-Day Song for North Oxford" (1945), Betjeman conveys this along with the growing cynicism of the new generation of students:

Oh! well-bound Wells and Bridges! Oh! earnest ethical search

For the wide high-table λοΥος of St. C.S. Lewis's Church.[51]

Betjeman left Oxford without a degree, an event he remembers in *Summoned by Bells* (1960) and links to his relationship with his Magdalen tutor Lewis:

> ... I'd seen myself a don,
> Reading old poets in the library,
> Attending chapel in an M.A. gown
> And sipping vintage port by candlelight.
> I sought my tutor in his arid room,
> Who told me, "You'd have only got a Third."[52]

Betjeman enjoyed teasing the "earnest" Lewis, who had little patience for Betjeman's aestheticism and eccentricities.[53] Nevertheless, Lewis and Betjeman had plotted in the early days of their acquaintance to submit parodies of T. S. Eliot's poems—"Eliotic verse"—to *The Dial* and *The Criterion* (which Eliot himself edited).[54]

Roger Lancelyn Green (1918–1987) enjoyed a very different relationship with Lewis. Green attended Lewis's lectures while studying for a BLitt at Oxford, became a scholar of Lewis Carroll (editing his diaries for Oxford University Press), and was a prolific writer of children's books retelling Greek mythology and the Arthurian legends. He gave Lewis important feedback while the latter was writing the *Chronicles of Narnia*, and became a biographer of Lewis seemingly by designation of his teacher as early as 1953.[55] Sharing an aversion to what Lewis termed "chronological snobbery," Green was on occasion brought into the Oxford literary group that took a collective stand against modernity and modernism by restoring the power of mythopoeia in literature: the Inklings.

The Inklings

The one Oxford undergraduate who would have the most impactful connection to both C. S. Lewis and J.R.R. Tolkien was Edward Tangye Lean. The younger brother of film director David Lean, Edward Lean published an Oxford novel in 1932 (while still an undergraduate) called *Storm in Oxford: A Fantasy*. Around 1931 he founded a small literary club of students and dons called The Inklings, which would meet regularly in his University College rooms to read and critique each other's works in progress. Lewis and Tolkien joined the group, and when Lean graduated they resurrected the club after a short hiatus. As Tolkien described its origins to an American academic in 1967,

> The Inklings had no recorder and C. S. Lewis no Boswell. The name was not invented by C.S.L. (nor by me). In origin it was an undergraduate jest, devised as the name of a literary (or writers') club. The founder was an undergraduate at University College, named Tangye-Lean. . . . He was, I think, more aware than most undergraduates of the impermanence of their clubs and fashions. . . . Tangye-Lean proved quite right. The club soon died . . . but C.S.L. and I at least survived. Its name was then transferred (by C.S.L.) to the undetermined and unelected circle of friends who gathered about C.S.L. and met in his rooms at Magdalen.[56]

Tolkien had already been meeting with Lewis and other Inklings at his Kolbitár ("Coal-biters"), an Old Norse reading group he started in 1926. Tolkien and Dyson were regulars in Lewis's rooms at Magdalen by 1931 when, on a warm September night, they accompanied Lewis on his spiritual journey to Christianity on Addison's Walk. The new version of the Inklings met often twice a week—Tuesday mornings at the Eagle and Child ("The Bird & Baby") or another Oxford pub, Thursday evenings in the college rooms of one of the members, usually Lewis's Magdalen rooms—for more than twenty years.[57] The Inklings would become the storm in Oxford that would spread—through their fiction and (in Lewis's case) apologetics—unabated to the present day, with books outstretching in sales and influence anything produced by their critics and ideological competitors.

The Inklings, and even their three intellectual leaders—Lewis, Tolkien, and Charles Williams—varied quite a lot in personality and temperament. The elegant and aristocratic Lord David Cecil, who joined in the late 1930s, had even been a friend of Virginia Woolf and member of the Garsington crowd. So, too, had Henry Victor "Hugo" Dyson, a worldly, boisterous lecturer at Reading who usually vetoed all talk of elves at Inkling meetings. Tolkien, in explaining to an American fan in 1965 why he was not influenced by and did not care for several of the works of Lewis and Williams, admitted that "it is an exhibition of my own limits of sympathy" more so than criticism of his friends:

> Lewis was a very impressionable man, and this was abetted by his great generosity and capacity for friendship. The unpayable debt that I owe to him was not 'influence' as it is ordinarily understood, but sheer encouragement. He was for long my only audience. Only from him did I ever get the idea that my 'stuff' could be more than a private hobby.[58]

All male and all Christian, like-minded (according to Tolkien), but brutally frank in their criticisms of each other's words and thoughts, the Inklings loved beer, laughter, and harpooning common enemies, including "atheists, totalitarians, modernists, and anyone with a shallow imagination."[59] They exalted in the ordinary and plain—beer, beef, pipes, tweed—almost as an act of rebellion against the dandies and aesthetes who had dominated Oxford undergraduate culture since the days of Oscar Wilde. The Inklings "were consistent in the one thing that mattered to the University," writes G. R. Evans in a recent history of Oxford. "They lived the life of the mind and they lived it socially."[60] But they also had scholarly expertise in and passion for the pre-modern world, "A sense of the ongoing value of the medieval . . . and ancient."[61] Tolkien was an acclaimed philologist of Anglo-Saxon and Middle English; Coghill was a Chaucerian and Dyson a Shakespearean; Lewis wrote literary criticism on medieval romance, Spencer, and Milton; his older brother, Major Warren "Warnie" Lewis, wrote histories of seventeenth-century France; Colin Hardie was a classicist; Owen Barfield wrote about Coleridge and Romanticism; and Charles Williams lectured in Oxford on Dante.

This last member, Charles Williams, remains the most enigmatic and problematic of all the Inklings.[62] Beginning his career in the publishing world of London in 1908 at Oxford University Press in Amen Corner on Paternoster Row, he would eventually enter the acquaintance of W. B. Yeats, T. S. Eliot, and Ottoline Morrell. It was Lady Ottoline, in fact, who recommended Williams's novels *The Place of the Lion* (1931) and *War in Heaven* (1930) to Eliot, and introduced the two poets at a tea party in London in 1934.[63] Eliot (then at Faber & Faber) commissioned a study of Dante and Romantic theology from Williams, and the two became friends. Just two years later Lewis would become a great admirer of Williams's *The Place of the Lion*, while simultaneously Williams had been reading Lewis's *Allegory of Love*, and they, too, became friends. Williams was brought into the Inklings by Lewis when, in 1939, the London offices of O.U.P. were relocated to the safer environs of Oxford for the duration of World War II. Williams would have a major influence on Lewis (much to the chagrin of Tolkien) until his death in 1945.

In addition to Williams, the poetry of Dante was one common link between the Inklings and Eliot. Another was—after Eliot's and Lewis's conversions—Christianity. Paul Elmer More, an American journalist and Christian apologist whom Lewis called his "spiritual uncle," related to Lewis a story about Eliot visiting him at Oxford in 1933 when, at a luncheon in Magdalen College, a Magdalen tutor mentioned to them the rumor that Lewis had been secretly going to chapel for weeks without any of the fellows knowing about it. Eliot, at this, gave a sly smile and remarked, "Why, it's quite evident that if a man wishes to escape detection at Oxford, the only place for him to go is the college chapel."[64]

In September 1947 a portrait of Lewis graced the cover of *Time* magazine in America, the caption reading, "Oxford's C. S. Lewis: His Heresy—Christianity." The accompanying article mentioned a number of similar heretics—T. S. Eliot, W. H. Auden, Charles Williams, Dorothy Sayers, Graham Greene—and what is interesting about this list is that, apart from their Christianity, they have two things in common: 1) a connection to Oxford (all but Williams had been students there), and 2) an interest in things medieval. One could, of course, add J.R.R. Tolkien, Evelyn Waugh, and writers of lesser fame to this list of contemporary Oxonian Christians who at least dabbled in the Middle Ages. These English writers have all found a large audience in America, perhaps none larger than the quite diverse throng of admirers of Lewis. Macmillan editor William Griffin relates a quite telling incident when, in 1979, a reviewer in the *New York Times* commented dismissively, "No one reads C. S. Lewis these days except children and Christians."[65] Macmillan was then selling more than a million copies a year of Lewis's fiction alone, and thus the publishing community found this a hilariously inaccurate pronouncement. *New York Times* reviewers, literary critics like Edmund Wilson, and most academics had completely underestimated the influence of Lewis and Tolkien, and many still display an ignorance about how the Inklings' scholarly understanding of medieval languages and literature make their creative writing so appealing to a vast—and still growing—worldwide audience.

Fitzgerald's Epic Grandeur and Medievalism

None had such promise then, and none
Your scapegrace wit or your disarming grace;
For you were bold as was Danaë's son,
Conceived like Perseus in a dream of gold. . .
—John Peale Bishop, "The Hours"
(describing F. Scott Fitzgerald)

As a young man, Fitzgerald's first introduction to the Middle Ages was through such standards of nineteen-century medievalism as Sir Walter Scott's *Ivanhoe* (1820) and Sir Arthur Conan Doyle's *The White Company* (1891). According to a conversation he had with Edmund Wilson in 1924, when Fitzgerald was twelve he wrote *Elavo*, "a novel in verse, dealing with knights of old, Roman strongholds, drawbridges, et cetera."[66] Father Fay introduced a teenage Scott to his friend Henry Adams, Harvard's first medieval historian. But he became truly enamored with medieval history and literature while at Princeton, as he wrote years later to Zelda: "I got nothing out of my first two years—in the last I got my passionate love for poetry and historical perspective and ideas in general. . . ."[67] In particular, he confessed to an interviewer, he was enthusiastic about "all books about that period which lies between the V and XV centuries."[68] Similarly, to Wilson he offered: "I'd like to have been a young Spaniard about 1550 in the glory of the Armada . . . [or] a young Venetian when Venice was the thoroughfare of the civilized world and all the crusaders passed through her gates."[69]

Fitzgerald's earliest prose shows the influence of the medieval and medievalism. In the short story "The Spire and the Gargoyle," published in the *Nassau Literary Magazine* a few months after his return to Princeton in 1915, the emphasis is on medieval symbolism in the collegiate Gothic aesthetic.[70] The image of the Gothic spire as symbolic of the writer's idealism and aspirations is carried over in his first novel, whose original title—*The Romantic Egotist*—quite accurately describes Amory Blaine and, arguably, Fitzgerald himself. In *This Side of Paradise* (a more neutral title), Monsignor Darcy and Amory find they share an enthusiasm for the medieval, the aristocratic, the romantic, and the lost cause. Darcy introduces Amory to his friend, the prominent medieval historian Thornton Hancock, and later tells Amory that he is also a "mediævalist" because he has "a passion for classifying and finding a type"—fitting C. S. Lewis's description of the medieval mind in his last book, *The Discarded Image* (1964).

Just as with Scott, Princeton began "to live up to its Gothic beauty" for Amory during his third year, when he immersed himself in what he christened "quest books" (111). Amory's brief love affair with Eleanor Ramilly included a walk "while the moon rose and poured a great burden of glory over the garden until it seemed fairy-land with Amory and Eleanor, dim phantasmal shapes, expressing eternal beauty in curious elfin love moods" (217). The novel concludes with Amory returning to Princeton to come to terms with his fleeting youth and amorous and professional failures: "Long after midnight the towers and spires of Princeton were visible, with here and there

CHRISTOPHER A. SNYDER

a late-burning light—and suddenly out of the clear darkness the sound of bells. An endless dream it went on; the spirit of the past brooding over a new generation . . ." (260). In his notes for a possible film treatment of *This Side of Paradise*, Fitzgerald writes: "some nurse might point out St. Francis of Assisi or Sir Galahad to [Amory] as a great saint and Amory might be thrilled, but his mother might angrily snatch him away and point to Lord Chesterfield as a better model for a boy."[71]

In *The Beautiful and Damned*, Anthony Patch graduates from Harvard and heads to Rome, where he takes up painting, the violin, and poetry: "[he] wrote some ghastly Italian sonnets, supposedly the ruminations of a thirteenth-century monk on the joys of the contemplative life" (15). Returning to New York City in 1912, he takes an apartment on 52nd Street where, he confesses to his grandfather, he intends to write history:

> "History? History of what? The Civil War? The Revolution?"
> "Why—no, sir. A history of the Middle Ages." Simultaneously an idea was born for a history of the Renaissance popes, written from some novel angle. Still, he was glad he had said "Middle Ages."
> "Middle Ages? Why not your own country? Something you know about?"
> "Well, you see I've lived so much abroad—"
> "Why you should write about the Middle Ages, I don't know. Dark Ages, we used to call 'em. Nobody knows what happened, and nobody cares, except that they're over now." (21)

Anthony does not write his medieval history, but he later tells a story about "a creature of my splendid mind," a character called Chevalier O'Keefe, exiled from Ireland "in the late days of chivalry . . . a sentimentalist . . . a romantic, a vain fellow, a man of wild passions" (80). Chevalier retires to the French monastery of St. Voltaire (!) and climbs to his cell at the top of the Tower of Chastity, only to tumble literally "head over heels" when he spies a young peasant girl below

166

adjusting her garter. Suspected by the monks of suicide, he "was not buried on consecrated ground, but tumbled into a field near by, where he doubtless improved the quality of the soil for many years afterward." Anthony is making the story up over cocktails with a girl he is trying to impress, a sort of Jazz Age parody of Lewis Carroll creating tales for the young Alice.

Chivalric imagery and allusions to classical and medieval literature in *The Great Gatsby* abound—Jimmy Gatz serving as Dan Cody's squire, Gatsby's faux-castle, Daisy as "the king's daughter . . . high in a white palace, the golden girl," the bridge to an enchanted isle, the questing knight astride his liveried horse (or shiny automobile), the chivalric colors of cars and shirts (white, green, silver, blue), the rose, the Grail itself—and many scholars have tread this ground before.[72] Here I would like to focus on two areas: the ancient war epic and the medieval questing knight. Fitzgerald failed to prove himself in war, but, I would contend, he would continue to test the medieval ideals of his youth through the literary trope of the quest in autobiographical fiction throughout his life.

Like Amory and Anthony in his previous two novels, Jay Gatsby wore the natural good looks of Scott Fitzgerald. "Gatsby bore about him the marks of his [Olympian] birth. He is a kind of exiled Duke in disguise," writes Marius Bewley. "We know him by his bearing. . . . one feels that [his pathetic old father] is only the kindly shepherd who once found a baby on a cold hillside."[73] Like Theseus, the mythical king of Athens (Shakespeare makes him duke of Athens), Gatsby has both a divine and a mortal father, he leaves the isolated land of his birth and proves himself in battle, then ventures to the great city to prove that he is the rightful heir, ultimately coming to rule in his own palace overlooking the sea. Through guile and help from others he navigates a labyrinth of wealth and power, and win's the love of the king's daughter. He leaves her, though unwillingly and on the advice of another, and she marries someone else. Like Theseus, Gatsby's closest friend is a fellow warrior, who helps him "abduct" a beautiful daughter of a king, but she is taken back to her palace home, and Gatsby is left in darkness to the Furies. Ultimately, Gatsby/Theseus is betrayed by a beautiful and wealthy woman, and dies violently at the hands of a suspicious and vengeful man, surrounded by water. As with Gatsby, many stories surrounded Theseus!

Though I have found no references explicitly to Theseus in the writings of Fitzgerald, his statement about reading Homeric literature during the writing of *Gatsby* would lead us naturally to look for comparisons in *The Iliad* and *The Odyssey*. Some have recognized in the famous party-list from Chapter Four of *The Great Gatsby* a mock-epic style, recalling, for example, the lists of combatants in *The Iliad* and the parade of famous shades in *The Aeneid*.[74] "The combination of erotic feeling and heroism" in *Gatsby*, writes Ronald Berman, "is Vergilian rather than Homeric."[75]

Looking at heroic epic might be heading down the wrong ancient path, given Fitzgerald's explicit connections of Gatsby with *The Satyricon* of the Roman satirist Petronius (ca. A.D. 27–66). Early titles for *Gatsby* included *Trimalchio at West Egg* and *Trimalchio*, the last attached to a manuscript submitted to Maxwell Perkins in November 1924. Trimalchio is the name of the former slave who throws a lavish banquet in *The Satyricon*, a 1913 translation of which was owned by Fitzgerald. "It was when curiosity about Gatsby was at its highest that the lights in his house failed to go on one Saturday night," writes Fitzgerald, "and, as obscurely as it had begun, his career as Trimalchio was over" (88). Churchwell has cataloged many of the possible *Satyricon* influences on *Gatsby*: "Trimalchio is given to false claims [and] self-aggrandizing tales of his life among the rich and powerful, . . . his banquets are adorned by tales of burnished gems and unfaithful women, . . . insatiable luxury, a cauldron of gluttony, . . . the emerald green, the glass bauble."[76] While Jazz Age parties may have reminded the New York *literati* of *The Satyricon*, Jay Gatsby is more than a lewd, boastful freedman. By the end of the novel, asserts Robert Long, Fitzgerald is working mythopoeically: floating lifelessly among the first leaves of autumn, Gatsby has become "a slain god, a youthful deity of spring . . . sacrificed to the progression of time."[77]

As for the Middle Ages in *The Great Gatsby*, Fitzgerald displays a true knowledge of medieval primary sources, but he is also influenced by the medievalism of the nineteenth century. "When [Gatsby] shows Daisy his collection of shirts, the moment is heraldic," writes Berman,[78] but it is hard to disentangle the colors of actual medieval heraldry from those restored by the Romantic poets and the Pre-Raphaelites. One finds the same dilemma in reading the fiction of Lewis and Tolkien. Even in Thomas Malory's great opus *Morte D'Arthur* (1475)—a subject of the last conversation between Tolkien and Lewis before the latter's death[79]—there is already a romanticization of the Middle Ages going on, delivering to us an idealized (though hardly sanitized) version of the medieval knight that many a poet, painter, and novelist have found irresistible. While Romantic and perhaps even at times quixotic, Fitzgerald was also capable of the satirical touch of Chaucer, Rabelais, and Cervantes in dealing with chivalric romance.[80] He also followed contemporary thought on the Middle Ages, particularly that of Oswald Spengler. The medieval questing knight became, for Spengler in 1918, symbolic of an aspirational phase of western civilization pre-Enlightenment, when "Faustian man" had an imagination that soared "like his Gothic cathedrals to encompass his ideas of infinity."[81]

Both Fitzgerald and Gatsby dreamt of the heroic quest; if both ultimately fell short of their goals, this, too, was oft the fate of the Arthurian knight. In particular, Gatsby's sojourn in Oxford is akin to the knight of the twelfth- and thirteenth-century French romances who is temporarily distracted from his amorous quest. In Chrétien de Troyes's *Yvain, or The Knight of the Lion* (written between 1177 and 1181) for example, the young Arthurian hero Yvain is distracted by knight errantry and does not keep his vow to return to his recently wed wife, Laudine. After a period of soul-searching in exile, Yvain wins back the love of Laudine *and* his reputation for courtesy (literally, the way a young man is to behave at court).

By contrast, in Chrétien's *Lancelot, or The Knight of the Cart* (written in the same period as *Yvain*), Lancelot overcomes several obstacles to rescue Guinevere, with whom he is carrying out an adulterous affair. In both romances, however, it is the woman who dishes out the punishment to her lover for breaking vows (in Guinevere's case she spurns Lancelot for merely hesitating in his rescue of her). In *Gatsby*, Daisy thinks that Gatsby has broken his vow by going to Oxford (or is hesitating returning to her) and so she breaks her vow by marrying Tom. Daisy's punishment is Tom's marital infidelity, Gatsby's is not having a conventional reunion and marriage to Daisy, and so having to build a castle of lies in order settle for an unsatisfying and short-lived affair.

In the thirteenth-century *Prose Lancelot* as well as in Malory's *Morte D'Arthur*, Lancelot conquers in the name of Guinevere—not that of Arthur (hence the subversive nature of the Lancelot romances)—sending the queen trophies of his devotion, and eventually carries her off to his castle, Joyeuse Guarde. Gatsby showers Daisy with parties and beautiful shirts in his faux-castle with its "feudal silhouette," but it is not enough.[82] "I've gotten these things for her, and now she wants to run away," Gatsby complains in the *Trimalchio* manuscript. As Barbara Tepa Lupack has observed, Gatsby lives for the seeking, while Daisy delights in the having.[83]

While Fitzgerald does not evoke Lancelot by name in the novel, he does mention the ultimate Arthurian quest object with which Lancelot had a rather complicated relationship in the late romances: the Holy Grail. Grail imagery abounds in *The Great Gatsby*, perhaps not so surprisingly given that Fitzgerald had recently read and admired Eliot's *The Waste Land*.[84] In *Gatsby*, "God has withdrawn from this . . . wasteland world," writes Lehan.[85] Jay Gatsby is, perhaps, America's Fisher King: he fished for salmon when he was young, he spent time on a mysterious boat (from which he emerged with a new name), he has a "castle," he is impure (bootlegging, adultery) and a materialist, and he has associations with both the sun and the sea. Lancelot, however, is not the hero of Chrétien's grail poem, *Perceval, or The Story of the Grail* (ca. 1190, the first written version of the grail legend). It is Perceval (in German romances Parzifal), one of many Arthurian manifestations of *le bel inconnu*, "the fair unknown," who shows up at court disguised (or unrecognized) needing to show by his martial actions that he is worthy of his noble bearing.[86] The Fair Unknown frequently stumbles in his quest, but is usually rewarded with both the love of a beautiful lady and an honored place at Arthur's court. Jay Gatsby is America's Fair Unknown, but the ending of *his*

FIG. 1 (ABOVE): "Aesthetics vs. Athletics," *Punch* (1881). Oscar Wilde and a group of Oxford Aesthetes are chased by Oxford Hearties across Christ Church Meadow. FIG. 2 (BELOW): Photo of Tommy Hitchcock, Jr. and Thomas Hitchcock, Sr. at a polo match (date unknown).

FIG. 3 (ABOVE): Photo of Alain Locke (standing, third from right) with members of the Oxford Cosmopolitan Club, ca. 1908. FIG. 4 (BELOW): Photo of Garsington Manor, Oxfordshire. View of the back of the house from the ornamental "bathing pond" (pool).

FIG. 5 (LEFT): Photo of Ottoline Morrell and T.S. Eliot at Garsington, possibly taken by Ottoline Morrell, 1920. The historian David Cecil, a friend to Ottoline, described her as "a princess of the Renaissance risen to shame our drab age."

FIG. 6 (RIGHT): Photo of Major William M. Rogers, the Rhodes scholar (Mississippi and St. John's, 1911) who led the contingent of American soldier-students to Oxford in 1919.

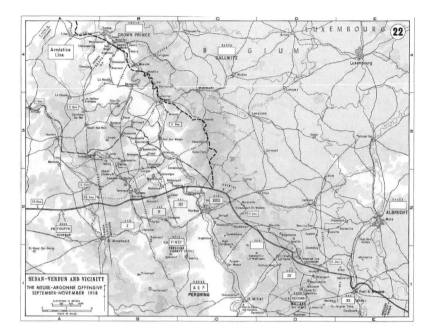

FIG. 7 (ABOVE): Map of the Western Theater of World War I, September to November 1918, showing the Meuse-Argonne Offensive. FIG. 8 (BELOW): Photo of U.S. Army students at Oxford, Summer Term, 1919.

FIG. 9: A.E.F. students at University College, Oxford (clockwise from back left): Lieutenant Theodore Futch, Lieutenant Harold Flack, Lieutenant Edward Strater, Captain Everett Brown, and Captain John Gammell.

FIG. 10 (ABOVE): Photo of the 1919 Summer Eights Crew from Pembroke (Lieutenant Donald H. Tyler in uniform). FIG. 11 (BELOW): Photo of the Oxford Encaenia, Summer 1919. Left to right: Field Marshal Sir Douglas Haig, Admiral Sir David Beatty, Marshal Joseph Joffre, and General John J. Pershing.

FIG. 12 (ABOVE): "How Mordred was slain by Arthur, and how by him Arthur was hurt to the death," illustration by Arthur Rackham from *The Romance of King Arthur and His Knights of the Round Table* (1917). Rackham's illustration for this abridged version of Malory's *Morte D'Arthur* was partly inspired by the trench warfare of the Western Front. FIG. 13 (BELOW LEFT): Photo of Cleveland Tower, Princeton University. The 173-foot tower and carillon are part of Princeton's Graduate College. FIG. 14 (BELOW RIGHT): Photo of Holder Tower, Princeton University. Holder Tower and Holder Hall, on Nassau Street, are now part of Princeton's Rockefeller College.

FIG. 15 (ABOVE LEFT): F. Scott and Zelda Fitzgerald, 1923. FIG. 16: (ABOVE RIGHT): Robert Byron and Harold Acton at Oxford ca. 1922. FIG. 17 (BELOW): Photo of the Bright Young People attending the Second Childhood Party in London, 1929.

quest calls into question both his own worth and that of America's aspirations.

Gatsby is also the broken knight. In both the *Prose Lancelot* and in *Morte D'Arthur*, Lancelot calls himself "Le Chevalier Mal Fet," which Malory translates as "The Knight that Hath Trespassed" and T. H. White as "The Ill-Made Knight."[87] Either way, Lancelot is unable to achieve the Grail Quest because of his unrepentant love for Guinevere. Like Lancelot, Gatsby is a knight whose remarkable accomplishments and physical beauty belie spiritual corruption, or at least a falling short of spiritual perfection, required in the medieval Grail Quest. Both Lancelot and Gatsby carry around with them a sin that, despite given glimpses of their grail, prevents them from ultimately attaining it, whereas Tom Buchanan, like Malory's Gawain, is a purely physical and worldly man who boasts but has no vision at all. Tom may have been the equestrian—"Tom Buchanan, the polo player"—but Gatsby rode horses in war and wears the heraldic trappings of the knight.[88] Tom expresses his physicality through sports and abusing women; Gatsby displays his through bravery in real battles and the medieval *courtoisie* he has brought to West Egg. Tom's adulterous affairs are with a chambermaid and a mechanic's wife; Gatsby's affair with Daisy conforms to the rules of Courtly Love. That Daisy does not end up with Gatsby only reminds us that Lancelot does not end up with Guinevere, and that Camelot ends in corruption and betrayal.

Daisy Fay and Jay Gatsby are both associated with gold—the color of the sun and the color long associated with wealth—and Daisy, "the golden girl," becomes the grail, the ultimate object of the ultimate quest. That Daisy becoming Gatsby's grail may be an overestimation of her character should not deter us from acknowledging the spiritual dimension of his quest. Thus what Nick describes as Gatsby's "Platonic image of himself" survives—in the prose of Nick/Scott—though his body perishes. Neoplatonism was at the heart of the Gothic impulse of the late twelfth and thirteenth centuries, a philosophy of ascendance that can be glimpsed in everything from Chartres Cathedral to *The Divine Comedy*. Similarly, in the early thirteenth-century prose romance, *Quest of the Holy Grail*, Sir Galahad achieves the Quest but lets go of his mortal body—though young, vigorous, and beautiful—so that his spirit can follow the Grail as it ascends to Heaven, an image captured *twice* in poems by Tennyson. "Rose, silver, and golden light are the colors of Gatsby's imagination," observes Robert Long, just as they were for Tennyson in his description of the Grail's first appearance, to the nun who is Perceval's sister:

'O my brother, Percivale,' she said,
'Sweet brother, I have seen the Holy Grail:
For, waked at dead of night, I heard a sound
As of a silver horn from o'er the hills
. . . and then
Streamed through my cell a cold and silver beam,
And down the long beam stole the Holy Grail,
Rose-red with beatings in it, as if alive,
Till all the white walls of my cell were dyed
With rosy colours leaping on the wall;
And then the music faded, and the Grail
Past, and the beam decayed, and from the walls
The rosy quiverings died into the night.[89]

Tennyson's language and phallic/vaginal imagery capture and expand the eroticism of the medieval romance. In seeking the Holy Grail, however, we must remember that Galahad loses his spiritual lover, Perceval's sister. In the Cistercian-influenced thirteenth-century remake of romance's knight-errantry, as well as in Tennyson's medievalism, spiritual transcendence—not physical love—is the true ending of *the* Quest. Like both Tolkien and Lewis, Fitzgerald was drawn to the ability of *eros* to transcend the physical realm, and like them he usually avoided descriptions of actual sexual acts between his fictional lovers apart from the kiss.[90] Henry Dan Piper discusses Gatsby's "mythopoeic nature" at length, comparing him to the Great or Noble Fool archetype of Celtic and Arthurian literature (in particular Perceval/Parzival).[91] He suggests that Fitzgerald is drawing unconsciously on the medievalism of Sir Walter Scott, Sir James Barrie, and John

William Locke (the last two mentioned as among Amory's favorite authors in *This Side of Paradise*) and converting the Grail knight into a Horatio Alger poor-boy hero.

The young Jimmy Gatz starts out on a quest built on the American Dream of the self-made man who wins fortune and influence through the exertion of great physical rigor married to charisma. But instead of finding a love that will elevate his soul, he discovers an intelligent but fragile young woman who turns out to be *La Belle Dame Sans Merci*, the lovely, heartless creature feared by the Romantic poets (here we enter the realm of medievalism, rather than the medieval). There are indications of this in her name, Daisy Fay. "Daisy," the beautiful flower whose pure white petals lead to an inner core of gold and, in some English varieties, are tipped in crimson (violence/blood). [92] "Fay," indicating the beautiful faeries that lure questing knights away from their world of masculine accomplishment into otherworldly exile or death. The most infamous of these was Morgan le Fay, remembered for her attempts to seduce Lancelot and usurp the power of King Arthur. Some scholars have seen Daisy Fay as a Morgan le Fay reincarnate! [93]

Perhaps this is unfair to Daisy—she does not set out to destroy Gatsby, who probably has less of a real understanding of who she is than does her husband. Daisy and Tom are famously described by Nick as "careless people," but no one seems to care much about the death of Myrtle Wilson (except for her husband). Myrtle was neither old money aristocracy (like Tom, Daisy, and Nick) nor a parvenu craving Old World style (like Gatsby), but only a lower middle-class woman desiring bourgeois American respectability. She is ultimately trampled by the horse, left in the Valley of Ashes, and soon forgotten in the drama of those who live in the Long Island castles.

There is yet another, essentially medieval tradition to be found in *The Great Gatsby*—the "carnivalesque." Chronicled by Mikhail Bakhtin, Emmanuel Le Roy Ladurie, and other modern scholars, *carnival* encompasses the manifold pageants, ceremonies, and other festivities held at the beginning of Lent throughout medieval Christendom and surviving in many Catholic countries and regions. The social order was temporarily turned upside down during *carnival*, with peasants and craftsmen using costume, music, and dance to mock ecclesiastical and political power. Chaucer and Rabelais are just two of the many authors who have borrowed from the humor of *carnival*. Joan Allen has written about the symbolism of the carnival and circus in both Fitzgerald's short stories and his novels, contrasting the flashing lights, ferris wheels, and freak shows of the American carnival with the steady solemnity of the liturgical candle—City of Man tempting Fitzgerald's alter egos from the City of God.[94] *The Great Gatsby*—described in its earliest stage by Fitzgerald as a Catholic novel—is filled with pageants and parties that are subversive to social and ethical norms.[95] Jay Gatsby wears a mask (figuratively) and bright costumes, drives a yellow roadster Tom calls "a circus wagon," lives in a fake castle, throws parties attended by actors and dancers, does business with underworld creatures, and displays his enormous wealth as a challenge to old-moneyed East Egg. Nick witnesses a procession of carnivalesque images—Myrtle Wilson's chaotic party, the three affluent Negroes driven by a white chauffeur, a Jewish gangster with human molars as cuff links—when he crosses the bridge into the city. Gatsby's lavish parties are themselves an attempt to bring the subversive culture and social intermingling of uptown Manhattan to otherwise staid Long Island. Nick—"his modest stature . . . a reminder of Gatsby's heroic size"—serves as something of a squire to Gatsby's knight in this pageant.[96] While not exactly comic like Sancho Panza, Nick at first sees Gatsby's dreams, costumes, and mannerisms as absurd and attempts (unsuccessfully) to ground him in reality.[97] In Malory, the realism and sarcastic commentary is delivered by a fellow knight, Sir Dinidan, like Nick an unheroic companion to heroic lovers like Sir Tristram, Sir Launcelot, and Sir Palomides.

"For a model of a new emergent culture," writes James Meredith, Fitzgerald "looked deep into history to the medieval age, especially to the Dark Ages of the ninth century," in his plan for the historical novel, *Philippe, Count of Darkness*.[98] Nowhere else does Fitzgerald's intense interest in the Middle Ages manifest itself more than in the preparation for this project, a ninety-thousand-word novel following the gritty adventures of the Frankish baron Philippe. The four finished stories were published in October 1934, June and August 1935, and (posthumously) in November 1941.[99] They are not very good, marred by what Peter Hays describes as "laughable dialogue, a movie version of imagined medieval slang" and possibly written under the influence of alcohol.[100] And while they also contain many historical inconsistencies and anachronisms, they do give us a glimpse into Fitzgerald's longstanding love affair with the Middle Ages.

In a notebook, now in the Fitzgerald Collection at Princeton University Library, Fitzgerald kept his "Notes for Medieval Stories."[101] The notebook includes a list of "The Medieval Library" volumes (edited by Sir Israel Gollancz) that included *Trobador Poets*, *Cligés*, *Pearl*, *Early Lives of Charlemagne*, *Piers Plowman*, *Ancren Riwle*, and *Beowulf*.[102] There is a typed list of "Books Used in Medieval Stories" that includes the following works: *Histoire de France*; Murray, *The Witch-Cult in Western Europe*; Weston, *From Ritual to Romance*; Lytton, *Harold, the Last of the Saxon Kings*; Taylor, *The Medieval Mind*; Belloc, *Europe and the Faith—The Dark Ages*; Calverton, *The Making of Man*; Young, *Mediaeval Towns, Rome*; Barrow, *Growth of Europe through Dark Ages*; and articles on "Arms and Armour," "Charlemagne," "Falconry," "Knighthood and Chivalry," etc. from *Encyclopedia Britannica*. His "Notes from Library Books for Medieval Series" includes typescript and handwritten notes on such subjects as "Ramparts," "Lange d'oc," "Ivory horn-Michelet," "Wolves," and "A.D. 877 Countships hereditary." There is a handwritten list/timeline, titled "Men of the Dark Thousand (970 years)," that runs from 476 (Odoacer) to 1446 (Henry Navigator), and a hand-drawn and notated timeline of events from 840 to 890.

Fitzgerald chose the setting of France in the ninth-century because he saw it as the dawn of chivalry and feudalism. The stories are written in a realist style, lacking all sentimentality and romanticism. Philippe, whom Fitzgerald claims to have based on Ernest Hemingway, returns from Spain to his native France to confront Vikings, organize the peasants, jump-start the local economy (with the help of Syrian merchants), mistreat his concubine, and manipulate a pagan fertility cult. One single, small note among his medieval papers reads: "Phillipe as an act of morality killing ugly little tart and then as an act of morality taking her to her parents." Another note, written on a torn half of page of paper: "On Witchcraft–After yielding she holds Phillipe and baby like Zelda & me in summer 1917." The crude behavior and violence of Phillipe make him a naïf like Parzival, observes Peter Hays, and Fitzgerald seems to be clumsily trying to combine a medieval bildungsroman with prose epic in the creation of a realist, historical novel.[103]

Of the projected thirteen chapters for the novel, only four *Phillipe* stories were finished—" In the Darkest Hour," "The Count of Darkness," "The Kingdom in the Dark," and "Gods of Darkness"—published serially in *Redbook*.[104] In the finished stories, observes Meredith, "medieval allegory allowed him to communicate his vision of the dark future augured by the fascist threat of the 1930s. . . . The real solution to the threat of fascism, Fitzgerald implies, is a resurgence of aristocratic nobility," with Philippe as a benevolent feudal lord and precursor to the High medieval knight.[105] Countering the darkness (the word "dark" appears in all four titles) is a "vigorous feudalism," writes Hays, "an organizing principle" for post-Roman European politics and economy, with anachronistic doses of democracy and Marxism thrown in.[106] Such modern *noblesse oblige*, Fitzgerald indicates in a composition note, has even been displayed by his former Long Island neighbor and friend, Mary Harriman Rumsey.[107]

The *Philippe* project betrays Fitzgerald's fascination with the medieval class system and feudalism, odd for a self-described Socialist. "Whereas Marxists looked forward to an age of large-scale labor organization," writes Fitzgerald biographer Paul S. Brown, "Scott looked back to the preindustrial era of small-scale localism."[108] Like the Jazz Age, the European Middle Ages witnessed the rise of an urban merchant class whose money and tastes were destined to replace the power and culture of the rural aristocracy. Nick's family background shows European aristocracy giving way to New World mercantile, bourgeois success, and respectability.[109] Gatsby, on the other hand, must climb toward respectability based on his own wits, concocting a story about wealthy parents that parodies Nick's biographical narrative. "Gatsby expects to be a gentleman," writes Berman, and "shows a kind of linguistic noblesse oblige" in deferring to Nick's preferences for the tea with Daisy and offering to share his "sideline business" with Nick. "Gatsby is being literary-honorable, imitating the gentry he has read about in magazines or those whom he has briefly known at Oxford, to whom any business would indeed be a sideline."[110]

Fitzgerald was clearly ambivalent about the rise of the mercantile—both in the Renaissance and in the Gilded Age—and like Chaucer and other late medieval poets he recognized the need to adapt for different patrons and different audiences. *The Great Gatsby*, like *The Canterbury Tales*, is able to capture the spirit of the age from different perspectives, offering social satire and biting criticism without giving up on the ideals. Fitzgerald himself "believed in the sanctity of chivalry," writes Meredith, "and he saw its loss as a powerful indicator of the spiritual and cultural depravity of the modern age" that the Great War had created.[111] In the contest between the old-moneyed, equestrian crowd of Tom Buchanan versus the *nouveau riche*, automotive culture of Jay Gatsby, it is Tom who wins the tarnished trophy.[112]

Fitzgerald's life was hardly a heroic quest, but it may have been, as Bruccoli observes, "a quest for heroism."[113] He hoped for success on the football field at Princeton and the fields of France in World War I that would bring him great renown, but he missed his chance at both. The honors he did receive at Princeton failed to win his first love, Ginevra King, whose wealthy father built a mock Rhenish castle for his family in Chicago's "Gold Coast" district.[114] Ginevra ultimately rejected Scott to marry a wealthy Chicago businessman. Zelda, too, would break off her engagement to Scott when she became nervous about his chances of succeeding as a writer, but he would convince his princess to marry him not (as he joked) by locking her in an ivory tower, but by publishing his first novel.

In 1941, just months after Scott's death, Zelda produced a water and graphite triptych titled *Morgan Le Fay*, portraying Morgan as heroic and rather masculine. This appears to be part of a sequence of paper dolls made for her grandchildren, a practice she had begun for Scottie in the 1920s. In the 1940s Zelda returned to painting—part therapy, part pure artistic expression—and much of it was inspired by the medieval. "I have painted King Arthur's round table," she wrote in a 1941 letter to Maxwell Perkins, perhaps with the intention of illustrating a children's book of her own.[115] "I have painted Jeanne d'Arc and coterie, Louis XIV and court, Robin Hood are [all] under way." In many of the surviving figures gender is hard to identify. "Males and females alike are heavily muscled," writes art curator Jane Livingston, with many of the male figures "displaying startlingly effeminate attributes."[116] Zelda, who had rebuked Scott for wanting her to be a princess locked up in a tower,[117] seems to have been asserting her artistic voice at last, and with some of the same medieval subject matter that had so captivated Scott.

Scott and Zelda shared many of the same talents, and many of the same vices. We explored the probable fairy origins of Daisy's last name. But in its variant spelling FEY, the word can mean "excessively refined," "unconventional," and even "fated to die" (Scottish). These could all describe Guinevere and Zelda Sayre. Zelda's flamboyant lifestyle and mental instability led to institutionalization, but it was Scott's excesses that marked him as doomed to a premature death, his neo-medieval and romantic spirit living on in his greatest literary creation, Jay Gastby.

8

"A Meadow Lark Among the Smoke Stacks": Oxford and Princeton

Looking back over a decade one sees the ideal of a university become a myth, a vision, a meadow lark among the smoke stacks. Yet perhaps it is there at Princeton, only more elusive than under the skies of the Prussian Rhineland or Oxfordshire; or perhaps some men come upon it suddenly and possess it, while others wander forever outside. Even these seek in vain through middle age for any corner of the republic that preserves so much of what is fair, gracious, charming and honorable in American life.

—F. Scott Fitzgerald, "Princeton" (1927)

In Scott Fitzgerald's reflections on Princeton ten years after he left the school, we see a nostalgia tinged with reality, yet nevertheless a dream-vision similar to the reflections on Oxford in the contemporary Oxford Novel. Princeton is Fitzgerald's Oxford. It was where he learned to be a poet and a student of poetry, where he honed his aestheticism in fashion as well as in writing, and where he came to respect (if not live up to) the ideals of a liberal education. He came with dreams of being a football star, and left clinging to the modest success he had writing musicals and short stories. Princeton dominates his first novel, and in the guise of Harvard and Yale it plays a significant role in the next two. In turn, the New Jersey university would come to embrace its native son, but only decades after his death.

The Education of Scott Fitzgerald

In his autobiographical essay, "Author's House" (1936), Fitzgerald writes that as a young boy he clung to the belief that he "wasn't the son of [his] parents but a son of a king . . . who ruled the whole world."[1] In a satirical family tree he sent to Edmund Wilson in 1920, he claimed "F. Scott Fitzgerald (drunkard)" descended from "Duns Scotus (philos.)," "Mary, Queen of Scotts (Queen)," "Sir Walter Scott (Ivanhoe)," "Duke Fitzgerald (Earl of Leinster)," and "Francis Scott Key (hymnalist)."[2] As a boy in St. Paul, Minnesota, Fitzgerald carried a cane when he went with his father to have their shoes shined on Sunday mornings.[3] Amory Blaine displays this youthful dandyism, while Fitzgerald calls both Anthony Patch (at Harvard and after, in New York) and his father dandies.

As Joan Allen points out, Fitzgerald was the first Irish Catholic to become a major American writer. The St. Paul of Fitzgerald's youth included a large number of Irish (about 8 percent of the city's population), both new immigrants and the descendants of those who arrived in large numbers in the middle of the nineteenth century. It was a time in which WASP America began to fear and turn against these new Irish immigrants, from social-Darwinist views of their racial inferiority to comparisons with the African Americans with whom they competed for wage labor.[4] Fitzgerald's Irish heritage descended from both his father and mother: his paternal grandfather, Michael Fitzgerald, had roots going back to civil service in Colonial America, while his maternal grandfather, Philip Francis McQuillan, emigrated at the age of eight from County Fermanagh, Ireland, settling first in Galena, Illinois (hometown of Ulysses S. Grant), and eventually in St. Paul, where he became a successful wholesale grocer.[5] Fitzgerld's father, Edward Fitzgerald, grew up in Rockville, Maryland, with Confederate sympathies. Edward had rowed Confederate spies across the Potomac and helped a member of Mosby's Raiders avoid arrest.[6] Chivalric and courtly, he struggled as a businessman in both Minnesota and upstate New York, finally accepting the humiliation of McQuillan subsidies.

Francis Scott Fitzgerald was born to Edward Fitzgerald and Mollie McQuillan on September 24, 1896, in St. Paul. Many of the St. Paul Irish bought homes and rose steadily into the upper middle-class, competing with older city elites, English and German Protestants on one hand and French Catholics on the other. Mollie had inherited money and Edward was a member of the White Bear Yacht Club, though they could not afford a summer home there like other members had.[7] In *This Side of Paradise*, Fitzgerald identifies both Ireland and Catholicism with the Romantic lost cause; just as important is his struggle to be accepted by older, mostly Anglo-Protestant elites. He was "in the mix" at the non-sectarian St. Paul Academy, near the affluent Summit Avenue. Though clearly intelligent and creative, he nevertheless made poor grades and few school friends at St. Paul's.

Fitzgerld's parents decided an East Coast finishing school might improve his academics and self-discipline. The Newman School for Boys in Hackensack, New Jersey, where Scott attended from the age of fifteen to seventeen, was an altogether different environment than St. Paul's.[8] Here prosperous Catholic families could send their boys for a "gentleman's education" in imitation of the mostly Protestant private preparatory schools of the northeast—like Groton and Andover—that were feeder-schools for Harvard, Princeton, and Yale. Less academic than Jesuit-run colleges, leadership and sports were stressed for young men who were assumed to be the next captains of industry and political leaders. Fitzgerald's passion was for football and writing, and he had modest success in both by his senior year. At the Newman School he also made the acquaintance of one of the school's trustees, Monsignor

Cyril Sigourney Webster Fay, a priest from a wealthy Philadelphia Irish family who was then living in Baltimore and teaching at the pontifical Catholic University of America in Washington, D.C. Well-read and worldly, the flamboyant Cyril Fay was an adult convert to Catholicism and a socialite who let Scott into his adult world of writers and academics. A student of medieval church history, Monsignor Fay was an avid reader of Oscar Wilde and something of an aesthete himself.[9] His fondness for the young Fitzgerald and their intimacy can be glimpsed in the frank conversations between Monsignor Darcy and Amory in *This Side of Paradise*.

As discussed in Chapter Two, Father Fay also introduced Fitzgerald to the English writer Shane Leslie while Fitzgerald was at the Newman School. Like Fay an adult convert to Catholicism, Leslie came from the Irish gentry and attended King's College, Cambridge. Fay and Leslie both read and encouraged Fitzgerald's early writing, and they made him reassess his attitude toward both Ireland and the Catholic Church as experienced in St. Paul. They "made of that church a dazzling, golden thing," and gave its ritual "the romantic glamour of an adolescent dream."[10]

Academic success did not come to Fitzgerald during his time at the Newman School, however, yet he had his heart set on attending Princeton. Drawn to Princeton in part by its football team, which often lost to rival Yale, "his image of the group he wished to join—romantic young men destined to suffer loss—is telling," observes Edward Gillin.[11] He may also have admired the university's appeal among the sons of Southern elites, as he alludes to in the "lost cause" romanticism of the teenage Amory Blaine in *This Side of Paradise*. Scott did not do well on his entrance exams, and was required to interview at Princeton. In person his charm just barely carried the day, and he joined the rest of the 58 percent of Princetonians who were admitted "on conditions" in 1913.[12]

At Princeton Fitzgerald studied Old English poetry (in translation) and Chaucer.[13] He also read Plato as well as Plutarch and Petronius. Only a few of his professors drew Fitzgerald's admiration, while the preceptors he found dull and uninspiring.[14] Frequently absent and failing in many of his studies, Fitzgerald nonetheless came to cherish the Princeton honor code and told the 1917 yearbook that he intended to do postgraduate study in English at Harvard. One of Fitzgerald's favorite professors was Christian Gauss, Class of 1900 Professor of Modern Languages and a former dean of the college who had begun his Princeton career as one of Wilson's first preceptors in 1905. Before that, Gauss had been a journalist working in Paris, where he hung out in cafes with Oscar Wilde. A guide and friend of the *Nassau Literary Magazine,* Gauss taught courses on Dante, Flaubert, and the French Romantics. In addition to Fitzgerald, Gauss would have a formative influence on both Edmund Wilson and John Peale Bishop.[15]

Fitzgerald's social aspirations depended on being part of either the athletic or club cultures at Princeton. Since he got cut from the football team after the first day of tryouts, he turned strategically to the club scene. Fitzgerald became a member of the Triangle Club as a freshman and was soon writing for the club's 1914–15 show, *Fie! Fie! Fi-Fi!,* adding social satire to the opening chorus.[16] "I spent my entire freshman year writing an operetta for the Triangle Club," he later confessed. "I failed in algebra, trigonometry, coordinate geometry and hygiene, but the Triangle Club accepted my show."[17] He contributed to two more Triangle productions, and appeared in drag as a chorus girl, later wearing the same costume to a dance at the University of Minnesota.[18] He also wrote several short pieces for the university's humor magazine, the *Princeton Tiger,* and contributed both poetry and short stories to the *Nassau Literary Magazine,* Princeton's major undergraduate literary periodical.

To be accepted into a community dominated by boys from the top private schools in the northeast, however, Fitzgerald sought admission into the most prestigious of the university's eating clubs, those selective social institutions that had replaced the banned fraternities in the late nineteenth century. Fitzgerald received bids to four of the eating clubs and chose The University Cottage Club of Princeton, known simply as Cottage, the second oldest (founded in 1886), housed in a spacious Georgian Revival mansion on Prospect Avenue, "The Street." *Ubi Amici Ibidem Sunt Opes* is the Cottage motto—"Where there are friends, there are riches"—and Fitzgerald desired both. "An impressive mélange of brilliant adventurers and well-dressed philanderers" is how Fitzgerald described Cottage in his first novel. Weekend parties at Cottage included debutantes bussed in from New York and Philadelphia to dance with the Princeton men and mingle in the patio gardens. Cottage even had an elaborate upper-floor library, paneled in English oak with carved ceilings and cornices and modeled specifically on the fourteenth-century Merton College Library at Oxford.[19] In this library Fitzgerald began writing the novel that would become *This Side of Paradise*. The Charles McKim designed house, finished in 1915, may have inspired Tom and Daisy's Georgian mansion in *The Great Gatsby*.[20]

One of the most autobiographically interesting of his early works is the short story, "The Spire and the Gargoyle," which first appeared in the *Nassau Literary Magazine* in 1917.[21] It is the story of an unnamed boy who, though recovering from epicurean revelry to collegiate ideas, flunks out of an unnamed university at the end of his freshman year. After failing an exam, the boy is unable to win the sympathy of the little, bespectacled preceptor, whom he names "the gargoyle." Five years later, in a Manhattan art museum, he runs into the gargoyle and finds that he, too, has left the university to teach in a Brooklyn high school. Both men make the journey by train back to the university a week later, but the younger man realizes, through fog and tears, that "the spirit that should have dominated his life" has forever vanished for him.

Fitzgerald scholars have commented on the timing of the story—Scott had just himself recovered from illness and poor performance to return to Princeton—and how it fits with his "lost Eden" writings lamenting his early academic and amorous failures.[22] Of note here is the narrator's descriptions of the university during his first year there and the symbolism of institution and architecture. In the opening scene, the night mist "clustered about the spires and towers, and then settled bellow them so that the dreaming peaks seemed still lofty in aspiration toward the stars."[23] Breaking through the "careless shell" of his freshman indulgences was "a deep and almost reverent liking for the grey walls and Gothic peaks and all they symbolized in the store of the ages of antiquity."[24] The boy "had learned that Gothic architecture with its upward trend was peculiarly adapted to colleges, and the symbolism of this idea had become personal to him." Outside his window "a tower sprang upward, grew into a spire, yearning higher," and the "pure" and "chaste" tower "led and directed and called" to him until "the spire became an ideal." Expelled from this kingdom because of a proctor who "looked like one of the gargoyles that nested in dozens of niches in some of the buildings," a "grotesque . . . of gargoyle origin, or at least gargoyle kinship," the boy becomes a man in the mindless vacuum of Fifth Avenue commerce and skepticism.[25] Yearning to return from "exile" to his idyllic college, he takes the train back to the university, but where "before the spirit of spires and towers had thrilled him and had made him dreamily content," now the vision "overawed him" and made him realize "his own impotence and insufficiency."[26] Now "the battlemented walls fronted him" while "the college dreamed on," and his eyes sought "where the spire began—and with his eyes went his soul. But the mist was upon both. He could not climb with the spire."[27]

Gerald Pike's fine study of authorial voice, animism, and structure in this example of Fitzgerald's "apprenticeship fiction" counters the overly easy dismissal of the short story as mere indulgent autobiography of Fitzgerald's own indolence at Princeton. One could go further, however, and extend sympathies for these early frustrated hopes of the author by noting how Gothic Princeton serves as the aesthetic connector of youthful dreaming and academic/professional accomplishment in both "The Spire and the Gargoyle" and *This Side of Paradise*. "The story is not simply about the boy," observes Pike, but also "about the relationship between the spire and the gargoyle, . . . between heaven and earth."[28] As Oxford, in part, inspired Princeton's aesthetic, so, too, does it serve as such a connector "between heaven and earth" for the Oxford Novels that influenced Fitzgerald in writing *The Great Gatsby*. Like *Gatsby*, this short story explores the capacity for hope, but also, as Edward Gillin points out, the often great distance between that hope "and the general human tragedy of its frustration."[29]

In his essay "Princeton," which first appeared in *College Humor* in 1927, Fitzgerald writes about the impression the university makes on approach from the surrounding New Jersey Countryside:

Princeton is in the flat midlands of New Jersey, rising, a green phoenix. . . . Two tall spires and then suddenly all around you spreads out the loveliest riot of Gothic architecture in America, battlement linked on to battlement, hall to hall, arch-broken, vine-covered, luxuriant and lovely. . . . Alfred Noyes has compared Princeton to Oxford. To me the two are sharply different. Princeton is thinner and fresher, at once less profound and more elusive.[30]

In a 1920 letter to Princeton President John Grier Hibben, who had lamented the portrayal of the University in *This Side of Paradise*, Fitzgerald wrote, "I have no fault to find with Princeton that I can't find with Oxford and Cambridge. I simply wrote out of my own impressions, wrote as honestly as I could a picture of its beauty. That the picture is cynical is the fault of my temperament."[31] It is significant that, in trying to describe Princeton after he left the school, Fitzgerald went not to Harvard or Yale for comparison, but here and often did he turn to Oxford.

Oxford Comes to Princeton: Woodrow Wilson and the American Collegiate Gothic

Princeton does not attempt to make good citizens, but to create a respect for ideas and to make the student aware how intolerably men have suffered that beauty and wisdom might have form.

—John Peale Bishop, "Princeton" (1921)

F. Scott Fitzgerald describes the Princeton of his day as growing out of the post-Civil War "fortunes of New York and Philadelphia" to include sports and clubs and "keg parties" and yet reflecting "[Woodrow] Wilson's cloistered plans for an educational utopia."[32] Woodrow Wilson had been a student at Princeton and a distinguished member of its faculty before being named president of the university in 1902, serving eight years as leader of the institution as it morphed from country club college to modern research university. While Fitzgerald never directly experienced Wilson as either faculty member or president, he certainly felt the presence of the progressive reformer during his three-plus undistinguished years at Princeton.

A child of the Reconstruction South, Thomas Woodrow Wilson began post-secondary education at Davidson College in North Carolina in 1873 but soon transferred to the College of New Jersey (as Princeton was then called) where he studied history and political philosophy and wrote for the *Nassau Literary Review*. After graduating in 1879, Wilson attended the University of Virginia Law School for one year before briefly practicing law in Georgia. In 1883 he began doctoral study at Johns Hopkins University, completing his dissertation on Congress and receiving his PhD in 1886, then commenced a teaching career that took him to Cornell, Bryn Mawr (where he taught ancient Greek and Roman history), and Wesleyan University (where he also coached the football team). In 1890 he was elected to the Chair of Jurisprudence and Political Economy at Princeton, and remained on the faculty for twenty years.

Woodrow Wilson was a lifelong Anglophile and an avid reader of the British Romantic poets, spending much time in Wordsworth's beloved Lake District. His first visits to Oxford and Cambridge came in 1896.[33] "A mere glance at Oxford is enough to take one's heart by storm," he wrote to his wife Ellen, and dreamt of moving there if a position was offered to him. He returned in 1899 and informed his daughter Jessie that "Oxford is England's great university town. We hope that Princeton will be like it [someday]." On the second visit he explored the colleges' quadrangles and "secluded gardens" and attended Professor Albert Dicey's lecture on comparisons between American and British universities. He was similarly impressed by the Gothic architecture and quads of Cambridge and Trinity College Dublin. His third and final trip to Oxford and Cambridge occurred in 1903, when, accompanied by his wife, he tried to visit all the colleges he had missed in his previous visits. In his five trips across the Atlantic, he only went to the Continent twice and there is no indication that he ever visited any universities there.

When he became president of Princeton in 1902, Wilson set out to accomplish many things, including founding a graduate school, creating new residential colleges, reorganizing the administration, building new structures in the "Collegiate Gothic" style, organizing the faculty into departments, recruiting top faculty who were researchers, instituting the preceptorial system and majors, and raising admissions standards. As historian James Axtell points out, the disappointment that Wilson felt in leaving office in 1910 distorts that fact that he accomplished many of his ambitious goals.[34] Wilson wanted to make Princeton one of the country's premiere universities, and he is largely responsible for its ascendance to that status. "Cambridge and Oxford had put dreams into his head," wrote Wilson's close friend, Edith Reid, even if other forces conspired against these dreams.[35]

A significant part of Wilson's 1904 reforms was increased rigor in the entrance examinations.[36] These included, for the bachelor of arts (AB) degree, exams in English, Latin, mathematics (through plane geometry), Greek, and French or German. These exams were given in cities and prep schools throughout the country for a fee of $5, equivalent to over $100 today, which served to deter many poor students from public schools. Only 23 percent of students who entered Princeton in the fall of 1904 did so without "conditions," the required remedial work with which Fitzgerald and many of his contemporaries struggled. Another deterrent for many students was high tuition—in 1908 fees were between $382 and $730 per academic year, excluding the costs of books, club fees, room furnishings, and travel. At the time of Fitzgerald's first year at Princeton, the school was becoming even more affluent and exclusive than it had ever been. Even though the stringent entrance exams were dropped in 1916 and mandatory Greek in 1919, the Princeton student demographic changed little until after World War II. In Fitzgerald's day, Princeton had no black students, no women, and few international students. ". . . while there is nothing in the law of the University to prevent a negro's entering," wrote Wilson in 1904, "the whole temper and tradition of the place are such that no negro has ever applied for admission."[37] There were very few Jewish students at Princeton either, and they were blackballed from the eating clubs.[38] Though he would appoint the first Catholic and Jewish members of the faculty at Princeton, Wilson actively discouraged black and Chinese students from applying and resisted co-education.[39]

The primary method of instruction at Princeton when Fitzgerald attended was the preceptorial system, introduced by President Wilson in 1905. The preceptorial was a modification of the Oxford tutorial system, with standard lectures given by professors supplemented by one-hour meetings with younger faculty or graduate students called "preceptors." The preceptors would meet once a week with three to six students, and grades were done on the Oxford system as well, with firsts through sevenths.[40] Wilson's hope was to foster "close and personal contact" between faculty and student, especially as his goal to make Princeton an elite research university necessitated enrollment growth.[41] Wilson's preceptors were to be more like the Oxonian tutors in their reformed Victorian guise, the intellectual companions and guides envisioned by John Henry Newman and Benjamin Jowett. After their first two years of a broad liberal education, Princeton undergraduates would move into newly created "majors." These were also partly inspired by Oxford's Greats program and its honours examinations.

President Wilson launched major fundraising initiatives soon after coming into office and accelerated the rebuilding of the campus in Collegiate Gothic style "to signal the university's medieval, and particularly English, heritage."[42] While Gothic Revival architecture on American college campuses began at Trinity College (CT) in the 1870s, many of the "ancient" structures that Fitzgerald praises in his 1927 "Princeton" essay dated back only a decade or so before his arrival on campus, including those "two tall spires"—Holder and Cleveland Towers—which date respectively to 1910 and 1913 (Figs. 13 and 14).[43] Both structures were designed on Oxford models, in particular St. Mary's Tower in Magdalen College. Wilson demanded that every building, even the science buildings, "should be beautiful." Fitzgerald's friend and classmate John Peale Bishop, writing in 1921, confirms the connection between Princeton's Gothic architecture and its pretensions to be the American Oxford:

The campus accepts this tradition [i.e., its Colonial roots] and attempts an air of even greater age by borrowing an architecture of Oxonian medievalism. It is the fashion just now among intellectuals to decry this imitation of the English collegiate Gothic. But . . . I am unfortunately fond of the grave beauty of these towers and spires trembling upward, intricately labored and grey; of these grey quadrangles and deep slate roofs . . . and Holder, enclosing with cloisters and arches a square of sunlight and sod. [44]

Wilson's efforts to remake Princeton along Oxbridge lines were paralleled, before and after the war, at many American institutions of higher learning. [45] "In a large number of the colleges and universities of the country—notably in Princeton, Columbia, Yale, Harvard, Oberlin, University of Minnesota, and the University of Washington—attempts are being made to apply English methods to the solution of American educational problems," wrote Frank Aydelotte in an editorial in 1917. The tutorial system is also singled out by Aydelotte, who saw its popularity in America expanding in the years following the establishment of the Rhodes scholarships.

One of the aspects of Oxford that appealed most to the early American Rhodes scholars was the community inherent in the collegiate model. One wartime scholar even recommended it over the American fraternity:

After being in war-time Oxford for three or four months and in the good fellowship of a very small college—there are about an even dozen of us at Trinity—I wonder whether it would be necessary to insist on a large fraternity on the model of the college in ordinary times in order to secure all the advantages of the Oxford system. . . . The bonds of fellowship, I believe, are very much closer in this reduced college than it would be possible for them to be when it is at its full strength. We all sit at the same table in Hall and we all gather around the same fire in the Common Room.

We have gotten to know each other's antecedents, habits of thought, and peculiarities. [46]

Woodrow Wilson attempted, in 1906, to establish "quads" at Princeton—which were his version of the Oxbridge residential colleges with their monastic quadrangles—in part to break the exclusivity and extracurricular "sideshows" that the eating clubs had become. [47] Not only were the eating clubs notorious for prodigious drinking, their pervasive discrimination in favor of the affluent particularly drew Wilson's ire as he sought to democratize the student body (at least in terms of social class). In the years between the wars Harvard University had acquired "houses" modeled on the Oxford and Cambridge colleges (Yale's residential college system dates to 1933), and at many other American colleges and universities the English Gothic collegiate style of their buildings introduced something of the collegiate reality: "the well-rounded and unspecialized training of an elite drawn from first-degree students in a residential setting." [48]

The most purely Gothic quadrangle went to the residential Graduate College, established in 1913 on the edge of campus (not in its center as Wilson wished) by Dean Andrew Fleming West. [49] West had been a longtime ally of Wilson's and had traveled to study closely both Oxbridge and the rising German universities. Wilson was so committed to the idea of the liberal arts as building intellectual community that he wished to extend the liberal arts to graduate education. He did not want Princeton to develop purely professional or technical schools, rejecting plans for law, industrial, and forestry schools as president. The Harvey S. Firestone Memorial Library was not built until 1948, but it is a magnificent Gothic structure that (appropriately) houses special collections and rare books, including the papers of Scott and Zelda Fitzgerald.

Public attention on Princeton grew, of course, when Woodrow Wilson won the U.S. presidential election in 1912 and even more so when Wilson arrived as the great American savior in Paris for the Versailles peace talks in 1919. Fitzgerald wrote a letter to Princeton friend Bishop in March of 1925 while living abroad:

Dear John:

I am quite drunk. I am told that this is Capri; though as I remember Capri was quieter. . . . I am full of my new work, a historical play based on the life of Woodrow Wilson.[50]

What follows is a précis of four acts, the first taking place at Princeton and the last at Versailles. President Wilson, in the "play," has a bastard son in Trenton who shows up at Versailles in a Prussian uniform; both the Princeton football team and the Triangle Club make appearances on stage, as does John Grier Hibben, Al Jolson, Clemenceau, and Gilbert Seldes. "Oh Christ!" interrupts the playwright from his description, "I'm sobering up!"

Scott Joins the Army

After four years at Princeton, what remains . . . beyond the recollection of torchlight processions . . . and the gargoyles creeping out into the crimson glare; . . . of arriving drunk to the Phi Beta Kappa dinner and passing out before the roast; of students leaving a little sorrowfully and without illusion for the war, after farewell parties which began on Perrier Jouet '93 and ended on Great Western . . . ?
—John Peale Bishop, "Princeton" (1921)

F. Scott Fitzgerald "sticks in the public consciousness as a sort of perpetual undergraduate: charming, talented, and rather irresponsible," writes Scott Donaldson.[51] He certainly had neither the academic talent nor the discipline of his Princeton friends Bishop and Wilson. Illness his junior year saw him back in St. Paul for recovery, but it also gave him an excuse to withdraw from classes he was failing. Returning to Princeton in the Fall of 1916, he faced the prospect of repeating his junior year. He was also failing in love: Ginevra King, the daughter of a wealthy Lake Forest family, with whom he had been carrying on a passionate (if mostly epistolary) love affair since Christmas 1914, broke off with Fitzgerald in January 1917. As he would later comment wryly in his *Ledger*, "Poor boys shouldn't think of marrying rich girls." Struggling at the same time with his January exams at Princeton, he saw a new way to save his reputation: America was about to enter the war. Princeton offered its students the option of withdrawing from their courses without losing credit if they joined the armed forces, and Fitzgerald did just that. Getting little from the formal academic course at Princeton, he nevertheless was formed by the books he read there, by the campus aesthetic, and by the small community of intelligent and creative souls with whom he ate, drank, and argued.

Fitzgerald enlisted in the army in October 1917, though many of his Princeton classmates had already enlisted before May.[52] He was commissioned as a second lieutenant in the infantry (he had his uniforms tailored in New York City at Brooks Brothers) and sent to training camp at Fort Leavenworth, Kansas, where his platoon captain was Dwight D. Eisenhower (neither man made much of an impression on the other). After short stints at Camp Taylor in Louisville, Kentucky, and Camp Gordon, in Georgia, Fitzgerald landed in June 1918 at Camp Sheridan near Montgomery, Alabama, where he was promoted to first lieutenant in the 45th Infantry Regiment of the 9th Division and served as *aide-de-camp* to General J. F. Ryan ("the big goopher"). Fitzgerald was not a natural soldier and displayed little talent as an officer, spending much time drinking and writing. After an aborted attempt to produce a collection of poems, he hurriedly wrote his first novel, then titled *The Romantic Egotist*, on weekends while preparing to leave for the battlefields of France. "I just went and purely for social reasons," he wrote his mother. "If you want to pray, pray for my soul and not that I won't get killed—the last doesn't seem to matter and if you are a good Catholic the first ought to."[53] Fitzgerald was not given a platoon (his superiors had little trust in his ability to lead men) and he expected to die in the war. "Of course when he is killed, [his novel] will also have a commercial value," wrote a friend recommending *The Romantic Egotist* to the publisher Scribner and Sons.[54] Scribner's declined to publish twice, but the soft criticisms offered by an anonymous editor in August were salient: neither love affairs nor war resulted in growth for Amory Blaine, who seemingly joined the army just as he had gone to college, "because it is simply the thing to do."[55]

But Fitzgerald was having too good a time in Montgomery to think much of dying in a war. Lawton Campbell, a local boy he had known at Princeton, took him to dances and introduced him to the local belles. It was purely by chance, however, that in July, at the Country Club of Montgomery, Scott Fitzgerald met seventeen-year-old Zelda Sayre, daughter of Judge Anthony D. Sayre of the Alabama Supreme Court. The youngest of six children, a descendant of Confederate generals and U.S. senators, Zelda Sayre was already a local celebrity by the time she met Scott Fitzgerald. She and her childhood friend, the actress Tallulah Bankhead, would often stage "dramas" on the steps of the Alabama State Capitol Building; her mother even wrote a play about "fairy land" in which Zelda played the jester "Folly." In a more patriotic pageant sponsored by the Montgomery Rotary Club, Zelda represented England and delivered a rousing call to arms:

> Interrupted in these benevolent pursuits, for over three years
> I have been engaged in bloody warfare and the end is not
> yet. O, America, young republic of the West, blood of my
> blood and faith of my faith, for humanity's sake together
> we fight![56]

"Zelda seemed licensed at birth to express the freedom and romance of the fictional gypsy for whom she was named," observed her grand-daughter, Eleanor Lanahan.[57] Zelda was a dancer and a great flirt, the months surrounding her high school graduation in June 1918 filled with tea parties, dances, and a string of adoring young men, including several football players and aviation officers. Scott's persistent wooing of Zelda paid off late that summer when, shortly before he was sent north to prepare for embarkation, their love was consummated.

It was a love, however, surrounded by the tragedy of war and pestilence. The Spanish Flu epidemic of 1918 hit Camp Sheridan hard and dozens died in the fall of 1918. Among the Red Cross volunteers at

Camp Sheridan was Lydia Eustis of Birmingham, who was to marry Major William Rogers after the war. While living at Hostess House at Camp Sheridan, Lydia was engaged in more than just rolling bandages and dancing with soldiers. She took on serious public health work for the Red Cross, chairing the Health and Sanitation Committee and collecting health and morbidity statistics in the Mississippi Delta. She wrote reports for the New York offices of the Red Cross on health and sanitation issues in some of the poorest counties in the country, made recommendations on government aid and medical needs, carrying out her work from 1918 to 1920. "Popular Society Girl of This City Becomes a Veritable Oracle at Hostess House," read one headline in *The Birmingham News*, but it sold her wartime contributions short to describe her as a hostess. [58]

Fitzgerald was ordered to Camp Mills, Long Island, assigned duties as a supply officer in preparation for the 9th Division's embarkation for France. He had ventured off to Princeton and it was there that he received the news: a truce was signed, and the Great War was over. Fitzgerald's reaction was to go on a long drinking binge in New York City. Eventually he was caught by the house detective with a naked girl at the Hotel Astor, and was thus AWOL when his troop train left to return to Alabama, showing up instead in Washington, D.C. with a bottle and two more girls! [59]

Fitzgerald explores his feelings about the war and its ending first in *This Side of Paradise*. Like Scott himself, Amory joins the army before graduating from Princeton. Writing to Amory in January 1918 when he was at the infantry embarkation point on Long Island, the Monsignor Darcy offers advice to his young friend about to see battle:

> Of one thing I'm sure—Celtic you'll live and Celtic you'll die; so if you don't use heaven as a continual referendum for your ideas you'll find earth a continual recall to your ambitions. . . .
>
> We [both] can attract people, we can make atmosphere, we can almost lose our Celtic souls in Celtic subtleties . . . (146).

He then closes his letter with a "keen" written for Amory titled "A Lament for a Foster Son, and He going to the War Against the King of Foreign." An actual poem written for Fitzgerald by Father Fay, each stanza begins with a phrase in Gaelic, the last stanza mimicking the early medieval Irish prayer known as *Saint Patrick's Breastplate*:

> May Patrick of the Gael and Collumb of the Churches and the
>   five thousand Saints of Erin be better than a shield to him
> And he go into the fight.
>   Och Ochone. (148).

Amory survives the war and writes a letter from France to his Princeton friend, Thomas D'Invilliers, suggesting they take an apartment together in Manhattan when he returns:

> I don't know what I'm going to do but I have a vague dream of going into politics. Why is it that the pick of the young Englishmen from Oxford and Cambridge go into politics and in the U.S.A. we leave it to the muckers? . . . Sometimes I wish I'd been an Englishman; American life is so damned dumb and stupid and healthy. (149)

In *Tender is the Night*, we get the contrast between Dick Diver—excited about the war as a moment in history—and Abe North, who actually saw combat and is nonchalant. Dick attempts to impress upon his traveling companions the scale of the slaughter as they walk along the trench near Thiepval. "He was full of excitement and he wanted to communicate it to them," writes Fitzgerald, "to make them understand about this, though actually Abe North had seen battle service and he had not." Abe asserts:

> "General Grant invented this kind of battle at Petersburg in sixty-five."
> "No, he didn't—he just invented mass butchery. This kind of battle was invented by Lewis Carroll and Jules Verne

and whoever wrote Undine, and country deacons bowling
and marraines in Marseilles and girls seduced in the back
lanes of Wurtemburg and Westphalia. Why, this was a love
battle—there was a century of middle-class love spent here.
This was the last love battle." (64).

Is Fitzgerald declaring that it takes a poet to understand war, rather
than a warrior? Why the association of a World War I battle with
fantasy, science fiction, and love?

Fitzgerald biographer David Brown argues that Fitzgerald saw
further than most writers the true meaning and consequences of
the Great War, despite never having seen combat, because he acted
the part of a cultural historian and perceived "a higher interpretive
truth."[60] James Meredith points to "Fitzgerald's personal sense of loss
and his profound understanding of what was also culturally lost for
a generation" to define him as war writer.[61] Influenced by medieval
and Romantic literature as a student, Fitzgerald saw the Great War as
an opportunity for Americans to test masculine chivalric ideals on a
European battlefield, and although *he* was deprived of the battle test,
Fitzgerald "infused his romantic fiction with the facts of the war."[62]
Nick and Gatsby *were* battle tested, and the latter displayed a battlefield
heroism inspired in part by the American war hero Sergeant Alvin
York. For Nick, however, like Rupert Brooke and many of the British
war poets, disillusionment characterizes the postwar era because of
the crushing victory of military machines, materialist consumption,
and moral corruption.

Once back at Camp Sheridan, Scott resumed his affair with Zelda,
who accepted an engagement ring from him. The ambitious pair
plotted marriage and a glamorous life in New York, but Zelda made it
clear that this could only happen if he became a published author and
earned a respectable income. Fitzgerald was discharged from the army
in February 1919 and took a job writing advertising copy for the New
York agency Barron Collier. He hated the job and was miserable and
lonely in his humble apartment on the Upper West Side of Manhattan.
To make matters worse, Zelda was becoming increasingly restless and,

despite Scott making three trips to Montgomery to see her, she suddenly called off the engagement in June. All his dreams, personal and professional, were in danger of dying. He called these "the four most impressionable months" of his life, as he tried to find meaning among the paradoxes he encountered in New York:

> When I got back to New York in 1919 I was so entangled in life that a period of mellow monasticism in Washington Square was not to be dreamed of . . . . New York had all the iridescence of the beginning of the world. The returning troops marched up Fifth Avenue and girls were instinctively drawn East and North toward them—this was the greatest nation and there was gala in the air. As I hovered ghost-like in the Plaza Red Room of a Saturday afternoon, or went to lush and liquid garden parties in the East Sixties or tippled with Princetonians in the Biltmore Bar I was haunted always by my other life—my drab room in the Bronx, . . . my shabby suits, my poverty, and love. . . . I was a failure—mediocre at advertising work and unable to get a start as a writer. Hating the city, I got roaring, weeping drunk on my last penny and went home.[63]

These were also the months that Jay Gatsby and the A.E.F. soldier-students spent in Oxford, Gatsby wondering about his fate, his fortune, and his future with Daisy Fay, who could not wait for her young officer to return to her. But it would take nearly two years before Fitzgerald discovered Major Gatsby among the ghosts meandering on the High in Oxford.

9

Scott and Zelda, Meet the Churchills

There had been a war fought and won and the great city of
the conquering people was crossed with triumphal arches
and vivid with thrown flowers of white, red, and rose.
                    —F. Scott Fitzgerald, *May Day* (1920)[1]

Prefacing the short story/novelette *May Day* when it was collected in *Tales of the Jazz Age*, F. Scott Fitzgerald explains that
he wrote the story in 1919 by collecting together three events
during the May celebrations of the ending of the Great War—an Ivy
League fraternity dance, a riot in which demobilized soldiers attacked a
radical socialist newspaper office, and the drunken adventures of "Mr.
In and Mr. Out" (two wealthy frat boys) at Columbus Circle. Fitzgerald
commented that these semi-historical events made a great impression
on him, "unrelated, except by the general hysteria of that spring, which
inaugurated the Jazz Age."[2] While Jay Gatsby paced the medieval
side streets of Oxford fretting over Daisy that May, Scott Fitzgerald
was a member of that "younger generation" restlessly following the

party crowds spilling out of the clubs and cafes onto Broadway. He saw these celebratory days between the Armistice and the signing of the Treaty of Versailles as the beginning of the Jazz Age, but beneath these intoxicated adventures lay uncertainties about his writing career and the commitment of Zelda to their relationship.

Love and Prohibition

Scott and Zelda were in love, but Zelda would not agree to marriage until he proved himself—financially—as a writer. Fitzgerald settled into a one-room apartment in Morningside Heights and a day job with the advertising agency Barron Collier while he worked on revising his first novel and selling his short stories. He refers to this obstacle—and his own doubts about his talent—in *This Side of Paradise*, as Mrs. Connage warns her daughter, Rosalind, about Amory: "You've already wasted over two months on a theoretical genius who hasn't a penny to his name . . . a nice, well-born boy, but a dreamer—merely *clever*" (179). Fitzgerald quit his job after a few months and—following desperate and pleading visits to Zelda in Montgomery—moved back to St. Paul to live on the McQuillan dime while he polished his novel.

As with Amory in 1919, alcohol was then playing an ever more important role in the lives of Scott and Zelda. Just eight days after their surreptitious wedding in the rectory of St. Patrick's Cathedral on April 4, 1920, Fitzgerald's novel *This Side of Paradise* was published by Scribner's, due in large part to the efforts of Maxwell Perkins. Charles Scribner took a risk on publishing the novel, but it proved an instant success. Scott and Zelda celebrated that success with extravagant parties, binges, and Zelda jumping into public fountains across Manhattan. In the first year of their marriage, they managed to get expelled from both the Biltmore and Commodore hotels. Newspaper gossip columns delighted in describing their escapades at the beginning of the Jazz Age.

America's Jazz Age was also the beginning of the Prohibition Era. The Eighteenth Amendment to the U.S. Constitution was ratified on January 16, 1919, and nine months later Congress passed the Volstead

Act, or National Prohibition Act, which provided for the enforcement of Prohibition through a special unit of the Treasury Department. Cocktails, rumrunners, bootleggers, and speakeasies rose to prominence in many American cities with the enforcement of the Volstead Act. Cheap rum was smuggled into the southern United States from the Caribbean, while barges just off the shore of Long Island distributed illicit liquor to New Yorkers who took their small boats out for frequent visits. British gin and Canadian whisky also made their way into the hands of tourists and smugglers, as attested in this verse that the Prince of Wales shared with his father after returning from a visit to Canada:

> Four and twenty Yankees, feeling very dry,
> Went across the border to get a drink of rye.
> When the rye was opened, the Yanks began to sing,
> 'God bless America, but God save the King!'[3]

The poet W.B. Yeats and his wife George, recently over from Oxford, stayed at the Algonquin Hotel when they arrived in New York in January 1920.[4] The Algonquin Round Table, which first met as "the Vicious Circle" in 1919, would include many of the 1920s' greatest newspaper writers, editors, and critics—Franklin Pierce Adams, George S. Kaufman, Dorothy Parker, Harold Ross, and Alexander Woolcott, among others. But there was also a host of writers and celebrities who would drift in for conversation, gambling, and drinking, including Carl Van Vechten, Tallulah Bankhead, Ring Lardner, Noël Coward, Harpo Marx, Herbert Bayard Swope, and Deems Taylor, most of whom became friends or drinking associates of the Fitzgeralds.

Exhausted and expelled from New York City, Scott and Zelda rented a Colonial house at 244 Compo Road South in Westport, Connecticut, for five months in late 1920 and early 1921 for Scott to write without distractions. The Gray House, just a few blocks from both the beach and the Saugatuck River, was built for William Gray II in 1758 and had been updated many times before the Fitzgeralds arrived. They hired a Japanese man to cook and clean while both Scott and Zelda worked on their novels, respectively *The Beautiful and Damned* and *Save*

Me the Waltz (1930). A mysterious millionaire named Frederick E. Lewis lived on the 175-acre Longshore estate adjacent to the Gray House and was known locally for his extravagant parties.[5] Scott and Zelda invited their New York friends out for dinners and parties that extended for days, meaning they were much distracted from their writing.

London: Shane Leslie and the Churchills

A more extensive break, it seems, was needed. The Fitzgeralds set sail for England on the Cunard steamship *Aquitania* on May 3, 1921, traveling first class from New York and docking at Southampton on May 10. Maxwell Perkins had set up a meeting for Scott with the author John Galsworthy and the Scribner's representative in London, Charles Kingsley, arranged meetings with other literary people, and Scott had a reunion with Shane Leslie.[6] Zelda was two months pregnant. Little documentation of the first European trip exists. Zelda kept a few photos in her scrapbook, while Scott recorded in his ledger spare details (and frequent misspellings):

> May–Sailed the 3rd. Tullocks, Heywards, Engalicheff. Celebrities. London 10th Kingsley, Leslie, Galesworthy. Lady Churchill. The Cecil. Oxford. Paris 17th Folies, Kay Laurel, Café de la Paix. Cherbourge. Cabino. Wapping Venice 26th The Sturtevant, Robbins. Pietro. Versaille. Mal Maison. Clothes.

> June–Florence 3rd Rome 8th John Carter, Americans. Embassy. Paris the 22nd Quai Dorsay–before the St James London 30th Claridges, Cavendish, Bob Handley, Jim Douglass, Brown Baker. Dancing in Savoy. The 4th. Venice–man kicked in stomach because he wasn't a Roman. The woman weeping in Vatican. The loot of 20 centuries.

> July the 4th Cambridge. Clothes in London. The Celtic. The Duncans & Lord Brice. The Biltmore New York . . .

They returned on the White Star liner *Celtic* that July. Scott wrote about his disappointment after dinner with Galsworthy, and Bruccoli relates an incident with Leslie leading Scott and Zelda in a nighttime walking tour of the London docks, showing them where Jack the Ripper had slain his victims, Zelda dressed (for safety) in men's clothing.[7] Scott spent handily on English tailored suits from Davies & Sons and shirts from Hilditch & Key; as of 1928 he was still ordering his clothes from both of these London shops, complemented by ties and hand-kerchiefs "all brightly colored."[8]

Some of the material in the *Ledger* made it into the story "Show Mr. and Mrs. F. to Number ___," with the byline Scott and Zelda Fitzgerald when it first appeared in *Esquire* (May-June 1934) but credited to Zelda in the *Ledger*. The story is a whirlwind, alternately lyrical and flippant recounting of all the hotels that Scott and Zelda stayed in from their honeymoon in the Biltmore to their trip to Bermuda in 1933. The 1921 trip to England gets only two sentences:

> They were respectful in the Cecil in London; disciplined by the long majestuous twilights on the river and we were young but we were impressed anyway by the Hindus and the royal processions. . . .
>
> Claridge's in London served strawberries in a gold dish, but the room was an inside room and gray all day, and the waiter didn't care whether we left or not, and he was our only contact.[9]

On their first stay in London, Scott and Zelda lodged at the Hotel Cecil in London and Zelda kept a picture of the room in her scrapbook. On their return to London they stayed at Claridges and at the Cavendish. They spent a Fourth of July at Cambridge (Zelda keeping a photo memory) and also visited Grantchester, home of one of Scott's favorite poets, Rupert Brooke.

The "Engalicheff" that Scott mentions in his *Ledger* is Prince Vladimir N. Engalitcheff, the son of the Prince Nicholas Engalitcheff, the Russian Imperial Vice Consul in Chicago, and Chicago heiress Evelyn

Florence Partridge.[10] Prince Vladimir (b. 1902) studied at Brown University and then went to work for a New York stoke broker. Scott and Zelda met the man they called "Val" on the voyage to England and would reconnect with him in New York in the autumn of 1922, including a week spent together in drunken revelry "equaled only by ancient Rome *and* Nineveh," records Zelda.[11] Scott would write in the *Ledger* in 1923, "Val Engalitcheff kills himself," though there is no other evidence of his death being a suicide.[12]

In her scrapbook, Zelda also kept an invitation card from Lady Randolph Spencer Churchill, inviting the Fitzgeralds to tea at her home in Hyde Park. Scribbled on the card are directions: "Lancaster Tube No. 2." Jennie Jerome, Lady Churchill, was born Jeanette Jerome in Brooklyn, New York, in 1854. She was the second daughter of Leonard Jerome, a financier, editor, and sportsman, and Clarissa Hall. Leonard Jerome made his fortune speculating in stocks, and passed on to Jennie his love of music and horses. After suffering a loss on the stock market in 1867, Leonard moved his wife and daughters to Paris, where they entered the circle of Napoléon III and empress Eugénie. The family reunited in London in 1870 and moved shortly thereafter to Cowes on the Isle of Wight. There, in 1873, Jennie met Lord Randolph Henry Spencer-Churchill, second son of the Duke of Marlborough, who had read History at Oxford (Merton College). Jennie and Randolph fell in love and were married (despite family opposition) in April 1874 in Paris. Their first son, Winston Leonard Spencer-Churchill, was born later that year.

As Leonard's fortunes continued to decline (the dowry was not sizeable), Randolph and Jennie struggled continuously to obtain the money needed to sustain their lavish lifestyle. They spent much time apart, and Jennie seldom saw her sons. Would she have seen herself in Beatrice, the eccentric and absent mother of *This Side of Paradise*? Would Winston have seen himself in Amory? After Randolph resigned from the government in 1886, the couple's estrangement led to rumors that Jennie was having affairs with several prominent men, including Edward, Prince of Wales, and the Austrian diplomat Count Karl Kinsky. After Randolph's death in 1895, Jennie turned her attentions and ambitions toward her eldest son. She married twice more, to younger men, and continued life as both a socialite and a social activist, embracing the suffragette movement, for example, and helping out with the Red Cross during World War I.

Zelda recalls talking at length at lunch with Winston Churchill, then Secretary for the Colonies. She also commented on the dessert: "strawberries as big as tomatoes." Winston's younger brother, Jack, took Scott to a cricket game, which bored the Americans and hence they left early. Sadly, just days after her visit with the Fitzgeralds, Jennie Jerome slipped while wearing new heels and fell down a flight of stairs. Gangrene set in from the broken ankle and she died of a hemorrhage at her London home. One cannot help but wonder if Evelyn Waugh got wind of the Fitzgeralds' visit as he skewered the Bloomsburies and Garsingtonians in a 1930 article for *Harper's*: "There are many kind, elderly ladies in London who think that they are attaining this modernity, by inviting coloured people or the authors of the latest bestsellers to luncheon."[13]

F. Scott Fitzgerald Meets Zuleika Dobson on the High

Scott and Zelda also visited Oxford shortly after their time with the Churchills. Scott shared his first impression of Oxford with Maxwell Perkins in a letter dated May 26, 1921:

> Dear Mr. Perkins:
> After a wonderful time in England and a rotten time in France, we're in Venice & enjoying ourselves hugely. . . . My book [*This Side of Paradise*] comes out in England today.
> The most beautiful spot in the world is Oxford, without a doubt.[14]

In 1921 Oxonians were pouring out their love and admiration (romantically as well as satirically) for their alma mater in novels, memoirs, and poems. Aldous Huxley wrote his first novel, *Crome Yellow*, satirizing the Garsington parties; the aesthete Beverley Nichols penned *Patchwork*; and Gerard Hopkins described Oxford thus in *A City in the Foreground*:

She has all the treasures of the world hidden in the fold
of her garments, and he who is lucky enough to be able to
search for them and find them has the greatest education
the world can give. . . . It doesn't matter what the professors
teach, it's what the *place* teaches, it's the young spirit that
breathes in the hearts of those who are taught.[15]

There appears to have been a second visit to Oxford, documented
only in the enigmatic end of Fitzgerald's essay "Three Cities," published
in the magazine *Brentano's Book Chat* that fall.[16]

We had been to Oxford before—after Italy we went back
there arriving gorgeously at twilight when the place was
fully peopled for us by the ghosts of ghosts—the characters, romantic, absurd or melancholy, of *Sinister Street*,
Zuleika Dobson and *Jude the Obscure*. But something was
wrong now—something that would never be right again.
Here was Rome—here on the High were the shadows
of the Via Appia. In how many years would our descendants approach this ruin with supercilious eyes to buy
postcards from men of a short, inferior race—a race that
were once Englishmen. How soon—for money follows
the rich lands and the healthy stock, and art follows
begging after money. Your time will come, New York,
fifty years, sixty. Apollo's head is peering crazily, in new
colors that our generation will never live to know, over
the tip of the next century.

Scott explains some of his reaction to Oxford, London, Paris, and
Rome in a letter he wrote to Edmund Wilson in July 1921:

God damn the continent of Europe. It is of merely antiquarian interest. . . . My reactions were all philistine, anti-
socialistic, provincial + racially snobbish. I believe at last
in the white man's burden. We are far above the modern

frenchman as he is above the negro. Even in art! . . . You may have spoken in jest about N.Y. as the capitol [sic] of culture but in 25 years it will be just as London is now. Culture follows money + all the refinements of aestheticism can't stave off its change of seat (Christ! What a metaphor). We will be the Romans in the next generation as the English are now.[17]

It is hard to know what to make of this spewing of honesty, racism, and outrageous prophecy. One could conclude that Europe, as a whole, seemed to Fitzgerald in his first encounters to be all history and ghosts, faded artistic glory, a cautionary tale for America. London and Oxford were becoming Rome—beautiful ruins and postcards for the tourist—and New York would go the same way in a generation. In September of that year the novel *Simon Called Peter*, written by the former Anglican minister and missionary Robert Keable (1887–1927), was published in America. It tells the story of an English clergyman who has an illicit affair with a Red Cross nurse and a subsequent crisis of faith in France during the Great War.[18] The novel was an enormous commercial success and was made into a Broadway play in 1924. It is the book that, ironically, Nick Carraway reads outside the bedroom where Tom and Myrtle are conducting *their* affair. Both Nick and Fitzgerald hated the book, but it is perhaps present in *Gatsby* as a symbol of the moral crisis that Fitzgerald saw at the time, one swallowing up Europe and making its way across the Atlantic.

Zelda recalled the trip many years later, whimsically, in a letter to her daughter, Scottie:

> We went to London to see a fog and saw Tallulah Bankhead which was, perhaps, about the same effect. Then the fog blew up and we reconstituted Arnold Bennett's *Pretty Lady* and the works of Compton McKenzie [sic] which Daddy loved so, and we had a curious nocturnal bottle of champagne with members of the British polo team. We dined with Galsworthy and lunched with Lady Randolph Churchill and had tea in the mellow remembrances of Shane

Leslie's house, who later took us to see the pickpockets pick in Wopping [sic]. They did.[19]

Of note is the association, in Zelda's mind at least, of Scott's favorite Oxford novelist with champagne and polo. Zelda also kept a picture of herself in her scrapbook, evidently taken by Scott, of her standing in a quad in front of Gothic spires—Trinity College quad, in fact, though the Cambridge Trinity rather than the Oxonian one.

Minnesota and the Arrival of Scottie

When Scott and Zelda returned to America in the summer of 1921 they went to Montgomery and intended to stay until Zelda gave birth. The heat drove them instead to Minnesota that autumn, renting a house at Dellwood on White Bear Lake (outside St. Paul) found for them by their wealthy St. Paul friends, Oscar and Zandra Kalman. Zelda met Scott's family for the first time, and they began to settle into the circle of married couples at the White Bear Yacht Club. Despite the anticipation of the birth of his first child, however, Scott was in a dark mood as he contemplated his next novel. As he wrote to Perkins, complaining about his lack of progress:

> Loafing puts me in this particularly obnoxious and abomi-nable gloom. My 3d novel, if I ever write another, will I am sure be as black as death with gloom. . . . I am sick alike of life, liquor and literature. If it wasn't for Zelda I think I would disappear out of sight for three years.[20]

On October 26, after a long hard labor, Frances Scott Key Fitzgerald was born. Coming out of the anesthesia, Zelda announced to her husband, "Oh God, goofo, I'm drunk. . . . I hope it's beautiful and a fool—a beautiful little fool." Scott recorded the episode and would give a version of these lines to Daisy in *The Great Gatsby*.

After a trip to New York the Fitzgerald's were back at White Bear Yacht Club for the Summer of 1922. Scott began to plan for his third novel while in Minnesota, and it was to be a "catholic" novel set in the Midwest after around 1885. "I want to write something new," he wrote to Perkins in July, "something extraordinary and beautiful and simple + intricately patterned." When exactly its protagonist emerged is not clear. Asked, in 1934, about the origins of Jay Gatsby, Fitzgerald wrote: "He was perhaps created on the image of some forgotten farm type of Minnesota that I have known and forgotten, and associated at the same moment with a sense of romance."[21] The gloom had parted with the arrival of Scottie, and Scott and Zelda were about to throw themselves back into the gaiety of Jazz Age New York to experience, for two years, what would provide the new backdrop for the third novel.

Gold-hatted Lovers along the Gold Coast

It was an age of miracles, it was an age of art, it was an age of excess, and it was an age of satire.
—F. Scott Fitzgerald, "Echoes of the Jazz Age" (1931)

Scott and Zelda were asked to leave the White Bear Yacht Club because of the disturbances made at their raucous parties. They were bored with Minnesota in any case and wanted to return to New York. From Manhattan they went house-hunting with novelist John Dos Passos (whom they had just met), driving out for a memorable tour of Long Island that included calling on sportswriter Ring Lardner, getting drunk, and Zelda dragging Dos Passos onto a Ferris wheel!

The house hunting was a success, however, and Scott and Zelda rented a bungalow at 6 Gateway Drive in Great Neck, New York, that October. There they hosted parties, went to parties hosted by their Long Island neighbors, and continued to make visits to the city. Great Neck had recently attracted a large number of actors, directors, editors, and others from the New York publishing and entertainment worlds, while across Manhasset Bay were the mansions of wealthy businessmen and industrialists.[22] Among those Fitzgerald records meeting in his *Ledger* during the Great Neck period (mostly at parties) are Lardner and his wife Ellis; the Bucks (songwriter Gene Buck and his wife Helen) and the Swopes (Herbert Bayard Swope and his wife Margaret); Mrs. Mary Harriman Rumsey and Tommy Hitchcock; the financier Clarence Mackay; the painter Augustus Johns and the English socialite and writer Princess Bibesco,[23] both Garsington regulars; and filmmaker Allan Dwan and actors Gloria Swanson and Ernest Truex. A similar list of Great Neck celebrities the Fitzgeralds met appears in a 1922 letter written by Scott to his cousin Cecilia ("Ceci"), inviting her to visit: joining Buck, Swope and Lardner are dancer/actress Mae Murray, actor/playwright Frank Craven, Broadway producer Arthur Hopkins, actress/playwright Jane Cowl, actor/film-maker Joseph Santley, movie mogul Samuel Goldwyn, cartoonist Fontaine Fox, Broadway actor Donald Brian, actor Tom Wise, General John J. Pershing (!), Irish tenor John McCormack, British novelist Sir Hugh Walpole, painter/illustrator Neysa McMein, Canadian illus-trator Arthur William Brown, composer Rudolf Friml, and composer/music critic Deems Taylor.[24] These gatherings were altogether "like a sustained concert" he assured Ceci.

In the eighteen months that the Fitzgeralds lived at Great Neck, Scott was only able to write three chapters of his next novel. "I spent it uselessly," he would write to Perkins, "neither in study nor in contempla-tion but only in drinking and raising hell generally."[25] Leaving the Long Island parties (and bills) behind, the Fitzgeralds sailed for Paris in May 1924 where Scott hoped to concentrate on writing *The Great Gatsby*. Like Tom and Daisy, Scott and Zelda slipped quietly away to France.

In item number three in the *Man's Hope* list outline for *Gatsby*—"Goddards. Dwanns Swopes"—Fitzgerald includes three figures of riches, fame, and glamour in Jazz Age New York: playwright Charles William Godard (or perhaps stockbroker Charles Howard Goddard); movie director Allan Dwan; and Herbert Bayard Swope, executive editor of the *New York World*. But the list of partygoers that appears in Chapter Four of *Gatsby* reaches back further in history: there are the Chester Beckers, the Leeches, a man called Bunsen, Dr. Webster Civet, the Willie Voltaires, the Blackbucks, the Hornbeams, the Ismays, the Christies, Beluga and Baedeker, Edgar Beaver and Clarence Endive, a bum named Etty, the Cheadles, the Stonewall Jackson Abrams, a Ulysses (but not a Grant), the Fishguards and the Ripley Snels, the Hammerheads and the Whitebaits, a Catlips, Maurice A. Flink, the Poles and the Mulreadys, Cecil Roebuck and Cecil Schoen, Gulick the state senator, Arthur McCarty and G. Earl Muldoon, the gamblers Da Fontano and Ed Legros, James B. "Rot-Gut" Ferret, George Duckweed and Francis Bull, Benny McClenahan with his four girls (always four), a prince who was called Duke, and of course the piano-playing boarder, Ewing Klipspringer.

This list has been much studied by Fitzgerald scholars, some seeing here the influence of Eliot and Joyce on Fitzgerald.[26] Many of the names suggest rodents, scavengers, fish, weeds, and mundane vegetables. Some "recall renowned figures—scientists and philosophers—from a more heroic age," writes Ruth Prigozy. "All are debasements of the real thing."[27] The guests have "burlesque names, suggesting tastelessness, violence, bathos," observes Sarah Churchwell. "This is café society, the promiscuous mingling of old and new money, aristocracy and industry, debauchery and criminality, comedy and death."[28] For Robert Long the list is a "satire of democracy," their names and biographies suggesting that they are the lesser sons of great and heroic figures of the Victorian Age.[29] The list functions, then, as a satirical bridge from the Victorian and Gilded Age aristocrats and captains of industry to the "fishy" figures of Jazz Age New York. It is a hybrid crowd—Gatsby's crowd, but not Tom's. And it would become an unforgettable memorial to the twilight of Gold Coast parties that sparkled as a mirror reflection of Prohibition era New York.

Gatsby's Money: Bootleggers, Max von Gerlach, and the Fuller-McGee Case

The two years that Scott and Zelda spent on Great Neck, Long Island, provided much inspiration for locations, characters, and plot lines for Scott's next novel. Jay Gatsby's extravagant lifestyle and his drug store business, for example, may have been suggested by a story that Maxwell

Perkins related to Scott involving their mutual friend, Ring Lardner.[30] Lardner described a Great Neck "newcomer" who had made his money "in the drug business—not dope but the regular line." One morning this man showed up at Lardner's house with two strangers, who turned out to be his personal manicurist and barber, which the "drug man" had, due to his loneliness, made companions!

Churchwell reminds us that there were other infamous New York bootleggers who would have been known to Fitzgerald in 1922. Larry Fay rose from the streets of Hell's Kitchen to become Jazz Age aristocracy through his fleet of taxis—outfitted with blinking lights and melodious horns—which he used to run liquor and launder his bootlegging profits. He boasted of having "trunk loads of tailored colored shirts shipped to him every year from London."[31] One of the investors in his El Fay nightclub was none other than Arnold Rothstein, the real life Wolfsheim who fixed the 1919 World Series, and "muscle" was provided by the Irish gangleader Owney Madden, brewer of "Madden's No. 1 Beer" (New Yorkers' Prohibition-era favorite) and owner of the Hotel Harding with its basement speakeasy, Club Intime. Then there was the German-born "King of the Bootleggers," George Remus, a lawyer from Cincinnati who made a fortune selling illegal liquor from drugstores in the months following the Volstead Act. Remus bought and extravagantly remodeled a huge Price Hill mansion, adding an indoor marble pool where he threw extravagant parties with water ballets, orchestras, and party gifts for his guests—$100 bills, Elgin watches, diamond tie clasps, and even new automobiles.[32] On the grounds of his estate there was a garden, racehorse stables, and houses for his servants and chauffeurs. Remus was eventually convicted and sentenced to two years, and soon after his release he shot his wife for having an affair—with a prohibition agent.

Unconvinced that bootlegging could have earned Gatsby so much money in such a short amount of time, John Randall has attempted to identify the source of Gatsby's great wealth in an actual financial scandal of the early 1920s: the Teapot Dome Scandal.[33] During the first few months of his administration, President Warren G. Harding transferred control of the naval oil reserves to the Department of the

Interior. Then Secretary of the Interior Albert B. Fall, in April 1922, secretly leased (at a very low rate) the oil reserves at Teapot Dome, Wyoming, to Mammoth Oil Company and received a $260,000 kickback (in Liberty Bonds) from Mammoth president Harry F. Sinclair. Congress became suspicious of Sinclair and other oilmen and traced some of their quick oil profits back to Fall, releasing their findings in early 1924. Gatsby admits to Nick that it took him only three years to earn the money to buy his Norman "castle" and that, in addition to drug stores, he was "in the oil business." Of course, he also offered to Nick—a seller of bonds—a little "side business."

Shortly before her death in 1947, Zelda identified several figures as influencing her husband's creation of Jay Gatsby: Edward M. Fuller, William F. McGee, Robert C. Kerr, and Max Gerlach. While Scott Fitzgerald met only Kerr and Gerlach, each of these men contributed to the story of Jimmy Gatz/Jay Gatsby. None of them, however, account for Gatsby's valor in combat in France nor for his sojourn in Oxford.

While revising the novel in December 1924, Fitzgerald wrote to Max Perkins from Rome that he was searching his mind and his files for details of "the Fuller Magee case."[34] Edward M. Fuller, a neighbor of the Fitzgerald's in Great Neck, along with his brokerage partner, William F. McGee, declared bankruptcy in June 1922 with $6 million in debts.[35] Rumored associates of Arthur Rothstein, they had gambled away millions of their clients' money and were indicted in October for larceny and "bucketing" fraud. We do not know that Fitzgerald ever met Fuller or McGee, but he did meet Arnold Rothstein, the notorious gangster widely believed to have fixed the 1919 World Series. We have no details of that meeting, but Rothstein would inspire the character of Gatsby's underworld associate, Meyer Wolfsheim.

In the summer of 1923 Fitzgerald did meet his Great Neck neighbor Robert C. Kerr, who provided him with important details for the Dan Cody episode in Gatsby's life.[36] Kerr told Fitzgerald (while they were both "buzzing," according to Kerr) about his own rags-to-riches story, when, as a fourteen-year-old living in Brooklyn in 1907, he saw a yacht drifting dangerously into the shallows of Sheepshead Bay. Kerr rowed out to warn its owner, Edward Robinson Gilman, who subsequently hired Kerr to join his crew. Gilman had embezzled nearly half a million dollars from Iron Clad Manufacturing, and was rumored to be having an affair with the much younger wife of Iron Clad's owner, Robert L. Seaman. The wife was none other than Nellie Bly, the famous journalist, and Fitzgerald may have enjoyed a little revenge for Bly's negative review of his first novel by making her the greedy Ella Kaye of *Gatsby*.

The most mysterious of these figures is Max Gerlach. Zelda would tell Fitzgerald scholar Henry Dan Piper in 1947 that Gatsby was "based on a neighbor named von Guerlach or something who was said to be General Pershing's nephew and was in trouble over bootlegging." Fitzgerald himself did not offer any info about this Gerlach other than a 1923 news clipping in his scrapbook, a photo of him, Zelda, and Scottie under the words "Enroute from the coast—Here for a few days on business—How are you and the family, old sport?"[37] In the 1950s a man named Gerlach surfaced claiming to be "the real Gatsby," contacting Fitzgerald's first biographer, Arthur Mizener, but Mizener declined to interview him, leading most Fitzgerald scholars to conclude that Gerlach was just one of many New York bootleggers who may have contributed to the literary portrait.[38]

Recently Horst Kruse has championed Max Gerlach's candidacy, painstakingly tracking down Gerlach (in U.S. and German archives) and filling in some more biographical details about this shadowy—and shady—character.[39] Kruse found no evidence that Gerlach ever lived on Long Island nor that he was living a life of grandeur. Born in Berlin in 1885, the son of a reserve officer in the Royal Prussian Army, Max Gerlach immigrated to America with his mother, sister, and stepfather, a German merchant named Andreas Stork, in 1894. The young Max Gerlach worked as a messenger and mechanic in New York, moved with his mother briefly to Chicago, and then was back in New York City, married and divorced, by 1912. Working his way up in the booming automobile industry, Gerlach traveled to Mexica, Cuba, and Germany, and served as first lieutenant in the U.S. Army's automotive support unit in New Jersey from August 15, 1918, to October 31, 1919. After the war he lived in Manhattan and was tried in 1927 in the U.S. District Court for possession and sale of liquor, violations of the Volstead Act that landed Gerlach fines of $200 and $10. Given that he was in possession of "a quantity of labels, corks and tops," Max Gerlach was indeed a bootlegger, if a minor and unsuccessful one.[40] In December 1939, driven by financial misfortunes, he attempted suicide, blinding himself permanently when he put a bullet in his head. He died on October 18, 1958, then living destitute at the Van Cortlandt Hotel on West 49th Street in Manhattan.

While certainly interesting, there is nothing in the factual biography of Max Stork Gerlach that would have necessarily compelled Fitzgerald to base his most famous literary creation on him. But, as Kruse forcefully argues, Gerlach viewed himself in grander terms, and lied to many people about his background and occupation. He gave false information to the U.S. Embassy in Berlin in order to avoid being drafted into the German army in 1914; lied in 1917 to the Justice Department about having been born in Germany; claimed falsely on his U.S. Army application of 1918 that he was born in Yonkers, New York, and that he was a friend of Judge Aaron J. Levy (George Bauchle, who did provide a reference for Gerlach, was a gambler and associate of Arnold Rothstein); lied again about his birth place and stay in Germany on a U.S. passport application in 1919; styled himself as German nobility after the war by using the name "Max von Gerlach"; and seems to have told some people that he was a major rather than a lieutenant. Some of these lies, however, were recorded well after *The Great Gatsby* had appeared in print, and even Kruse admits that many of Gerlach's delusions could have come about because he had convinced *himself* that he was the original Jay Gatsby.

Even if we take Gerlach to be "the one man I knew" in the confession Fitzgerald made to Bishop in August 1925, we need to return to the context of that statement: " . . . you are right about Gatsby being blurred and patchy. I never at any one time saw him clear myself—for he started as one man I knew *and then changed into myself*—the amalgam was never complete in my mind" [emphasis added]. In giving birth to Jay Gatsby, Fitzgerald was creating an amalgam of which the author himself was the most important piece. Ever the autobiographical novelist, Fitzgerald created many characters who began as figures like himself, developed according to plot lines, and then returned to some aspect of Fitzgerald's own character, aspirations, or depravations.

France and Italy

Scott, Zelda, and Scottie arrived in France in May 1924 and stayed a few days in Paris before heading south. "We were going to the Old World to find a new rhythm for our lives," wrote Scott shortly after arriving in France, "with a true conviction that we had left our old selves behind forever."[41] After a short stay at a hotel in Hyères the family settled in June at Villa Marie, Valescure, St. Raphaël. ". . . a clean cool villa set in a large garden on a hill above town," said Scott. "It was what we had been looking for all along. There was . . . a gardener who called me milord."[42] It was at the villa that Fitzgerald wrote the bulk of the first draft of *Gatsby*.

Their closest friends in France were the American expatriates and patrons extraordinaire Gerald and Sara Murphy, who lived in Paris and later in a villa near Antibes from 1921 to 1934, where the Fitzgeralds visited on more than one occasion. Just before the arrival of Scott and Zelda in Paris the Murphys threw a legendary party on a barge on the Seine; among the attendees were Igor Stravinsky and Sergei Diaghilev (the party was in honor of the premiere of their ballet, *Les Noces*), Pablo Picasso, Darius Milhaud, Jean Cocteau, and Scofield Thayer (editor of *The Dial*). Cocteau at one point put on a captain's uniform and announced "*On coule*"—"We're sinking!"—while Stravinsky leapt through an enormous laurel wreath.[43] Scott would later include the barge party in his short story, "One Trip Abroad."

Ring Lardner and his wife visited the Fitzgeralds at St. Raphaël shortly after they had relocated. "They left the United States last May," wrote Lardner in a *Liberty* article, "because New Yorkers kept mistaking their Long Island home for a road house."[44] "We are living in a sort of idyllic state," Fitzgerald wrote to Carl Van Vechten, and "at present I am content to work and become excruciatingly healthy under Byron's and Shelley's and Dickens' sky." He did work, finishing the first draft of *The Great Gatsby* and sending it to Maxwell Perkins in October. Scott and Zelda were also at this time trying to work through the ramifications of Zelda's affair with the French aviator Edouard Jozan.[45]

The family relocated to Italy for the winter of 1924–25, arriving in Rome in November so Scott could work on revisions of *Gatsby*. "With the aid you've given me I can make *Gatsby* perfect," he assured Perkins in December, having revised the Plaza Hotel scene according to his editor's advice. Scott and Zelda spent much time in the company of the film crew shooting the epic *Ben Hur*, including befriending the lead actress, Carmel Myers.[46] It was then that Scott began to realize the great potential of film, that the novel "was becoming subordinated to a mechanical . . . art."[47] In January they moved on to Capri to warm up and recover from illnesses. Zelda took up painting and Scott got to meet the literary idol of his youth, the Oxford novelist par excellence Compton Mackenzie.

The Great Gatsby was published by Scribner's in April 1925. It sold well at first, competing with titles by Edith Wharton, Somerset Maugham, and Janet Fairbank. Congratulations came in from Edmund Wilson and H.L. Mencken and others, and reviews were generally favorable. Gertrude Stein wrote to Scott, after she had finished reading *Gatsby* in May 1925, "it is a good book . . . and it shows that you have a background of beauty and tenderness."[48] Edith Wharton also complimented him for "the great leap" he had accomplished with *Gatsby*, though wishing he had revealed more of Gatsby's early career.[49] T. S. Eliot confessed, as we have seen, that he had read it three times by December of that year. As Fitzgerald reveled in the novel's early success, he and Zelda moved back to Paris where they were to meet new friends among the bohemian expatriates who would pull them back into a life of alcoholic excess and drive a wedge through their marriage. In May, at the Dingo American Bar and Restaurant on the Left Bank, Fitzgerald would meet the writer whom he came most to admire and from whom he most sought approval—Ernest Hemingway. He "has a brilliant future" Fitzgerald wrote to Perkins, recommending the war-wounded journalist to his editor.

Scott's Oxford Dream

Fitzgerald had taken the Midwestern Jimmy Gatz to the battlefields of France, where he proved heroic, and thence to Oxford. Would the life of a celebrated novelist in Oxford have suited Scott and Zelda in their post-*Gatsby* years? In 1925 Fitzgerald wrote to his friends Bishop and Gilbert Seldes that he and Zelda intended to spend the spring of 1926 in Nice and the summer in Oxford.[50] He had likely heard (perhaps from General Pershing himself) about the positive experiences of the A.E.F. Oxford students like Major William Rogers and Captain Frank Markoe, remembered Oxford from his own 1921 visit as one of the most beautiful places he had ever seen, and admired the image of war-hero Tommy Hitchcock leaving Harvard to play polo in Oxford in 1920. Above all, Oxford was the setting of many of his favorite novels, and the home or inspiration of many of his literary heroes. Fitzgerald "embraced [Oxford] in all its literary associations," writes Kruse, even comparing the Gothic-faced High Street with the Via Appia of ancient Rome.[51]

England in general may also have appealed to Fitzgerald because of his admiration of the Bloomsbury/Garsington crowd and other resident modernists. After receiving great praise from T. S. Eliot for *Gatsby*, Fitzgerald wrote to Perkins in February 1926:

> Now, confidential. T. S. Eliot for whom you know I have profound admiration—I think he's the greatest living poet in any language—wrote me. He'd read Gatsby 3 times *and* thought it was the *1st step forward* American fiction had taken since Henry James.[52]

Eliot had just offered his press, Faber and Gwyer, as a possible publisher for the UK edition of *Gatsby*, and requested Fitzgerald short stories for the *Criterion*. Fitzgerald wrote back to Eliot enthusiastically while traveling through the Pyrenees that same month, telling him that *Gatsby* was already set to be published in England by Chatto and Windus, but that he might have something for the *Criterion*: "I can't express just how good your letter made me feel—it was easily the nicest thing that's happened to me in connection with *Gatsby*. Thank you."[53] Fitzgerald also told Eliot that it was John Peale Bishop who had introduced him, at Princeton, to Eliot's poetry, and asked if Eliot might be on the Riviera that summer.

Scott and Zelda never made it back to Oxford, indeed, never made it back to England. But Fitzgerald's novels and short stories of America's Jazz Age would have a great impact on Oxford students and Oxford writers. The postwar generation in England—at least the public school Oxonians and the smart set of London—began to embrace jazz music, American slang, and flapper couture, and received from the British tabloids the ironic label, the Bright Young People. Oxonian Evelyn Waugh would be the chronicler of their exploits as the 1920s came to a raucous end.

10

England's Jazz Age: Evelyn Waugh and the Bright Young People

Tho' you're only seventeen
Far too much of life you've seen
Syncopated child.
Maybe if you only knew
Where your path was leading to
You'd become less wild.

—Noël Coward, lyrics to the song
"Dance Little Lady" (1928)

It was 1929. Prohibition was nearing its end in America, but the New York Stock Market crashed and the Great Depression had just begun. William Faulkner's *The Sound and the Fury* and Ernest Hemingway's *A Farewell to Arms* are published. The editor of the *Oxford English Dictionary* is living in Chicago—the Chicago of Al Capone and the Saint Valentine's Day Massacre, of Louis Armstrong and Bennie Goodman—working on a dictionary of American English. In Germany, World War I veteran Erich Maria Remarque publishes his novel, *All Quiet on the Western Front*, soon to be banned and burned by the Nazis, while Belgian comic book hero Tintin first appears, battling the Soviets. Jean-Paul Sartre and Simone de Beauvoir meet while studying in Paris, while George Orwell leaves the city to return to Britain. There, Oxonians Graham Greene and Robert Graves publish, respectively, their first novel (*The Man Within*) and autobiography (*Good-Bye to All That*), and Grave's friend from Oriel College, Richard Hughes, publishes *A High Wind in Jamaica*. R. C. Sherriff's World War I play *Journey's End* premiers at the Savoy. Diana Mitford, who grew up just outside of Oxford at Asthall Manor, marries Bryan Guinness, heir to the brewing fortune. In 1929 Faber and Faber publishing house is established in London, with American expat T. S. Eliot as literary editor, and Virginia Woolf pens *A Room of One's Own*. Scotland Yard seizes from a Mayfair gallery thirteen male and female nudes painted by D. H. Lawrence, while E. B. White and James Thurber ask the question, *Is Sex Necessary?* G. K Chesterton writes *The Everlasting Man*, C. S. Lewis gives up his New Look and submits to God, and Mahatma Gandhi finishes his serialized autobiography, *The Story of My Experiments with Truth*. In Oxford, the Herbert Baker-designed Rhodes House opens as a new home for the Rhodes scholars, complete with its own impressive library and opulent reception hall.

While Fitzgerald was splitting his time between Paris and Cannes in 1929, Oxonian Evelyn Waugh was writing a novel called *Vile Bodies* depicting London's Jazz Age and its celebrities, the Bright Young People. An undergraduate at Hertford College at the beginning of the decade, Waugh served as chronicler of Oxford's last-gasp aestheticism and of the Jazz Age in England. Oxford and London play major roles in his greatest novel, *Brideshead Revisited*, for many readers *the* literary portrait of Oxonian aesthetic excesses. But like Nick Carraway, *Brideshead*'s narrator Charles Ryder is problematic—looking back in time and giving us idiosyncratic and selective personal history. Both *Brideshead* and *Gatsby* tackle issues of wealth and privilege, aspirational climbers who love beautiful things, young women who struggle with love and emancipation, modern war and its aftermath, and spiritual truths contesting with material success and excess. Waugh shows us in both his novels and nonfiction the effects of American cultural inventions—jazz, flappers, cocktails, and speakeasies—on England in the 1920s, and is thus an English counterpart to Fitzgerald and a fitting guide through to the end of England's Jazz Age in 1929.

Of Flappers and Knickerbockers

. . . flapper epics present a glamorous dream of youth and gaiety and swift, tapping feet. Youth—actual youth—is essentially crude. But the movies idealize it, even as Gershwin idealizes jazz in *Rhapsody in Blue*.

—F. Scott Fitzgerald, interview in
Motion Picture Magazine (1927)

Changing tastes and fashions—be it in music, dance, clothing, or language—defined the Jazz Age in both America and Britain. The younger generation looked different and sounded different than their parents, celebrating postwar survival and the gradual return of material consumption—often to excess. Members of the press were intrigued, parents mostly annoyed, as freedom and rebellion were exercised as never before and a generation gap was created almost overnight. Columns in *The Times* starting in October 1919 warned the British public about the deleterious effects of "the frivolous scantily-clad jazzing flapper."[1] Soon they were reading about these wild young women and their gin-soaked beaus in the first two novels of F. Scott Fitzgerald.

Young men drifted away from their fathers' tastes for the Edwardian formal frock coats, morning suits, gloves, and top hats in the 1920s. Either the "sport coat" or blazer (often with a crest decorating the top pocket) or the Norfolk coat (with a wide belt around the waist) were chosen to be worn over looser fitting pants. Athletes like Bill Tilden and Bobby Jones inspired sportswear that young men frequently opted to wear, whether they played sports or not, including knickerbockers, baggy sweaters, and V-neck sweater vests paired with white flannel trousers. Knickerbockers took off in England and America, inspiring the long and extremely baggy "Oxford bags" when, in 1925, Oxford students tried to find a way around the university's ban on knickerbockers by wearing "bags" over them. Evelyn Waugh and his friends purchased their "bags" and silk shirts and ties at Hall Brothers on Magpie Lane, and, after Oxford, hit the more fashionable tailors on London's Bond Street and Savile Row.[2] Edward, Prince of Wales, set the style standard for many young Britons with his tuxedos, tweed plus-fours, and knitted sweaters. Bowlers and top hats began to be replaced by fedoras and caps, while gold cigarette cases were the flashy accessory of British men.

Women's fashion changed even more radically, as young women emancipated themselves from the Victorian frilly hats and dresses, high collars, restrictive corsets, long dresses and high heels of their mothers. In came the simple and elegant—though often risqué—look epitomized by the *garçonne* design of Coco Chanel. Young women chose slimming looks over curves, while necklines of dresses plunged as their hems rose to just above the knee, frequently ending in tassels that exaggerated the movement of frenetic dancing. Gone were the high heels and wide-brimmed hats, sheer rayon stockings now clung to exposed legs, long hair pinned up gave way to short "bobs" (straight or shingled, sometimes wrapped in bands or scarves), capping faces whose cosmetics emphasized dark, shining eyes and vampish red lips. Coco Chanel also introduced "illusion" or costume jewelry in the 1920s, and strands of glass beads or fake pearls became a common accessory, while Josephine Baker helped make heavy ivory bracelets exotically fashionable. Gold and silver metallic handbags, or else clutches with extravagant designs, completed the look.

The new style of dress for women of the Jazz Age became synonymous with the flapper, who, most people assumed, was an American innovation. In Scott Fitzgerald's mind, however, the origin of the flapper was in England:

Just before the war, a new type of girl had appeared in England. You remember Stephen McKenna's books, don't you? Well, most of his heroines were flappers. There was an outbreak of new heroines in English life and letters. They wanted independence. They loved danger and were excitement-mad and faintly neurotic. . . . They discussed subjects which had hitherto been considered taboo for women; they lived independently of their families; they were to be seen everywhere unchaperoned. In short . . . they did as they pleased. [3]

Scott was right about the flapper's place of origin. A term used at least since the eighteenth century to describe a young bird unable to rise in flight, it began to be applied to English girls in the 1880s who were too young to dress and coif like their upright mothers, then in the Edwardian period to young women who were well-educated, honest, talkative but not the least bit sentimental. [4] Zelda Fitzgerald also weighed in frequently with comments about the style and attitude of the flapper. She wrote a June 1922 piece for *Metropolitan* magazine titled "Eulogy on the Flapper," wherein she described the flapper's ascendance from style to attitude to philosophy:

. . . the Flapper awoke from her lethargy of sub-deb-ism, bobbed her hair, put on her choicest pair of earrings and a great deal of audacity and rouge and went into the battle. She flirted because it was fun to flirt and wore a one-piece bathing suit because she had a good figure, she covered her face with powder and paint because she didn't need it and she refused to be bored chiefly because she wasn't boring. . . . Now audacity and earrings and one-piece bathing suits have become fashionable. . . . Flapperdom had become a game; it is no longer a philosophy.

Androgyny was also an important element in women's fashion. Photos staged for Fitzgerald's 1920 article, "The Cruise of the Rolling Junk," showed he and Zelda both wearing knickerbockers, a fashion statement recalled later by Zelda in her story, "Show Mr. and Mrs. F. to Number —." "At the O. Henry in Greenville [South Carolina] they thought a man and his wife ought not to be dressed alike in white knickerbockers in nineteen-twenty and we thought the water in the tubs ought not to run red."[5]

The new fashions in men's and women's clothing—though often associated with London aristocrats, Manhattan socialites, and film stars like Clara Bow—actually caused a democratization in the textile industry. Expensive tailors and dressmakers gave way to mass-produced suits and off-the-peg dresses. Men wanted to look like the Arrow Collar Man, women wanted to follow the fashion trends of *Vogue*, which began to focus exclusively on women and printed in Britain and France after the end of the war. The affluent young also desired the new sports cars that began to appear after the war, and they too became a fashion accessory of the Jazz Age. Everything seemed to be moving faster in the 1920s.

England's Jazz Age

A fearsome thing called "Jazz music" has reached us from the other side of the Atlantic: it has been described as "syncopation runs riot." What its effect will be, time alone can show.

Thus warned the British magazine *Dancing Times* in January 1918, but the warning may have been too late to prevent the advent of Britain's Jazz Age. By 1917 sheet music of American jazz songs had already invaded the island and sound recordings were soon to follow.[6] Already in 1915 syncopated music played by black American musicians could be heard in London clubs and in 1919 American jazz bands were touring throughout England and the Continent. As the 1920s began, the first short stories and novels by F. Scott Fitzgerald would give British readers a glimpse of the lifestyle of American flappers and their baggy-panted dancing partners—the rebellious youth of Prohibition who would inspire the Bright Young People of Oxford and London.

The origins and development of jazz music in America is a long, complex, and oft disputed story. The polyrhythmic drumming of African slaves in New Orleans' Congo Square in the mid-nineteenth century; that same city's saloons, brothels, and street parades; brass bands traveling up the Mississippi River on gambling riverboats; blues and gospel singing originated by freed slaves in the South; ragtime and European classical music; Tin Pan Alley lyrics from New York—all these elements (and more) blended in the gumbo of jazz music in America. New Orleans, Memphis, St. Louis, Kansas City, Chicago, and New York were all developing distinctive types of jazz by the time Fitzgerald began to take note of the new musical style. Cultural appropriation happened almost immediately. "All the musical references provided in *The Great Gatsby* are to vaudeville type numbers popularized by such [white] artists as Al Jolson," observes musicologist Art Gottschalk, "and written by well-trained Tin Pan Alley types like Gus Kahn."[7] All, that is, except for a reference in *Gatsby* to a song written in 1916 by the man known as the Father of the Blues, W.C. Handy (1873–1958):

> All night the saxophones wailed the hopeless comment of the "Beale Street Blues" while a hundred pairs of golden and silver slippers shuffled the shining dust. At the gray tea hour there were always rooms that throbbed incessantly with this low, sweet fever, while fresh faces drifted here and there like rose petals blown by the sad horns around the floor. (118)

This scene from *Gatsby* refers to Louisville in 1919, where "orchestras set the rhythm of the year," white Southern debutantes coming alive again after the war to the sounds of a black musical genius from Memphis. As Ronald Berman observes, Daisy's sexuality is being reawakened by this jazz music with its "low, sweet fever" and its down 'n' dirty lyrics: "If Beale Street could talk."[8] Fitzgerald was one of the few whites who recognized at the time that "jazz" was, in semantic origin, a euphemism for sex, and that its rhythms gloried in the mimicry of the act of making love.

In his 1936 book *The Negro and His Music*, Alain Locke traced the history of African-American music, defining the period 1918–26 "the jazz age" and 1926–36 "the classical age of jazz, which is characterized by the dawn of classical Negro music."[9] Locke observed that composers like Duke Ellington were no longer simply entertaining the white bourgeoisie after 1926, but rather creating complex and sophisticated music that was a match for that of their white classical counterparts. "I've a hearty liking for jazz music, especially Irving Berlin's," confessed Zelda in a 1923 interview. "It's most artistic. One of the first principles of dancing is abandon, and this is a quality that jazz music possesses. It's complex. It will, I believe, occupy a great place in American art."[10] She was right about the place of jazz in American art music, but Berlin's lyrics were only an ingredient, added relatively late, in the lyrical improvisation of black artists like Louis Armstrong, Ella Fitzgerald, and Billie Holiday.

It is also simplistic to see jazz as suddenly appearing in England in 1919. In the mid-nineteenth century many American musicians and musical groups came to Britain, including black and black-faced performers and minstrel groups. More often than not these were gross stereotypes of American plantation life fit for the burlesque music halls of Britain, not a clear conveyance of black musical innovation from America. One notable exception was the Fisk Jubilee Singers, who toured Britain in the early 1870s to raise money for their university, giving a well-received performance before the Queen at Argyll House.[11] In 1903 the all-black musical comedy *In Dahomey* came to London's West End, followed a few years later by American ragtime revues. Rhodes scholar singing groups like the Oriel Quartette introduced Oxford to ragtime music.[12] American students there in the early 1920s attempted to start dances in which Oxford scholars could mix with town girls, but the movement was quickly quashed by Vice-Chancellor Farnell.[13]

The "jazz and cocktail" scene in London was made possible by the altering of the wartime Licensing Act in 1921, allowing for alcohol to be served in public places until 12:30 A.M. (as long as food was also served). But jazz music had already made its way there during the war. Dan Kildare's black orchestra sailed from New York to London on the White Star Line's *Megantic* and played syncopated music in Ciro's Restaurant in the West End in 1915. Pianist Kildare, an American of Jamaican heritage, drummer Louis Mitchell, and five others formed the Seven Spades, when the London police closed Ciro's, and toured England playing "ragged" dance music. The all-white Original Dixieland Jass Band (ODJB, later spelled "Jazz") arrived in London in 1919 (two years after they released their first real jazz record) along with the Southern Syncopators Orchestra. The ODJB played the Hammersmith Palais, the Palladium, and even a command performance at Buckingham Palace at the request of the jazz-loving Edward, Prince of Wales. The Southern Syncopators Orchestra, a classically influenced American "symphonic" jazz band, played at the Royal Albert Hall to mark the first anniversary of the Armistice. Clarinetist Sidney Bechet came to London with the Syncopators and stayed until he was deported in 1922, moving on to Paris. Bert Ambrose, London's most celebrated bandleader, began his musical career in New York before starting his seven-piece orchestra at the Embassy Club in London. Florence Mills and her Blackbird troupe first appeared in London in 1926, and singer-pianist Leslie A. Hutchison (aka "Hutch") played at the Victor in addition to private West End parties.[14]

New dances imported from America were another ingredient in the success of jazz in 1920s Britain. The American dance act the Dolly Sisters returned from London to New York in 1922, and in 1925 American flapper and actress Louise Brooks became the first person to dance the Charleston in London, at the Café de Paris.[15] Evelyn Waugh records that Olivia Plunkett Greene and other members of the Bright Young People were learning the Charleston from Barbara Back in London in December 1925, with Olivia mad to try it out in a subsequent trip to Paris.[16] While Louise Brooks went on to become a silent film star, she was followed in London by the American dancer Bee Jackson, who toured the Charleston in New York, London, and Paris, becoming a sensation at London's Piccadilly Hotel and the Kit Cat Club in Haymarket. The nightclub at 100 Sink Street visited by Charles Ryder and a friend in *Brideshead Revisited* is a likely reference to Kate Meyrick's 43 Club in Soho.[17]

The popularity of jazz in Britain was boosted by the magazine *Melody Maker*, edited by Edgar Jackson, which first appeared in January 1926, as well as by radio programs from the recently launched British Broadcasting Corporation (BBC). While *Melody Maker* charted the popularity in Britain of "hot" jazz recordings from American artists like Fletcher Henderson and Bix Beiderbecke, insular jazz artists also began making a name for themselves. Jack Hylton, Bert Firman, Fred Elizalde, Spike Hughes, and Ted Heath formed jazz ensembles of British musicians that competed with the touring American bands, sometime luring away their members.[18] Dance halls not only showed off the abilities of the jazz musicians, jazz dancing showed off the new short, fringed dresses of the flappers. Young women in Britain, as in America, found these halls to be places of freedom where dancing, flirting, smoking, and drinking could be enjoyed apart from the judgments of their Victorian parents. One unfortunate extreme of this emancipation was drug use, cocaine in particular appealing to young women.[19]

New technologies, new dances, sexual freedom, drugs, the exotic primitivism of African American music and rhythms—these are just some of the ingredients that went into the heady cocktail of the British Jazz Age. R.W.S. Mendl, in his *The Appeal of Jazz* (1927), wrote that "even if [jazz] disappears altogether it will not have existed in vain. For its record will remain as an interesting human document—the spirit of the age written in the music of the people."[20] It has not disappeared altogether, in part because Fitzgerald's stories and novels keep taking us back to the Jazz Age. It is perhaps no coincidence that the original and iconic jacket art for *The Great Gatsby* was a gouache painting called "Celestial Eyes" done by Francis Cugat (1896–1981), older brother of the famous jazz bandleader, Xavier Cugat.

The Bright Young People

To the woman of this period thus set forth, restless, seductive, greedy, discontented, craving sensation, unrestrained . . . neurotic and vigorous, a worshipper of tinsel gods at perfumed altars.

—Warner Fabian (né Samuel Hopkins Adams),
Flaming Youth (1923)

Too young to fight in the Great War, but old enough to remember the somberness and the sacrifices, a new generation of young Britons entered Oxford and Cambridge in the early 1920s. Many of them then moved on to London and to legend as their tastes in clothes, music, and parties came to define Britain's Jazz Age. It was their wild, themed parties and urban escapades in particular that grabbed the attention of the press, who dubbed the group the Bright Young People (sometimes, Bright Young *Things*). The title was ironic, as was the lifestyle of this tight-knit group of London's smart set.

Membership in the Bright Young People was fluid, with a celebrated core and various associates, some of whom would deny their affiliation when things began to sour in 1929: Elizabeth Ponsonby and her cousin Loelia; Eleanor Smith, daughter of Lord Birkenhead; actress and addict Brenda Dean Paul; John Betjeman; playwright Noël Coward; war poet Siegfried Sassoon; Cecil Beaton, the Cambridge dandy and society photographer; sisters Zita and Teresa "Baby" Jungman; Bryan Guinness, Lord Moyne; Harold Acton; the poet Brian Howard; Oliver Messel; Tom Driberg, future Labour MP; Stephen and David Tennant, sons of the Earl of Glenconnor; the novelists Anthony Powell, Beverley Nichols, Barbara Cartland, and Evelyn Waugh; Nancy and Diana Mitford; Eddie Gathorne-Hardy; siblings Richard, David, and Olivia "Babe" Plunkett Greene; Cyril Connolly; Patrick Balfour; and the American actresses Adele Astaire and Tallulah Bankhead, childhood friend of Zelda Fitzgerald, who moved from early stage success in New York to London's West End in 1923, starring in *The Dancers* and *They Knew What They Wanted*.

Many of the Bright Young People met at public schools like Eton (Harold Acton, Brian Howard, Anthony Powell, Henry Yorke, Oliver Messel) and Lancing (Evelyn Waugh, Tom Driberg). Other groups, like the "Guinness set" and Brian Howard's the Hearts, formed at Oxford.[21] Acton, Powell, Howard, and Waugh were also members of the Hypocrites Club at Oxford, attending its fancy-dress parties in the early 1920s. Brian Howard recalls his Oxford years as "a sort of passionate party all the time—one rushed from one amusement to another until one's sense of proportion and self-control gradually vanishes." Howard was of American parentage, educated at Eton and Oxford. Acton declared him to be completely amoral, while Waugh famously described him as "mad, bad and dangerous to know."[22] The Oxford University Railway Club, which specialized in cross-country excursions to the Midlands, was an excuse for heavy drinking and lavish banquets in its dining car, led by future Bright Young People like Acton, Howard, Waugh, Bryan Guinness, and Patrick Balfour.[23]

There were also connections to the Bloomsbury/Garsington crowd: Clive Bell and Lytton Strachey attended Bright Young People events like the Sailor Party in the summer of 1927 (Strachey arriving dressed as an admiral).[24] While London hotel bars, speakeasies, and other night clubs were their favorite haunts for most of the year, they would also retreat to country houses, like the Mitfords' Oxfordshire homes, Asthall Manor and Swinbrook House.

The fellowship started with smart and well-bred young women like Zita Jungman and Lady Eleanor Smith chasing around London in cars and buses, leaving clues for their friends to find them in 1922–23. Later this was replaced with clues to hidden treasures and scavenger parties, and a July 26, 1924 article in the *Daily Mail* described one such treasure hunt as a meeting of "The Society of Bright Young People," as they were now officially dubbed. One treasure hunt led hoards of young Londoners to the gates of Buckingham Palace looking frantically for clues and panicking the Captain of the Guard.[25]

The next manifestation of the ennui of the Bright Young People included the exotic charades of the Jungman sisters (Teresa, dressed in black hair and mink, once pretended to be a Russian refugee), lots of drinking in underground nightclubs, fake weddings, and outrageous fancy-dress parties known as "freak parties." Two common threads to these London speakeasies and parties were jazz and cocktails, both American imports. Even the upscale Ritz Carlton and Savoy hotels in London boasted American bars and bartenders.

Some claim that the era of the Bright Young People began to wane with the infamous Bath and Bottle Party of 1928, jointly hosted by Babe Plunkett Greene, Elizabeth Ponsonby, Eddie Gathorne-Hardy, and Brian Howard at St. George's swimming baths in Buckingham

Palace Road. A band of black jazz musicians was hired, adding an exotic air to the scandalous affair. Londoners on their way to work in the early morning saw police breaking up the party, the scantily clad and inebriated young aristocrats proving an unsavory contrast with their more responsible neighbors. Londoners, this time, were not amused.

But 1929 saw a brilliant, last burst of bacchanalia across high-society London. Harold Acton threw a Wild West party at his Lancaster Gate home, Brian Howard hosted the Great Urban Dionysia (complete with Greek costumes), and designer Norman Hartnell tried to top all with his Circus Party—250 guests dressed as circus performers with live circus animals.[26] Even Edward, Prince of Wales, and his brother Bertie dressed as baby boys for one Mayfair soiree. While not officially a member of the Bright Young People, the Prince of Wales led a parallel existence in Mayfair cocktail parties and London nightclubs in the 1920s, dancing to jazz at the Café de Paris.

The press began to turn against the Bright Young People following the Red and White Party hosted by art dealer Arthur Jeffress at the house of dancer Maud Allan on November 21, 1931. Guests were instructed to only wear red and white, and the lavish buffet and cocktails matched the attire (red caviar, champagne, salmon, red and white wines, gin, etc.).[27] There was also, in 1931, the American Party, a fancy-dress affair over which Elizabeth Ponsonby and Brian Howard presided. At the Second Childhood Party, thrown by Rosemary Sanders at Rutland Gate, party guests arrived in prams and played on rocking horses in the garden (Fig. 17). "Cocktails were served in nursery mugs," wrote the reporter for the *Daily Express*, "and the 'bar' was a babies' pen."[28]

The Bright Young People were easy targets for social criticism. At a Mozart party in Piccadilly, they all got bored, according to Beverley Nichols, and disrupted work on the gas mains at Hyde Park Corner, grabbing construction equipment (in full eighteenth-century finery) and laborers to pose with them for pictures.[29] Parents and older relatives were sometimes the harshest critics of their actions. Dorothea Ponsonby described her niece, Olivia Plunket Greene, as "a chit—a rude, egotistical frivolous vain painted child who takes no truck whatever with anyone over 40—unless they are smartly dressed."[30]

The Bright Young People made up slang words and phrases (e.g., sprinkling "mad" and "divine" into their conversations) to distinguish themselves from the crowd, as did the hipsters of American jazz. In fact, the Bright Young People borrowed many Americanisms. Partly these cultural borrowings came from American films and music, but they also came from visiting Americans. These American bohemians also, on occasion, brought with them drugs, particularly cocaine and heroin, and alcoholism and drug addiction afflicted several members of the society.

The "dandy posturing," observes D. J. Taylor, was "undercut by an occasionally lacerating self-awareness," as when Brian Howard is said to have quipped to someone at the Gargoyle Club, "At least I'm a has-been, and that's something you can never be."[31] Several members of the set were writers who could not resist depicting their Mayfair and Belgravian friends in their own novels and memoirs. Nancy Mitford described the Bright Young People in her novels *The Pursuit of Love* (1945) and *Love in a Cold Climate* (1949), as did Henry Green (born Henry Yorke) in *Party Going* (1939), Harold Acton in *Memoirs of an Aesthete* (1948), and Anthony Powell in his series *A Dance to the Music of Time* (1951–75). Photographer Cecil Beaton provided a visual chronicle of the Bright Young People, drawing attention to their elaborate costumes and the striking beauty of several members.

While the Bright Young People produced many writers, it was Evelyn Waugh, ever on the fringe of the crowd, who became the most trenchant observer of their highs and their lows in novels like *Decline and Fall* (1928), *Vile Bodies* (1930), and *Brideshead Revisited* (1945). Agatha Runcible in *Vile Bodies* is thought to be based on Elizabeth Ponsonby (the novel is dedicated to Bryan Guinness and Nancy Mitford), while Teresa "Baby" Jungman is partially reflected in *Brideshead*'s Lady Julia Flyte. Brian Howard and Harold Acton inspired Anthony Blanche ("2/3 Brian and 1/3 Harold Acton" confessed Waugh) while Sebastian Flyte is perhaps a mixture of aesthete Stephen Tennant and Oxonians Alistair Graham and Hugh Patrick Lygon.[32]

In a 1929 piece for *The Evening Standard*, Waugh wrote in praise of the writers who emerged from the party crowd and challenged Bloomsbury to take notice:

> In Society indefatigable maiden ladies of Chelsea and Mayfair, dyspeptic noblemen and bald old wits still caper in the public eye as "the Bright Young People." There are the Peter Pans of Bloomsbury, the skittish old critics who will not grow up, who must always be in the movement. Is there no one who will gently remind them . . . that *there is a younger generation*? . . . I see certain common tendencies [in Acton, Byron, Hollis, Quennell, and Stokes] which may be called the Spirit of the Age. One is a tendency to be bored with the problems of Sex and Socialism, which so vexed our seniors; another is . . . a disposition to regard very seriously mystical experience and . . . religion; another is a complete freedom from any kind of prudery. [33]

None of these writers, however, would succeed at the same level as did Waugh himself. The Bright Young People and the Oxonians of the 1920s remain vibrant and alive in the novels of the poor boy who partied with aristocrats and dreamed of marrying the rich girl.

Evelyn Waugh

> Life here is very beautiful. Mayonnaise and punts and cider cups all day long. One loses all ambition to be an intellectual. I am reduced to writing light verse for the *Isis* and taking politics seriously.
> —Evelyn Waugh, letter to Tom Driberg (1922) [34]

In writing his history of English letters during the era of the Bright Young People, Humphrey Carpenter confesses that Evelyn Waugh gradually dominates the narrative: "This is because, in his person and his writings, increasingly as the years passed, he displayed the characteristics and conflicts of the group more intensely and dramatically, and more entertainingly, than any other member."[35] Waugh was the Brightest of the Young People in terms of literary talent, many would argue, and he certainly became the lens through which subsequent readers would view England's Jazz Age and the Oxonian contribution. As such, he performs a role very close to that of F. Scott Fitzgerald, even though the two never met nor took much notice of each other.

Evelyn Arthur St. John Waugh was born on October 28, 1903, in Hampstead, the son of Arthur Waugh, a London writer and publisher who had studied at New College and won the Newdigate Prize for poetry in 1888 (though he obtained only a double-third in Mods and Greats). In his memoir, *One Man's Road* (1931), Arthur offered his recollection of Oxford during the Great War: "Everything for which Oxford stood was at a standstill; the Colleges were barracks, the meadows drill yards; the long tradition of manners which 'makyth man' was broken."[36] Arthur had built a modest villa for his family called Underhill, close to Golders Green. The eldest son Alec—"The heir of Underhill"—was expelled from Sherborne for being caught in a homosexual affair; he would write about the incident in the scandalously autobiographical novel, *The Loom of Youth* (1915), and was a prisoner of war. Barred from attending Sherborne, Evelyn landed instead at another public school, Lancing. "His early intellectual tastes were romantic," writes Michael Davie, editor of Waugh's diaries, "in architecture, he was drawn to the medieval . . . in books, to *Morte d'Arthur*."[37] At Lancing he read the *Divine Comedy* and Andrew Lang, wrote an essay on "Fairytales," worked on a cover design for the *Chanson de Roland* (to be published by his father), and planned "Spenserean stanzas on any incident from Malory" for the poetry prize. Waugh also made his first visit to a London club, Valhalla, to hear a jazz band play.[38]

"I am reading *Sinister Street* Vol II again to get the Oxford atmosphere," he records in his diary in June 1920, "since father and I have started discussing what college I am to go to. It is incomparably good and I am quite enchanted." A few months later he made his first visit to

Oxford: "I have never seen anything so beautiful. In places like Wells there are beautiful buildings and closes, but I have never seen anything like New College Cloisters or Tom Quad or the Founder's Tower."[39] While he and his father hoped to land a place at New College, Waugh also saw the advantage of being at one of the smaller colleges. Desperate to leave Lancing, he took the scholarship exam at Oxford in December 1921 and won a scholarship to Hertford College, worth more than the New College scholarship.[40] He went up to Oxford in January 1922 to read Modern History at Hertford, "a respectable but dreary little college" with "a good kitchen," as he describes it in his memoir, *A Little Learning* (1964).[41] Hertford, medieval but only a college since 1874, had neither roll call nor compulsory chapel, as other colleges did, and this suited Waugh for he never attended chapel.

The happiness of his first two terms was marked by "learning to smoke a pipe; getting drunk for the first time; walking and bicycling about the surrounding villages; making an unremarkable maiden speech at the Union [on February 8]; doing enough work to satisfy the examiners in History Previous."[42] For his first speech at the Oxford Union, he opposed the resolution: "This House Would Welcome Prohibition." He began walking with a cane and was drawn to childish pranks, while his clothing became increasingly dramatic—"sea-green plus-fours and tight-fitting blue tweeds," according to one biographer.[43] Waugh also tells us that, like the young Fitzgerald, his imagination was awakened by his reading of Matthew Arnold and the Oxford novels *Zuleika Dobson*, *Sinister Street*, *Verdant Green*, and *Patchwork*.[44] Waugh would later refer to Max Beerbohm as his "Master," "an idol of my adolescence to whom every year . . . deepened my devotion."[45] Like Beerbohm, Waugh was also a talented illustrator, and his artwork was featured regularly in the *Isis* and the *Oxford Broom*. He also read *Alice in Wonderland* his first year, declaring it "an excellent book," and the poetry of Rupert Brooke.[46]

Hertford had just added Neo-Gothic touches and its iconic imitation of the Bridge of Sighs only a generation before Waugh arrived. Oxford in 1922, however, was still very much like the Oxford of his father and great-grandfather:

The town was still isolated among streams and meadows. Its buildings proudly displayed their grey and gold. . . . The motor works at Cowley existed, but were far from sight or sound of the university. During term tourists were few.[47]

After moving to larger rooms on the ground floor of the front quad at Hertford, Waugh began hosting large, boisterous gatherings of undergrads and drank prodigiously day and night. He had the misfortune of having as tutor the Dean of Hertford, C.R.M.F. Cruttwell, whom he pranked, lampooned in print, and accused of sexual attraction to dogs! "I do not work here and never go to chapel," he confessed to old Lancing friend Tom Driberg, and was too bad to play football for Hertford; when asked once by a drunken student "what he did for the college," Waugh responded that he "drank for it."[48] Much of his carousing came from his membership in the Hypocrites Club, an association of public school boys that included many future members of the Bright Young People. As he recalled the events of 1923 in his memoir, Waugh writes:

by the time I joined, [the Hypocrites was] in process of invasion and occupation by a group of wanton Etonians who brought it to speedy dissolution. It then became notorious not only for drunkenness but for flamboyance of dress and manner which was in some cases patently homosexual. . . . The Hypocrites, like Gatsby's swimming pool, saw the passage, as members or guests, of the best and the worst of that year.[49]

Whispered as a den of all-males orgies (in reality, women were often smuggled in from London), the Hypocrites Club was a place where openly gay men like Driberg could enjoy camaraderie, but it was primarily a drinking society where music and singing played a large role. David Plunket Green would play Harlem blues on the piano before evenings dissolved in high spiritedness.[50]

Waugh destroyed the diaries recording most of his time at Oxford, but gives us a selectively reconstructed narrative in *A Little Learning*. Of the many important friends he made at Oxford—Terence Greenidge, Christopher Hollis, Patrick Balfour, Robert Byron, Anthony Powell, Cyril Connolly, Brian Howard, Alfred Duggan—the most significant relationships were with Harold Acton (1904–1994) and Alistair Graham. The Etonian Acton, who came up to Christ Church in October 1922, had been brought up in a villa outside Florence and was the most cosmopolitan and modern of Waugh's Oxford friends, introducing him, for example, to modernist artists and the works of Gertrude Stein and T. S. Eliot.[51] The two first met at a talk given by G. K. Chesterton to the Newman Society. A year younger than Waugh, Acton was a flamboyant dresser (Fig. 16) and poet who introduced Oxford Bags to the university, and Waugh would dedicate his first novel to Acton "in homage and affection."[52]

Waugh may have had multiple romantic relationships with men at Oxford, including fellow history student Richard Pares and aristocrat Hugh Lygon.[53] It was Waugh's relationship with Graham, however, whom Waugh calls "Hamish Lennox," "the friend of my heart," in *A Little Learning*, that would be memorialized in the aesthetic eroticism shared by Charles Ryder and Sebastian Flyte in *Brideshead*. Graham's mother was a wealthy American and his father was a grandson of the Duke of Somerset, and Waugh spent a good deal of time at the Graham estate near Stratford-upon-Avon. Waugh and Graham would remain close friends until 1932.

The lavish and hyper-social lifestyle of dress, luncheons, dinners, and drinks led to enormous debt for Waugh. Although he made a little money for his many contributions to the *Isis* (he penned a regular film review column) and from selling some of his illustrations, Waugh borrowed heavily from his friends, not the richest—like Alfred Duggan, the Balliol stepson of Lord Curzon, Chancellor of Oxford, who then "lived in an alcoholic haze," later becoming a famous historical novelist—but instead from "his poorer cronies." Some seven short stories written by Waugh during his undergraduate years survive, showing an interest in history, the macabre, class distinctions . . . and all with marks of the Wavian wit.[54]

As an undergraduate at Oxford, Waugh was not well-known as a writer, but rather it was his drawings that brought him a little attention.

Acton commissioned a story from Waugh in 1923, but it showed little promise and Waugh thought, in any case, that his career would be that of an illustrator. It was certainly not going to be an academic career. "These tiresome historians always find causes for their wars in national expansion and trade rivalry and religion and such things," he complained in the *Isis* in 1924. "I don't know about these things because . . . I am never up in time to read the newspapers."[55] Neither did Waugh read much in history books. "I was uneasily aware as I left Examination Schools," he recalls much later in his memoir, "that the questions had been rather inconvenient. I did not even then despair," but rather chose to show up "tipsy" at a dinner thrown by his tutor for the history candidates and "further alienated their sympathies by attempting . . . to sing a Negro spiritual."[56] The result of his exam and *viva* was a low third, and his father decided the expense of another term at Oxford was not a wise investment, enrolling his son instead at an art school (Heatherley) that autumn. Failing to fulfill his residency requirement, Waugh received no degree from Oxford.

When Waugh went down from Oxford he was first employed as a schoolmaster in North Wales and later in Buckinghamshire and Notting Hill Gate, but he continued to write and draw; more prolifically, he indulged in Mayfair and Oxford drinking parties, collecting new friends and acquaintances like the actresses Gwen Farrar and Tallulah Bankhead.[57] In December 1924 he records that he was falling in love with Olivia Plunkett Greene, one of the younger members of the Bright Young People, and from the fringe of that group he began making observations that would show up in his satirical homage, *Vile Bodies*. He also asked, looking back from a 1930 trip to Oxford, whether the money and years spent at Oxford had been worthwhile: certainly not, in terms of guaranteed employment and higher wages, he concluded:

> But there is another side. Oxford is architecturally a city of peculiar grace and magnificence. . . . The truth is that Oxford is simply a very beautiful city in which it is convenient to segregate a certain number of the young of the nation while they are growing up. . . . It puts them out of the way of

their fellow-citizens while they are making fools of themselves. . . . After that they can begin on the dreary and futile jobs that wait for most of them, with a great deal more chance of keeping their sense of humour and self-respect. [58]

After one wild party back in Oxford in 1925, during which he fell out of a hotel window and badly sprained his ankle, Waugh turned in his convalescence to writing about the artists with whom he shared the most affinity: the Pre-Raphaelites. "I was deep in the study of the Pre-Raphaelites," he writes in November of that year:

I want to write a book about them. . . . I have lived with them night and day. Early in the morning with Holman Hunt—the only Pre-Raphaelite—untiring, fearless, conscientious. Later in the day with Millais. . . . How he shines through Holman Hunt's loyal pictures of him. Later, when firelight and rum and loneliness have done their worst, with Rossetti, soaked in chloral. [59]

The result was a pamphlet titled *PRB: An Essay on the Pre-Raphaelite Brotherhood, 1847–1854* (1926), privately published by Alistair Graham. Waugh hoped to change the learned public's attitude toward William Holman Hunt (who had married two of Waugh's relations), John Everett Millais, and Dante Gabriel Rossetti. The Pre-Raphaelites were utterly dismissed by Garsington/Bloomsbury artists and critics like Lytton Strachey, Clive Bell, and Roger Fry. The young Waugh was, in the words of art historian Christopher Wood, "a lone voice crying in the modernist wilderness." [60]

A year later Waugh was commissioned by Duckworth to write a biography of PRB founder Dante Gabriel Rossetti, *Rossetti: His Life and Works* (1928). This was his first published book, followed soon after by his first novel, *Decline and Fall*. Waugh was just twenty-five years old. Waugh defends Rossetti (despite his technical flaws) as a "literary" painter devoted to female beauty and through beauty portraying spiritual devotion, most successfully in *Beata Beatrix* (1863).

Rossetti's *Arthur's Tomb* (1855), depicting the last meeting of Lancelot and Guinevere over Arthur's effigy, is described by Waugh as "a painful picture," "endowed by Rossetti with a guilt all his own."[61] Waugh and his Oxford friend John Betjeman would together do much to encourage serious study of Victorian art and architecture, and Waugh became a collector of Pre-Raphaelite works when he could eventually afford them.

Like *This Side of Paradise*, Waugh's first novel, *Decline and Fall*, is heavily autobiographical, narrating comically the plight of promising middle-class student Paul Pennyfeather, "sent down for indecent behavior" from Oxford—unfairly accused of being a member of the riotous "Bollinger Club," who terrorize him because they mistake him for an aesthete—and sentenced to work as a schoolmaster at a bottom-tier public school in Wales. Housed in Llanabba Castle, the school loosely mirrors the experiences of Waugh teaching in Wales. There is neither nostalgia nor romanticizing of Oxford in this early work; Scone College is home to venal college authorities and philistine aristocratic students.[62] Nothing has changed there when Paul returns to Oxford posing as his cousin.

To nearly everyone's surprise, Waugh quite suddenly married Evelyn Gardner, the androgynous daughter of the 1st Baron Burghclere, in London on June 27, 1928. Even in his diary he gives no reason other than being bored: let's "see how it goes," he told Evelyn during his proposal over dinner at the Ritz Grill.[63] It did not go well. She-Evelyn (as many of his friends called her) was often ill and could not keep pace with the social life and drinking of her husband. While He-Evelyn was off in the country writing his next novel, She-Evelyn recovered and fell in love with the young Etonian editor for the BBC, John Heygate. She confessed the affair to Waugh and he agreed on a divorce, announced in January 1930.

Waugh's second novel, *Vile Bodies*, was published in 1930. "Bright Young People and others kindly note," ran the prefatory warning in the novel's typescript, "that all characters are entirely imaginary (and you get far too much publicity already whoever you are)." Waugh was then writing a column for the *Daily Mail* in which his Oxford and

London friends made frequent appearances. One of these was Teresa "Baby" Jungman, Catholic and eccentric, with whom Waugh fell desperately in love and proposed marriage several times. Teresa was still very young and would not agree to be either his lover or his wife (Waugh's divorce from She-Evelyn would need to be recognized by the Church as an annulment), though Waugh would write her some seventy-five love letters between 1930 and 1935.[64] Still, Waugh was now a very successful novelist with a widening set of influential friends and patrons: Cunards, Guinnesses, Mitfords, Coopers, et al. One new acquaintance was Carl Van Vechten, the Fitzgeralds' friend and rival of Alain Locke, who Waugh called "the playboy of the western world" and claimed, at a 1930 cocktail party thrown in his honor, "He was so drunk he could not speak, only bark and bite."[65] Another new friend was Noël Coward, who "talked Catholicism" and encouraged Waugh to "go around the world." He seems to have taken the flippant Coward seriously: Waugh was received into the Roman Catholic Church on September 29, 1930, and would travel from Abyssinia to the Arctic over the next five years.

Both Patey and Parsonage point out that Britain's Jazz Age can be understood through looking at the subtle changes in characters and plots between Waugh's two novels, *Decline and Fall* and *Vile Bodies*.[66] *Vile Bodies* opens with two epigraphs from *Through the Looking Glass* and begins in gaiety, but devolves into a darker world of political and social unrest, of corruption of good characters and decay leading to death and war. "With its treasure hunts, nightclubs, parties, sexual experimentation, motor racing, ocean liners and aeroplane travel," writes Paula Byrne, "*Vile Bodies* is *the* English novel of the Jazz Age, as the very different *Great Gatsby* is the definitive American imagining of the era."[67] 1934's *A Handful of Dust* serves as something of a requiem for the Bright Young People. Its title is derived from a line from *The Waste Land*, and it's two main characters live in a country house whose rooms are named after characters in Malory.

No novel about Oxford student life has had such a lasting impression as Waugh's *Brideshead Revisited*, first published in 1945. It was, he told his second wife Laura, to be his "magnum opus."[68] He wrote this novel in a state of great boredom while recovering from a broken leg and serving as an officer in the Special Services Brigade, billeted in an army base near Sherborne. While the novel's framing device echoes that drab military camp atmosphere, in contrast, Book One (*Et in Arcadia Ego*) launches with some of the most beautiful prose Waugh ever composed. First, time is established as the divine summer of youth: ". . . it was a day of peculiar splendor, such as our climate affords once or twice a year, when leaf and flower and bird and sun-lit stone and shadow seem all to proclaim the glory of God." Then, the aestheticism is completed with the incantation of place:

> Oxford—submerged now and obliterated, irrecoverable as Lyonesse, so quickly have the waters come flooding in—Oxford, in those days, was still a city of aquatint. In her spacious and quiet streets men walked and spoke as they had done in Newman's day; her autumnal mists, her grey springtime, and the rare glory of her summer days—such as that day—when the chestnut was in flower and the bells rang out high and clear over her gables and cupolas, exhaled the soft vapours of a thousand years of learning. [69]

Waugh did not invent Oxonian Aestheticism, but this passage may come closer than any in encapsulating its crucial elements: the evocative power of the name "Oxford," comparing it to an ancient fabled city (the Arthurian "Lyonesse"), vivid colors (white, blue, gold), ghosts of great Oxonians (Newman) walking the streets, flowers in bloom, the chimes of the bells, Gothic architecture, and academics (last, and in Waugh's case, perhaps least). Neither the verse of Shelley nor the prose of Arnold can match this ode to Oxford by Waugh. He establishes his Oxonian Arcadia in Book One then immediately depicts a disruptive threat—a "rabble of womankind" come for the Summer Eights and college balls (a template borrowed from Beerbohm and Mackenzie)—which sends Charles Ryder and Sebastian Flyte on the idyllic, escape cum picnic that leads to Charles' first encounter with Brideshead.

Charles says that his "eyes were opened" when Sebastian, one day, read from Clive Bell's book *Art* (1913): "'Does anyone feel the same kind of emotion for a butterfly or a flower that he feels for a cathedral or a picture?' Yes. *I* do" (28). Their bond of friendship was formed, then, over aesthetic theory. Sebastian equated his appreciation of natural beauty with religious devotion, and Charles, artist and religious skeptic, was intrigued if not convinced. Sebastian was "magically beautiful," frequented the Botanic Gardens, and wrote "in a style of remote fantasy" (31, 33). He shows Charles Brideshead Chapel on their first visit to his home: "It was an aesthetic education to live within those walls," declares Charles (38–39). The shared aesthetic pleasures of Charles and Sebastian that first summer are described by Charles as "a happy childhood" falling "little short of the joy of innocence" (45). At the same time they indulged in "wickedness" and "naughtiness high in the catalog of grave sins" (80).

Until recently, most critics have either downplayed or denied the homosexual love between Charles and Sebastian at the beginning of *Brideshead*.[70] But denying the strong element of *eros* in the novel—Charles and Sebastian are clearly enamored of each other and aesthetic partners, if not sexual partners—weakens the novel's spiritual journey. "Same-sex love does not triumph or survive in the novel," writes Peter Christensen, who nevertheless argues that Waugh treated homosexuality with great dignity.[71] Neither does heterosexual love triumph: Charles and Julia join in sexual union, but their love is never completed because Catholicism, ever-present at Brideshead, stands in the way. ". . . to know and love one other human being is the root of all wisdom," is Charles's simple response to his cousin Jasper's remonstrance of his aesthetic lifestyle.

Charles remembers most fondly the summer after his first year at Oxford, spent with Sebastian at Brideshead wandering together "through that enchanted palace" (79). Brideshead had been a castle, Sebastian explains, its stones torn apart and reassembled into a grand country house. Like Fitzgerald in *Gatsby*, Waugh here combines medieval and fairy imagery with male aestheticism of the 1920s. Painting, wine tasting, the trip to Venice—all add to the sensuous and erotic first chapters of the novel; but in the background is the constant of the Catholic Church, with Brideshead's chapel, the Venetian *carnival*, and the medieval origins of the Marchmains. Paula Byrne and Jane Mulvagh have argued that the depiction of Brideshead owes much to Madresfield, the estate of the disgraced Lord Beauchamp (father of Waugh's Oxford friend Hugh Lygon) where Waugh spent much time in the 1930s.[72]

Interviewed for *The Paris Review* in 1962, Waugh was asked, did you write a novel at Oxford? "No," he replied. "I did sketches and that sort of thing for the *Cherwell* and for a paper Harold Acton edited—*Broom*, it was called. The *Isis* was the official undergraduate magazine: it was boring and hearty, written for beer drinkers and rugger players. The *Cherwell* was a little more frivolous."[73] Asked about his career after going down from Oxford, he answered, "I became a prep-school master. It was very jolly and I enjoyed it very much. I taught at two private schools for a period of nearly two years and during this I started an Oxford novel which was of no interest. After I had been expelled from the second school for drunkenness I returned penniless to my father."

Such behavior became the tragic narrative of Sebastian Flyte in *Brideshead*. Most of Sebastian comes from Waugh's remembrances of Alistair Graham. In the handwritten manuscript of *Brideshead*, the name "Alistair" appears in several places before being replaced by "Sebastian." Anthony Blanche—"the 'aesthete' *par excellence*"—flamboyant and bisexual, provoking the "boatmen" in Christ Church Meadow by reciting *The Waste Land* through a megaphone—is Waugh's homage to an antic of Harold Acton's. But Charles also compares Anthony to the Wandering Jew and "held him in considerable awe."[74] Anthony goes to Garsington to discuss the latest books, like Aldous Huxley's *Antic Hay* (1923), and fights duels over continental duchesses. Anthony Blanche in *Brideshead* plays the part of a more cosmopolitan but cruel Meyer Wolfsheim. Like Wolfsheim with Nick, he interviews Charles to see if he is a suitable companion for his school friend Sebastian; he tells wild stories and probes to see if Charles is really a gold-digger; and he fails, ultimately, to save his rich, flamboyant young protégé.

As Sebastian spirals into alcoholism in exile while Charles and Julia engage in an extramarital affair, the novel turns to last things and the deaths of Lord and Lady Marchmain. Lord Marchmain returning to his faith in extreme unction ends the romance of Charles and Julia but takes the novel to a higher, sublime level that has troubled some readers, and is ignored by others. In a typed memorandum "for the guidance of script-writers and all engaged in the production of the film of *Brideshead Revisited*," Waugh offers the following commentary on "the essential structures and features of the book":

> THEME: The theme is theological. It is in no sense abstruse and is based on principles which have for nearly two thousand years been understood by millions of simple people, and are still so understood. But . . . they are antithetical to much of the current philosophy of Hollywood. . . .
>
> 1. The novel deals with what is theologically termed, "the operation of Grace," that is to say, the unmerited and unilateral act of love by which God continually calls souls to Himself.
>
> 2. Grace is not confined to the happy, prosperous and conventionally virtuous. . . . God has a separate plan for each individual by which he or she may find salvation. The story of *Brideshead Revisited* seeks to show the working of several such plans in the lives of a single family.
>
> 3. The Roman Catholic Church has the unique power of keeping remote control on human souls which have been part of her.[75]

In this memorandum, Charles Ryder is described as "an intelligent, artistic and lonely young man," and Sebastian Flyte as "the idol of the fashionable aesthetic set which was prominent in English university life in the 'twenties."[76] As he recalls his experience at Oxford some twenty-two years later, Waugh has sanitized his memories and written a revisionist, spiritual history that has proved problematic for some readers. "Waugh is so eloquent on the beauty of lost youth, hope and *joie de vivre* that the novel's closing promise of spiritual comfort can be less convincing than its glowing evocation of the past," writes Cooke. "The consolations of faith are not as obvious [as] the joys, or even memory, of youth. They are, however, profound and lasting."[77]

Fitzgerald did not live to see the publication and success of the novel that became an English counterpart to *The Great Gatsby*, but one of his closest friends weighed in on *Brideshead*. Edmund Wilson shared his dislike of the novel in a 1945 letter to Elizabeth Huling: "I saw Evelyn Waugh again. The great topic of conversation was his new novel which . . . is partly extremely trashy and unintentionally—which is sad for Waugh—comic. . . ."[78]

Brideshead Revisited is not documentary history of the Oxford of the 1920s, and was never meant to be. But does it capture the spirit of the age? "For the generation that was young in the 1920s and 1930s, and for whom Waugh was in some ways the blithe spirit, the unresolved question was this: Were they living in a postwar world or a pre-war one?" writes Christopher Hitchens. "The suppressed hysteria of this time—the echo of the preceding bloodshed and the premonition of more impending—was never captured better, except perhaps by F. Scott Fitzgerald. . . . *Brideshead* . . . evokes almost to perfection the atmosphere of Oxford just after World War I, populated by young men who are acutely conscious of having barely missed the great test of combat."[79]

Waugh died on Easter Sunday 1966. Years of heavy drinking had taken their toll, but, as with Fitzgerald, alcohol and Waugh had become so intertwined that it would be hard to think of his novels without thinking about cocktails. "Do let me seriously advise you to take to drink," he wrote to Driberg, still at Lancing, in 1922. "There is nothing like the aesthetic pleasure of being drunk and if you do it in the right way you can avoid being ill next day. That is the greatest thing Oxford has to teach."[80] "From the first I regarded Oxford as a place to be enjoyed for itself," he wrote in *A Little Learning*, "not as a preparation for something else."[81]

Waugh did, I would argue, develop a distinctly Oxonian aesthetic, at first merely comical but eventually, as in the early parts of *Brideshead*, rhapsodic and sublime. Realism was never the goal in his later descriptions of Oxford, but rather capturing the spirit of the place in the 1920s the way Max Beerbohm and Compton Mackenzie had done a generation before. "He remains a legend at the University," writes biographer Martin Stannard, "warmly remembered as a modern Hamlet," inspiring the the Vile Bodies Dining Club in the 1970s where members came dressed in period costume to honor their Oxonian Bacchus.[82]

Evelyn Waugh and F. Scott Fitzgerald, though little aware of each other's work, shared much in common.[83] Both were solidly middle class young aesthetes who were drawn to the rich and titled. Neither attended a top prep school though both made it into elite universities where they drank much, acted a little, and made significant contributions to campus literary periodicals. Both writers left their universities without taking degrees but soon after published their first novels and got married. Both spent their twenties in a drunken whirl of social affairs, where alcohol formed part of their aesthetic sensibilities, yet both also commented wryly on the decline around them of the Jazz Age. As satirists they drew inspiration from Lewis Carroll and Max Beerbohm, while embracing the modernist verse of T. S. Eliot. They were drawn to and critical of the power of motion pictures. Catholic writers who struggled with issues of faith, military officers who served during wartime, both were, for periods, absentee husbands and fathers. Each carried memories of unrequited love, of women who rejected their proposals but inspired portraits of unattainable women in their fiction. In the two novels for which they are most remembered, each has a narrator at times conceited and snobbish, at other times an acute observer of human nature and the one character most appreciative of beauty.

Evelyn Waugh and Charles Ryder were both students of history with artistic talent and a penchant for parties and travel; F. Scott Fitzgerald and Nick Carraway were aspiring writers drawn to the fêtes of Long Island castles. Both Fitzgerald and Waugh attempted to define their generation, to defend the young writers and intellectuals who stepped out of the darkness of the Great War with cocktail in hand and a ready quip.

11

Dreaming in Oxford

I wonder anybody does anything at Oxford but dream and remember, the place is so beautiful. One almost expects the people to sing instead of speaking. It is all like an opera.
—W. B. Yeats (1888)[1]

I n 1919 the Irish poet William Butler Yeats moved to Oxford and took up residence at 4 Broad Street, a seventeenth-century house opposite Balliol College.[2] Two years later, the great man invited the American-born cleric and poet William Force Stead to pay him an evening visit, and Stead brought along a young Oxford undergraduate named C. S. Lewis. Lewis recorded this meeting with "the mighty Yeats," and one the following week, in letters to his father, his brother Warnie, and his friend Arthur Greeves.[3] Sitting on antique chairs surrounded by William Blake etchings of Job and Dante, their conversations turned often to literature, mysticism, and magic. Yeats's dramatic flair and obsession with spiritualism did not appeal to Lewis, who was then at the height of his stage of atheism and skepticism. But

Yeats did impress Lewis with stories about Andrew Lang and William Morris.[4] The old man could still dream great dreams and remember great Victorians.

Yeats also made several trips to America, his father living for a while in New York City. During one such trip he came out to Long Island, to the estate of Mary Harriman Rumsey, and read for her friends. The Barnard-educated widow of polo-player Pad Rumsey, Mary was quite interested in the Irish Literary Revival. In 1923 a frequent guest at her parties was another writer with interest in Irish literature: F. Scott Fitzgerald.[5] *The Great Gatsby* ends with an aspiring writer from the Midwest contemplating "the last and greatest of all human dreams" held by the first arrival to Long Island from the Old World, man "face to face for the last time in history with something commensurate to his capacity for wonder" (140).

Dreaming and Remembering

Dreaming—romanticism, metaphysics, imagination—and *remembering*—cognition, history, the collective memory—these are indeed important characteristics of Oxford, even as the medieval town made its turn toward modernity. Dreaming and remembering also make Oxford an appropriate destination for Jay Gatsby. When Dante Gabriel Rossetti met the Oxford students William Morris and Edward Burne-Jones, he told his friends that they were two of the nicest young men in "Dreamland." While the three painters dreamed Arthurian dreams at the Oxford Union in 1857, Lewis Carroll was about to tell new stories about Dreamland to the young daughters of the Dean of Christ Church.

Youth and dreaming had been connected by Fitzgerald in his 1922 novella, *The Diamond as Big as the Ritz*. The narrator comments, of the story's young protagonist, "It is youth's felicity as well as its insufficiency that it can never live in the present, but must always be measuring up the day against its own radiantly imagined future—flowers and gold, girls and stars, they are only prefigurations and prophecies of that incomparable, unattainable young dream."[6] In Nick's remembrance of his last conversation with Gatsby, he contrasts Gatsby's wealth—gotten from corrupt business—with "his incorruptible dream" (120). Nick wonders whether Gatsby, waiting for that phone call from Daisy that never came, finally recognized the world as a colder place than that of his golden dream. "He must have looked up at an unfamiliar sky through frightening leaves and shivered as he found what a grotesque thing a rose is and how raw the sunlight was upon the scarcely created grass. A new world, material without being real . . ." (126).

Gatsby's dreams are so powerful that they approach Platonic forms, and thus are more *real* than the reality perceived by those around him. Gatsby "sprang from his Platonic conception of himself," asserts Nick. "He was a son of God . . . and he must be about His Father's business" (7), a reference to Luke 2:49. As Julian Cowley observes, Fitzgerald "was interested in the way that symbolism could produce a kind of magical transformation in which the physical world might, through an act of imagination, come to assume the quality of the ideal."[7] The Christian Platonism of the Renaissance leads us in this direction, as, for example, in Pietro Bembo's rapturous description of the lovers' kiss in Castiglione's *The Book of the Courtier* (1528): "For this reason all chaste lovers desire the kiss as a union of souls . . . to signify the wish that his soul be transported through divine love to the contemplation of heavenly beauty."[8]

Unfortunately, pathos results from Gatsby's first kiss of Daisy, for instead of the union of two great souls this kiss prevents Gatsby's mind from climbing the Platonic ladder and "romping with the mind of God." *The Great Gatsby* is, nevertheless, a philosophic novel. Berman argues that "*Gatsby* . . . asks, if implicitly, what is the good life?"[9] Nick's existential crisis, Daisy's moral dilemmas, Tom's philandering, Jordan's dishonesty, Wilson's sickness—all of these characters are struggling in different ways with making ethical decisions in conflict with societal norms, personal worldviews, marital oaths. Only Gatsby with his winning smile seems to have a clear vision of the Good, and the tragedy seems to be that the one character "worth more than the whole lot put together" sacrificed everything to this vision, metaphysical yet reliant upon a physical and flawed object of devotion. It is the problem with dreams: They transcend reality and can offer a glimpse of the Good, but it is often distorted and always ephemeral.

History, on the other hand, is collective remembrance grounded in fact. Fitzgerald's fascination with history comes through in *Gatsby* in many ways. There are the explicit references to historical events and figures: the Middle Ages, the Dutch explorers of the New World, the Dukes of Buccleuch, the Restoration and Marie Antoinette, the American Civil War, the Great War. "Fitzgerald never wavered from his view that World War I represented a dramatic break from the past," writes James Meredith. "No Fitzgerald novel better conveys the socio-logical role World War I played in the break from the past than *The Great Gatsby*."[10] And yet, despite the break, the past remains present in the novel. It comes back again and again through flashbacks of Gatsby's youth and of his meeting Daisy and Dan Cody. Fitzgerald's handling of time in the novel is "masterful," judges Robert Long, creating nar-rative layers and textures.[11] Clocks, timetables, changing seasons, tides and currents, deceased characters—the reader is constantly reminded of history and of the passage of time.

There are also the differing views of the characters in the novel about how history and the past work. Meyer Wolfsheim, for example, is sentimental about the bad old days at the Metropole, "Filled with faces dead and gone" (56). For Tom, history is static and rigid, a drama in which the superior men of the superior races are destined to come out on top. For Gatsby, history can be relived and rewritten. When Nick advises Gatsby about Daisy—"I wouldn't ask too much of her. . . . You can't repeat the past"—Gatsby famously replies, "Can't repeat the past? . . . Why of course you can!" (86). Gatsby's claims about Oxford, observes Jeffrey Meyers, are commented on by nearly all the major characters in the novel—Nick, Jordan, Daisy, Tom, Wolfsheim—and emphasize Gatsby's "obsessive need to change as well as to repeat the past."[12] Nick's last words in the novel seem to indicate a somewhat revised position on history. Not only can it be relived, we are all forced back into the past incessantly: "So we beat on, boats against the current, borne back ceaselessly into the past" (141).

John Callahan writes about Fitzgerald's unique use of history and myth in *The Great Gatsby*.[13] "History, myth, and personality together illuminate the vision of America" in *Gatsby*, asserts Callahan. For Nick, "we are doomed to repeat [history's] pattern in our lives even if individual minds and hearts resist its course. Past history has taken away *our* freedom." Gatsby's great "capacity for hope" becomes "crushed in Carraway by the burden of history."[14]

There are, of course, many references to and uses of history in Fitzgerald's other works. He had, on occasion, used history as allegory: in the Philippe stories, for example, with Count Philippe representing Modern Man, battling the chaos and darkness brought about by the organized thuggery of the Vikings, i.e., Hitler and Mussolini's followers.[15] "Fitzgerald's historical awareness was at its core sentimental, nostalgic, and conservative," writes David Brown, and he found cohesion "both emotionally and intellectually in the chivalry, paternalism, and Catholic sensibility of the Middle Ages."[16] Brown places Fitzgerald in the company of Henry Adams and Oswald Spengler as Historical Decline thinkers who doubted the survival of even the best ancien régime ideas and institutions in modernity, with Fitzgerald giving us romantic heroes whose dreams are destroyed by the bureaucrats, materialists, and femmes fatales of the early twentieth century.

Beauty and Aesthetics

Yeats also was overwhelmed by the *beauty* of Oxford. In 1865, Matthew Arnold had described an Oxford "whispering from her towers the last enchantments of the Middle Ages," calling its students and dons "to the true goal of all of us, to the ideal, to perfection—to beauty, in a word, which is only truth seen from another side."[17] Walter Pater and his disciple, Oscar Wilde, began a mission to spread aesthetic appreciation from Oxford to the rest of the world—even if the world was not yet ready for challenging notions of masculinity and male sartorial beauty. Fitzgerald took up the challenge, exploring dandyism—through Amory Blaine, Anthony Patch, Jay Gatsby, and Dick Diver—as well as the flapper phenomenon. Furthermore, he and Zelda performed beauty and style on "stages" from St. Paul to Montgomery, from Long Island to the French Riviera. And, finally getting a chance to see Oxford for himself (rather than through his beloved Oxford Novels) in 1921, he pronounced it the most beautiful place he had ever seen. He would fall for the beauty of other mistresses—in France, in Italy, and in Hollywood—but Oxford remains an important early love.

Harold Bloom, champion of literary aesthetics, connects beauty with the transcendent in *Gatsby*. "If there is an American sublime, going beyond irony, in modern American fiction, then it is located most centrally in *The Great Gatsby*."[18] Bloom recognizes the influence of both Keats and Yeats on Fitzgerald's depiction of the transcendent imagination in *The Great Gatsby*. "The man of imagination, however compromised," writes Bloom,

> quests perpetually for an immortal female, more daemonic than human. Poor Daisy . . . is precisely a possible American Belle Dame Sans Merci of 1925, and Gatsby is her inevitable victim, who does not want to know better, and so is not deceived. . . . It cannot matter that Daisy is an absurd object, because Gatsby's drive is Transcendental. What matters is what the Yeatsian quester of *A Full Moon in March* calls 'the image in my head.' In love with that image, Gatsby . . . dies more than adequately.

This, of course, brings us back to Plato, whose mentor Socrates confessed to be moved by the daemon *Eros*, ultimately costing him his life, and also recalls the death of Sir Galahad, in both the thirteenth-century *Queste del Saint Graal* and in Tennyson's poetry, who dies far too young (but also far more than adequately) in pursuit of the Grail. The combination in *Gatsby* of dreams, imagination, and history are very close to how Yeats envisioned literature. "Yeats argued the people needed 'imaginative' literature, not sociological or political treatises," writes Jeffrey Stewart, "to incite them to dream a new future for themselves based on their glorious past."[19]

When it comes to the spiritual dimension of *The Great Gatsby*, critics are conflicted. Can the great modernist novel, with its crass materialism, decadence, and skepticism, be considered a religious work? The conflict, however, is inherent in the author himself, and, indeed, in the Oxford of the early twentieth century, where the venerable humanities battled the burgeoning sciences, the Magdalen Metaphysicals confronted the Oxford Realists, and High Church struggled against commerce on High Street. Fitzgerald stood on the High in 1921 and felt the forces of past and present struggling over Oxford's future. "It was not the modernists themselves," points out Oser, "but a cadre of specialists, usurping cultural authority, that ruled out the dialectic between religion and literature."[20] Realists like Joseph Conrad, Thomas Hardy, and Henry James did not think religion the enemy of art and culture, and their modernist successors Virginia Woolf, James Joyce, and Samuel Beckett at least remained interested in the soul. While Fitzgerald struggled with his religion, he never lost interest in transcendence.

Berman summarizes the critical judgment of Gatsby's idealism: a failure of reasonableness, a folly or illusion, a misdirected search for transcendence. "Gatsby is an unrealist, an immature romantic, childish, and even paranoid," say these critics. "Even when we are sympathetic to Gatsby, we tend to think that he has not only mistaken the object of his quest but misconceived the idea of the quest. He seems to have parodied spirituality."[21] Does Gatsby choose illusion over truth? Anthony Patch in *The Beautiful and Damned* "cherished all beauty and all illusion" (61). Fitzgerald, describing *The Great Gatsby* at the very time he was writing it, calls it "a new thinking out of the idea of illusion," stating that "the whole burden of this novel . . . [is] the loss of those illusions that give such color to the world so that you don't care whether things are true or false as long as they partake of the magical glory."[22] Daisy says she is crying because of the enormous beauty of Gatsby's collection of London shirts, but is she really crying, as Catherine Mintler suggests, because she recognizes it as an illusion of class status?[23]

Fitzgerald returns to the theme of beauty and illusion in his last novel, the unfinished *The Last Tycoon*. Here the narrator describes

Hollywood producer Monroe Stahr as a modern and more successful Icarus:

> He had flown up very high to see, on strong wings, when he was young. And while he was up there he had looked on all the kingdoms, with the kind of eyes that can stare straight into the sun. Beating his wings tenaciously—finally frantically—and keeping on beating them, he had stayed up there longer than most of us, and then, remembering all he had seen from his great height of how things were, he had settled gradually to earth.[24]

Monroe Stahr is a movie producer, creating glamour and illusions for a living. Fitzgerald was brought to Hollywood to do the same thing with his scriptwriting, and in Hollywood—the land of illusion—Fitzgerald's magic failed him just as his health, too, was failing him. Fitzgerald had been a performer all his life, had created characters who performed their identities, and had fallen in love with dancers and movie stars. It is perhaps fitting that his life should end among the beautiful people, whose newly acquired riches had built a magical kingdom in the western wilderness of America.

Romping Like the Mind of God

Categorizing Fitzgerald as a member of the Lost Generation of postwar writers, critics have emphasized disillusionment in *The Great Gatsby* and pointed to the almost complete absence of God and institutional religion in the novel. Contrasting *Gatsby* with the more overtly Catholic *This Side of Paradise*, Brown calls the former "a parable of Elysian loss and spiritual decline."[25] In part this is because Fitzgerald purposely excised the original Catholic background story of young Jimmy Gatz, reworking it for his short story "Absolution," which appeared first in H. L. Mencken's *American Mercury* (1924). In the novel, Gatsby receives a Lutheran funeral, and none of the main characters in the novel appeal to scripture, faith in the divine, or clerical guidance. When George Wilson, speaking morbidly after accusing his wife of adultery and seeing Myrtle killed by Gatsby's car, says of the eyes of Doctor T. J. Eckleburg, says, "God sees everything," his neighbor Michaelis[26] replies, "that's an advertisement," suggesting that George go for spiritual help to a church—"Don't belong to any," is George's cold reply (157–60). Science and advertising have, seemingly, replaced God and scripture in the Valley of Ashes.

But we should not be so obtuse as to ignore Fitzgerald's essentially Catholic worldview, whatever his spiritual condition. "His Catholic heaven," wrote his friend, literary critic Ernest Boyd, "is not so far away that he can be misled into mistaking the shoddy dream of a radical millennium as a substitute for Paradise."[27] Joan Allen explores in great detail the Catholic influences on Fitzgerald the man and the writer in *Candles and Carnival Lights: The Catholic Sensibility of F. Scott Fitzgerald* (1978). She points to the influence of St. Augustine, Cardinal Newman, and Compton Mackenzie on Fitzgerald, but views Gatsby as "a Trimalchio, not a Christ, and the God he worships is Mammon."[28] I think this is too severe a judgment, and ignores the fact that Gatsby's materialism is a means—to win Daisy—rather than an end.

"Like Gatsby I have only hope," wrote Fitzgerald to Gertrude Stein as he awaited the reception of his novel. James Meredith has written eloquently about that hope in the writings of Fitzgerald, especially in those works of fiction which explore both the personal and cultural aftermath of the Great War:

> There is a pervasive sense of loss in Fitzgerald's work, as there is in so much modernist fiction, and the single most important event that caused that sense of loss was World War I. Yet, there is also deeply embedded in Fitzgerald's fiction an abiding hope and faith that the idyllic old world could once again be possible if only the modern times, brought on by a terrible modern war, could somehow cease to cast a deep and darkening shadow upon the everlasting light of the modern day.[29]

Gatsby is "true to poetic sources of imagination," writes Berman, "that teach us first to love things human as if they were spiritual."[30]

Marius Bewley writes that Gatsby's "doomed but imperishable spiritual beauty . . . is defined by his contrast with Tom."[31] But there is also a contrast between the beauty of Gatsby and the beauty of Daisy. Both manifest physical beauty supported by material wealth; but Gatsby dreams of transcending the material world, while Daisy settles for its comforts at the expense of love. Oser describes this as a Christian humanist tempering of classical ideas about beauty, a lesson that "appearances can be deceiving" and a common theme running through the writings of "Wilde, Chesterton, Eliot, Tolkien, Fitzgerald, [and] Waugh."[32] Christian humanism remained a vital intellectual strain in both Catholic and Oxonian writers well into the twentieth century, and one could add C. S. Lewis, Charles Williams, and Graham Greene to this list.

In the Oxford of the 1920s, as we have seen, there was a conflict in philosophy between the Oxford Realists and the Magdalen Metaphysicals.[33] From the latter group, C. S. Lewis observed: "The world is full of imposters who claim to be disenchanted and are really unenchanted: mere 'natural' men who have never risen so high as to be in danger of the generous illusions they claim to have escaped from."[34] *Generous illusions* could describe Gatsby's parties, Gatsby's conversations with Nick, and even Gatsby's love for Daisy.

Through most of the first half of the twentieth century, it was dreaming and beauty that most captivated those Oxonians and visitors who left us written testimony. To them Oxford was an English Athens, a western Shangri-La *not* open to all, reminds John Dougill. "To have youth, talent and wealth, to enjoy the opportunity for self-development in beautiful surroundings, to spend one's prime amidst gifted contemporaries, to lead a life of leisurely study with access to lawn and river and meadow—this is indeed the stuff of dreams."[35]

Fitzgerald throughout his life seems to have wavered between youthful romanticism—beautiful dreams—and the glib realism of New York nightclubs and Parisian cafes. ". . . I'm not a realist," declares Anthony Patch in his early wooing of Gloria. "No, only the romanticist preserves the things worth preserving" (61). Fitzgerald preserved beautiful things from the past in his prose, just as Gatsby tried to preserve his past with Daisy, his golden girl kissed beneath the silver moonlight. Oxford and its American stand-in, Princeton, were two of the beautiful things full of history preserved in the writings of Fitzgerald. When he wrote the last words of his greatest novel—"borne back ceaselessly into the past"—Fitzgerald was himself a boat borne back into America's past, into the Old World. From France he tried to capture the sparkle, the glamour of Jazz Age New York, of the Roaring Twenties, but to convey true meaning he reached into a very old cultural vocabulary. It is this aspect of Fitzgerald and of *The Great Gatsby* that has been most elusive to critics looking for the new.[36] The "tremendous detail" that Nick defines for us readers, however, is Oxford, an ancient city whose medieval dreams can still be glimpsed in the modern.

The Last Enchantments of the Middle Ages

All in the golden afternoon
Full leisurely we glide. . . .
The dream-child moving through a land
Of wonders wild and new.
       —Lewis Carroll, "The Dream Child" (1862)

Fitzgerald stood on the High in Oxford in 1921 seeing the ghosts of Oxford's literary past and bemoaned the decay of tradition. If there is a distinctly Oxonian aestheticism, one that Fitzgerald had at least partly grasped from his reading of *Zuleika Dobson* and *Sinister Street*—it combines the elements of history, dreaming, and beauty. The Romantic poets Shelley and Keats had glimpsed this aestheticism a century earlier, and Arnold and Pater had attempted to describe it in formal theory. Carroll made it part of his dream "in the golden afternoon," while Wilde had made it part of his look and his very being. Tolkien and Lewis, more Hearties than Aesthetes, had nevertheless described Oxford's beauty and ancientry in their earliest poems and reminded the world through their enormously popular fiction that the enchantments of the Middle Ages were not quite exhausted. Even Eliot became increasingly a champion of tradition and religion, as did Waugh, and both were partly indebted to Oxford for their faith journeys.

The Great Gatsby is a novel explicitly built, according to its author, on ancient and medieval foundations. It is a novel about history—of the Old World and the New—about dreaming—American dreams wrapped in medieval chivalric colors—and about beauty—of golden girls and movie stars, of shining cars and pink suits, of fairy-tale castles and the enchanting lights of Manhattan. F. Scott Fitzgerald chronicled America's Jazz Age, but his pen and mind were sharpened on medievalism and Romanticism. The Princetonian Fitzgerald was not really "an Oxford man," but he understood what that term meant well enough to give us Jay Gatsby, a war hero who spent as much time at Oxford as did Shelley and many other students who have been sent down. Gatsby photographed in cricket attire standing in Trinity Quad is an image that is composed of many layers of meaning, not least the important role that sport has played in attracting American students to Oxford. He may not have been a Rhodes scholar, but Gatsby was nonetheless a war hero, a soldier-student, and one of the most memorable Americans ever to inhabit the City of Dreaming Spires.

APPENDIX A
Oxford Writers, ca. 1829–1929

A representative group of major writers living in and/or working at Oxford.

Mathew Arnold (1822–1888), poet and literary theorist, came to Balliol in 1841 to read Greats, became a Fellow of Oriel College in 1845.

Sir Max Beerbohm (1872–1956), studied at Merton College (1890–94), left without taking a degree, befriended Oscar Wilde, became famous as a humorist/caricaturist and dandy, author of one novel, *Zuleika Dobson* (1911).

Robert Bridges (1844–1930), educated at Eton and Corpus Christi, friend of Gerard Manley Hopkins at Oxford, retired as a physician and was Britain's poet laureate 1913–30.

Vera Brittain (1893–1970), awarded an exhibition to Oxford (Somerville College) to study English Literature in 1914, left Oxford to serve as a nurse during the war, returned to Oxford to read History in 1918, caricatured Oxford dons in her first novel, *The Dark Tide* (1923).

John Buchan, 1st Baron Tweedsmuir (1875–1940), studied *Literae Humaniores* at Brasenose College (1895–1900) and was President of the Oxford Union.

Rev. Charles Lutwidge Dodgson (Lewis Carroll) (1832–1898), came to study mathematics and Classics at Christ Church in 1851, was appointed lecturer in 1855.

T. S. Eliot (1888–1965), came to Oxford (Merton College) on a traveling research fellowship in 1914.

Robert Graves (1895–1985), studied English and Classics at St. John's (1919).

Henry Graham Greene (1904–1991), read History at Balliol, earning a second in 1925 and publishing his first book (a volume of poetry) while at Oxford.

Gerard Manley Hopkins (1844–1889), studied Classics at Balliol (1863–67) and was briefly curate at St. Aloysius's Church.

Aldous Huxley (1894–1963), grandson of biologist T. H. Huxley, read English literature at Balliol and graduated with an honors first in 1916, edited *Oxford Poetry*, spent much of the war years at Garsington Manor.

Andrew Lang (1844–1912), Scottish writer and journalist who studied Greats at Balliol and became a fellow at Merton in 1870, teaching at Oxford for five years before moving to London.

T. E. Lawrence ("Lawrence of Arabia") (1888–1935), studied History at Jesus College (1907–10), began postgraduate work at Magdalen before becoming a practicing archaeologist, won a research fellowship at All Souls (1919).

C. S. Lewis (1898–1963), came to Oxford as a student in 1917 (University College) and lived there the rest of his life, fellow and tutor in English Literature at Magdalen (1925–54).

Sir Compton Mackenzie (1883–1972), studied modern history at Magdalen and wrote the classic Oxford Novel *Sinister Street* (1914).

John Masefield (1878–1967), British poet laureate 1930–67, lived on Boar's Hill just outside Oxford, received an Honorary Doctorate of Literature from the university, organized the annual *Oxford Recitations* in 1923.

William Morris (1834–1896), studied Classics at Exeter College (1852–56), co-founded *The Oxford and Cambridge Magazine*, and was married at the Church of St. Michael at the North Gate (1859).

John Ruskin (1819–1900), studied Greats at Christ Church (1836–42), appointed first Slade Professor of Fine Art (1869), founded the Ruskin School of Drawing and Fine Art (1871).

Dorothy Sayers (1893–1957), born in Oxford to the chaplain of Christ Church, studied modern languages and medieval literature at Somerville College (finished with a first in 1915), author of *Gaudy Night* and other detective fiction, Christian humanist and Dante translator, friend of C. S. Lewis.

J.R.R. Tolkien (1892–1973), came to Oxford as a student in 1911 (Exeter College), receiving a first in English in 1916, worked on the *Oxford English Dictionary* after the war, became Rawlinson and Bosworth Professor of Anglo-Saxon and Fellow at Pembroke in 1925, Merton Professor of English Language and Literature in 1945.

Arnold J. Toynbee (1889–1975), British historian and philosopher of history, studied *Literae Humaniores* at Balliol (1907–11), tutor and fellow of ancient history at Balliol until the war, married daughter of Gilbert Murray, father of writer and communist Philip Toynbee.

Evelyn Waugh (1903–1966), read Modern History at Hertford College (1922–24) but left without taking a degree.

Oscar Wilde (1854–1900), read Greats at Magdalen College, earning a first in 1878.

William Butler Yeats (1865–1939), moved to Oxford in April 1919, lived there intermittently for two years.

APPENDIX B

A.E.F. Soldier-Students
at British Universities, 1919

District 1		*Officers*	*Soldiers*
London	University College	29	94
	King's College	36	107
	Imperial College of Science & Technology	6	10
	London School of Economics	74	156
	Goldsmith's College	0	2
	New College	5	11
	Regent's Park College	2	4
	Battersea Polytechnic	0	15
	Birkbeck College	3	24
	Royal Veterinary College	11	0
	Royal College of Music	1	0
	Trinity College of Music	1	3
	Royal Normal College	1	0
	Royal Architectural Association	1	1
	Law Society Hall	5	23
	Inns of Court	45	68
	Fellowship of Medicine	90	8
	Subtotals for London	310	526

Oxford	University of Oxford	123	31
Bristol	University of Bristol	5	17
Reading	University College	1	4
	Totals for District 1	439	578
District 2			
Aberystwyth	University College of Wales	6	28
Birmingham	University of Birmingham	9	65
Cambridge	University of Cambridge	147	48
Harpenden	Rothamstead Experiment Station	1	3
Leeds	University of Leeds	5	5
Liverpool	University of Liverpool	10	24
Manchester	University of Manchester	22	47
Nottingham	University College	1	9
Sheffield	University of Sheffield	4	13
	Totals for District 2	205	242
District 3			
Aberdeen	University of Aberdeen	3	23
Aberdeen	North of Scotland College of Agriculture	6	21
Belfast	Queen's University	0	9
Cork	National University of Ireland, University College	1	2
Dublin	University of Dublin, Trinity College	23	39
Dublin	National University of Ireland, University College	0	4
Edinburgh	University of Edinburgh	82	160
Galway	National University of Ireland, University College	0	4
Glasgow	University of Glasgow	14	48
St. Andrews	University of St. Andrews	0	2
	Totals for District 3	131	334
	Total Students Assigned	775	1154

Bibliography

ARCHIVES

Princeton University Library contains most of the correspondence, notes, photos, manuscripts, and ephemera of F. Scott and Zelda Fitzgerald. The Firestone Library at Princeton also contains several original photographs taken by Lewis Carroll.

The Matthew J. Bruccoli Papers, a collection of Fitzgerald and Great War papers put together by the leading Fitzgerald scholar, is housed at the University of South Carolina Library. It includes *F. Scott Fitzgerald's Ledger, 1919–1938*, now available online.

The Bodleian Library, University of Oxford, holds most of the academic papers (and some letters and manuscripts) of J.R.R. Tolkien, C. S. Lewis, Charles Williams, and Owen Barfield. Vivienne Eliot's diaries are also held by the Bodleian.

Marquette University, in Milwaukee, has an important collection of Tolkien manuscripts.

The Marion E. Wade Center at Wheaton College (Illinois) holds a major collection of materials by and about Owen Barfield, G. K. Chesterton, C. S. Lewis, George MacDonald, Dorothy L. Sayers, J.R.R. Tolkien, and Charles Williams.

The Merton College Library, Oxford, has important collections of papers and manuscripts relating to Old Mertonians Sir Max Beerbohm and T. S. Eliot.

The Harry Ransom Center, University of Texas at Austin, contains the diaries of Evelyn Waugh and important collections of letters, artwork, manuscripts, and other materials of or relating to Waugh, Sir Max Beerbohm, Sir Edward Burne-Jones, Lewis Carroll, John Keats, Compton Mackenzie, Lady Ottoline Morrell, William Morris, Percy Shelley, T. S. Eliot, T. H. White, and Oscar Wilde.

Houghton Library, Harvard University, contains an important collection of manuscripts and papers of T. S. Eliot, whose student records are held at the Harvard University Archives.

The Alain Locke Papers are housed at the Moorland-Spingarn Research Center, Founders Library, Howard University, in Washington, D.C. Other information related to his student years are kept in the Harvard University Archives. Harvard kept good records of the activities of most of their A.E.F. students at Oxford.

Horace Kallen's papers are located at the America Jewish Archives, Hebrew Union College (Cincinnati, Ohio), and YIVO Institute for Jewish Research, New York.

The Rhodes Trust Archive, containing documents and other media relating to the history of the Rhodes scholarship, is located at Rhodes House, Oxford.

The Vera Brittain Archives are housed at Somerville College, Oxford.

ONLINE RESOURCES

The First World War Poetry Digital Archive, University of Oxford. http://www.oucs.ox.ac.uk/ww1lit/collections

"Globalising and Localising the Great War," History Faculty/TORCH, University of Oxford. http://greatwar.history.ox.ac.uk

The University of Oxford WWI Resources. http://www.ox.ac.uk/world-war-1/ww1-oxford-resources

PRINT RESOURCES

Ackroyd, Peter. *T. S. Eliot: A Life*. New York: Simon and Schuster, 1984.

Alberge, Dalya. "Lost Evelyn Waugh letters reveal thwarted love for 'bright young thing.'" *The Guardian*, July 20, 2013, https://www.theguardian.com/books/2013/jul/21/evelyn-waugh-love-letters.

Alexander, David. "The American Scholarships." In *The History of the Rhodes Trust 1902–1999*, edited by Anthony Kenny, 100–202. Oxford: Oxford University Press, 2001.

Alexander, Michael. *Medievalism: The Middle Ages in Modern England*. New Haven and London: Yale University Press, 2017.

Allen, C. K., ed., *The First Fifty Years of the Rhodes Trust and the Rhodes Scholarships 1903–1953*. Oxford: Basil Blackwell, 1955.

Allen, Joan M. *Candles and Carnival Lights: The Catholic Sensibility of F. Scott Fitzgerald*. New York: New York University Press, 1978.

The American Soldier-Student. The student detachment of the U. S. Army in Great Britain, 1919, 5 nos.

Arnold, Matthew. In *Lectures and Essays in Criticism*, edited by R.H. Super. Ann Arbor, MI: University of Michigan Press, 1962.

Assadi, Jamal and William Freedman, eds., *A Distant Drummer: Foreign Perspectives on F. Scott Fitzgerald*. New York: Peter Lang, 2007.

Axtell, James. *The Making of Princeton University: From Woodrow Wilson to the Present*. Princeton, NJ: Princeton University Press, 2006.

Aydelotte, Frank. *The Vision of Cecil Rhodes: A Review of the First Forty Years of the American Scholarships*. London: Oxford University Press, 1946.

———. *The Oxford Stamp and Other Essays*. Freeport, New York: Books for Libraries Press, 1967 (first edition 1917).

———. "What the American Rhodes Scholar Gets from Oxford." *Scribner's Magazine*, June 1923, 677–88.

Baker, Joseph Ellis. *The Novel and the Oxford Movement*. New York: Russell & Russell, 1965.

Beerbohm, Max. *Zuleika Dobson, or An Oxford Love Story*. New York: The Heritage Press, 1960.

———. In *The Prince of Minor Writers: The Selected Essays of Max Beerbohm*, edited by Phillip Lopate. New York: New York Review Books, 2015.

Berman, Ronald. *The Great Gatsby and Modern Times*. Urbana, IL: University of Illinois Press, 1996.

———. *The Great Gatsby and Fitzgerald's World of Ideas*. Tuscaloosa, AL: University of Alabama Press, 1997.

Betjeman, John. *John Betjeman's Oxford*. Oxford: Oxford University Press, 1990. First published under the title *An Oxford University Chest* (London: John Miles, 1938).

———. *Collected Poems*. New York: Farrar, Straus & Giroux, 2006.

Betjeman, John and David Vaisey. *Victorian and Edwardian Oxford from Old Photographs*. London: B.T. Batsford, 1971.

Bieri, James. *Percy Bysshe Shelley: A Biography, Vol. I, Youth's Unextinguished Fire, 1792–1816*. Newark, DE: University of Delaware Press, 2004.

Blake, Robert, ed. *The Private Papers of Douglas Haig 1914–1919*. London: Eyre & Spottiswoode, 1952.

Blazek, William. "Literary Influences." In *F. Scott Fitzgerald in Context*, edited by Bryan Mangum, 45-55. New York: Cambridge University Press, 2013.

Bloom, Harold, ed. Introduction to *F. Scott Fitzgerald's The Great Gatsby*. New York: Chelsea House Publishers, 1986.

Bogen, Anna. "Compton Mackenzie, Liberal Education, and the Oxford Novel." *English Literature in Transition 1880–1920* 49, no. 1 (Winter 2006): 14–30.

———. *Women's University Fiction, 1880–1945*. London: Routledge, 2016.

———, ed. *Women's University Narratives, 1890–1945, Part II, Volume II*. New York: Routledge, 2018.

Bowering, Peter. *Aldous Huxley: A Study of the Major Novels*. London: Bloomsbury, 2013.

Boyd, Ernest. "Aesthete: Model 1924." *The American Mercury*, January 1924, 51–56.

Brock, M. G. and M. C. Curthoys, eds. *The History of the University of Oxford, Vol. VI: Nineteenth-Century Oxford, Part I*. Oxford: Clarendon Press, 1996.

Brockliss, L.W.B. *The University of Oxford: A History*. Oxford: University of Oxford Press, 2016.

Brockliss, L.W.B., ed. *Magdalen College Oxford: A History*. Oxford: Magdalen College, 2008.

Brown, David S. *Paradise Lost: A Life of F. Scott Fitzgerald*. Cambridge, MA: Harvard University Press, 2017.

Bruccoli, Matthew J. "'How Are You and the Family Old Sport'—Gerlach and Gatsby." *Fitzgerald/ Hemingway Annual* (1975), 33–36.

———. *Some Sort of Epic Grandeur: The Life of F. Scott Fitzgerald*, second revised edition. Columbia, SC: University of South Carolina Press, 2002.

Bruccoli, Matthew J., ed. *F. Scott Fitzgerald's The Great Gatsby: A Literary Reference*. New York: Carroll & Graf, 2000.

———. *F. Scott Fitzgerald: Inscriptions*. Columbia, SC: Bruccoli, 1988.

———. *F. Scott Fitzgerald on Authorship*. Columbia, SC: University of South Carolina Press, 1996.

———. *The Collected Writings of Zelda Fitzgerald*. Tuscaloosa, AL: University of Alabama Press, 1991.

Bruccoli, Matthew J. and Jackson R. Bryer, eds. *F. Scott Fitzgerald in His Own Time*. Kent, OH: Kent State University Press, 1971.

Bruccoli, Matthew J. and Judith S. Baughman, eds. *Conversations with F. Scott Fitzgerald*. Jackson: University Press of Mississippi, 2004.

Bruccoli, Matthew J. and Margaret M. Duggan, eds. *Correspondence of F. Scott Fitzgerald*. New York: Random House, 1980.

Bruccoli, Matthew J., Scottie Fitzgerald Smith, and Joan P. Kerr, eds. *The Romantic Egoists: A Pictorial Autobiography from the Scrapbooks and Albums of F. Scott and Zelda Fitzgerald*. Columbia, SC: University of South Carolina Press, 1974.

Bruce, Homer L. "Organizing the Invasion." *The American Oxonian* 7, no. 1 (January 1920): 1–6.

Bryer, Jackson R., ed. Introduction to *New Essays on F. Scott Fitzgerald's Neglected Stories*. Columbia, MO: University of Missouri Press, 1996.

Bryer, Jackson R. Alan Margolies, and Ruth Prigozy, eds. *F. Scott Fitzgerald: New Perspectives*. Athens, GA: University of Georgia Press, 2000.

Byrne, Paula. *Mad World: Evelyn Waugh and the Secrets of Brideshead*. London: Harper, 2009.

Calderon, George. *The Adventures of Downey V. Green*. London: Smith, Elder & Co., 1902.

Callahan, John F. *The Illusions of a Nation: Myth and History in the Novels of F. Scott Fitzgerald*. Chicago: University of Illinois Press, 1972.

Callow, Simon. *Oscar Wilde and His Circle*. London: National Portrait Gallery, 2000.

Carnutt, Keith. "Literary Style." In *F. Scott Fitzgerald in Context*, edited by Bryant Mangum, 34–43. New York: Cambridge University Press, 2013.

Carnutt, Keith (ed.). *A Historical Guide to F. Scott Fitzgerald*. Oxford: Oxford University Press, 2004.

Carpenter, Humphrey. *The Brideshead Generation: Evelyn Waugh and His Friends*. London: Faber and Faber, 1990.

———. *J.R.R. Tolkien: A Biography*. Boston: Houghton Mifflin, 2000.

Carroll, Lewis. *Alice's Adventures in Wonderland and Through the Looking-Glass*. Edited by Peter Hunt. Oxford: Oxford University Press, 2009.

Catto, J.I. *et al.*, eds. *The History of the University of Oxford, Volumes I–III*. Oxford: Oxford University Press, 1984–93.

Chenoweth, C. W. "An American's Impressions of Oxford and Mansfield." *Mansfield College Magazine* 10, no. 17 (July 1919): 281–84.

Churchwell, Sarah. *Careless People: Murder, Mayhem, and the Invention of* The Great Gatsby. New York: Penguin, 2013.

Clark, Timothy and Jerrold E. Hogle, eds. *Evaluating Shelley*. Edinburgh: Edinburgh University Press, 1996.

Collini, Stefan. *Matthew Arnold: A Critical Portrait*. Oxford: Clarendon Press, 1994.

Cooke, Barbara. *Evelyn Waugh's Oxford*. Oxford: Bodleian Library, 2018.

Corbin, John. *An American at Oxford*. Boston: Houghton Mifflin, 1903.

———. "The Latin Quarter of England." Review of *Impressions of Oxford* by Paul Bourget, *The Lamp* XXVI (February/July 1903): 123–27: https://archive.org/stream/lamp00sonsgoog#page/n112/mode/2up.

Cornebise, Alfred Emile. *Soldier-Scholars: Higher Education in the AEF, 1917–1919*. Philadelphia: American Philosophical Society, 1997.

Cornwell, John. *Newman's Unquiet Grave: The Reluctant Saint*. London: Continuum, 2010.

Corrigan, Maureen. *So We Read On: How* The Great Gatsby *Came to Be and Why It Endures*. New York: Little, Brown & Co., 2014.

Corso, Joseph. "One Not-Forgotten Summer Night: Sources for Fictional Symbols of American Character in *The Great Gatsby*." *Fitzgerald/ Hemingway Annual* (1976): 8–33.

Cowley, Malcolm and Robert Cowley. *Fitzgerald and the Jazz Age*. New York: Scribner's, 1966.

Crawford, Robert. *Young Eliot: From St. Louis to "The Waste Land."* New York: Farrar, Straus & Giroux, 2015.

Crook, J. Mordaunt. *Brasenose: The Biography of an Oxford College*. Oxford: Oxford University Press, 2008.

Crosby, Laurence A. and Frank Aydelotte. *Oxford of Today: A Manual for Prospective Rhodes Scholars*. New York: Oxford University Press, 1922.

Cuneo, Andrew P. *Selected Literary Letters of C. S. Lewis*. 2 vols. Doctoral thesis, University of Oxford, 2001.

Curnutt, Kirk, ed. *A Historical Guide to F. Scott Fitzgerald*. Oxford: Oxford University Press, 2004.

Darroch, Sandra Jobson. *Ottoline: The Life of Lady Ottoline Morrell*. London: Chatto and Windus, 1976.

———. *Garsington Revisited: The Legend of Lady Ottoline Morrell Brought Up-to-Date*. East Barnet, Hertfordshire: John Libbey Publishing, 2017.

Donaldson, Scott. *Fool for Love: F. Scott Fitzgerald*. New York: Congdon and Weed, 1983.

Dougill, John. *Oxford in English Literature: The Making, and Undoing, of "The English Athens."* Ann Arbor, MI: University of Michigan Press, 1998.

Douglas-Fairhurst, Robert. *The Story of Alice: Lewis Carroll and the Secret History of Wonderland.* Cambridge, MA: Harvard University Press, 2015.

Duff, David. *Romance and Revolution: Shelley and the Politics of a Genre.* Cambridge: Cambridge University Press, 1994.

Duke, Alex. *Importing Oxbridge: English Residential Colleges and American Universities.* New Haven and London: Yale University Press, 1996.

Duriez, Colin. "Lewis and Military Service: War and Remembrance (1917–1918)." In *C. S. Lewis: Life, Works, and Legacy, Vol. 1: An Examined Life*, edited by Bruce L. Edwards, 79–101. Westport, CT: Praeger, 2007.

Dyer, John R. "What the A.E.F. Thought of Oxford." *The American Oxonian* 7, no. 1 (January 1920): 13–14.

Eade, Philip. *Evelyn Waugh: A Life Revisited.* London: Weidenfeld & Nicolson, 2016.

Eliot, Valerie and Hugh Haughton (eds.). *The Letters of T. S. Eliot, Vol. 1: 1898–1922*, revised edition. London: Faber and Faber, 2009.

———. *The Letters of T. S. Eliot, Vol. 2: 1923–25.* London: Faber and Faber, 2009.

Eliot, Valerie and John Haffenden, eds. *The Letters of T. S. Eliot, Vol. 3: 1926–27.* New Haven, CT: Yale University Press, 2012.

Ellmann, Richard. *Oscar Wilde at Oxford: A Lecture Delivered at the Library of Congress on March 1, 1983.* Washington, D.C.: Library of Congress, 1984.

Elton, Godfrey, ed. *The First Fifty Years of the Rhodes Trust and the Rhodes Scholarships, 1903–1953.* Oxford: Basil Blackwell, 1955.

Fimi, Dimitra. *Tolkien, Race, and Cultural History: From Faeries to Hobbits.* New York: Palgrave Macmillan, 2009.

Fitzgerald, F. Scott. *Afternoon of an Author: A Selection of Uncollected Stories and Essays.* New York: Scribner's, 1957.

———. *All the Sad Young Men.* New York: Scribner's, 1926.

———. *Babylon Revisited and Other Stories.* New York: Macmillan, 1960.

———. *The Beautiful and Damned.* New York: Modern Library, 2002. Cambridge: Cambridge University Press, 2008.

———. *The Collected Letters of F. Scott Fitzgerald.* E-artnow, 2015.

———. *The Great Gatsby.* New York: Charles Scribner's Sons, 1925; MacMillan, 1980.

———. *The Great Gatsby.* Edited by Matthew J. Bruccoli. New York: Cambridge University Press, 2013.

———. *I'd Die for You and Other Lost Stories.* Edited by Anne Margaret Daniel. New York: Scribner's, 2017.

———. *The Letters of F. Scott Fitzgerald.* Edited by Andrew Turnbull. New York: Scribner's, 1963.

———. *The Love of the Last Tycoon: A Western.* Edited by Matthew J. Bruccoli. New York: Cambridge University Press, 1994.

———. *May Day.* Smart Set Company, 1920. Brooklyn, NY: Melville House, 2009.

———. *My Lost City. Personal Essays, 1920–1940.* Edited by James L.W. West III. Cambridge: Cambridge University Press, 2005.

———. *The Popular Girl.* Foreword by Helen Dunmore. London: Hesperus Press, 2005.

———. Review of *The Celt and the World*, by Shane Leslie. *Nassau Literary Review* (May 1917).

———. *Spires and Gargoyles: Early Writings, 1909–1919.* Edited by James L.W. West III. Cambridge: Cambridge University Press, 2010.

———. *Tender is the Night.* New York: Scribner, 2003.

———. *This Side of Paradise.* Edited by James W. West III. Cambridge: Cambridge University Press, 1995.

———. "Three Cities." *Brentano's Book Chat* 1 (Sept–Oct 1921), 15, 28. Fitzgerald's impressions of Paris, Florence, Rome, and Oxford.

Fitzgerald, Zelda. *Save Me the Waltz: A Novel.* New York: Scribner, 1932.

———. *The Collected Writings.* Edited by Matthew J. Bruccoli. Collier Books, 1992.

Forrey, Robert. "Negroes in the Fiction of F. Scott Fitzgerald." *Phylon: The Atlanta University of Journal of Race and Culture* 48 (1967): 293–98.

Foster, R.F. *W.B. Yeats: A Life, Vol. II.* Oxford: Oxford University Press, 2003.

Froehlich, Maggie Gordon. "Jordan Baker, gender dissent, and homosexual passing in *The Great Gatsby.*" *The Space Between: Literature and Culture, 1914–1945* 6, no. 1 (2010): 81–103.

———. "Gatsby's mentors: queer relations between love and money in *The Great Gatsby.*" *The Journal of Men's Studies* 19, no. 3 (Fall 2011).

Fruoco, Jonathan. "C. S. Lewis and T. S. Eliot: Questions of Identity." In *Persona and Paradox: Issues of Identity for C. S. Lewis, His Friends and Associates.* Cambridge Scholars Publishing, 2012.

Gandal, Keith. *The Gun and the Pen: Hemingway, Fitzgerald, Faulkner, and the Fiction of Mobilization.* Oxford: Oxford University Press, 2008.

Garth, John. *Tolkien and the Great War: The Threshold of Middle-earth.* London: HarperCollins, 2003.

———. *Tolkien at Exeter College: How an Oxford Undergraduate Created Middle-earth.* Oxford: Exeter College, 2014.

Gathorne-Hardy, Robert, ed. Introduction to *Ottoline at Garsington: Memoirs of Lady Ottoline Morrell, 1915–1918.* London : Faber and Faber, 1974.

Gillin, Edward. "Princeton, New Jersey, Princeton University, and the *Nassau Literary Magazine.*"In *F. Scott Fitzgerald in Context*, edited by Bryant Mangum, 126–35. New York: Cambridge University Press, 2013.

Graham, Malcolm. *Oxford in the Great War.* Barnsley: Penn & Sword Military, 2014.

Green, Roger Lancelyn and Walter Hooper. *C. S. Lewis: The Authorised and Revised Biography.* London: HarperCollins, 2003.

Greenidge, Terence. *Degenerate Oxford? A Critical Study of Modern University Life.* Chapman and Hall, 1930.

———. *Evelyn Waugh in Letters.* Edited by Charles E. Linck. Commerce, TX: Cow Hill Press, 1994.

Griffin, William. *Clive Staples Lewis: A Dramatic Life*. San Francisco: Harper and Row, 1986.

Hale, Robert. "Oxford Again—A Rhodes Scholar Goes Back." *Outlook* (July 11, 1923): 378–80.

Hargrove, Nancy Duvall. *T. S. Eliot's Parisian Year*. Gainesville, FL: University of Florida Press, 2009.

———. "'Une Présent Parfait': Eliot and La Vie Parisienne, 1910–1911." In *T. S. Eliot at the Turn of the Century*, edited by Marianne Thormählen. Lund, Sweden: Lund University Press, 1994, 33–58.

Harris, Leonard. *Alain L. Locke: Biography of a Philosopher*. Chicago: University of Chicago Press, 2008.

———, ed. *The Philosophy of Alain Locke: Harlem Renaissance and Beyond*. Philadelphia: Temple University Press, 1989.

Harrison, Brian, ed. *The History of the University of Oxford: Volume VIII: The Twentieth Century*. Oxford: Clarendon Press, 1994.

Harrold, Charles Frederick. *John Henry Newman: An Expository and Critical Study of His Mind, Thought and Art*. Hamden, CT: Archon Books, 1966.

Heilbrun, Carolyn G., ed. *Lady Ottoline's Album*. Lord David Cecil (intro). London: Michael Joseph, 1976.

Higgins, Sørina, ed. *The Inklings and King Arthur*. Berkeley, CA: Apocryphile Press, 2017.

Higginson, Thomas Wentworth. *Cheerful Yesterdays*. Boston: Houghton Mifflin, 1898.

———. *Letters and Journals, 1846–1906*. Edited by Mary Potter Thatcher Higginson. Boston: Houghton Mifflin, 1921.

Hindus, Milton. *F. Scott Fitzgerald: An Introduction and Interpretation*. New York: Holt, Rinehart, and Winston, 1968.

Hoare, Philip. "John Ruskin: Mike Leigh and Emma Thompson have got him all wrong." *The Guardian*, 7 October 2014. http://www.theguardian.com /artanddesign/2014/oct/07/john-ruskin-emma-thompson-mike-leigh-film-art.

Hogg, Thomas Jefferson. *The Life of Percy Bysshe Shelley*. London: George Routledge & Sons, 1906.

Holmes, Richard. *Shelley: The Pursuit*. London: HarperCollins, 1994.

Hooper, Walter, ed. *The Collected Letters of C. S. Lewis*. 3 vols. San Francisco: HarperCollins, 2004.

Hopkins, Clare. *Trinity: 450 Years of an Oxford College Community*. Oxford: Oxford University Press, 2005.

Hunt, John Dixon. *The Pre-Raphaelite Imagination 1848–1900*. Lincoln, NE: University Nebraska Press, 1968.

Huxley, Aldous. *Crome Yellow*. 1921. Columbia, SC, 2018.

———. *Antic Hay*. London: Dalkey Archive Press, 1923; 2006.

———. *Letters of Aldous Huxley*. Edited by Grover Smith. London: Chatto & Windus, 1969.

Johnston-Jones, D.R. "Some Other Yanks at Oxford." *Oxford* 33, no. 1 (May 1981).

Joseph, H.W.B. "Oxford in the Last War." *Oxford Magazine* May 1941, 96–8.

Kallen, Horace M. "Alain Locke and Cultural Pluralism." *Journal of Philosophy* 54, no. 5 (Feb 1957): 119–27.

———. *The Education of Free Men.* New York: Farrar, Straus & Giroux, 1949.

Kallen, Horace M. and Sidney Hook, eds. *American Philosophy Today and Tomorrow.* New York: Lee Furman, 1935.

Karabel, Jerome. *The Chosen: The Hidden History of Admission and Exclusion at Harvard, Yale, and Princeton.* Boston: Houghton Mifflin, 2005.

Keats, John. *Selected Poems and Letters of Keats.* Selected by Robert Gittings, edited by Sandra Anstey. Oxford: Harcourt, 1995.

Keene, Anne. *Oxford: The American Connection.* Oxford: Temple Rock Publications, 1990.

Keith, Charles A. *Fast Balls and College Halls: An Autobiography.* New York: Vantage Press, 1959.

Kenny, Anthony, ed. *The History of the Rhodes Trust 1902–1999.* Oxford: Oxford University Press, 2001.

Ker, Ian. *John Henry Newman: A Biography.* Oxford: Clarendon Press, 1988.

Kruse, Horst H. *F. Scott Fitzgerald at Work: The Making of* The Great Gatsby. Tuscaloosa, AL: University of Alabama Press, 2014.

———. "F. Scott Fitzgerald and Marry Harriman Rumsey: An Untold Story." *The F. Scott Fitzgerald Review* 13, no. 1 (2015): 146–62.

———. "The Real Jay Gatsby: Max von Gerlach, F. Scott Fitzgerald, and the Compositional History of *The Great Gatsby.*" *The F. Scott Fitzgerald Review* 1 (2002): 45–81.

Kuehl, John and Jackson R. Bryer, eds. *Dear Scott/Dear Max: The Fitzgerald-Perkins Correspondence.* New York: Scribner's, 1971.

Laffaye, Horace A., ed. *Profiles in Polo: The Players Who Changed the Game.* London: McFarland, 2007.

Lanahan, Eleanor, ed. *Zelda, An Illustrated Life: The Private World of Zelda Fitzgerald.* New York: Harry N. Abrams, 1996.

Lancaster, Marie-Jacqueline, ed. *Brian Howard: Portrait of a Failure.* London: Anthony Blond, 1968.

Lang, Andrew. *Oxford: Brief Historical and Descriptive Notes.* London: Seeley and Co., 1902.

Langstaff, J. Brett. *Oxford—1914.* New York: Vantage Press, 1965.

Leach, Karoline. *In the Shadow of the Dreamchild: A New Understanding of Lewis Carroll.* London: Peter Owen, 1999.

Leacock, Stephen. "The Horrors of Oxford." *Living Age* (June 24, 1922): 779–81.

———. "Oxford as I See It." *Harper's* (May 1922): 738–45.

———. *My Discovery of England.* New York: Dodd, Mead & Co., 1922.

Lehan, Richard. *The Great Gatsby: Limits of Wonder.* Boston: Twayne Publishers, 1990.

Leslie, W. Bruce. "Dreaming Spires in New Jersey." In *The Educational Legacy of Woodrow Wilson: From College to Nation*, edited by James Axtell. University of Virginia Press, 2012.

Lewis, C. S. *Rehabilitations and Other Essays*. Freeport, NY: Books for Libraries Press, 1939; reprinted 1972.

———. *All My Road Before Me: The Diary of 1922–1927*. Edited by Walter Hooper. London: HarperCollins, 1991.

———. *The Collected Poems of C. S. Lewis*. Edited by Walter Hooper. London: HarperCollins, 1994.

Lewis, C. S. and Owen Barfield. *Mark vs. Tristram: Correspondence between C. S. Lewis and Owen Barfield*. Edited by Walter Hooper. Cambridge, MA: Lowell House, 1967.

Lewis, David M. *The Jews of Oxford*. Oxford: Oxford Jewish Congregation, 1992.

Lewis, Janet. "Fitzgerald's Philippe, Count of Darkness." *Fitzgerald/ Hemingway Annual* 7 (1975): 7–32.

Linnemann, Russell J. (ed.). *Alain Locke: Reflections on a Modern Renaissance Man*. Baton Rouge: Louisiana State University Press, 1982.

Little, Matthew. "'I Could Make Some Money': Cars and Currency in *The Great Gatsby*." *Papers on Language & Literature* 51, no. 1 (Winter 2015).

Locke, Alain LeRoy. "Oxford: By a Negro Student." *The Colored American Magazine* 17 (1909): 184–90.

———. "Oxford Contrasts." *The Independent* (July 15, 1909): 139–42. Reprinted in *The American Oxonian* 94, no. 2 (Spring 2007): 225–31.

———. "The Rhodes Scholar Question." Written in 1910 and transcribed by Jack Zoeller in *The American Oxonian* 94, no. 2 (Spring 2007): 232–36.

———. *The New Negro: An Interpretation*. New York: Albert and Charles Boni, 1925. Reprinted New York: Arno Press and the *New York Times*, 1968.

———. "Values and Imperatives." In *American Philosophy Today and Tomorrow*, edited by Horace M. Kallen and Sidney Hook, 313–33. New York: Lee Furman, 1935.

Long, Robert Emmet. "The Vogue of Gatsby's Guest List." *Fitzgerald/Hemingway Annual* 1 (1969): 23–25.

———. *The Achieving of* The Great Gatsby. Lewisburg, PA: Bucknell University Press, 1981.

Lupack, Alan and Barbara Tepa Lupack. *King Arthur in America*. Cambridge: D.S. Brewer, 1999.

Lupack, Barbara Tepa. "F. Scott Fitzgerald's 'Following of a Grail.'" *Arthuriana* 4, no. 4 (Winter 1994): 324–47.

Machann, Clinton. *Matthew Arnold: A Literary Life*. London: Macmillan, 1998.

Mackrell, Judith. *Flappers: Six Women of a Dangerous Generation*. New York, Farrar, Straus & Giroux, 2013.

MacLean, George E. "British Universities and American Soldier-Students." *The Landmark* 1 (June 1919): 365–70.

Madden, O.E. "Keats and Oxford." *Oxford Magazine* 42, no. 2 (December 1990): 88–91.

Makurath, Paul A. "Another Source for *Gatsby*," *Fitzgerald/ Hemingway Annual* (1975), 115–16.

Maloney, Alison. *Bright Young Things: Life in the Roaring Twenties*. London: Virgin Books, 2012.

Mangum, Bryant, ed. *F. Scott Fitzgerald in Context*. New York: Cambridge University Press, 2013.

Marsh, Jan. *The Pre-Raphaelite Circle*. London: National Portrait Gallery, 2005.

Martindale, Charles, Stefano Evangelista, and Elizabeth Prettejohn, eds. *Pater the Classicist: Classical Scholarship, Reception, and Aestheticism*. Oxford: Oxford University Press, 2017.

Massie, Allan. "The magnum opus of Compton Mackenzie: On Capri in 1925 Scott Fitzgerald met his 'old idol' Compton Mackenzie and found him 'cordial, attractive and pleasantly mundane.'" *The Spectator*, Sept 26, 2007.

McGrath, Alistair. *The Intellectual World of C. S. Lewis*. Oxford: Wiley-Blackwell, 2014.

McMullen, Bonnie Shannon. "'This Tremendous Detail': The Oxford Stone in the House of Gatsby." In *A Distant Drummer: Foreign Perspectives on F. Scott Fitzgerald*, edited by Jamal Assadi and WIlliam Freedman, 11–20. New York: Peter Lang, 2007.

Mead, Frederick S., ed. *Harvard's Military Record in the World War*. Boston: Harvard Alumni Association, 1921.

Mendelssohn, Michèle. *Making Oscar Wilde*. Oxford: Oxford University Press, 2018.

Meredith, James H. "World War I." In *F. Scott Fitzgerald in Context*, edited by Bryant Mangum, 136–43. New York: Cambridge University Press, 2013.

Meyers, Jeffrey. *Scott Fitzgerald: A Biography*. New York: HarperCollins, 1994.

———. *Edmund Wilson: A Biography*. Boston: Houghton Mifflin, 1995.

Miller, James E., Jr. *T. S. Eliot: The Making of an American Poet, 1888–1922*. University Park, PA: Penn State Press, 2005.

Mintler, Catherine. "From Aesthete to Gangster: The Dandy Figure in the Novels of F. Scott Fitzgerald." *F. Scott Fitzgerald Review* 8, no. 1 (2010): 104–29.

Mitchell, Sally. *The New Girl: Girl's Culture in England, 1880–1915*. New York: Columbia University Press, 1995.

Mizener, Arthur. *The Far Side of Paradise: A Biography of F. Scott Fitzgerald*. Boston: Houghton Mifflin, 1949; Reprinted New York: Vintage, 1959.

Molesworth, Charles, ed. *The Works of Alain Locke*. Oxford: Oxford University Press, 2012.

Moore, Hilary. *Inside British Jazz: Crossing Borders of Race, Nation and Class*. Aldershot, United Kingdom: Ashgate, 2007.

More, Paul Elmer. *Pages from an Oxford Diary*. Princeton: Princeton University Press, 1937.

Moreland, Kim. *The Medievalist Impulse in American Literature: Twain, Adams, Fitzgerald, and Hemingway*. Charlottesville, VA: University of Virginia Press, 1996.

Murray, Nicholas. *A Life of Matthew Arnold*. London: Hodder and Stoughton, 1996.

Newman, John Henry. *John Henry Newman Autobiographical Writings.* Edited by Henry Tristram. New York: Sheed and Ward, 1956.

——. *The Idea of a University.* New Haven, CT: Yale University Press, 1996.

——. *The Letters and Diaries of John Henry Newman.* Edited by Charles Stephen Dessain *et al.* 32 vols. Oxford: Oxford University Press, 1961–2008.

Nicolay, Theresa Freda. *Tolkien and the Modernists: Literary Responses to the Dark New Days of the 20th Century.* Jefferson, NC: McFarland, 2014.

O'Brien, Michael. *Death Did Not Divide Them: The American Rhodes Scholars Who Died in World War One.* Brighton, United Kingdom: Reveille Press, 1913.

O'Gorman, Francis, ed. *The Cambridge Companion to John Ruskin.* Cambridge: Cambridge University Press, 2015.

O'Neill, Michael. *Percy Bysshe Shelley: A Literary Life.* London: Macmillan, 1989.

Oser, Lee. *The Return of Christian Humanism: Chesterton, Eliot, Tolkien, and the Romance of History.* Columbia, MO: University of Missouri Press, 2007.

Parsonage, Catherine. *The Evolution of Jazz in Britain, 1880–1935.* Aldershot, United Kingdom: Ashgate, 2005.

Patey, Douglas Lane. *The Life of Evelyn Waugh: A Critical Biography.* Oxford: Blackwell, 1998.

Patrick, James. *The Magdalen Metaphysicals: Idealism and Orthodoxy at Oxford, 1901–1945.* Macon, GA: Mercer University Press, 1985.

Peberdy, R. B. "F. Scott Fitzgerald and Merton College, Oxford." Oxford: published by author, 2000: 1–10.

Pike, Gerald. "A Style is Born: The Rhetoric of Loss in 'The Spire and the Gargoyle.'" In *New Essays on F. Scott Fitzgerald's Neglected Stories*, edited and introduction to by Jackson R. Bryer, 9–23. Columbia, MO and London: University of Missouri Press, 1996.

Piper, Henry Dan. *F. Scott Fitzgerald: A Critical Portrait.* New York: Holt, Rinehart and Winston, 1965.

——. *Fitzgerald's* The Great Gatsby. New York: Scribner's, 1970.

Prigozy, Ruth. "Gatsby's Guest List and Fitzgerald's Technique of Naming." *Fitzgerald/Hemingway Annual* 4 (1972): 99–112.

Prigozy, Ruth, ed. *The Cambridge Companion to F. Scott Fitzgerald.* New York: Cambridge University Press, 2002.

Pursglove, Glyn and Alistair Ricketts, eds. *Oxford in Verse.* Oxford: Perpetua Press, 1999.

Record of War Service of Rhodes Scholars from the Dominions Beyond the Seas and the United States of America. Oxford: Vincent Works, 1920.

Rinn, Anne. "Rhodes Scholarships, Frank Aydelotte, and Collegiate Honors Education." *Journal of the National Collegiate Honors Council* 127 (Spring 2003): 27–39.

Risden, E.L. *Tolkien's Intellectual Landscape.* Jefferson, NC: McFarland & Co., 2015.

Robbins, William. *The Newman Brothers.* Cambridge, MA: Harvard University Press, 1966.

Roberts, Pamela. *Black Oxford: The Untold Stories of Oxford University's Black Scholars.* Oxford: Signal Books, 2013.

Robertson, C. Grant. "An Oxford Impression of the American Army Students." *The American Oxonian* 7, no. 1 (January 1920): 15–19.

Roditi, Edouard. *Oscar Wilde.* Norfolk, CT: New Directions, 1947.

Ross, Cathy. *Twenties London: A City in the Jazz Age.* Philip Wilson Publishers, 2003.

Saddlemyer, Ann. *Becoming George: The Life of Mrs. W. B. Yeats.* Oxford: Oxford University Press, 2002.

Schaeper, Thomas J. and Kathleen Schaeper. *Rhodes Scholars: Oxford, and the Creation of an American Elite.* New York: Berghahn Books, 2010.

Schlacks, Deborah Davis. "Echoes of the Middle Ages: Teaching the Medieval in *The Great Gatsby*." In *Approaches to Teaching Fitzgerald's* The Great Gatsby, edited by Jackson R. Bryer and Nancy P. VanArsdale, 162–68. New York: MLA Publications, 2009.

———. "St. Paul, Minnesota, St. Paul Academy, and the *St. Paul Academy Then and Now*." In *F. Scott Fitzgerald in Context*, edited by Bryant Mangum, 105–14. New York: Cambridge University Press, 2013.

Secor, Robert. *John Ruskin and Alfred Hunt: New Letters and the Record of a Friendship.* Victoria, BC: University of Victoria Literary Studies, 1982.

Shelley, Percy Bysshe. *The Letters of Percy Bysshe Shelley, Vol. 1: Shelley in England.* Edited by Frederick L. Jones. Oxford: Oxford University Press, 1964.

Shippey, Tom. *J.R.R. Tolkien: Author of the Century.* Boston: Houghton Mifflin, 2001.

———. *The Road to Middle-earth.* Boston: Houghton Mifflin, 2003.

Shuchard, Ronald. "Burbank with a Baedeker, Eliot with a Cigar: American Intellectuals, Anti-Semitism, and the Idea of Culture." *Modernism/Modernity* 10, no. 1 (January 2003): 1–26.

Sklar, Robert. *F. Scott Fitzgerald: The Last Laocoön.* New York: Oxford University Press, 1967.

Smith, Philip E. and Michael Helfand, eds. *Oscar Wilde's Oxford Notebooks: A Portrait of Mind in the Making.* Oxford: Oxford University Press, 1989.

Snyder, Christopher. *The Making of Middle-earth: A New Look Inside the World of J.R.R. Tolkien.* New York: Sterling, 2013.

Stanford, Derek (ed.). *Pre-Raphaelite Writing: An Anthology.* London: Dent, 1984.

Stannard, Martin. *Evelyn Waugh: The Early Years, 1903–1939.* New York: W.W. Norton, 1987.

Stewart, Jeffrey C. "Alain LeRoy Locke at Oxford: The First African-American Rhodes Scholar." *The Journal of Blacks in Higher Education* 31 (Spring 2001): 112–17.

———. *The New Negro: The Life of Alain Locke.* New York: Oxford University Press, 2018.

Stokes, Anson Phelps, John Erskine, and Reginald Aldworth Daly. *Educational Plans for the American Army Abroad.* New York: Association Press, 1918.

Stone, Edward. "More About Gatsby's Guest List." *Fitzgerald/Hemingway Annual* 4 (1972): 315–16.

Svarney, Erik. *"The Men of 1914": T. S. Eliot and Early Modernism*. Philadelphia: Open University Press, 1988.

Taylor, D. J. *Bright Young People: The Lost Generation of London's Jazz Age*. New York: Farrar, Straus & Giroux, 2010.

Taylor, Kendall. *The Gatsby Affair: Scott, Zelda, and the Betrayal that Shaped an American Classic*. New York: Random House, 2018.

Taylor, R. T. "The Social Side of the Invasion." *The American Oxonian* (January 1920): 7–12.

Tolkien J.R.R. *The Letters of J.R.R. Tolkien*. Ed. by Humphrey Carpenter. Boston: Houghton Mifflin, 2000.

Toll, William. "Horace M. Kallen: Pluralism and American Jewish Identity." *American Jewish History* 85, no. 1 (March 1997).

Tredell, Nicolas, ed. *F. Scott Fitzgerald: The Great Gatsby*. Columbia Critical Guides. New York: Columbia University Press, 1997.

Trowbridge, A. Buel. *An Auld Acquaintance Who'll Never Be Forgot: Memories of a Rhodes Scholar at University College, Oxford, 1920–23*. Boston: Branden Press, 1976.

Turnbull, Andrew. *Scott Fitzgerald*. New York: Charles Scribner's Sons, 1962.

Turner, Frank. *John Henry Newman: The Challenge to Evangelical Religion*. New Haven: Yale University Press, 2002.

Vogel, Joseph. "'Civilization's Going to Pieces': *The Great Gatsby*, Identity, and Race, From the Jazz Age to the Obama Era." *The F. Scott Fitzgerald Review* 13 (2015): 29–54.

Wagner-Martin, Linda. *Zelda Sayre Fitzgerald: An American Woman's Life*. New York: Palgrave Macmillan, 2004.

Watt, Judith. "The Lonely Princess of Bohemia." *The Guardian*, Nov 18, 2000, https://www.theguardian.com/theguardian/2000/nov/18/weekend7 .weekend2.

Waugh, Evelyn. *Brideshead Revisited*. New York: Little, Brown and Co., 1944; 1999.

———. *The Complete Stories of Evelyn Waugh*. Boston: Little, Brown and Co., 2000.

———. *The Diaries of Evelyn Waugh*. Edited by Michael Davie. London: Penguin, 1986.

———. *Edmund Campion*. Boston: Little, Brown, 1946.

———. *The Letters of Evelyn Waugh*. Edited by Mark Amory. New Haven, CT: Ticknor & Fields, 1980.

———. *The Life of the Right Reverend Ronald Knox*. London: Chapman & Hall, 1959

———. *A Little Learning*. London: Penguin, 2011.

———. *A Little Order: A Selection from His Journalism*. Edited by Donat Gallagher. Boston: Little, Brown, 1977.

———. *PRB: An Essay on the Pre-Raphaelite Brotherhood, 1847–1854*. Westerham, Kent: Dalrymple Press, 1982.

———. *Rossetti: His Life and Works*. Introduction by John Bryson. London: Duckworth, 1975.

———. *Vile Bodies*. New York: Little, Brown and Co. 1930; 2012.

———. "Was Oxford Worth While?" *Daily Mail*, June 21, 1930.

Weatherby, Harold L. *Cardinal Newman in His Age*. Nashville, TN: Vanderbilt University Press, 1973.

Weinfeld, David. "What Difference Does the Difference Make? Horace Kallen, Alain Locke, and the Development of Cultural Pluralism in America." PhD dissertation. New York University, 2014.

Welland, D.S.R. *The Pre-Raphaelites in Literature and in Art*. London: George G. Harrap & Co., 1953.

White, Edward. *The Tastemaker: Carl Van Vechten and the Birth of Modern America*. New York: Farrar, Straus & Giroux, 2014.

White, Patti. *Gatsby's Party: The System and the List in Contemporary Narrative*. Purdue University Press, 1992.

White, Roger, Judith Wolfe and Brendan N. Wolfe, eds. *C. S. Lewis and His Circle: Essays and Memoirs from the Oxford C. S. Lewis Society*. Oxford: Oxford University Press, 2015.

White, William Luther. *The Image of Man in C. S. Lewis*. London: Hodder and Stoughton, 1970.

Wilde, Oscar. *Literary Criticism of Oscar Wilde*. Ed. by Stanley Weintraub. Lincoln: University of Nebraska Press, 1968.

———. *The Artist as Critic: Critical Writings of Oscar Wilde*. Edited by Richard Ellmann. New York: Random House, 1969.

———. *The Complete Letters of Oscar Wilde*. Edited by Merlin Holland and Rupert Hart-Davis. New York: Henry Holt, 2000.

Williams, Heathcote. *Shelley at Oxford: Blasphemy, Book-Burning and Bedlam*, second edition. Oxford: Huxley Scientific Press 2012.

Wilson, A. N. *C. S. Lewis: A Biography*. London: Collins, 1990.

Wilson, Edmund (ed.). *The Crack-Up*. New York: New Directions, 1945.

Wilson, John Howard. "A Walking Tour of Evelyn Waugh's Oxford." In *A Handful of Mischief: New Essays on Evelyn Waugh*, edited by Donat Gallagher et al. Lanham, MD: Rowman & Littlefield, 2011.

Winchester, Simon. *The Alice Behind Wonderland*. Oxford: Oxford University Press, 2011.

Wood, Ralph C., ed. *Tolkien among the Moderns*. Notre Dame, IN: University of Notre Dame Press, 2015.

Woodward, David R. *The American Army and the First World War*. Cambridge: Cambridge University Press, 2014.

Wylie, Francis. "The Rhodes Scholars and Oxford 1902–31." Pp. 59–128 in Godfrey Elton (ed.), *The First Fifty Years of the Rhodes Trust and the Rhodes Scholarships, 1903–1953*. Oxford: Basil Blackwell, 1955.

BIBLIOGRAPHY

Zaleski, Philip and Carol Zaleski. *The Fellowship: The Literary Lives of the Inklings: J.R.R. Tolkien, C. S. Lewis, Owen Barfield and Charles Williams.* New York: Farrar, Straus & Giroux, 2015.

Ziegler, Philip. *Legacy: Cecil Rhodes, the Rhodes Trust and Rhodes Scholarships.* New Haven: Yale University Press, 2008.

Zoeller, Jack C. "Alain Locke at Oxford: Race and the Rhodes Scholarships," *The American Oxonian* 94, no. 2 (Spring 2007): 183–224.

Endnotes

PREFACE

1   R. T. Taylor, "The Social Side of the Invasion," *The American Oxonian* 7, no. 1 (January 1920): 7–12 (7).

2   Hans Bertens, *Literary Theory: The Basics* (London: Routledge, 2001), 177.

3   Max Beerbohm, *Zuleika Dobson: An Oxford Love Story* (New York: Heritage Press, 1960), 143. First published in 1911; blame Beerbohm for the pun.

4   Alain Locke, "Oxford Contrasts," *The Independent* (15 July 1909), 139–42, reprinted in *The American Oxonian* 94 no. 2 (Spring 2007), 225–31.

5   Bruccoli (ed), *The Great Gatsby* (New York: Cambridge University Press, 1993), 211.

I: JAY GATSBY: AN OXFORD MAN

1   Unless otherwise noted, all page references to *Gatsby* refer to the standard critical edition, F. Scott Fitzgerald, *The Great Gatsby*, edited by Matthew J. Bruccoli (Cambridge: Cambridge Univ. Press, 2013).

2   On the importance of Fitzgerald choosing 1922—the year in which both *Ulysses* and *The Wasteland* were published—as the setting for *Gatsby*, see Michael North, *Reading 1922: A Return to the Scene of the Modern* (Oxford: Oxford Univ. Press, 1999).

3   In Fitzgerald's first complete submitted manuscript, titled *Trimalchio*, there is conversation at the first supper with three men, one a Yale graduate, who "all affected the Oxford mush-mouth accent," according to Nick: see F. Scott Fitzgerald, *Trimalchio: An Early Version of The Great Gatsby*, edited by James L. West (Cambridge: Cambridge University Press, 2002), 38.

4   In the *Trimalchio* manuscript, Nick adds: "Have you got some prejudice against Oxford?" (41).

5   In one study of a possible source for the name Gatsby, Paul Makurath points out that George Elliot's 1860 novel *The Mill on the Floss* mentions a figure named

Gadsby who resides in the community of *St. Oggs* and whose first cousin is said to have been "an Oxford man." See Makurath, "Another Source for 'Gatsby,'" *Fitzgerald/ Hemingway Annual* (1975), 115–16.

6 For a possible connection between Fitzgerald and Merton College, see R. B. Peberdy, "Merton College, Oxford" (2000).

7 In a 1935 letter to Fitzgerald, Ernest Hemingway joked about having Scott killed so Zelda could cash in on his insurance policy, then volunteers to scatter Fitzgerald's remains around the world, donating "your liver . . . to the Princeton Museum, your heart to the Plaza Hotel . . . [and] if we can still find your balls I will take them via the Ile de France to Paris." Quoted in Maureen Corrigan, *So We Read On: How* The Great Gatsby Came *to Be and Why It Endures* (New York: Little, Brown & Co., 2014), 29.

8 The Oxford conversation at the Plaza is not in the *Trimalchio* manuscript. Apparently, Fitzgerald created it following the advice of his editor, Maxwell Perkins, to release some of the details about Gatsby's past little by little throughout the novel.

9 F. Scott Fitzgerald, "Sentiment—and the Use of Rouge," *Nassau Literary Magazine* 73 (June 1917), 107–23; reprinted in *Spires and Gargoyles: Early Writings, 1909–1919*, edited by James L. W. West III (Cambridge: Cambridge Univ. Press, 2010), 199–213.

10 *Spires and Gargoyles*, 211.

11 All page references are to F. Scott Fitzgerald, *This Side of Paradise*, edited by James L. W. West III (Cambridge: Cambridge Univ. Press, 1995).

12 Compare this to the language in Fitzgerald's letter (July 18, 1933) to author John O'Hara: "So if I were elected King of Scotland tomorrow after graduating from Eton, Magdalene to Guards, with an embryonic history which tied me to the Plantagenets, I would still be a parvenu." Andrew Turnbull (ed), *The Letters of F. Scott Fitzgerald* (New York: Scribner's, 1963), 503.

13 For discussion of Scott Fitzgerald's early years, see Chapter Eight below.

14 Letter to Frances Newman (Feb 26, 1921), in *Letters*, 469.

15 C. S. Lewis makes this same association in *The Discarded Image* (1964), arguing, against romantic notions of the Middle Ages, that medieval minds were obsessed with classification.

16 F. Scott Fitzgerald, "The I.O.U." in *'I'd Die for You': And Other Lost Stories*, edited by Anne Margaret Daniel (New York: Scribner's, 2017), 1–16.

17 Fitzgerald, *I'd Die for You*, 3.

18 All page references hereafter are to F. Scott Fitzgerald, *The Beautiful and Damned* (Cambridge: Cambridge Univ. Press, 2008).

19 The F. Scott Fitzgerald Collected Papers, Box 33, Folder 11: *A Yank at Oxford* (Carbon copy of typescript), 1.

20 Bonnie Shannon McMullen, "'This Tremendous Detail': The Oxford Stone in the House of Gatsby," in Jamal Assadi and William Freedman (eds), *A Distant Drummer: Foreign Perspectives on F. Scott Fitzgerald* (New York: Peter Lang, 2007), 11–20.

21   For discussion of the Fitzgeralds' visit to Oxford and their plans to return, see Chapter Nine.

22   In the Introduction to the New Directions printing of *The Great Gatsby* (1946).

23   Arthur Mizener, *The Far Side of Paradise: A Biography of F. Scott Fitzgerald* (Boston: Houghton Mifflin, 1949; New York: Vintage, 1959), xiii. Maxwell Perkins and Ernest Hemingway also contributed material to this biography.

24   Andrew Turnbull, *Scott Fitzgerald* (New York: Charles Scribner's Sons, 1962); idem. (ed), *The Letters of F. Scott Fitzgerald* (New York: Scribner's, 1963).

25   Henry Dan Piper, *F. Scott Fitzgerald: A Critical Portrait* (New York: Holt, Rinehart and Winston, 1965), viii.

26   Ibid., 121–23. See discussion in Chapter Seven below.

27   Matthew Bruccoli, *Some Sort of Epic Grandeur: The Life of F. Scott Fitzgerald*, 2nd rev. ed. (Columbia, SC: Univ. of South Carolina Press, 2002).

28   David S. Brown, *Paradise Lost: A Life of F. Scott Fitzgerald* (Cambridge, MA: Harvard Univ. Press, 2017).

29   Ruth Prigozy (ed), *The Cambridge Companion to F. Scott Fitzgerald* (New York: Cambridge Univ. Press, 2002); Keith Carnutt (ed), *A Historical Guide to F. Scott Fitzgerald* (Oxford: Oxford Univ. Press, 2004); and Bryant Mangum (ed), *F. Scott Fitzgerald in Context* (New York: Cambridge Univ. Press, 2013).

30   Sarah Churchwell, *Careless People: Murder, Mayhem, and the Invention of* The Great Gatsby (New York: Penguin, 2013).

31   Richard Lehan, *The Great Gatsby: Limits of Wonder* (Boston: Twayne Publishers, 1990), 13.

32   Lehan, *The Great Gatsby*, 94.

33   Ibid., 101.

34   Michael Alexander, *Medievalism: The Middle Ages in Modern England* (New Haven and London: Yale Univ. Press, 2017), xx.

35   James Nagel, "American Literary Realism," in Mangum (ed), *F. Scott Fitzgerald in Context*, 171.

36   Ibid., 175.

37   Quoted in Charles Scribner III's introduction to F. Scott Fitzgerald, *The Great Gatsby* (New York: Macmillan, 1980), xv.

38   See Peh Li Qi, "Class, Taste and Social Mobility in The Great Gatsby," *Folio* 2010, 8.

39   Olivia Sung, "He's an Oxford man, you know," *Cherwell* (January 5, 2016): www .cherwell.org. Sung asks the question for the contemporary Oxford student: "Do you, like me, ever feel vaguely uneasy: do you ever wonder if you, like Gatsby, are trespassing on a territory you weren't made for, and that one day, perhaps, they will find out your fraud?"

2 "OUR YOUNG BARBARIANS ALL AT PLAY": OXFORD FROM PERCY SHELLEY TO OSCAR WILDE

1   For the early history of Oxford, see J. I. Catto (ed.), *The History of the University of Oxford, Volume I: The Early Oxford Schools* (Oxford: Oxford Univ.

Press, 1984); and L.W.B. Brockliss, *The University of Oxford: A History* (Oxford: University of Oxford Press, 2016).

2   Charles Frederick Harrold, *John Henry Newman: An Expository and Critical Study of His Mind, Thought and Art* (Hamden, CT: Archon Books, 1966), 6.

3   Max Beerbohm, "Diminuendo," in *The Prince of Minor Writers: The Selected Essays of Max Beerbohm*, edited by Phillip Lopate (New York: New York Review Books, 2015), 185–86.

4   John Ruskin, *The Storm-Cloud of the Nineteenth Century*, Lecture 1, delivered February 4, 1884 at the London Institution: https://www.wwnorton.com/college/english /nael/noa/pdf/27636_Vict_U08_Ruskin.pdf.

5   Brockliss, *The University*, 490.

6   Cuthbert Bede, *The Adventures of Mr. Verdant Green, A Freshman, Volume 1* (London: Nathaniel Cooke, 1853), 43.

7   Brockliss, *The University*, 453ff.

8   Ibid., 456–61.

9   Evelyn Waugh, "The Youngest Generation," editorial in *Lancing College Magazine* (December 1921), reprinted in Waugh, *A Little Order: A Selection from His Journalism*, Donat Gallagher (ed) (Boston: Little, Brown, 1977), 2.

10   Milton Hindus, *F. Scott Fitzgerald: An Introduction and Interpretation* (New York: Holt, Rinehart, and Winston, 1968), 37.

11   For Shelley's brief stay in Oxford, see *The Letters of Percy Bysshe Shelley, Vol. 1: Shelley in England*, edited by Frederick L. Jones (Oxford: Oxford University Press, 1964); Michael O'Neill, *Percy Bysshe Shelley: A Literary Life* (London: Macmillan, 1989), ch. 2; Richard Holmes, *Shelley: The Pursuit* (London: Harper Collins, 1994), ch. 2; James Bieri, *Percy Bysshe Shelley: A Biography, Vol. I Youth's Unextinguished Fire, 1792–1816* (Newark, DE: Univ. of Delaware Press, 2004), 119ff; Heathcote Williams, *Shelley at Oxford*, 2nd edition (Oxford: Huxley Scientific Press 2012); and (with caution) Thomas Jefferson Hogg, *The Life of Percy Bysshe Shelley* (London: George Routledge & Sons, 1906).

12   Letter to Lady Charlotte Campbell (March, 15 1811), quoted in Bieri, *Percy Bysshe Shelley*, 126, 129.

13   Hogg, *The Life*, 45.

14   Heathcote Williams, *Shelley at Oxford: Blasphemy, Book-Burning and Bedlam* (Oxford: Huxley Scientific Press, 2012), vii.

15   Shelley, *Letters*, no. 22.

16   Brockliss, *The University of Oxford*, 270.

17   Holmes, *Shelley*, 37.

18   Hogg described Oxford as "chartered laziness . . . destitute of every literary attainment . . . vulgar sons of vulgar fathers," while Shelley said simply that they were "all very dull people here." See Hogg, *The Life of Percy Bysshe Shelley*, 68–69.

19   Shelley's description of himself in a letter to William Godwin. On Shelley's political agitation in Ireland, see O'Neill, *Percy Bysshe Shelley*, 22ff.

20 Mary Shelley, editorial note on *Queen Mab*, quoted in David Duff, *Romance and Revolution: Shelley and the Politics of a Genre* (Cambridge: Cambridge Univ. Press, 1994), 112.

21 Duff (*Romance and Revolution*, 143) suggests that Shelley defends chivalry—the law that governs "the religion of love"—as celebrating sexual love, leading to sexual equality, and rescuing Europe from "anarchy and darkness."

22 See Ralph Pite, "Shelley, Dante and *The Triumph of Life*," in Timothy Clark and Jerrold E. Hogle (eds.), *Evaluating Shelley* (Edinburgh: Edinburgh Univ. Press, 1996), 197–214.

23 Sklar, 174.

24 Kuehl and Bryer (eds), *Dear Scott/Dear Max*, 71.

25 C. S. Lewis, "Shelly, Dryden, and Mr. Eliot," in *Rehabilitations and Other Essays* (Freeport, NY: Books for Libraries Press, 1939; repr. 1972), 3.

26 See O.E. Madden, "Keats and Oxford." *Oxford Magazine* 42, no. 2 (December 1990): 88–91.

27 *Keats: Selected Poems and Letters of Keats*, selected by Robert Gittings, edited by Sandra Anstey (Oxford: Harcourt, 1995), 23.

28 John Keats, "Lines Rhymed in a Letter received (by J.H.R.) from Oxford," in idem., 25.

29 Keith Carnutt, "Literary Style," in Bryant Mangum (ed), *F. Scott Fitzgerald in Context* (New York: Cambridge Univ. Press, 2013), 34–43 (43).

30 See William Blazek, "Literary Influences," in Bryant Mangum (ed), *F. Scott Fitzgerald in Context* (New York: Cambridge Univ. Press, 2013), 46–47; and Bruccoli (ed), *Life in Letters*, 460.

31 Turnbull (ed), *Letters*, 464.

32 Robert Sklar, *F. Scott Fitzgerald: The Last Laocoön* (New York: Oxford Univ. Press, 1967), 100ff.

33 Sklar, 265.

34 F. Scott Fitzgerald, "Who's Who—and Why," in *Afternoon of an Author: A Selection of Uncollected Stories and Essays* (New York: Scribner's, 1957), 84.

35 Sklar, 170.

36 Ibid., 172.

37 Nicholas Murray, *A Life of Matthew Arnold* (London: Hodder and Stoughton, 1996), 4.

38 Qtd. in Murray, *A Life*, 52.

39 Clinton Machann, *Matthew Arnold: A Literary Life* (London: Macmillan, 1998), 11.

40 From Arnold, *Discourses in America*, "Emerson," qtd. in Murray, *A Life*, 39.

41 Lee Oser, *The Return of Christian Humanism: Chesterton, Eliot, Tolkien, and the Romance of History* (Columbia, MO: Univ. of Missouri Press, 2007), 12ff.

42 Murray, *A Life*, 49; M.C. Curthoys and C.J. Day, "The Oxford of Mr. Verdant Green," in M.G. Brock and M.C. Curthoys (eds), *The History of the University*

of Oxford, Vol. VI: Nineteenth-Century Oxford, Part I (Oxford: Clarendon Press, 1996), 282.

43 Reminiscence of tutor William Charles Lake, quoted in Murray, *A Life*, 57.

44 C.S. Lewis, *Surprised by Joy* (London: Harcourt, 1955). See also James P. Helfers, "A Time for Joy: The Ancestry and Apologetic Force of C.S. Lewis's *Sehsucht*," *C.S. Lewis Journal* 1, no. 1 (1997), 7–18.

45 Stefan Collini, *Matthew Arnold: A Critical Portrait* (Oxford: Clarendon Press, 1994), 46.

46 See Clinton Machann, *Matthew Arnold: A Literary Life* (London: Macmillan, 1998), 8, 65ff.

47 Arnold, *Selected Letters*, 165, and Arnold, Preface to *Essays in Criticism*; quoted in Machann, *Matthew Arnold*, 67.

48 Matthew Arnold, *Poetical Works of Matthew Arnold* (London; New York: Macmillan, 1893), Rare Books (Ex) 3610.1893, Princeton University Library.

49 McMullen, "'This Tremendous Detail,'" 17.

50 Anna Bogen, "Compton Mackenzie, Liberal Education, and the Oxford Novel," *English Literature in Transition 1880–1920* 49, no. 1 (Winter 2006): 14–30. See Mathew Arnold, "Literature and Science," *The Complete Prose Works of Matthew Arnold*, edited by R.H. Super (Ann Arbor, MI: Univ. of Michigan Press, 1960), vol. 10, p. 53.

51 T.S. Eliot, "The Ultimate Belief," *International Journal of Ethics* 27, no. 1 (October 1916), 127.

52 Henry Tristram (ed.), *John Henry Newman Autobiographical Writings* (New York, 1956), 49–50.

53 John Cornwell, *Newman's Unquiet Grave: The Reluctant Saint* (London: Continuum, 2010), 26–27. For good critical biographies of Newman that deal with his Oxford career, see also Harold L. Weatherby, *Cardinal Newman in His Age* (Nashville: Vanderbilt Univ. Press, 1973); Ian Ker, *John Henry Newman: A Biography* (Oxford: Clarendon Press, 1988); and Frank M. Turner, *John Henry Newman: The Challenge to Evangelical Religion* (New Haven and London: Yale Univ. Press, 2002).

54 Cornwell, *Newman's Unquiet Grave*, 29–30.

55 Robbins, *Newman Brothers*, 22–23.

56 Charles Stephen Dessain et al. (ed.), *The Letters and Diaries of John Henry Newman* (Oxford: Oxford University Press, 1961–2008), vol. I, 160–61.

57 See Weatherby, *Cardinal Newman*, 99–101.

58 On Disraeli and Newman, see Joseph Ellis Baker, *The Novel and the Oxford Movement* (New York: Russell & Russell, 1965): "Like many Anglo-Catholic novelists, [Disraeli] tended to look upon Victorian life as if it were Medieval" (52).

59 Quoted in Evans, *The University*, 254–55.

60 *Reports of the Royal Commissions on the Universities of Oxford and Cambridge, 1852–53*, in J. Stuart Maclure (ed.), *Educational Documents, Vol. II: England and Wales 1816 to the Present Day* (London: Routledge, 2006), 63.

61 Bogen, "Compton Mackenzie," 18.

62 See discussion in Chapter Five below.

63 Qtd. in John Betjeman and David Vaisey, *Victorian and Edwardian Oxford from Old Photographs* (London: B.T. Batsford, 1971), 9.

64 Newman, *Idea*, 5.

65 Ibid., 9.

66 Ibid., 77.

67 Ibid., 79–81, 89.

68 Joan M. Allen, *Candles and Carnival Lights: The Catholic Sensibility of F. Scott Fitzgerald* (New York: NYU Press, 1978), 27.

69 *Letters*, 453.

70 Brown, *Paradise Lost*, 35.

71 See Allen, *Candles*, 46ff.

72 See discussion of Mackenzie and the Oxford Novel in Chapter Three below.

73 Cornwell, *Newman's Unquiet Grave*, 207.

74 Paul Elmer More, *Pages from an Oxford Diary* (Princeton: Princeton Univ. Press, 1937), 5.

75 Martha McMackin Garland, "Newman in His Own Day," in Newman, *Idea*, 265–81 (266).

76 F. Scott Fitzgerald, *'I'd Die for You' and Other Lost Stories*, ed. by Anne Margaret Daniel (New York: Scribner's, 2017).

77 John Ruskin, *Time and Tide*.

78 Richard Ellmann, "Oscar at Oxford," *The New York Review of Books* (March 29, 1984): http://www.nybooks.com/articles/1984/03/29/oscar-at-oxford/.

79 William Michael Rossetti, "The Brotherhood in a Nutshell," *The Germ* (1850), reprinted in Derek Stanford (ed.), *Pre-Raphaelite Writing: An Anthology* (London: Dent, 1984), 15.

80 See Walter Pater, "Dante Gabriel Rossetti," in D.S.R. Welland, *The Pre-Raphaelites in Literature and in Art* (London: George G. Harrap & Co., 1953), 188–91; and John Dixon Hunt, *The Pre-Raphaelite Imagination 1848–1900* (Lincoln, NE: Univ. Nebraska Press, 1968), 34–35.

81 The painting is sometimes identified as *Queen Guinevere*, and Morris's best known poem is the proto-feminist "The Defense of Guenevere" (1857).

82 Fitzgerald, *Spires and Gargoyles*.

83 Brockliss, *The University*, 378. See also Harold Pollins, *A History of Ruskin College* (Oxford, 1984).

84 Ruskin's inaugural lecture as Slade Professor of Art (1870), quoted in Schaeper and Schaeper, 5.

85 On the controversial child photography of Dodgson, see Karoline Leach, *In the Shadow of the Dreamchild: A New Understanding of Lewis Carroll* (London: Peter Owen, 1999); Simon Winchester, *The Alice Behind Wonderland* (Oxford: Oxford Univ. Press, 2011); and Robert Douglas-Fairhurst, *The Story of Alice: Lewis Carroll and the Secret History of Wonderland* (Cambridge, MA: Harvard Univ. Press, 2015), 59.

86   Welland, *The Pre-Raphaelites*, 43.

87   See Christopher A. Snyder, *The Making of Middle-earth: A New Look Inside the World of J.R.R. Tolkien* (New York: Sterling, 2013), 86–90; and Chapter Seven below.

88   *Letters of Oscar Wilde*, 720.

89   Dougill, *Oxford in English Literature*, 165.

90   M. Jean Fayard, *Oxford and Margaret* (London: Jarrolds, 1925), 253.

91   Ellmann, *Oscar Wilde at Oxford: A Lecture Delivered at the Library of Congress on March 1, 1983* (Washington, D.C.: Library of Congress, 1984), 9. See also Ellmann's seminal biography of Wilde, *Oscar Wilde* (Vintage, 1988).

92   Edouard Roditi, *Oscar Wilde* (Norfolk, CT: New Directions, 1947), 203–4.

93   Brockliss, *The University*, 495–96.

94   Wilde, *Letters*.

95   See Philip E. Smith II and Michael Helfand (eds.), *Oscar Wilde's Oxford Notebooks: A Portrait of Mind in the Making* (Oxford: Oxford Univ. Press, 1989). The two holograph notebooks are now at the William Andrews Clark Memorial Library of the University of California at Los Angeles.

96   Merlin Holland and Rupert Hart-Davis (eds.), *The Complete Letters of Oscar Wilde* (New York: Henry Holt, 2000).

97   Ellmann (*Oscar Wilde at Oxford*, 23–25) cites as evidence Wilde's first published prose, a review of the opening of the new Grosvenor Gallery in 1877, and an anonymous pamphlet titled *Boy Worship at Oxford* then circulating at Oxford.

98   See discussion in Michèle Mendelssohn, *Making Oscar Wilde* (Oxford: Oxford Univ. Press, 2018), 51–56.

99   See Mendelssohn, *Making Oscar Wilde*, plate 1. For context, see Lewis Perry Curtis, *Apes & Angels: The Irish in Victorian Caricature* (Washington, D.C.: Smithsonian Press, 1971); and R.F. Foster, *Paddy & Mr. Punch: Connections in Irish and English History* (London: Allen Lane, 1993).

100   Ibid., 71.

101   See Stanley Weintraub (ed.), *Literary Criticism of Oscar Wilde* (Lincoln: Univ. of Nebraska Press, 1968); and Richard Ellmann (ed.), *The Artist as Critic: Critical Writings of Oscar Wilde* (New York: Random House, 1969).

102   Lehan, *The Great Gatsby*, 62–63.

103   See Turnbull, *Scott Fitzgerald*, 27–28; Bruccoli, *Some Sort of Epic Grandeur*, 18; and Chapter Eight below.

104   Catherine Mintler, "From Aesthete to Gangster: The Dandy Figure in the Novels of F. Scott Fitzgerald," *F. Scott Fitzgerald Review* 8, no. 1 (2010), 104–29 (106, 114).

105   Lehan, *The Great Gatsby*, 31.

106   The actual quote can be found in the play *Vera, or The Nihilists*, Act II: "Experience, the name men give to their mistakes. I never commit any."

107   See Bruccoli and Baughman (eds.), *Conversations*, 4.

108   Ibid., *Conversations*, 83. It is followed by Compton Mackenzie's *Sinister Street*, the most influential novel he read at the age of twenty.

109 Simon Callow, *Oscar Wilde and His Circle* (London: National Portrait Gallery, 2000), 37.

110 James C. Stewart, *The New Negro: The Life of Alain Locke* (New York: Oxford Univ. Press, 2018), 79.

111 Wilde, "*Henry the Fourth* at Oxford," *Dramatic Review* (May 23, 1885), in *Literary Criticism of Oscar Wilde*, 123–26.

3 "OLD SPORT": THE FIRST AMERICAN RHODES SCHOLARS

1 Now in the F. Scott Fitzgerald Collection, Princeton University Library. See photo in Matthew J. Bruccoli (ed.), *F. Scott Fitzgerald's 'The Great Gatsby': A Literary Reference* (New York: Carroll & Graf, 2002), 55; and detailed discussion in Churchwell, *Careless People*.

2 According to the *Oxford English Dictionary*, "glamour" was first used by Sir Walter Scott as a synonym for "magic, enchantment, spell." However, in *The Road to Middle-earth* (Boston: Houghton Mifflin, 2003), Tom Shippey shows that Oxford's most famous philologist, Prof. J.R.R. Tolkien, knew that *glamour* had a far older history, and was related to Old English *glam/glaum*, "mirth, merriment," and was probably a corruption of *grammar*. "Word-magic" thus became, by Fitzgerald's day, glamour, "a showbiz word, an advertiser's word, false and meretricious . . . as [in] 'glamour-girl'" (51–53).

3 Brockliss, *The University*, 408.

4 See Anne Keene, *Oxford: The American Connection* (Oxford: Temple Rock Publications, 1990), 14.

5 Ibid., 16.

6 See Mary Potter Thatcher Higginson (ed.), *Letters and Journals of Thomas Wentworth Higginson, 1846–1906* (Boston: Houghton Mifflin, 1921), 291–92; Thomas Wentworth Higginson, *Cheerful Yesterdays* (Boston: Houghton Mifflin, 1898), 188–89; and Mendelssohn, *Making Oscar Wilde*, 31–38. Wentworth comments on the German research university surpassing Oxford and Cambridge in influence at Harvard and other top American schools.

7 Keene, 27.

8 J. Mordaunt Crook, Brasenose: *The Biography of an Oxford College* (Oxford: Oxford Univ. Press, 2008), 296.

9 See Horace A. Lafaye, *Polo in Britain: A History* (London: McFarland, 2012), 31; and Horace A. Laffaye (ed.), *Profiles in Polo: The Players Who Changed the Game* (London: McFarland, 2007).

10 Crook, 267, 296 n.31.

11 Nigel a Brassard, "Thomas Hitchcock Jr.: 'The best of America was in his veins,'" in Laffaye (ed), *Profiles*, 108–14.

12 Churchwell, 35–39.

13 On the importance of the automobile in *Gatsby*, see Matthew Little, "'I Could Make Some Money': Cars and Currency in the Great Gatsby," *Papers on Language & Literature* 51, no. 1 (Winter 2015).

14   Brassard, 113.

15   *Letters*, 491.

16   Fitzgerald, Letter to Scottie (Winter, 1939), in *Collected Letters*.

17   Horst H. Kruse, *F. Scott Fitzgerald at Work: The Making of "The Great Gatsby"* (Tuscaloosa, AL: University of Alabama Press, 2014), 87–89.

18   Meyers, *Scott Fitzgerald*, 234.

19   Brockliss, *The University*, 465.

20   Lee Oser, *The Return of Christian Humanism: Chesterton, Eliot, Tolkien, and the Romance of History* (Columbia, MO: Univ. of Missouri Press, 2007), 36.

21   See Thomas J. and Kathleen Schaeper, *Rhodes Scholars: Oxford, and the Creation of an American Elite* (New York and Oxford: Berghahn Books, 2010), 3.

22   Philip Ziegler, *Legacy: Cecil Rhodes, the Rhodes Trust and Rhodes Scholarships* (New Haven: Yale Univ. Press, 2008), 6–7.

23   Brockliss, *The University*, 408.

24   Quoted in Ziegler, *Legacy*, 14. Rhodes' 1877 "Confession of Faith," now in the archives of the Rhodes House, also mentions his dream of "the ultimate recovery of the United States of America an integral part of the British Empire."

25   Ziegler, *Legacy*, 16.

26   A facsimile of the will is in Ziegler, *Legacy*, appendix I. Rhodes adds that, "as the College authorities live secluded from the world and so are like children as to commercial matters I would advise them to consult my Trustees as to the investment of these various funds. . . ."

27   See, for example, the review of *An American at Oxford* (1902) by John Corbin in *The Harvard Graduate's Magazine* (December 1902), 320–21.

28   See Schaeper and Schaeper, 22–23.

29   G.K. Chesterton, *A Miscellany of Men* (London: Methuen and Co., 1912), 203–4.

30   David Alexander, "The American Scholarships," in Anthony Kenny (ed), *The History of the Rhodes Trust 1902–1999* (Oxford: Oxford Univ. Press, 2001), 105.

31   Ibid.

32   Memo of June 1903, Rhodes Trust File 1122. See also Kenny, "The Rhodes Trust," 6.

33   Francis Wylie, "The Rhodes Scholars and Oxford 1902–31," in Godfrey Elton (ed), *The First Fifty Years of the Rhodes Trust and the Rhodes Scholarships, 1903–1953* (Oxford: Basil Blackwell, 1955), 83.

34   Schaeper and Schaeper, 28.

35   Wylie, "The Rhodes Scholars," 88.

36   Michael O'Brien, *Death Did Not Divide Them: The American Rhodes Scholars Who Died in World War One.* Brighton: Reveille Press, 2013), 18.

37   Schaeper and Schaeper, 47.

38   *University of Texas Record* 5 (1904): 384–85.

39   Schaeper and Schaeper, 64.

40 Charles A. Keith, *Fast Balls and College Halls: An Autobiography* (New York: Vantage Press, 1959), 27.

41 Wylie, "The Rhodes Scholars," 89–90.

42 Schaeper and Schaeper, 55.

43 "A Programme," *The Alumni Magazine of the Association of American Rhodes* 1, no. 1 (December 1907), 9.

44 *The History of the University of Oxford*, vol. 7, p. 810.

45 Reprinted in *The American Oxonian* 94, no. 2 (Spring 2007), 237–40.

46 Sidney Ball, "Oxford's Opinion of the Rhodes Scholars," *The American Oxonian* 1, no. 1 (April 1914), 8–10.

47 According to Aydelotte, some 40 percent of American Rhodes Scholars between 1904–17 ended up teaching at colleges and universities. See Frank Aydelotte, "A Challenge to Rhodes Scholars," reprinted in Aydelotte, *The Oxford Stamp and Other Essays* (Freeport, NY: Books for Libraries Press, 1967; orig. ed. 1917), 66.

48 Alexander, "The American Scholarships," 119.

49 Crook, 328–29.

50 Alexander, "The American Scholarships, 119–120.

51 Frank Aydelotte, *The Oxford Stamp and Other Essays* (Freeport, NY: Books for Libraries Press, 1967; orig. ed. 1917), iii.

52 Aydelotte, *Oxford Stamp*, 21.

53 See discussion in Anne Rinn, "Rhodes Scholarships, Frank Aydelotte, and Collegiate Honors Education," *Journal of the National Collegiate Honors Council* 127 (Spring 2003): 27–39 (32).

54 Rinn, "Rhodes Scholarships," 37.

55 Ibid. See also Schaeper and Schaeper, 78–80 and *passim*.

56 Schaeper and Schaeper, 50.

57 Lehan, *The Great Gatsby*, 84.

58 F. Scott Fitzgerald, "Three Cities," *Brentano's Book Chat* 1 (Sept-Oct 1921), 15, 28; reprinted in Matthew J. Bruccoli (ed.), *F. Scott Fitzgerald on Authorship* (Columbia, SC: Univ. of South Carolina Press, 1996), 51–52. See also discussion in Chapter Seven below.

59 Max Beerbohm, *Zuleika Dobson* (New York: Heritage Press, 1911), 96–97.

60 Ibid., 100.

61 Ibid., 182.

62 Dougill, *Oxford in English Literature*, 169.

63 Beerbohm, *Zuleika*, 7.

64 See Bruccoli and Baughman, *Conversations*, 44 n2. Fitzgerald also mentioned *Tom Brown* in a review of Booth Tarkington's *Penrod and Sam* in 1917.

65 See Fitzgerald, *On Authorship*, 59; and Mintler, 125 n1. "Mr. Fitzgerald thinks Aldous Huxley great," wrote the editor of *The Bookman* (May 1922), quoting Fitzgerald, "'because he kids everybody and kids himself, and kids himself for kidding himself and for kidding everybody.'"

66   Fitzgerald's annotated copy of *Sinister Street* is now at Princeton University Library, Rare Books (Ex) 3839.9.385.1914.

67   See Turnbull (ed.), *Letters*, 468–69; and Blazek, "Literary Influences," 47.

68   Max Beerbohm, quoted in Andro Linklater, *Compton Mackenzie: A Life* (London: Hogarth, 1992), 131.

69   Letter to John Peale Bishop (April 1925), in *Letters*, 356. See also Allan Massie, "The magnum opus of Compton Mackenzie: On Capri in 1925 Scott Fitzgerald met his 'old idol' Compton Mackenzie and found him 'cordial, attractive and pleasantly mundane," *The Spectator*, September 26, 2007.

70   Bruccoli (ed.), *Collected Writings of Zelda Fitzgerald*, 422.

71   See Anna Bogen, "Compton Mackenzie, Liberal Education, and the Oxford Novel," *English Literature in Transition 1880–1920* 49, no. 1 (Winter 2006): 14–30.

72   Compton Mackenzie, *Sinister Street* (New York: D. Appleton and Company, 1914), 4.

73   Bogen, "Compton Mackenzie," 21.

74   Mackenzie, *Sinister Street*, 326–27.

75   Bogen, "Compton Mackenzie," 21. For American support of Oxonian liberal education, we can look to Rhodes Scholar Frank Aydelotte: "every son of Oxford will hope and believe that no desire for economy or efficiency or popularity will drive her to sacrifice the thoroughness and the humanity which were her glory before the war" (*Oxford Stamp*, v–vi).

76   Alain Locke, "The Rhodes Scholar Question," transcribed by Jack Zoeller in *The American Oxonian* 94, no. 2 (Spring 2007), 232–36 (236).

77   Bogen, "Compton Mackenzie," 27.

78   Robert Emmet Long, *The Achieving of* The Great Gatsby (Lewisburg, PA: Bucknell Univ. Press, 1981), 24–25.

79   Beverly Nichols, *Patchwork* (London: Chatto and Windus, 1921), 234.

80   John Dougill and Q.D. Leavis, respectively, quoted in Bogen, "Compton Mackenzie," 26.

81   Corbin came to Oxford in 1894–95 to turn his Harvard MA thesis (on *Hamlet*) into a published monograph: see John Corbin Papers (MS 011), Archives & Special Collections, University of Nebraska–Lincoln Libraries.

82   John Corbin, *An American at Oxford* (Boston: Houghton Mifflin, 1903), 8.

83   Ibid., 309.

84   John Corbin, "The Latin Quarter of England," review of *Impressions of Oxford* by Paul Bourget, *The Lamp* XXVI (February/July 1903), 123–27: https://archive .org/stream/lamp00sonsgoog#page/n112/mode/2up.

85   George Calderon, *The Adventures of Downy V. Green: Rhodes Scholar at Oxford* (London: Smith, Elder & Co., 1902).

86   James Saxon Childers, *Laurel and Straw* (New York: D. Appleton and Co., 1927), 31.

4 "MODISH NEGROES" AND MR. WOLFSHEIM: ALAIN LOCKE, HORACE KALLEN, AND CULTURAL PLURALISM

1   Churchwell, *Careless People*, 81.

2   See Edward White, *The Tastemaker: Carl Van Vechten and the Birth of Modern America* (New York: Farrar, Straus & Giroux, 2014), 208–13. Van Vechten became the literary executor of Gertrude Stein upon her death.

3   Letter to Fitzgerald (23 July 1934), F. Scott Fitzgerald Papers, Princeton. Qtd. in Brown, *Paradise Lost*, 190–91.

4   Richard Forrey, "Negroes in the Fiction of F. Scott Fitzgerald," *Phylon* 28, no. 3 (1967), 293–98 (295).

5   See discussion in Chapter Eight below. For ethnicity in Fitzgerald studies, see J. Rohrkemper, "Becoming White: Race and Ethnicity in *The Great Gatsby*," *Midwestern Miscellany* 31 (2003), 22–31; Suzanne del Gizzo, "Ethnic Stereotyping," in Mangum (ed.), *F. Scott Fitzgerald*, 224–33; and Joseph Vogel, "'Civilization's Going to Pieces': *The Great Gatsby*, Identity, and Race, From the Jazz Age to the Obama Era," *The F. Scott Fitzgerald Review* 13 (2015), 29–54.

6   Vogel, "'Civilization's Going to Pieces,'" 33.

7   A theory put forward first in a 2000 conference paper, then in Carlyle V. Thompson, *The Tragic Black Buck: Racial Masquerading in the American Literary Imagination* (New York: Peter Lang, 2004).

8   Matthew Bruccoli was particularly adamant in his opposition: see, e.g., Elizabeth Manus, "Was Gatsby Black?" *Salon*, August 9, 2000: https://www.salon.com /2000/08/09/gatsby/.

9   Locke's grandfather, Ishmael Locke, was a free black who attended the University of Cambridge, spent four years establishing schools in Liberia, and became principal of the Institute for Colored Youth in Philadelphia: see Pamela Roberts, *Black Oxford: The Untold Stories of Oxford University's Black Scholars* (Oxford: Signal Books, 2013), 11.

10   See Jack C. Zoeller, "Alain Locke at Oxford: Race and the Rhodes Scholarships," *The American Oxonian* 94, no. 2 (Spring 2007), 183–224. Locke's academic papers and personal correspondence are in the Alain L. Locke Archives, Moorland-Spingarn Center, Howard University in Washington, D.C. His student records and other documents are in the Harvard University Archives UAIII 15.88.10, 1890–1968, Box 2986.

11   Locke could alternatively have applied from New Jersey, where his mother resided but where he would have gone up against Princeton students, or from Massachussetts, where he would have competed for the Harvard endorsement with five of his fellow classmates. By choosing Pennsylvania, he was guaranteed (that year) of being endorsed by Harvard.

12   Letters to Mary Locke (February 28, 1907, and March 3, 1907), Alain Locke Archives.

13   A later recollection quoted in Arthur Fauset, *For Freedom: A Biographical Study of the American Negro* (Philadelphia: Franklin Publichin, 1934), 175.

14 Stewart, *The New Negro*, 101.

15 Rhodes Trust File 1122.

16 Alain Locke, letter to Mary Locke (1907); quoted in Jeffrey C. Stewart, "Alain LeRoy Locke at Oxford: The First African-American Rhodes Scholar," *The Journal of Blacks in Higher Education* 31 (Spring 2001): 112–17 (112).

17 See Roberts, Black Oxford, 2ff.; and Mendelssohn, *Making Oscar Wilde*, 37–41.

18 Alexander, "The American Scholarships," 108–10.

19 Reported in *The Washington Star* (May 1907).

20 Alexander, "The American Scholarships," 108. The University of Georgia, Emory, and Mercer had colluded to monopolize the three-year state cycle of awardees.

21 Ibid., 108–9, Alexander quoting correspondence between Parkin and Francis P. Venables, President of the University of North Carolina.

22 Rhodes Trust Report to Trustees 1903, 20.

23 Wylie, "The Rhodes Scholars," 99–100.

24 See Alexander, "The American Scholarships," 110.

25 Letter to Boyd, March 22, 1907, Rhodes Trust Files 1122. See Ziegler, *Legacy*, 65.

26 Schaeper and Schaeper, 57; Zoeller, "Alain Locke at Oxford," 196.

27 Challis, *Vicarious Rhodesians*, 22; Zoeller, "Alain Locke at Oxford," 204; Stewart, *The New Negro*, 173–75. Locke reported the incident to his mother and contemplated writing in angry response an essay titled, "April 1909, Southern Rhodes Scholars vs. English Tory Allies" (Alain Locke Papers).

28 Zoeller, "Alain Locke at Oxford," 199ff. Locke kept the many invitations he received to teas, dinners, and other social gatherings (Alain Locke Papers, 164–76). Christopher Hollis and Evelyn Waugh recall the prejudice with which black and brown Oxford students were treated in the 1920s, including the coordinated racism that kept S.W.R.D. Bandaranaike from becoming the first non-white President of the Oxford Union: see Barbara Cooke, *Evelyn Waugh's Oxford* (Oxford: Bodleian Library, 2018), 110–11.

29 Seme received his BA in Civil Law from Oxford in 1909 and was called to the Bar at the Middle Temple. Seme also arranged for Locke to meet with Theophilus Scholes (ca. 1858–1940), the Jamaican physician and Pan Africanist, soon after Locke's arrival in London. See Stewart, *The New Negro*, 118; and Roberts, *Black Oxford*, 51–53.

30 Haley had studied at Howard Law School and at Yale before arriving at Harvard, where he received an honors degree in Semitic languages in 1906. He was one of the first Oxford students to receive the Diploma in Anthropology from the Pitt Rivers Museum. See Roberts, *Black Oxford*, 16–19.

31 Letter to Mary Locke (December 1, 1907), Alain Locke Papers.

32 Zoeller, "Alain Locke at Oxford," 203–4. Kallen called the Thanksgiving dinner at the American Club "a dinner of inauthentic Americans," and Locke subsequently became a regular at Sunday dinners at the home of Dicey, a friend of Henry James: see Stewart, "Alain LeRoy Locke at Oxford," 114; idem., *The New Negro*, 122.

33   Alexander, "The American Scholarships," 113; Ziegler, *Legacy*, 65; Zoeller, "Alain Locke and Oxford," 197; and Wylie's letter to Boyd of March 20, 1907, RTF 1122.

34   Alain Locke file, Rhodes House. See Zoeller, "Alain Locke at Oxford," 215.

35   Stewart, *The New Negro*, 96.

36   Schiller had been recommended by Horace Kallen, and Locke and Schiller discussed the project amicably as they attended a lecture by a visiting William James. See Zoeller, "Alain Locke at Oxford," 215–16.

37   Alain Locke Papers 164–76 (9).

38   Stewart, *The New Negro*, 151–55.

39   Alain Locke, Letter to Mary Locke (October 7, 1907), Alain Locke Papers 164–47 (10).

40   Rhodes Trust Files 1122. See also Kenny, "The Rhodes Trust," 7.

41   See Alain Locke Papers, 164–76 (9). Stewart believes that, while Locke did not admit to romantic affairs in the letters he wrote to his mother, he and Downes had almost certainly become lovers by the time they traveled together to France.

42   For discussion of the phenomenon of the Black Dandy, see Monica Miller, *Slaves to Fashion: Black Dandyism and the Styling of Black Diasporic Identity* (Durham, NC: Duke Univ. Press, 2009).

43   Ibid., 51: "Locke used his dress to trouble White expectations of what a Negro looked like and replace them with an image of the New Negro, who created a new surprising identity through the art of dress."

44   Santayana had published *The Sense of Beauty* in 1898.

45   Mendelssohn, *Making Oscar Wilde*, 41.

46   Alain Locke, Letter to Mary Locke (Oxford, no date), Alain Locke Papers 164–47 (10).

47   Alain Locke, Letter to Mary Locke (October 23, 1907), Alain Locke Papers 164–47 (10). See Stewart, *The New Negro*, 118.

48   Stewart, *The New Negro*, 119. Wendell, a Francophile dandy and aesthetic crusader in Boston, had taught at the Sorbonne and returned to Harvard to become Locke's mentor.

49   Alain Locke, Letters to Mary Locke (October 7 and December 1, 1907), Alain Locke Papers 164–47 (10).

50   Alain Locke, "Oxford Contrasts," *The Independent* (July 15, 1909): 139–42; reprinted in *The American Oxonian* 94, no. 2 (Spring 2007): 225–31 (227).

51   Locke, "Oxford Contrasts," 230. The delay in publishing Locke's essay was apparently due to the publisher expecting Locke to focus more on race.

52   Stewart, *The New Negro*, 132.

53   General John J. Pershing, secret communiqué concerning African American troops sent to the French military stationed with the American army, August 7, 1918. See National Park Service Archives: http://web.archive.org /web/20060619181706/http://www.nps.gov/untold/banners_and_backgrounds /militarybanner/military.htm.

54   Harvard University Archives UA V.874.269.2, "War Records Office Personal Service Records," Box 21. While Harvard records list Locke as "Personnel Officer and 2nd Lieutenant, Infantry," Stewart (*New Negro*, 296) believes that Locke stretched the truth of his service to get a deferment from combat.

55   Letter from Alain Locke to William George (July 4, 1922), Alain Locke Papers. See also Stewart, *The New Negro*, 319–20.

56   Stewart, *The New Negro*, 431ff.

57   Ernest Boyd, "Æsthete: Model 1924," *Portraits: Real and Imaginary* (New York: George H. Doran Co., 1924), 11–25 (18).

58   See discussion in Chapter Seven below.

59   Much of the writing and collecting had first been done for the "Harlem, Mecca of the New Negro" issue of the magazine *Survey Graphic* (March 1925). Maxwell Perkins, Fitzgerald's editor at Scribner's, had liked Locke's idea of turning some of this material into a book, but only if it had a single author. See Stewart, *The New Negro*, 484.

60   See Leonard Harris (ed.), *The Philosophy of Alain Locke: Harlem Renaissance and Beyond* (Philadelphia: Temple Univ. Press, 1989), 6–8. Later in his career he would also support the "black proletarian" writers like Richard Wright.

61   Stewart, *The New Negro*, 82–87.

62   Vogel, "Civilization's Going to Pieces," 47.

63   Alain Locke (ed.), *The New Negro: An Interpretation* (New York: Albert and Charles Boni, 1925. Repr. New York: Arno Press and the *New York Times*, 1968), ix.

64   Stewart, *The New Negro*, 88.

65   Ibid., 239.

66   Horace M. Kallen and Sidney Hook (eds.), *American Philosophy Today and Tomorrow* (New York: Lee Furman, 1935), 312.

67   Brown, *This Side of Paradise*, 88.

68   *The Newark, N.J. Afro-American* December 29, 1962: "While we congratulate and are happy for the two men of color who qualified, we still believe it more than incredible that the committee had to search for more than a half century to find them." Oxford and Cambridge still struggle to recruit and admit students of color for first degrees: see Richard Adams and Helena Bengtsson, "Oxford accused of 'social apartheid' as colleges admit no black students," *The Guardian* (October 19, 2017).

69   Locke, "Oxford Contrasts," 230.

70   Penned anonymously, attributed to "A Gentleman of the University of Oxford." In an 1810 letter to John Joseph Stockdale, Shelley makes arrangements for the publication of this "Romance" and asks the bookseller if he has received the MS of his poem, "The Wandering Jew." See Shelley, *Letters*, nos. 19 and 23.

71   Keith Gandal, *The Gun and the Pen: Hemingway, Fitzgerald, Faulkner, and the Fiction of Mobilization* (Oxford: Oxford Univ. Press, 2008), 77ff.

72   David M. Lewis, *The Jews of Oxford* (Oxford: Oxford Jewish Congregation, 1992), 1.

73   Ibid., 22ff.

74   Ibid., 24.

75   See Jerome Karabel, *The Chosen: The Hidden History of Admission and Exclusion at Harvard, Yale, and Princeton* (Boston: Houghton Mifflin, 2005).

76   See the letter from Hutchins in Helene van Rossum, "Being Jewish at Princeton: From F. Scott Fitzgerald's Days to the Center for Jewish Life," *News from the Princeton University Archives & Public Policy Papers Collection* (posted April 29, 2011): https://blogs.princeton.edu/reelmudd/2011/04/printecons-jewish-students-from-the-days-of-scott-fitzgerald-to-the-center-of-jewish-life/.

77   Ibid. The first African American students admitted to Princeton came as part of the Navy V-12 program after World War II.

78   Judith Goldstein, *Inventing Great Neck: Jewish Identity and the American Dream*, quoted in Mary Jo Murphy, "Eyeing the Unreal Estate of Gatsby Esq.," *The New York Times* (September 30, 2010): http://www.nytimes.com/2010/10/01/nyregion/01gatsby.html.

79   Rutledge M. Dennis, "Relativism and Pluralism in the Social Thought of Alain Locke," in Russell J. Linnemann (ed.), *Alain Locke: Reflections on a Modern Renaissance Man* (Baton Rouge: Louisiana State University Press, 1982), 29–49 (31). Note that Kallen gives Locke credit for coining the phrase "cultural pluralism" or "the right to be different." See Horace Meyer Kallen, "Alain Locke and Cultural Pluralism," *Journal of Philosophy* 54, no. 5 (February 1957): 119–27.

80   Student records in the Harvard University Archives UAIII 15.88.10, 1890–1968, Box 2537.

81   The letters to Kallen are part of the Horace Kallen Papers (MS-1, Box 14, Folder 17) in the American Jewish Archives, Cincinnati, Ohio.

82   Letter from Horace Kallen to Barrett Wendell (October 22, 1907), Horace Kallen Papers. See discussion in Stewart, *The New Negro*, 121.

83   Stewart, *The New Negro*, 127.

84   James' testimonial included describing Kallen as "an originative mind" with "first rate pedagogic talent," his "energy, courage, and moral elevation are superlative." Harvard University Archives UAIII 15.88.10, 1890–1968, Box 2537.

85   Harvard University Archives UAIII 15.88.10, 1890–1968, Box 2537.

86   *New York Times* February 17, 1974.

87   See discussion in David Weinfeld, "What Difference Does the Difference Make? Horace Kallen, Alain Locke, and the Development of Cultural Pluralism in America," PhD dissertation, New York University, 2014.

88   Stewart, *The New Negro*, 95.

89   William Toll, "Horace M. Kallen: Pluralism and American Jewish Identity," *American Jewish History* 85, no. 1 (March 1997).

90   The Eliot-Kallen correspondence was discovered in 1997 at the American Jewish Archives in Cincinnati. Box 8, Folder 26 of the Horace M. Kallen

Papers, MS-1. Kallen was responding to that year's detention of Jewish scientists and intellectuals by Heinrich Himmler.

91 See Ronald Shuchard, "Burbank with a Baedeker, Eliot with a Cigar: American Intellectuals, Anti-Semitism, and the Idea of Culture" *Modernism/Modernity* 10, no. 1 (January 2003), 1–26. Shuchard's article set off a heated debate reassessing Eliot's alleged anti-Semitism.

92 Shuchard, "Burbank," 19.

93 In Horace M. Kallen, *The Education of Free Men* (New York: Farrar, Straus & Co., 1949), 15–35 (15–16).

94 See Chapter Two above.

95 Mintler, 118.

96 Eleanor Lanahan (ed.), *Zelda, An Illustrated Life: The Private World of Zelda Fitzgerald* (New York: Harry N. Abrams, 1996), 31.

97 Mintler, 107–8.

98 For discussion of the flappers, see Chapter Ten below.

99 See K. Fraser, "Another reading of The Great Gatsby," *English Studies in Canada* 5 (1979), 330–343; E. Wasiolek, "The sexual drama of Nick and Gatsby," *The International Fiction Review* 19, no. 1 (1992), 14–22; Maggie Gordon Froehlich, "Jordan Baker, gender dissent, and homosexual passing in The Great Gatsby," *The Space Between: Literature and Culture, 1914–1945* 6, no. 1 (2010), 81–103; and idem., "Gatsby's mentors: queer relations between love and money in The Great Gatsby," *The Journal of Men's Studies* 19, no. 3 (Fall 2011).

100 Froehlich, "Gatsby's Mentors."

101 See discussion in Donaldson, 73ff.

102 Scott did admit to having strong feelings for Hemingway: "I really loved him, but of course it wore out like a love affair. The fairies have spoiled all that." See *Notebooks*, 62.

103 F. Scott Fitzgerald Papers, Princeton University Libraries.

104 Nancy Milford, *Zelda* (New York: Harper & Row, 1970), 168, 175.

105 Mintler, "From Aesthete to Gangster," 109.

106 See Froehlich, "Gatsby's Mentors," n.22; and Sally Cline, *Zelda Fitzgerald: Her Voice in Paradise*, 173.

107 Sklar, 101.

108 Malcolm Bradbury, *The American Novel*, 65.

5 AN AMERICAN AT MERTON COLLEGE: T. S. ELIOT, GARSINGTON, AND THE WOMEN OF OXFORD

1 Evans, *The University of Oxford*, 27ff.

2 Sandra J. Darroch, *Garsington Revisited*, 40.

3 Sally Mitchell, *The New Girl: Girl's Culture in England, 1880–1915* (New York: Columbia Univ. Press, 1995), 53.

4 Brockliss, *The University*, 462.

5 Qtd. in Evans, *The University*, 32.

6   See Susan R. Grayzel and Tammy M. Proctor (eds.), *Gender and the Great War* (Oxford: Oxford Univ. Press, 2017). Of the recent centenary projects focusing on women and the Great War, see the Bodleian Library's "WWI Primary Resource Guide: Women during WWI" (last updated January 15, 2018): https://libguides .bodleian.ox.ac.uk/ww1-sources.

7   Vera Brittain, "The Point of View of a Woman Student," *Oxford Outlook* (1919). See also Anna Bogen, *Women's University Fiction, 1880–1945* (London: Routledge, 2016), 112–14, 153.

8   Bogen, *Women's University Fiction*, 113.

9   Evans, *The University*, 33.

10   Mitchell, *The New Girl*, 52.

11   Bogen, *Women's University Fiction*; and idem (ed.), *Women's University Narratives, 1890–1945, Part II, Volume II* (New York: Routledge, 2018). Bogen praises Trevelyn, in particular, for her experimental, stream-of-consciousness style, her "originality and bravery in melding together modernist styles with the Oxford novel."

12   Bogen, *Women's University Fiction*, 163.

13   See T.S. Eliot, *The Letters of T. S. Eliot: Volume 6: 1932–1933* (New Haven and London: Yale Univ. Press, 2016), 686.

14   E.H. Wells wrote to Tom's father on 4 Dec 1906: "This is not a record on which he would win promotion at the end of the year." Eliot's transcripts reveal that he actually earned Cs in German, History, and Government, though he did receive a D in German during his second year. In his third year his grades were all As and Bs. Harvard University Archives UAIII.15.88.10, 1890–1968, Box 120.

15   See Nancy D. Hargrove, "'Une Présent Parfait': Eliot and La Vie Parisienne, 1910–1911," in Marianne Thormählen (ed.), *T.S. Eliot at the Turn of the Century* (Lund, Sweden: Lund Univ. Press, 1994), 33–58; and idem, *T.S. Eliot's Parisian Year* (Gainesville, FL: University of Florida Press, 2009).

16   Harvard University Archives UAIII 15.88.10, 1890–1968, Box 120.

17   Ibid. For extensive discussion of Eliot's time at Oxford, see Robert Crawford, *Young Eliot: From St. Louis to 'The Waste Land'* (New York: Farrar, Straus and Giroux, 2015); and Brand Blanshard, "Eliot at Oxford," in James Olney (ed), *T.S. Eliot: Essays from the Southern Review* (Oxford: Oxford Univ. Press, 1988).

18   Crawford, *Young Eliot*, 214–15, 218–20.

19   Valerie Eliot and Hugh Haughton (eds.), *The Letters of T.S. Eliot, Vol. 1: 1898–1922* (rev. ed. London: Faber and Faber, 2009), 71.

20   G.R. Evans, *The University of Oxford: A New History* (London: I.B. Tauris, 2014), 20; *Letters, Vol. 1*, 61 and 81.

21   Merton College Debating Society Minute Book, 1902–1921 (Merton College Archives, MCR 12.1.21), 308.

22   *Letters, Vol. 1*, 77.

23 Crawford, *Young Eliot*, 210–11.

24 Erik Svarney, *'The Men of 1914': T.S. Eliot and Early Modernism* (Philadelphia: Open Univ. Press, 1988), 65ff.

25 Crawford, *Young Eliot*, 225ff.; James E. Miller Jr., *T. S. Eliot: The Making of an American Poet, 1888–1922* (University Park, PA: Penn State Press, 2005), 218. Eliot wrote to Thayer a year later: "Can it be a year ago you and I were charming the eyes (and ears) of Char-flappers . . . ?" (*Letters*, Vol. I, 137).

26 Harvard University Archives UAIII 15.88.10, 1890–1968, Box 120.

27 Judith Watt, "The Lonely Princess of Bohemia," *The Guardian* (18 Nov 2000): https://www.theguardian.com/theguardian/2000/nov/18/weekend7.weekend2.

28 Ann Saddlemyer, *Becoming George: The Life of Mrs. W.B. Yeats* (Oxford: Oxford Univ. Press, 2002), 231–32.

29 Miranda Seymour, "Why Garsington Manor was Britain's most scandalous wartime retreat," *The Guardian* July 25, 2014.

30 Aldous Huxley, *Crome Yellow* (Columbia, SC, 2018; 1921).

31 See Gathorne-Hardy, *Ottoline*, 78. Huxley at least, for his part, was remorseful of using details from Garsington.

32 See Peter Bowering, *Aldous Huxley: A Study of the Major Novels* (London: Bloomsbury, 2013), 33ff.

33 Quoted in Maev Kennedy, "The real Lady Chatterley: society hostess loved and parodied by Bloomsbury group," *The Guardian* October 10, 2006 (https://www.theguardian.com/uk/2006/oct/10/books.booksnews).

34 Ottoline wrote in her memoir that she at first found Eliot "dull, dull, dull. He never moves his lips but speaks in an even and monotonous voice. . . . Where does his queer neurasthenic poetry come from, I wonder. . . . How very foreign Eliot seemed to me then...." Gathorne-Hardy, *Ottoline*, 101–102.

35 Peter Ackroyd, *T.S. Eliot: A Life* (New York: Simon and Schuster, 1984), 73–74.

36 *Letters, Vol. 1*, xix.

37 Crawford, *Young Eliot*, 244. Vivienne records in her diaries (Bodleian MS.Eng. misc.f.532 is her 1919 diary) her frequent battle with migraine headaches.

38 Ackroyd, *T.S. Eliot*, 89.

39 See Vivienne's diaries, now in the rare books collections, Bodleian Library, Oxford.

40 His copy is at Princeton University Library: Jessie L. Weston, *From Ritual to Romance* (Cambridge, University Press, 1920), Rare Books (Ex)3758.7.96.2.

41 See Lawrence Rainey (ed.), *The Annotated Waste Land with Eliot's Contemporary Prose* (New Haven and London: Yale Univ. Press, 2005), 16, 37–38.

42 Vivienne records in her diary under January 8, 1919: "Cable came saying Tom's father is dead. Had to wait all day till Tom came home. . . . Most terrible. Slight migraine. A fearful day & evening" (Bodleian MS.Eng.misc.f.532).

43 For a discussion of the medievalism of Eliot and Pound, see Michael Alexander, *Medievalism: The Middle Ages in Modern England* (New Haven and London: Yale Univ. Press, 2017), chs. 11 and 12.

44 Weston, *From Ritual to Romance*, 177.

45 Ackroyd, *T.S. Eliot*, 155–57.

46 Letter to Ottoline Morrell (undated), Lady Ottoline Morrell Collection, Ransom Center, Univ. of Texas at Austin, 6.3. Compare with the letter to Ottoline dated June 18, 1923: "It means so much to find fresh and untried minds and unspoiled lives: one doesn't meet many in London. I should like nothing better than to give a course of lectures in Oxford, if we can arrange it."

47 Letter to Ottoline Morrell (dated Thursday, ?), Lady Ottoline Morrell Collection, Ransom Center, Univ. of Texas at Austin, 6.3: "I do wish that I could get a connection with Oxford. Will you advertise me, when you can?"

48 See Nigel Nicolson (ed.), *A Change of Perspective: Letters of Virginia Woolf, Vol. III, 1923–28* (1994), 457–58.

49 Ackroyd, *T.S. Eliot*, 162.

50 See Walter Hooper (ed.), *The Collected Letters of C.S. Lewis, Vol. I* (San Francisco: HarperCollins, 2004), 529; and discussion in Chapter Ten below.

51 Some of the details of this feud-turned-friendship are traced in James Patrick, *The Magdalen Metaphysicals: Idealism and Orthodoxy at Oxford, 1901–1945* (Mercer Univ. Press, 1985), xx–xxii; and Jonathan Fruoco, "C.S. Lewis and T.S. Eliot: Questions of Identity," in *Persona and Paradox: Issues of Identity for C.S. Lewis, His Friends and Associates* (Cambridge Scholars Publishing, 2012).

52 A war perhaps still reflected in the critical studies of Eliot and his works, almost none of which mention Lewis.

53 Valerie Eliot and Hugh Haughton (eds.), *The Letters of T.S. Eliot, Vol. 2: 1923–25* (London: Faber and Faber, 2009), 813–14.

54 Lord David Cecil, Introduction to Carolyn G. Heilbrun (ed.), *Lady Ottoline's Album* (London: Michael Joseph, 1976), 13.

55 Alexander, *Medievalism*, 207.

56 See T.S. Eliot, *The Letters of T. S. Eliot: Volume 6: 1932–1933* (New Haven and London: Yale Univ. Press, 2016), 686–87; and Matthew J. Bruccoli (ed.), *F. Scott Fitzgerald: A Life in Letters* (2005), 227.

57 J. Brett Langstaff, *Oxford—1914* (New York: Vantage Press, 1965), frontispiece.

58 Ibid., 23.

59 Ibid., 255.

60 Ibid., 275.

61 Ibid., 138.

62 Ibid., 190–91.

6 MAJOR GATSBY IN TRINITY QUAD: OXFORD AND THE GREAT WAR

1 This broadening of perspectives on the First World War is in large part due to the Great War projects sponsored by the Bodleian Library and the University of Oxford: see, for example, the War Poets Digital Archive (http://www.oucs.ox.ac.uk/ww1lit/) and the Great War Archive (http://www.oucs.ox.ac.uk/ww1lit/gwa). I was fortunate to be a part of the "Globalising and Localising

the Great War Programme" (http://greatwar.history.ox.ac.uk) one of the many research projects spawned at Oxford from the Great War centenary commemorations.

2   F. Scott Fitzgerald, Review of H.G. Welles' *God, the Invisible King* (1917), *The Nassau Literary Magazine* 73 (June 1917), 153.

3   Williams/Hadfield Papers, Bodleian Library, Box 5, Fol. 1.

4   See John Garth, *Tolkien at Exeter College: How an Oxford Undergraduate Created Middle-earth* (Oxford: Exeter College, 2014), 39–41.

5   Wylie, "The Rhodes Scholars," 104.

6   Materials relating to Hawkins were collected by Hilda Margaret Pickard-Cambridge and donated to the Bodleian Library, Oxford MSS.Top.Oxon.d.665.

7   Anne Keene, *Oxford: The American Connection* (Oxford: Temple Rock Publications, 1990), iii.

8   Wylie, "The Rhodes Scholars," 105.

9   Keene, *Oxford*, 34–35.

10   See Kenny, "The Rhodes Trust," 18; and *The History of the University of Oxford: Volume VIII: The Twentieth Century*, 18–20.

11   Frank Aydelotte, "Rhodes Scholars and the War," *The American Oxonian* 1, no. 2 (October 1914), 86.

12   "War-time Difficulties," *The American Oxonian* 4, no. 4 (October 1917), 143.

13   Wyatt Rushton, "A Note on Oxford Colleges and American Fraternities," *The American Oxonian* 4, no. 3 (July 1917), 112–15 (113).

14   Parkin, "The Scholarships Postponed During the War," *The American Oxonian* 4, no. 4 (October 1917), 143–45.

15   Numbers taken from *Oxford Magazine*. See the editorial, "Numbers in Residence at Oxford," *The American Oxonian* 5, no. 2 (April 1918), 61.

16   Clare Hopkins, *Trinity: 450 Years of an Oxford College Community* (Oxford: Oxford Univ. Press, 2005), 347.

17   Bodleian MSS.Top.Oxon.d.664, fol. 10.

18   Henry S. Canby, "Impressions of Oxford in War-time," *The American Oxonian* 5, no. 4 (October 1918), 116.

19   Philip and Carol Zaleski, *The Fellowship: The Literary Lives of the Inklings* (New York: Farrar, Straus & Giroux, 2016), 8.

20   Rushton, "A Note on Oxford Colleges," 112.

21   Canby, "Impressions of Oxford," 116.

22   *Letters of T.S. Eliot*, Vol. I, 75.

23   See "John Masefield," *The War Poets Association* (http://www.warpoets.org /poets/john-masefield-1878–1967/).

24   See John Masefield, "Roadways," in *The Story of a Round-house, and other poems* (New York: Macmillan, 1916); idem, *The Old Front Line* (London: William Heinemann, 1917); idem, *The Battle of the Somme* (London: Heinemann, 1919).

25   See John Masefield, *The War and the Future* (New York: The Macmillan Company, 1918); idem, *St. George and the Dragon* (London: William Heinemann,

1919); idem, *War Poems from the Yale Review* (New Haven: Yale University Press, 1919).

26   T. Means (Secretary), "Personal News by Classes," *The American Oxonian* 8 (1921), 108.

27   The Reserve Officer Training Corps had been created by the National Defense Act of 1916.

28   Michael S. Neiberg, "Pershing's Decision: How the United States Fought its First Modern Coalition War," www.army.mil (December 10, 2010).

29   Robert Blake (ed.), *The Private Papers of Douglas Haig 1914–1919* (London: Eyre & Spottiswoode, 1952), 318.

30   Ibid., 338.

31   It is the First Division in the *Trimalchio* manuscript and in the first printing of *The Great Gatsby*, then changed to the Third Division in subsequent printings of the novel.

32   Gatsby's and Nick's relating of these facts to the reader only makes sense historically if Gatsby fought with the Third Division (on the Marne) until July 1918 and then was transferred to either the Twenty-Eighth or Seventy-Seventh Divisions to participate in the Argonne Forest battle in September: see Lehan, *The Great Gatsby*, 4; and the explanatory notes by Bruccoli in Fitzgerald, *The Great Gatsby* (Cambridge, 2013), 188, 192.

33   Statistics from the U.S. Army: http://www.history.army.mil/html/reference/army_flag/wwi.html.

34   J.M. Winter, "Oxford and the First World War," in Brian Harrison (ed.), *The History of the University of Oxford: Volume VIII: The Twentieth Century* (Oxford: Clarendon Press, 1994), 10.

35   Anson Phelps Stokes, *Educational Plans for the American Army Abroad* (New York: Association Press, 1918), 3, 6.

36   George E. MacLean, "British Universities and American Soldier-Students," *The Landmark* 1 (June 1919): 365–70 (366). See also the announcement in *The Stars and Stripes* 1 no. 34 (27 Sept 1918), 1–2.

37   MacLean, "British Universities," 365.

38   *The Stars and Stripes* December 6, 1918, 3.

39   At Queen's College, Oxford, each accepted student was interview by the Pro-Provost, who wrote a brief description and attached it to the original, signed "Student's Record and Authorization" form (from the A.E.F. and the YMCA) in their College Entrance Book. Queen's College Archives, courtesy Michael Riordan, College Archivist.

40   Homer L. Bruce, "Organizing the Invasion." *The American Oxonian* (January 1920): 1–6.

41   R.T. Taylor, "The Social Side of the Invasion," *The American Oxonian* 7, no. 1 (January 1920), 7–12 (7).

42   Letter to his father (27 Jan 1919), *Letters*, vol. I, 428.

43   *Balliol College Register*, October 1918 to October 1919, 17.

ENDNOTES

44 Melvin L. Brorby, "Our A.E.F. Universities," in Robert S. Crawford (ed), *The Wisconsin Alumni Magazine* 20, no. 10 (August 1919), 299.

45 Bruce, "Organizing," 3.

46 Taylor, "The Social Side," 10.

47 Capt. Herbert Stolz (California and Queen's, 1910), a star player at Oxford, was drafted for the A.E.F. rugby team that competed in the Inter-Allied Games in June 1919: see *The Stars and Stripes* (May 2, 1919), 7.

48 Frederick S. Mead (ed.), *Harvard's Military Record in the World War* (Boston: Harvard Alumni Association, 1921), 679.

49 New College, for example, agreed to accept 15 officers, but only offered rooms for 10. See H.W.B. Joseph, Minutes of the Meeting of the Warden and Tutors for January 17, 1919, New College Archives.

50 T.G. Brown, "HELL, YES!" *The Stars and Stripes* (March 14, 1919), qtd. in Cornebise, Soldier-Scholars, iii–iv.

51 November, 1916, from *Songs for a Little House* (1916).

52 Taylor, "The Social Side," 11.

53 Ibid., 11.

54 Ibid., 10.

55 Ibid., 9–10.

56 H.W.B. Joseph, Minutes for the Meeting of the Warden and Tutors, 25 April 1919, New College Archives.

57 John R. Dyer, "What the A.E.F. Thought of Oxford," reprinted in *The American Oxonian* 7, no. 1 (January 1920): 13–14 (13).

58 C. Grant Robertson, "An Oxford Impression of the American Army Students." *The American Oxonian* 7, no. 1 (January 1920): 15–19 (15).

59 Robertson, "An Oxford Impression," 17–18.

60 Remarks from Keble College tutors on the A.E.F. students, Keble College Archives.

61 C.W. Chenoweth, "An American's Impressions of Oxford and Mansfield," *Mansfield College Magazine* 10, no. 17 (July 1919): 281–84.

62 Ibid., 295.

63 Dyer, "What the A.E.F. Thought," 14.

64 *Stars and Stripes* June 13, 1919, 4 col. 2.

65 Lydia Eustis had a distinguished, if short, service in the Red Cross and kept records of activities at Camp Sheridan, residing there in its Hostess House (the only place in camp where women could visit soldiers). "It is all very interesting," she wrote in a report of August 1918, "and like our Mothers we will be handing down war stories even unto the third and fourth generation." Lydia Eustis Rogers Papers, Birmingham Public Library Archives, 869.1.3.

66 After graduating from Princeton (where he studied History and was a member of the Triangle Club) and serving in the Navy, Wayne Rogers became a professional actor and achieved fame for his role as "Trapper" John McIntyre in

the television series *M*A*S*H* from 1972–78, and much later was a financial commentator on American television's FOX News.

67 J.M. Winter, "Oxford and the First World War, in Brian Harrison (ed.), *The History of the University of Oxford: Volume VIII: The Twentieth Century* (Oxford: Clarendon Press, 1994), 24.

68 *The Great Gatsby*, manuscript chapter 7, 2. Princeton University Library.

69 Fitzgerald, *Trimalchio*, 117.

70 Bruccoli (ed.), *The Great Gatsby* (NY: Cambridge University Press, 1993), 193. It may be significant that Nick claims that his family can trace their lineage back to the Dukes of Buccleuch.

7 THE CASTLE AND THE GRAIL: J.R.R. TOLKIEN, C. S. LEWIS, AND MODERN MEDIEVALISM

1   *F. Scott Fitzgerald: A Life in Letters*, 68.

2   The only Tolkien family sanctioned biography is the now somewhat dated Humphrey Carpenter, *J.R.R. Tolkien: A Biography* (Boston: Houghton Mifflin, 1977; 2000). For Tolkien as an academic medievalist (as well as author of medievalism), see Tom Shippey, *J.R.R. Tolkien: Author of the Century* (Boston: Houghton Mifflin, 2001); idem, *The Road to Middle-earth* (Boston: Houghton Mifflin, 2003); Dimitra Fimi, *Tolkien, Race, and Cultural History: From Faeries to Hobbits* (New York: Palgrave Macmillan, 2009); and Snyder, *The Making of Middle-earth* (2013).

3   Garth, *Tolkien at Exeter College*, 4–7.

4   In Stapledon *Magazine* (December 1913).

5   See John Garth, *Tolkien and the Great War: The Threshold of Middle-earth* (London: Harper Collins, 2003); idem, *Tolkien at Exeter College: How an Oxford Undergraduate Created Middle-earth* (Oxford: Exeter College, 2014); and Catherine MacIlwaine (ed.), *Tolkien: Maker of Middle-earth* (Oxford: Bodleian Library, 2018), the catalog accompanying the summer 2018 exhibition of the same name at the Westin Library of the Bodleian.

6   Garth, *Tolkien at Exeter College*, 12–13.

7   Ibid., 19.

8   Tolkien, *Letters*, 53.

9   See Tolkien, Letters, 95; and Garth, Tolkien at Exeter College, 37.

10 Gathorne-Hardy, *Ottoline at Garsington*, 92–93.

11 T. W. Earp, "Broceliande," in *Oxford Poetry 1916* (Oxford: Blackwell, 1916), 19–20.

12 J.R.R. Tolkien, "Goblin Feet," from *Oxford Poetry 1915*, G.D.H. Cole and T.W. Earp (eds.), (Oxford: Blackwell, 1915), 64–65. Earp, Dorothy Sayers, and Aldous Huxley also made contributions to this issue of *Oxford Poetry*.

13 J.R.R. Tolkien, "The Wanderer's Allegiance," quoted in Garth, *Tolkien and the Great War*, 132.

14 See McIlwaine (ed.), *Tolkien*, 16 and n.6. The club's minutes show that future Inklings Nevill Coghill and Hugo Dyson were present for the reading.

15   See Tom Shippey, "Tolkien and 'that noble northern spirit,'" in McIlwaine (ed.), *Tolkien*, 58–69.

16   From a letter to Anne Barrett, in *The Letters of J.R.R. Tolkien*, Humphrey Carpenter (ed.), (Boston: Houghton Mifflin, 2000), 350.

17   See, for example, *Letters of J.R.R. Tolkien*, 69–70.

18   Letter to Carole Batten-Phelps (Autumn 1971), in *Letters*, 412.

19   From a letter to Christopher Tolkien (July 31, 1944), in *Letters*, 89.

20   Michael D. Thomas, "Unlikely Knights, Improbable Heroes: Inverse, Antimodernist Paradigms in Tolkien and Cervantes," in Ralph C. Wood (ed.), *Tolkien Among the Moderns* (Notre Dame, IN: Univ. of Notre Dame Press, 2015), 79–94.

21   See Theresa Freda Nicolay, *Tolkien and the Modernists: Literary Responses to the Dark New Days of the 20th Century* (Jefferson, NC: McFarland, 2014).

22   E.L. Risden, *Tolkien's Intellectual Landscape* (Jefferson, NC: McFarland & Co., 2015), 84.

23   Yet, Tolkien's philosophy as expressed by Thorin in *The Hobbit*—"If more of us valued food and cheer and song above hoarded gold, it would be a merrier world"—seems close to that of Fitzgerald's mentor, Monsignor Fay, as described by a friend: "[he] clearly loved good company, good food and drink": see Brown, *Paradise Lost*, 36.

24   See Snyder, *The Making of Middle-earth*, 224–27; and Corrigan, *So We Read On*, 208.

25   Oser, 65–66.

26   Lehan, *The Great Gatsby*, 62.

27   See James Patrick, *The Magdalen Metaphysicals: Idealism and Orthodoxy at Oxford, 1901–1945* (Macon, GA: Mercer Univ. Press, 1985).

28   G. H. Claypole, Lewis's lieutenant and adjutant officer in O.T.C., remarked on April 30, 1917, "Likely to make a useful [infantry] officer but will not have had sufficient training for commission before end of June." Public Record Office ref. WO 339/105408, 58141, fol. 2 (copies of Lewis's war record are kept in the Bodleian Library, Oxford, MS Facs. b. 98).

29   Quoted in Brenton D. G. Dickieson, "Mixed Metaphors and Hyperlinked Worlds: A Study of Intertextuality in C. S. Lewis's Ransom Cycle," in *The Inklings and King Arthur*, edited by Sørina Higgins (Berkeley, CA: Apocryphile Press, 2017), 82. Lewis had begun calling his childhood friend, Arthur Greeves, "Galahad" in correspondence the year before.

30   Colin Duriez, "Lewis and Military Service: War and Remembrance (1917–1918)," in Bruce L. Edwards, (ed.). *C. S. Lewis: Life, Works, and Legacy, Vol. 1: An Examined Life* (Westport, CT: Praeger, 2007), 79–101 (83).

31   The report from the Army Medical Board indicated that Lewis was struck by shrapnel in his left chest, left wrist, and left upper leg and was having breathing trouble after the shrapnel wounds had healed because one piece was left in his left lung: P.R.O. ref. WO 339/105408, 58141, fol. 10 (Bodleian MS Facs. b. 98.).

32   Cuneo, *Selected Literary Letters*, 57.

33 *The Collected Letters of C. S. Lewis, Vol. 1: Family Letters 1905–1931*, edited by Walter Hooper (San Francisco: HarperCollins, 2004), 407. The sea-sickness joke is a reference to the poem "A Channel Passage," by Rupert Brooke.

34 "Lewis Papers: Memoirs of the Lewis Family 1850–1930," vol. VI, 98; quoted in C. S. Lewis, *The Collected Poems of C. S. Lewis*, ed. by Walter Hooper (London: HarperCollins, 1994), xiii.

35 Baker would become moderately successful on the London stage. When Lewis visited him at the Old Vic in the summer of 1922, Baker reminded Lewis of his prediction that "my chimney would turn into a spire" (Lewis, *All My Road Before Me*, 94). See also Zaleski and Zaleski, *The Fellowship*, 92–94.

36 Owen Barfield Papers, Bodleian Library, Dep.c.1072. A large group of these letters from 1928 (68 pages of Lewis prose plus another 15 pages of his notes on Barfield's reply) Lewis called *Clivi Hamiltonis Summae Metaphysices Contra Anthroposophos Libri II* ("Clive Hamilton's Treatise on Metaphysics Against the Anthroposophists in Two Books") is modeled on the great medieval *Summa* of Thomas Aquinas.

37 See Simon Blaxland-de Lange, *Owen Barfield: Romanticism Come of Age* (Temple Lodge, 2006).

38 Lewis, entry in his diary for July 9, 1922; idem., dedication in *Allegory of Love*.

39 McGrath, *The Intellectual World*, 36–39.

40 His diary and marginalia written in his textbooks single out his Old English tutor, Edith Elizabeth Wardale, for boring him, and especially philologist H. C. Wyld, for being a bully and a terrible lecturer. Tom Shippey, "The Lewis Diaries: C. S. Lewis and the English Faculty in the 1920s," in Roger White et al. (eds.), *C. S. Lewis and His Circle: Essays and Memoirs from the Oxford C. S. Lewis Society* (Oxford: Oxford Univ. Press, 2015), 135–49; and Simon Horobin (pers. comm.).

41 Patrick, *Magdalen*, xvii.

42 C. S. Lewis, "Shelley, Dryden, and Mr. Eliot."

43 For the epistolary debates between Lewis and Eliot, see Andrew P. Cuneo, *Selected Literary Letters of C. S. Lewis* (Doctoral thesis. Univ. of Oxford, 2001), Vol. II (and commentary in Vol. I, Chap. 1); and Jonathan Fruoco, "C. S. Lewis and T. S. Eliot: Questions of Identity," in *Persona and Paradox: Issues of Identity for C. S. Lewis, His Friends and Associates* (Cambridge Scholars Publishing, 2012).

44 The essay is included in his collection of 1939, *Rehabilitations and Other Essays* (Freeport, NY: Books for Libraries Press, 1939; repr. 1972). It was sparked by Eliot's 1932 essay on Dryden.

45 Cuneo, *Selected Literary Letters*, Vo. I, 4–5. Cf. Sir Philip Sidney, *The Defense of Poesy*. Lewis in a later epistle to Eliot (June 2, 1931, Bodleian MS. Eng. Lett. c. 220/2), describes his views as "a neo-Aristotelian theory of literature."

46 Alistair McGrath, *The Intellectual World of C. S. Lewis* (Oxford: Wiley-Blackwell, 2014), 39–40. McGrath is quoting from Eliot's Quartet No. 1, *Burnt Norton* (1935), Part I.

47   Lewis, *Surprised by Joy*, 209. See also Zaleski and Zaleski, *The Fellowship*, 161.

48   For relevant examples in medieval theology, see McGrath, *Intellectual World*, 107–8 and notes.

49   Patrick, *Magdalen*, xvii–xviii.

50   Lehan, *The Great Gatsby*, 73.

51   John Betjeman, *Collected Poems* (NY: Farrar, Straus & Giroux, 2006), 96.

52   Ibid., 475–6.

53   A. N. Wilson, *C. S. Lewis: A Biography* (London: Collins, 1990), 98–99. Several letters of C. S. Lewis to John Betjeman have been collected at the Wade Center, Wheaton College, with copies in the Bodleian Library (Oxford, MS.Facs.d.144., fols. 78–81).

54   Zaleski and Zaleski, *The Fellowship*, 168.

55   Roger Lancelyn Green and Walter Hooper, *C. S. Lewis: The Authorised and Revised Biography* (London: HarperCollins, 2003), xi. Green recalls that Lewis threw a lunch party in December 1949 at Magdalen for the soon-to-be illustrator of his *Chronicles*, Pauline Baynes, who had just illustrated Tolkien's *Farmer Giles of Ham* (1949). The party was, appropriately, in the Wilde Room at Magdalen.

56   See William Luther White, *The Image of Man in C. S. Lewis* (London: Hodder and Stoughton, 1970), 221–22.

57   See Humphrey Carpenter, *The Inklings* (1978; London: HarperCollins, 1997); and now Zaleski and Zaleski, *The Fellowship*, esp. 194ff.

58   From a letter to Dick Plotz (September 12, 1965), *Letters*, 359–62. Lewis's dogged encouragement was a major factor in Tolkien's completion of *The Lord of the Rings*, begun shortly after *The Hobbit* appeared in 1937 and published in three parts in 1954 and 1955. "Professor Tolkien's second Hobbit is still unfinished," wrote Lewis to one of his readers in 1947, "he works like a coral insect you know!" (Bodleian MS.Facs.d.144, folio 72).

59   Zaleski and Zalseski, 198.

60   G.R. Evans, *The University of Oxford: A New History* (London: I.B. Tauris, 2014), 18.

61   John Garth, "Tolkien and the Inklings," in McIlwaine (ed.), *Tolkien*, 24.

62   See Humphrey Carpenter, *The Inklings*; Zaleski and Zaleski, *The Fellowship*; and Grevel Lindop, *Charles Williams: The Third Inkling* (Oxford: Oxford Univ. Press, 2015). Williams's attraction to magic and the occult (troubling for Tolkien) and his obsessive relationship with female colleagues are dealt with in the last two. Letters, notes, and unpublished Williams material can now be viewed in the Charles Williams/Hadfield Papers at the Bodleian Library.

63   See Jonathan Fruoco, "C. S. Lewis and T. S. Eliot: Questions of Identity," in *Persona and Paradox: Issues of Identity for C. S. Lewis, His Friends and Associates* (Cambridge Scholars Publishing, 2012).

64   *The Collected Letters of C. S. Lewis, Vol. II*, 164 note 37.

65   William Griffin, *Clive Staples Lewis: A Dramatic Life* (San Francisco: Harper and Rowe, 1986), xix.

66 B. F. Wilson, "Notes on Personalities, IV—F. Scott Fitzgerald," *Smart Set*, 73 (April 1924), 29–33; repr. in Brucoli and Baughman (eds.), *Conversations with F. Scott Fitzgerald*, 60–66 (62).

67 Letter to Zelda (September 14, 1940).

68 Matthew J. Bruccoli and Jackson R. Bryer (eds.), *F. Scott Fitzgerald in His Own Time* (Kent, OH: Kent State Univ. Press, 1971), 270.

69 Brucoli and Baughman (eds.), *Conversations*, 65.

70 See discussion in Chapter Eight.

71 *F. Scott Fitzgerald Papers*, Box 33, Folder 3: *This Side of Paradise* (notes for film scenario). Princeton University Library.

72 See, for example, Deborah Davis Schlacks, "Echoes of the Middle Ages: Teaching the Medieval in *The Great Gatsby*," in Jackson R. Bryer and Nancy P. VanArsdale (eds.), *Approaches to Teaching Fitzgerald's* The Great Gatsby (MLA Publications, 2009), 162–68; Letha Audhuy, "*Waste Land* Myths and Symbols," in Harold Bloom (ed. and intro), *F. Scott Fitzgerald's The Great Gatsby* (New York: Chelsea House Publishers, 1986), 109–22; Barbara Tepa Lupack, "F. Scott Fitzgerald's 'Following of a Grail,'" *Arthuriana* 4, no. 4 (Winter 1994), 324–47; and Alan Lupack and Barbara Tepa Lupack, *King Arthur in America* (Cambridge: D.S. Brewer, 1999), ch. 5.

73 Bewley, 15.

74 See, for example, Berman, 89.

75 Berman, 111.

76 Churchwell, *Careless People*, 83–84.

77 Long, *The Achieving*, 158. Long also sees in Gatsby elements of Phoebus Apollo and of Adam.

78 Berman, 63.

79 Walter Hooper (pers. comm.), who was present along with Tolkien's son Christopher.

80 In his 1923 review of Sherwood Anderson's *Many Marriages*, Fitzgerald refers to the theme of "the noble fool which has dominated tragedy from Don Quixote to *Lord Jim*" (Herald Tribune [NY] March 4, 1923).

81 Lehan, *The Great Gatsby*, 84, referring to ideas in Spengler's *The Decline of the West* (1918–22) and their influence on Fitzgerald in *Gatsby* and in his *Count Philippe* stories.

82 Falaise, Harry Guggenheim's 216-acre estate at Sand's Point with its mansion based on a thirteenth-century Norman manor house, may have been the inspiration for Fitzgerald's description of Gatsby's mansion: see Churchwell, *Careless People*, 90.

83 Barbara Tepa Lupack, "F. Scott Fitzgerald's 'Following of a Grail,'" *Arthuriana* 4, no. 4 (Winter 1994), 324–47 (338).

84 See Letha Audhuy, "*Waste Land* Myths and Symbols"; and discussion in chapter three.

85 Lehan, *The Great Gatsby*, 32–33.

86 Christopher A. Snyder, "Jay Gatsby as the Fair Unknown: Arthurian Resonances in Fitzgerald," paper delivered to the International Medieval Congress, May 2017.

87 T. H. White, *The Ill-Made Knight* (1940), incorporated in White, *The Once and Future King* (1958). White wrote a thesis on Malory while an undergraduate at Queen's College, Cambridge in the 1920s, became an expert on falconry, and later translated a medieval Latin bestiary.

88 Kruse (*F. Scott Fitzgerald at Work*, 89) states that "riding a horse while serving as an officer had helped to make social disadvantage disappear" for Gatsby, but only for the duration of the War. Without horse and uniform on Long Island, Gatsby could not even use his newfound wealth to buy his way into the East Egg world of polo and leisure.

89 Tennyson, *Idylls of the King*, "The Holy Grail." In both the medieval original and Tennyson's retelling, Perceval's sister cuts off her long golden hair to make a sword-belt for Galahad, literally binding him to her.

90 For an author famous for his extravagant and rebellious lifestyle, Fitzgerald was remarkably conservative when it came to depicting sex in fiction: see Donaldson, 73–75.

91 Piper, *F. Scott Fitzgerald*, 121–23.

92 Schlacks, 165.

93 See, for example, William Bysshe Stein, "Gatsby's Morgan le Fay," *Fitzgerald Newsletter*, 67; and Allen, *Candles*, 111.

94 Allen, *Candles*, esp. 22–25 (the Basil stories), 76–78 and 81 (*This Side of Paradise*), 100–101 ("Absolution"), 111–15 (*Gatsby*), and 128–31 (*Tender is the Night*).

95 Vogel, "Civilization's Going to Pieces," 47.

96 The description of Nick is from Long, *The Achieving*, 145.

97 In an early draft, Gatsby's estate includes a windmill with a bar inside and flashing lights on its turning blades.

98 James H. Meredith, "Fitzgerald and War," in Kirk Curnutt (ed.), *A Historical Guide to F. Scott Fitzgerald* (Oxford: Oxford Univ. Press, 2004), 163–213 (166, 202–3).

99 For discussion of the publishing history, see Peter L. Hays, "Philippe, 'Count of Darkness,' and F. Scott Fitzgerald, Feminist?" in Bryer (ed.), *New Essays*, 291–304.

100 Ibid., 292.

101 *F. Scott Fitzgerald Papers*, Princeton University, Box 20.

102 J.R.R. Tolkien would, early in his career, work on new editions and translations of *Pearl*, *Ancrene Riwle*, and *Beowulf*: see Tom Shippey, *Road to Middle-earth*.

103 Hays, "The 'Count of Darkness' Stories," 297–98. Hays suggests that Eliot's *The Waste Land* and Weston's *From Ritual to Romance* are responsible for Philippe's similarities with Parzival, but "if Fitzgerald extended his reading of source material beyond Weston, he would have found that Chrétien de Troyes's patron . . . was Count Philip of Flanders" (298). Compare Fitzgerald's attempts to write a medieval novel with that of another American author imbued with *noblesse oblige*—John Steinbeck, whose unfinished, posthumous novel, *The Acts*

of King Arthur and His Noble Knights (1976), subjected Malory's *Morte D'Arthur* to a similar (though more successful) updating and modern realism.

104 See Janet Lewis, "Fitzgerald's Philippe, Count of Darkness," *Fitzgerald/Hemingway Annual* 7 (1975): 7–32.

105 Meredith, 206.

106 Hays, "The 'Count of Darkness' Stories," 295.

107 Horst H. Kruse, "F. Scott Fitzgerald and Marry Harriman Rumsey: An Untold Story," *The F. Scott Fitzgerald Review* 13, no. 1 (2015), 146–62.

108 Brown, *Paradise Lost*, 110.

109 Lehan, *The Great Gatsby*, 98–99.

110 Berman, 63, 120–21.

111 James H. Meredith, "World War I," in Bryant Mangum (ed.), *F. Scott Fitzgerald in Context*. (New York: Cambridge Univ. Press, 2013), 136–43 (141).

112 Kruse, "F. Scott Fitzgerald and Mary Harriman Rumsey," 158.

113 Matthew J. Bruccoli, *Some Sort of Epic Grandeur: The Life of F. Scott Fitzgerald* (New York: Harcourt, 1981), xx.

114 Brown, *Paradise Lost*, 58–59.

115 See Jane S. Livingston, "On the Art of Zelda Fitzgerald," in Lanahan (ed), *Zelda, An Illustrated Life*, 82–83.

116 Ibid., 83.

117 Zelda was contrite in a subsequent letter (dated February 1920): "Darling Heart, our fairy tale is almost ended, and we're going to marry and live happily ever afterward just like the princess in her tower who worried you so much." See Bruccoli (ed.), *Collected Writings of Zelda Fitzgerald*, 447.

8 "A MEADOW LARK AMONG THE SMOKE STACKS": OXFORD AND PRINCETON

1 F. Scott Fitzgerald, "Author's House," *Esquire* 6 (1936), 40, 138; reprinted in *Afternoon of an Author: A Selection of Uncollected Stories and Essays* (New York: Scribner's, 1957), 185.

2 Letter to Edmund Wilson (1920), in Bruccoli and Duggan (eds.), *Correspondence*, 76. See also Donaldson, *Fool for Love*, 2.

3 Bruccoli, *Some Sort of Epic Grandeur*, 18.

4 While Irish stereotypes (e.g., drunk, violent leprechauns) were abundant in eighteenth and nineteenth century Britain, xenophobia in Reconstruction America manifest in cartoons depicting both Irish and African Americans with simian features: see Lewis P. Curtis, *Apes and Angels*, 2nd ed. (Washington, D.C.: Smithsonian, 1997); and Noel Ignatiev, *How the Irish Became White* (NY and London: Routledge, 2009).

5 See Deborah Davis Schlacks, "St. Paul, Minnesota, St. Paul Academy, and the *St. Paul Academy Then and Now*," in Mangum (ed.), *F. Scott Fitzgerald in Context*, 105–14; and Brown, *Paradise Lost*, 17–22.

6 Brown, *Paradise Lost*, 22.

7 Donaldson, *Fool for Love*, 11.

8   See Pearl James, "A Catholic Boyhood: The Newman School, the *Newman News*, and Monsignor Cyril Sigourney Webster Fay," in Bryant Mangum (ed.), *F. Scott Fitzgerald in Context*. (New York: Cambridge Univ. Press, 2013), 114–25.

9   Brown, *Paradise Lost*, 35.

10   Quoted in Bruccoli, *Some Sort of Epic Grandeur*, 38. See also Allen, *Candles*, xii.

11   Edward Gillin, "Princeton, New Jersey, Princeton University, and the *Nassau Literary Magazine*" in Mangum (ed.), *F. Scott Fitzgerald in Context*, 126–35.

12   See J. Karabel, *The Chosen: The Hidden History of Admission and Exclusion at Harvard, Yale and Princeton* (Boston: Houghton Mifflin, 2005), 62.

13   His annotated copy of his Old and Middle English poetry textbook is now at Princeton University Library: Henry Spackman Pancoast and John Duncan Ernst Spaeth, *Early English Poems* (New York, H. Holt and Company, 1911), Rare Books (Ex) 3598.694.

14   Gillin, "Princeton," 127.

15   Alexander Leitch, *A Princeton Companion* (Princeton, NJ: Princeton Univ. Press, 1978).

16   Gillin, "Princeton," 128.

17   Interview with Charles C. Baldwin, in Matthew J. Bruccoli, Scottie Fitzgerald Smith, and Joan P. Kerr (eds.), *The Romantic Egoists: A Pictorial Autobiography from the Scrapbooks and Albums of F. Scott and Zelda Fitzgerald* (Columbia, SC: Univ. of South Carolina Press, 1974), 23.

18   See photo in Bruccoli, Smith, and Kerr, 24.

19   Gillin, "Princeton," 130.

20   See Anne Margaret Daniel "What Were F. Scott Fitzgerald's Real Models for the Houses of The Great Gatsby?" *The Huffington Post* (Dec 6, 2017): https://www.huffingtonpost.com/anne-margaret-daniel/great-gatsby-houses_b_3222775.html.

21   F. Scott Fitzgerald, "The Spire and the Gargoyle," *Nassau Literary Magazine* (February 1917); reprinted in James L. West (ed.), *Spires and Gargoyles: Early Writings, 1909–1919* (Cambridge: Cambridge Univ. Press, 2010).

22   See discussion in Gerald Pike, "A Style is Born: The Rhetoric of Loss in 'The Spire and the Gargoyle,'" in Jackson R. Bryer (ed. and intro), *New Essays on F. Scott Fitzgerald's Neglected Stories* (Columbia, MO: Univ. of Missouri Press, 1996), 9–23.

23   Fitzgerald, "The Spire," 161.

24   Ibid., 162.

25   Ibid., 163.

26   Ibid., 168.

27   Ibid., 168–9.

28   Pike, "A Style is Born," 22.

29   Gillin, "Princeton," 134.

30   F. Scott Fitzgerald, "Princeton," in idem, *Afternoon of an Author*, edited by Arthur Mizener (New York: Scribners, 1958), 72.

31   Letter to John Grier Hibben (June 3, 1920), in *Letters*, 461–62.

32   Fitzgerald, "Princeton," 72.

33   See discussion in W. Bruce Leslie, "Dreaming Spires in New Jersey," in *The Educational Legacy of Woodrow Wilson: From College to Nation*, ed. by James Axtell (University of Virginia Press, 2012). Leslie points out that these visits all occurred during summer vacation, not term time.

34   James Axtell, *The Making of Princeton University: From Woodrow Wilson to the Present* (Princeton and Oxford: Princeton Univ. Press, 2006).

35   Edith Reid, *Woodrow Wilson: The Caricature, the Myth, and the Man* (New York: Oxford Univ. Press, 1934), 100–101.

36   For discussion, see Axtell, *The Making of Princeton*, 112ff.

37   Axtell, *The Making of Princeton*, 9.

38   See Van Rossum, "Being Jewish at Princeton"; and Karabel, The Chosen.

39   See Axtell, *The Making of Princeton*, 7–10.

40   Bruccoli, *Some Sort of Epic Grandeur*, 46.

41   Axtell, *The Making of Princeton*, 5.

42   Ibid., 2.

43   Brown, *Paradise Lost*, 46.

44   John Peale Bishop, "Princeton," in *The Collected Essays of John Peale Bishop*, Edmund Wilson (ed.), (New York: Scribner's, 1948), 391–400; reprinted in Malcolm Cowley and Robert Cowley, *Fitzgerald and the Jazz Age* (New York: Scribner's, 1966), 10–16 (11).

45   See Alex Duke, *Importing Oxbridge: English Residential Colleges and American Universities* (New Haven, CT: Yale Univ. Press, 1996).

46   Wyatt Rushton, "A Note on Oxford Colleges and American Fraternities," *The American Oxonian* 4, no. 3 (July 1917), 113–15 (112).

47   Axtell, *The Making of Princeton*, 1–2, 14–17.

48   Brian Harrison, "College Life, 1918–1939," in idem (ed.), *The History of the University of Oxford: Volume VIII: The Twentieth Century* (Oxford: Clarendon Press, 1994), 81.

49   Axtell, *The Making of Princeton*, 17–18.

50   Turnbull (ed.), *The Letters*, 354–55.

51   Donaldson, *Fool for Love*, 18.

52   For a good recent assessment of Fitzgerald's military career and war stories, see James H. Meredith, "World War I," in Mangum (ed.), *F. Scott Fitzgerald in Context*, 136–43.

53   Scott Fitzgerald to his mother (November 14, 1917), in Bruccoli, Smith, and Kerr, 33.

54   Bruccoli, *Some Sort of Epic Grandeur*, 86.

55   The Scribner's letter of August 19, 1918, appears in Bruccoli, Smith, and Kerr, 34.

56   Newspaper articles from Zelda's scrapbook, Princeton University Library, reproduced in Bruccoli, Smith, and Kerr, 44–45.

57   "Introduction," in Eleanor Lanahan (ed.), *Zelda, An Illustrated Life: The Private World of Zelda Fitzgerald* (New York: Harry N. Abrams, 1996), 11.

58   Lydia Eustis Rogers Papers, Birmingham Public Library Archives, 869.1.6.

59   Bruccoli, *Some Sort of Epic Grandeur*, 93–94.

60   Brown, *Paradise Lost*, 74.

61   Meredith, "World War I," 136.

62   Ibid., 141.

63   Fitzgerald, "My Lost City," 108.

9 SCOTT AND ZELDA, MEET THE CHURCHILLS

1   F. Scott Fitzgerald, *May Day* (Smart Set Company, 1920; Brooklyn, NY: Melville House, 2009), 3.

2   *Tales of the Jazz Age* (1922).

3   Quoted in Alison Maloney, *Bright Young Things: Life in the Roaring Twenties* (Virgin Books, 2012), 72.

4   Ann Saddlemyer, B*ecoming George: The Life of Mrs. W. B. Yeats* (Oxford: Oxford Univ. Press, 2002), 239.

5   See Sam Dangremond, "Wait, Was *The Great Gatsby's* West Egg Actually Westport, Connecticut?" *Town & Country* (May 22, 2018): https://www.townandcountry mag.com/leisure/arts-and-culture/a20849751/west-egg-great-gatsby-westport -connecticut/.

6   See Bruccoli, *Some Sort of Epic Grandeur*, 149–51. Galsworthy had published C. S. Lewis's first professionally published poem, "Death in Battle," in his new periodical, *Reveille* 3 (February 1919).

7   Bruccoli, *Some Sort of Epic Grandeur*, 149; Turnbull, *Scott Fitzgerald*, 125.

8   See Bruccoli and Braughman (eds.), *Conversations*, 95. Edmund Wilson and John Peale Bishop teased Scott after the successful publication of *This Side of Paradise* that Scribner's should mount a Fitzgerald display in their bookstore window containing, among other items, "Copy of *Sinister Street*," "Original cocktail shaker used by Amory Blaine," and "First yellow silk shirt worn by Fitzgerald at the beginning of his great success": see Bruccoli, Smith, and Kerr, 61.

9   Bruccoli (ed.), *Collected Works of Zelda Fitzgerald*, 419–31 (420).

10   See Churchwell, *Careless People*, 86–87.

11   Letter to the Kalmans, Zelda Fitzgerald Papers, Princeton.

12   His obituary said he died suddenly of heart disease at his home on Fifth Avenue (Matthew Bruccoli Papers, University of South Carolina).

13   Waugh, "Let us Return to the Nineties: But not to Oscar Wilde," *Harper's Bazaar* (November 1930), reprinted in Waugh, *A Little Order*, 19–22.

14   John Kuehl and Jackson R. Bryer (eds.), *Dear Scott/Dear Max: The Fitzgerald-Perkins Correspondence* (New York: Scribner's, 1971), 37.

15   Hopkins, *A City in the Foreground* (London: Constable, 1921), 182.

16   F. Scott Fitzgerald, "Three Cities," *Brentano's Book Chat 1* (September–October 1921), 15, 28; reprinted in Matthew J. Bruccoli (ed.), *F. Scott Fitzgerald on Authorship* (Columbia, SC: Univ. of South Carolina Press, 1996), 51–52.

17   Quoted in Brucoli, *Some Sort of Epic Grandeur*, 150.

18   The novel was quite autobiographical. Keable, who rowed for Magdalene College, Cambridge, had Anglo-Catholic leanings and was ordained in 1911 but left the Church after an affair with a nurse while he was an army chaplain during the war. Living in Tahiti at the time *Gatsby* was written, Keable's prolific literary output included an essay on the origins of the cocktail (June 21, 1925, *New York Times*)! See Hugh Cecil, *The Flower of Battle: How Britain Wrote the Great War* (Secker and Warbury, 1995).

19   Zelda to Scottie, ca. 1944, quoted in Bruccoli, Smith, and Kerr (eds.), *The Romantic Egoists*, 84.

20   Letter to Maxwell Perkins, dated August 25, 1921. In Kuehl and Bryer (eds.), *Dear Scott/Dear Max*, 41.

21   Letter to John Jamieson (April 15, 1934), F. Scott Fitzgerald Papers, Princeton Libraries.

22   Piper, *F. Scott Fitzgerald: A Critical Portrait*, 102.

23   Born Elizabeth Asquith, daughter of the British Prime Minister Herbert Asquith, and wife of the Romanian ambassador to the United States. Elizabeth was photographed at Garsington in 1924, and Lady Ottoline described her as "like a quick ticker-tape machine, ticking out aphorisms and anecdotes. . . . She isn't unkind and I feel has rather a nice tolerant nature, but she is too conceited and vain." Fitzgerald seems to agree, quoting her in his *Ledger*, "I only write for intellectuals."

24   *Correspondence of F. Scott Fitzgerald*, 117.

25   F. Scott Fitzgerald, letter to Max Perkins (1924).

26   See, for example, Meyers, *Scott Fitzgerald*, 127.

27   Ruth Prigozy, "Gatsby's Guest List and Fitzgerald's Technique of Naming," *Fitzgerald/Hemingway Annual* 4 (1972): 99–112 (102).

28   Churchwell, *Carless People*, 112.

29   Quoted in Berman, 90.

30   See Perkins's letter to Scott dated Aug 8, 1924, in Kuehl and Bryer (eds.), *Dear Scott/Dear Max*, 74–75.

31   Churchwell, *Careless People*, 155ff.

32   Churchwell, *Careless People*, 210–12; Edward Behr, *Prohibition: Thirteen Years that Changed America* (New York: Arcade Publishing, 1996); William A. Cook, *King of the Bootleggers: A Biography of George Remus* (Jefferson, NC: McFarland, 2008).

33   John H. Randall III, "Jay Gatsby's Hidden Source of Wealth," *Modern Fiction Studies 13* (Autumn 1967), 247–57; reprinted in Piper, *Fitzgerald's* The Great Gatsby, 190–97.

34   Kuehl and Bryer (eds.), *Dear Scott/Dear Max*, 89.

35   For the fullest accounts of the Fuller-McGee case and its association with Gatsby, see Sarah Churchwell, *Careless People*, 133ff., Henry Dan Piper, "The Fuller-McGee Case," in *Fitzgerald's* The Great Gatsby, 171–84; and idem., *F. Scott Fitzgerald*, 112ff.

36   See Sarah Churchwell, *Careless People*, 196–97; and Joseph Corso, "One Not-Forgotten Summer Night: Sources for Fictional Symbols of American Character in *The Great Gatsby*," *Fitzgerald/ Hemingway Annual* (1976), 8–33.

37   F. Scott Fitzgerald Papers, Princeton University Library. See Matthew J. Bruccoli, "'How Are You and the Family Old Sport'—Gerlach and Gatsby," *Fitzgerald/ Hemingway Annual* (1975), 33–36; and Bruccoli (ed), *The Great Gatsby: A Literary Reference*, 20–21.

38   One of these bootleggers, Max Fleischmann, appears as a bootlegger living in extravagance in Edmund Wilson's play, *The Crime in the Whistler Room* (1924). Fitzgerald admitted that Fleischmann, who had built an estate at Sands Point Village on Manhasset Neck, gave him the idea of Gatsby's grandeur: see Matthew J. Bruccoli (ed.), *F. Scott Fitzgerald: Inscriptions* (Columbia, SC: Bruccoli, 1988), item 86.

39   Horst H. Kruse, "The Real Jay Gatsby: Max von Gerlach, F. Scott Fitzgerald, and the Compositional History of *The Great Gatsby*," *The F. Scott Fitzgerald Review* 1 (2002): 45–81; idem, *F. Scott Fitzgerald at Work: The Making of The Great Gatsby* (Tuscaloosa, AL: Univ. of Alabama Press, 2014).

40   See Kruse, *F. Scott Fitzgerald at Work*, 24 and 125 n.27.

41   F. Scott Fitzgerald, "How to Live to Live on Practically Nothing a Year" (September 1924).

42   Ibid.

43   Cowley and Cowley, *Fitzgerald and the Jazz Age*, 97–99.

44   Ring Lardner, "The Riviera," *Liberty* (September 1924), a copy of which was kept in Scott's scrapbook: see Bruccoli, Smith, and Kerr, 118.

45   On this affair, see now Kendall Taylor, *The Gatsby Affair: Scott, Zelda, and the Betrayal that Shaped an American Classic* (New York: Random House, 2018).

46   Mizener, *The Far Side of Paradise*, 181ff.

47   From "Handle with Care," in Edmund Wilson (ed.), *The Crack-Up*, 78.

48   Wilson (ed.), *The Crack-Up*, 308.

49   Ibid., 309.

50   *Letters*, 358 and 485.

51   Kruse, *F. Scott Fitzgerald at Work*, 50–51.

52   Matthew J. Bruccoli, *F. Scott Fitzgerald: A Life in Letters* (1994), 137. Fitzgerald had also told Hemingway that Eliot's compliment made him feel like "the biggest man in my profession."

53   Valerie Eliot and John Haffenden (eds.), *The Letters of T. S. Eliot, Vol. 3: 1926–27* (New Haven and London: Yale Univ. Press, 2012), 61–62.

10 ENGLAND'S JAZZ AGE: EVELYN WAUGH AND THE BRIGHT YOUNG PEOPLE

1   See Judith Mackrell, *Flappers: Six Women of a Dangerous Generation* (New York, Farrar, Straus and Giroux, 2013), 5.

2   See Barbara Cooke, *Evelyn Waugh's Oxford* (Oxford: Bodleian Library, 2018), 85ff.

3   Fitzgerald quoted in B. F. Wilson, "F. Scott Fitzgerald Says: 'All Women Over Thirty-five Should Be Murdered,'" *Metropolitan Magazine* 58 (Nov 1923), 34, 75–76; reprinted in Bruccoli and Baughman (eds.), *Conversations*, 55–59 (56).

4   See Irving Lewis Allen, *The City in Slang: New York Life and Popular Speech* (New York: Oxford Univ. Press, 1993), 69.

5   See photos in Bruccoli, Smith, and Kerr, 73.

6   See Catherine Parsonage, *The Evolution of Jazz in Britain, 1880–1935* (Aldershot, Hamp: Ashgate, 2005), 3.

7   Quoted in Esther Zuckerman, "Extremely Loud & Incredibly Contrived: Jazz Experts on the *Gatsby* Soundtrack," *Atlantic Monthly* (May 2013): https://www.theatlantic.com/entertainment/archive/2013/05/great-gatsby-soundtrack-reviews/315618/.

8   Ronald Berman, *The Great Gatsby and Modern Times* (Urbana and Chicago: Univ. of Illinois Press, 1996), 47.

9   See Russell J. Linnemann, "Alain Locke's Theory of the Origins and Nature of Jazz," in Linnemann (ed.), *Alain Locke: Reflections on a Modern Renaissance Man* (Baton Rouge: Louisiana State University Press, 1982), 109–121 (110).

10   Interview, "What a 'Flapper Novelist' Thinks of His Wife," *The Courier-Journal* (September 30, 1923)," reproduced in Bruccoli, Smith, and Kerr, 112–13.

11   Parsonage, *The Evolution of Jazz*, 8.

12   Schaeper and Schaeper, 53.

13   Brockliss, *The University*, 451n.

14   Taylor, *Bright Young People*, 117–18.

15   Maloney, *Bright Young Things*, 78, 81.

16   Waugh, *The Diaries*, 236–38. The group showed up at Waugh's place once "with a car full of Charleston records from London" (249).

17   Maloney, *Bright Young Things*, 98.

18   Parsonage, *The Evolution of Jazz*, 196ff.

19   See M. Kohn, *Dope Girls: The Birth of the British Drug Underground* (London: Lawrence and Wishart, 1992).

20   Quoted in Parsonage, *The Evolution of Jazz*, 44.

21   See Maloney, *Bright Young Things*, 21–23; and Marie-Jacqueline Lancaster (ed.), *Brian Howard: Portrait of a Failure* (London: Anthony Blond, 1968).

22   Stannard, *Evelyn Waugh*, 89.

23   Taylor, *Bright Young People*, 25–26.

24   Ibid., 27.

25   Described by Loelia Ponsonby in Maloney, *Bright Young Things*, 26.

26   Maloney, *Bright Young Things*, 40.

27   Ibid., 45–46.

28   Quoted in Maloney, *Bright Young Things*, 76.

29   Beverley Nichols, *All I Could Ever Be* (1949).

30   Diary entry of July 29, 1924, quoted in Taylor, *Bright Young People*, 56.

31   Taylor, *Bright Young People*, 10.

32   Waugh, *Letters*, 506; Maloney, *Bright Young Things*, 35. Sebastian's beloved teddy-bear Aloysius is a nod to John Betjeman's bear, Archibald Ormsby-Gore.

33   Waugh, "Too Young at Forty," *The Evening Standard* (January 22, 1929), reprinted in Waugh, *A Little Order*, 7–8.

34   Mark Amory (ed.), *The Letters of Evelyn Waugh* (New Haven, CT: Ticknor & Fields, 1980), 10.

35   Humphrey Carpenter, *The Brideshead Generation: Evelyn Waugh and His Friends* (London: Faber and Faber, 1990), ix.

36   Arthur Waugh, *One Man's Road* (London: Chapman and Hall, 1931), 371.

37   Evelyn Waugh, *The Diaries of Evelyn Waugh*, ed. by Michael Davie (London: Penguin, 1986), 17. The original diaries (kept from 1911 to 1965) are now in the Ransom Center at the University of Texas, Austin.

38   Waugh, *The Diaries*, 46.

39   Waugh, *The Diaries*, 100–101. For Waugh's Oxford years, see Martin Stannard, *Evelyn Waugh: The Early Years, 1903–1939* (New York: W.W. Norton, 1987), 67–96; and now Barbara Cooke, *Evelyn Waugh's Oxford* (Oxford: Bodleian Library, 2018).

40   Wilson, "Walking Tour,"

41   Evelyn Waugh, *A Little Learning* (London: Penguin, 2011), 232–33.

42   Waugh, *A Little Learning*, 236.

43   Douglas Lane Patey, *The Life of Evelyn Waugh: A Critical Biography* (Oxford: Blackwell, 1998), 9.

44   In *Brideshead Revisited*, Charles Ryder keeps a copy of *Sinister Street* in his Hertford College rooms.

45   Quoted in Carpenter, *The Brideshead Generation*, 155.

46   *Letters*, 9. Cooke points out (*Evelyn Waugh's Oxford*, 108) that, "as a schoolboy, Waugh had been captivated by the whimsy, humour and menacing undertones of the *Alice* stories."

47   Waugh, *A Little Learning*, 238.

48   Ibid., 164; Stannard, *Evelyn Waugh*, 67.

49   Ibid., 181.

50   Stannard, *Evelyn Waugh*, 83, 89.

51   Davie in Waugh, *The Diaries*, 158.

52   Cooke, *Evelyn Waugh's Oxford*, 27.

53   Waugh told Nancy Mitford years later that Pares was "his first homosexual love," and Pares's love letter to Waugh (in the British Library) confirms at least this affair: see Paula Byrne, *Mad World: Evelyn Waugh and the Secrets of Brideshead* (London: Harper, 2009); Philip Eade, *Evelyn Waugh: A Life Revisited* (London: Weidenfeld & Nicolson, 2016); and Cooke, *Evelyn Waugh's Oxford*, 9ff. Byrne argues that Waugh's relationship with Lygon and his family was of far greater import to his writing.

54   See Evelyn Waugh, *The Complete Stories of Evelyn Waugh* (Boston: Little, Brown and Co., 2000), 575–608.

55 Waugh, "Oxford and the Next War," *Isis* (March 12, 1924), reprinted in Waugh, *A Little Order*, 3–4.

56 Waugh, *A Little Learning*, 295.

57 Waugh, *The Diaries*, 163ff. Waugh indicates that many of these parties were thrown in honor of American actors, including Paul Robeson and Tallulah Bankhead.

58 Waugh, "Is Oxford Worth While?" *Daily Mail* (June 21, 1930), reprinted in Waugh, *A Little Order*, 15–17.

59 Waugh, *The Diaries*, 233–34.

60 Wood, "Postscript," in Evelyn Waugh, *PRB: An Essay on the Pre-Raphaelite Brotherhood, 1847–1854* (Westerham, Kent: Dalrymple Press, 1982), 41–44.

61 Evelyn Waugh, *Rossetti: His Life and Works* (London: Duckworth, 1975), 94, 95.

62 Cooke, *Evelyn Waugh's Oxford*, 70–71.

63 Waugh, *The Diaries*, 294, 305.

64 Jungman only recently shared Waugh's letters to her: see Dalya Alberge, "Lost Evelyn Waugh letters reveal thwarted love for 'bright young thing.'" *The Guardian* (July 20, 2013): https://www.theguardian.com/books/2013/jul/21/evelyn-waugh-love-letters.

65 Waugh, *The Diaries*, 316–17.

66 D. L. Patey, *The Life of Evelyn Waugh: A Critical Biography* (Oxford: Blackwell, 1998), 57ff.; Parsonage, *The Evolution of Jazz*, 58ff.

67 Byrne, *Mad World*, 123.

68 Alexander Waugh, "Foreword," in Cooke, *Evelyn Waugh's Oxford*, viii.

69 Evelyn Waugh, *Brideshead Revisited* (New York: Little, Brown and Co., 1999), 21.

70 See e.g. John Osborne, "Sebastian Flyte as a Homosexual," *Evelyn Waugh Newsletter and Studies* 23, no. 3 (Winter 1989), 7–8; David Bittner, "Sebastian and Charles—More than Friends?" *Evelyn Waugh Newsletter and Studies* 24, no. 2 (Autumn 1990), 1–3.

71 Peter G. Christensen, "Homosexuality in *Brideshead Revisited*: "Something quite remote from anything the [builder] intended," in Donat Gallagher, et al. (eds.), *"A Handful of Mischief": New Essays on Evelyn Waugh* (Lanham, MD: Rowman & Littlefield, 2011), 100.

72 Byrne, *Mad World*, 152ff.; Jane Mulvagh, *Madresfield* (Doubleday, 2007).

73 *The Paris Review*, Issue 30 (Summer–Fall 1963).

74 Waugh, *Brideshead*, 46.

75 Evelyn Waugh Papers, Ransom Center, Univ. of Texas at Austin, folder 2.1 "*Brideshead Revisited*: instructions for filming" (Feb 18, 1947), pp. 1–2.

76 Ibid., 3.

77 Cooke, *Evelyn Waugh's Oxford*, 51.

78 Edmund Wilson, Letter to Elizabeth Huling (July 4, 1945), in *Edmund Wilson on Writers and Writing*. Wilson's copy of the *Brideshead* MS can be found in the Evelyn Waugh Papers, Ransom Center, Univ. of Texas at Austin, folder 2.1–2 "*Brideshead Revisited* typed MS Bound in Harold Matson Folder."

79   Christopher Hitchens, "The Permanent Adolescent: His vices made Evelyn Waugh a king of comedy and of tragedy," *The Atlantic* (May 2003).

80   *Letters*, 10.

81   Waugh, *A Little Learning*, 171.

82   Stannard, *Evelyn Waugh*, 67.

83   These similarities are often overlooked by Waugh scholars. See, however, James J. Thompson, Jr., "Evelyn Waugh and 'The Bright Young Things,'" *New Oxford Review* 55, no. 4 (May 1988): http://www.newoxfordreview.org/reviews.jsp?did=0588-thompson.

II DREAMING IN OXFORD

1   W. B. Yeats, Letter to Katharine Tynan (Aug 25, 1888), in John Kelly (ed.), *The Collected Letters of W. B. Yeats, Vol. I* (1986).

2   For the Yeats family's years in residence in Oxford, see R. F. Foster, *W. B. Yeats: A Life, Vol. II* (Oxford: Oxford Univ. Press, 2003), 113–17, 121, 157–60, 186–87; and Ann Saddlemyer, *Becoming George: The Life of Mrs. W. B. Yeats* (Oxford: Oxford Univ. Press, 2002), ch. 10. Mrs. Yeats's father and brother had both attended Wadham College, and W. B. became president of the newly established Irish Society at Oxford.

3   Walter Hooper (ed.), *The Collected Letters of C. S. Lewis, Vol. I* (San Francisco: HarperCollins, 2004), 524–34, 564–65.

4   The Yeatses decorated their house on Broad St. with deep blue Morris hangings in the guest bedroom and a Rossetti painting in the lavatory! See Saddlemyer, 230–31.

5   See Horst H. Kruse, "F. Scott Fitzgerald and Marry Harriman Rumsey: An Untold Story," *The F. Scott Fitzgerald Review* 13, no. 1 (2015), 146–62.

6   F. Scott Fitzgerald, "The Diamond as Big as the Ritz," in *Tales of the Jazz Age* (New York: Vintage, 2010), 129–75 (146–47).

7   Julian Cowley, *The Great Gatsby: York Notes Advanced* (London: York Press, 1998), 89.

8   Baldesar Castiglione, *The Book of the Courtier*, trans. by Charles S. Singleton, edited by Daniel Javitch (New York: Norton, 2002), 253.

9   Berman, *The Great Gatsby*, 8.

10   James Meredith, "Fitzgerald and War," in Curnutt (ed.), *A Historical Guide*, 173, 180.

11   Long, *The Achieving*, 138–40.

12   Meyers, *Scott Fitzgerald*, 125.

13   John F. Callahan, *The Illusions of a Nation: Myth and History in the Novels of F. Scott Fitzgerald* (Chicago: Univ. of Illinois Press, 1972).

14   Ibid. 3, 33–34.

15   Meredith, 204.

16   Brown, *Paradise Lost*, 3–7, 191.

17   Matthew Arnold, Preface to the First Edition of *Essays in Criticism*, quoted in Zaleski and Zaleski, 6.

18   Harold Bloom (ed. and intro), *F. Scott Fitzgerald's The Great Gatsby* (New York: Chelsea House Publishers, 1986), 3.

19   Stewart, *The New Negro*, 88.

20   Oser, *The Return of Christian Humanism*, x.

21   Berman, *The Great Gatsby and Fitzgerald's World of Ideas*, 155.

22   F. Scott. Fitzgerald, letter to Moran Tudury, in Matthew J. Bruccoli and Margaret M. Duggan (eds.), *Correspondence of F. Scott Fitzgerald* (New York: Random House, 1980), 139; idem, *Afternoon of an Author: A Selection of Uncollected Stories and Essays* (New York: Scribner's, 1957), 9.

23   Mintler, "From Aesthete to Gangster," 118.

24   F. Scott Fitzgerald, *The Love of the Last Tycoon* (New York: Cambridge University Press, 1994), 283.

25   Brown, *Paradise Lost*, 174.

26   Michaelis is the first to comfort George after Myrtle's death, and Allen (*Candles*, 103–4) identifies the Greek as performing the role of the Archangel Michael.

27   Quoted in Turnbull, *Scott Fitzgerald*, 146.

28   Allen, *Candles*, 108.

29   Meredith, "World War I," 142.

30   Berman, 158.

31   Marius Bewley, "Scott Fitzgerald's Criticism of America," in Bloom, *The Great Gatsby*, 11–27 (24).

32   Oser, *The Return of Christian Humanism*, 129.

33   See Patrick, *The Magdalen Metaphysicals*.

34   Lewis, *Rehabilitations*, 17.

35   Dougill, *Oxford in English Literature*, 171.

36   Fitzgerald's views about Europe and American exceptionalism would evolve after his long sojourn in France and Italy (1924–26), as expressed, for example, in "The Swimmers" (1929) and *Tender is the Night* (1934).

Acknowledgments

The idea for this book came when my daughter challenged me to watch—with an open mind—the latest film adaptation of one of my favorite novels. Only then did I notice the repetition of the phrase "an Oxford man" in *The Great Gatsby*, so I must begin by thanking my daughter, Carys Glynne Snyder, for watching movies and discussing novels with me (despite my prejudices).

I am also grateful to my former student, Donald "Field" Brown (Mississippi and Christ Church, 2014), and to the staff at the Rhodes House, Oxford. Had I not been visiting Field's new "home away from home," and searching for information about Mississippi State's first Rhodes scholar, I would not have been able to make such a rich exploration of the American soldier-students who, like Jay Gatsby, left the Western Front to come to Oxford in the winter of 1919. Thank you, Field, for introducing yourself to the new dean and for letting him vicariously enjoy your experience as a Rhodes scholar.

I conducted most of the research for this book during my subsequent research fellowship at Oxford. For five years I was privileged to be affiliated with the History Faculty and the "Globalising and

Localising the Great War Programme." Thank you, especially, Dr. Jeanette Atkinson, for logistical assistance during my fellowship; to Bob, Tim, Adam, and Judson at WISC (friends ever-willing to help me in Oxford); to Dr. Tudor Jones, for his comments on the manuscript; and to the archivists and librarians at all of the Oxford colleges with whom I had the privilege to work. All the archivists are unsung heroes, but let me sing special praise for Robin Darwall-Smith, Claire Hopkins, Julian Reid, Emma Goodrum, Jennifer Thorp, Penelope Baker, Georgina Edwards, Eleanor Ward, Cliff Davies, and Michael Riordan.

I also want to thank Dean Frances Coleman and archivist Ryan Semmes of the Mitchell Library, Mississippi State University; the Special Collections librarians associated with the F. Scott and Zelda Fitzgerald Collections at Princeton University's Firestone Library, especially Brianna Cregle; Helen Thomas at the Bodleian Library, Oxford; the librarians and archivists at the Ransom Humanities Center at the University of Texas at Austin; Elizabeth Sudduth at the University of South Carolina Library; Elisa Ho at the Jacob Rader Marcus Center of the American Jewish Archives, Cincinnati; the Moorland-Spingarn Center at Howard University; the Rhodes College Library and Archives; and the British Library, London. Dr. Sarah Churchwell, thank you for your encouragement as I entered the world of Fitzgerald studies; and Ian Flintoff, for your kindness as I entered your world in Trinity Quad.

My research activities were generously supported by the Office of the Provost and the Shackouls Honors College at Mississippi State University. I especially want to thank my former provost, Dr. Jerry Gilbert, and current provost, Dr. Judy Bonner, for their constant support; Judy and Bobby Shackouls, for your enthusiasm for all we do in the college that bears your name; Mrs. Becky Gardner, for holding down the fort while I was (often) distracted by my research; Dr. Tommy Anderson, for patiently listening to me talk obsessively about this Gatsby project; Dr. Matt Little, who has generously shared his *Gatsby* sources and insights; and to my History Department colleagues, Dr. Kathryn Barbier and Dr. Richard Damms, for their comments on part of the manuscript in its early phase. Thanks also to the Honors faculty

(Eric, Kristin, Donna, Don, and Anthony), for letting me share some of my thoughts about the novel with them over tea (and pastries!); and to all of my Honors students at MSU: it is from you that I derive my energy and recognize my purpose.

To my wife, Dr. Renee Baird Snyder, to my father, Don Snyder, and to my dear friends, Dr. Charles R. Smith, Dr. Seth Oppenheimer, Dr. Scott Carnicom, Dr. Jason Kelsey, and Dr. Greg Dunaway, I offer gratitude for your presence in my life. Lastly, to my agent, Mark Gottlieb, and to my publisher, Claiborne Hancock, I give thanks for your belief in this book project and your guidance along the way to publication.

Image Sources

Index

INDEX

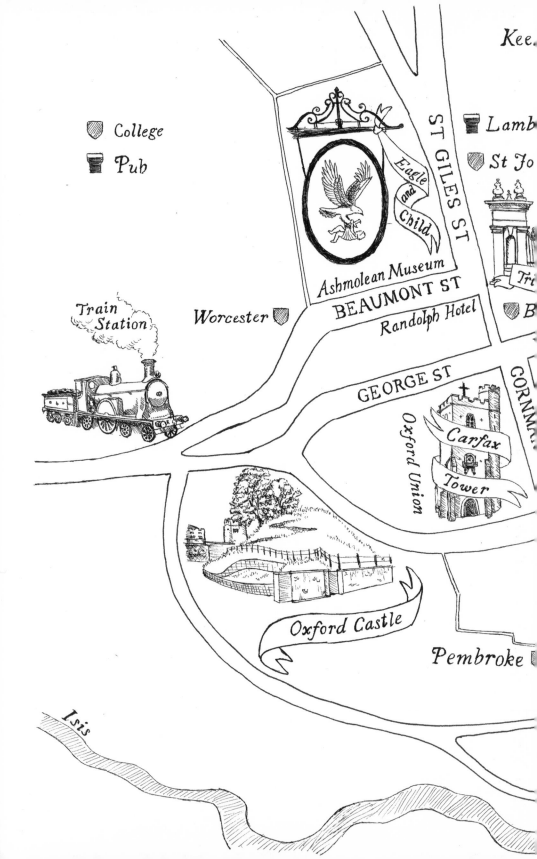

College

Pub

Kee...

Lamb

St Jo

Eagle and Child

Ashmolean Museum

BEAUMONT ST

Randolph Hotel

ST GILES ST

Tr

B

Train Station

Worcester

GEORGE ST

CORNMA

Oxford Union

Carfax Tower

Oxford Castle

Pembroke

Isis